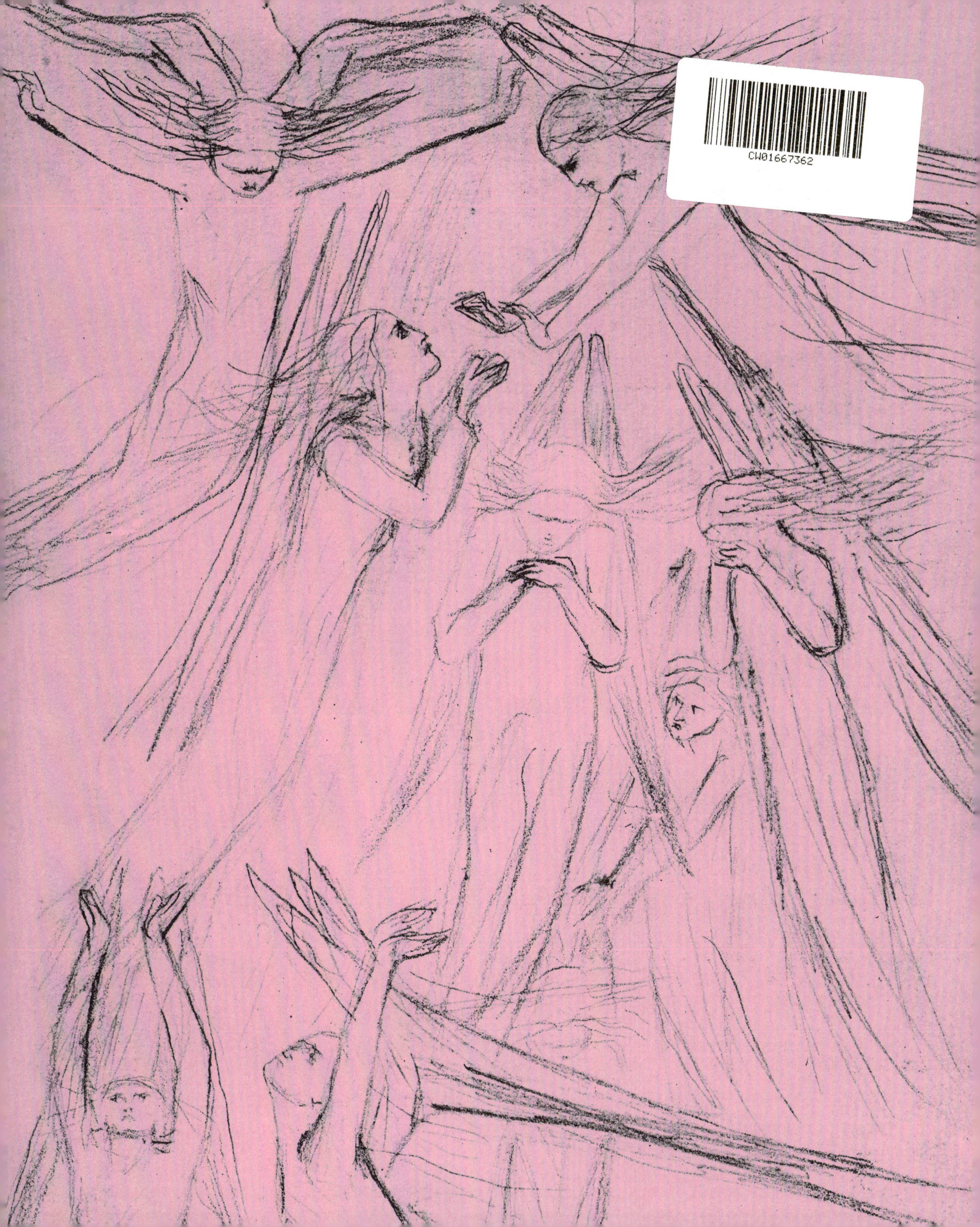

The Rossettis

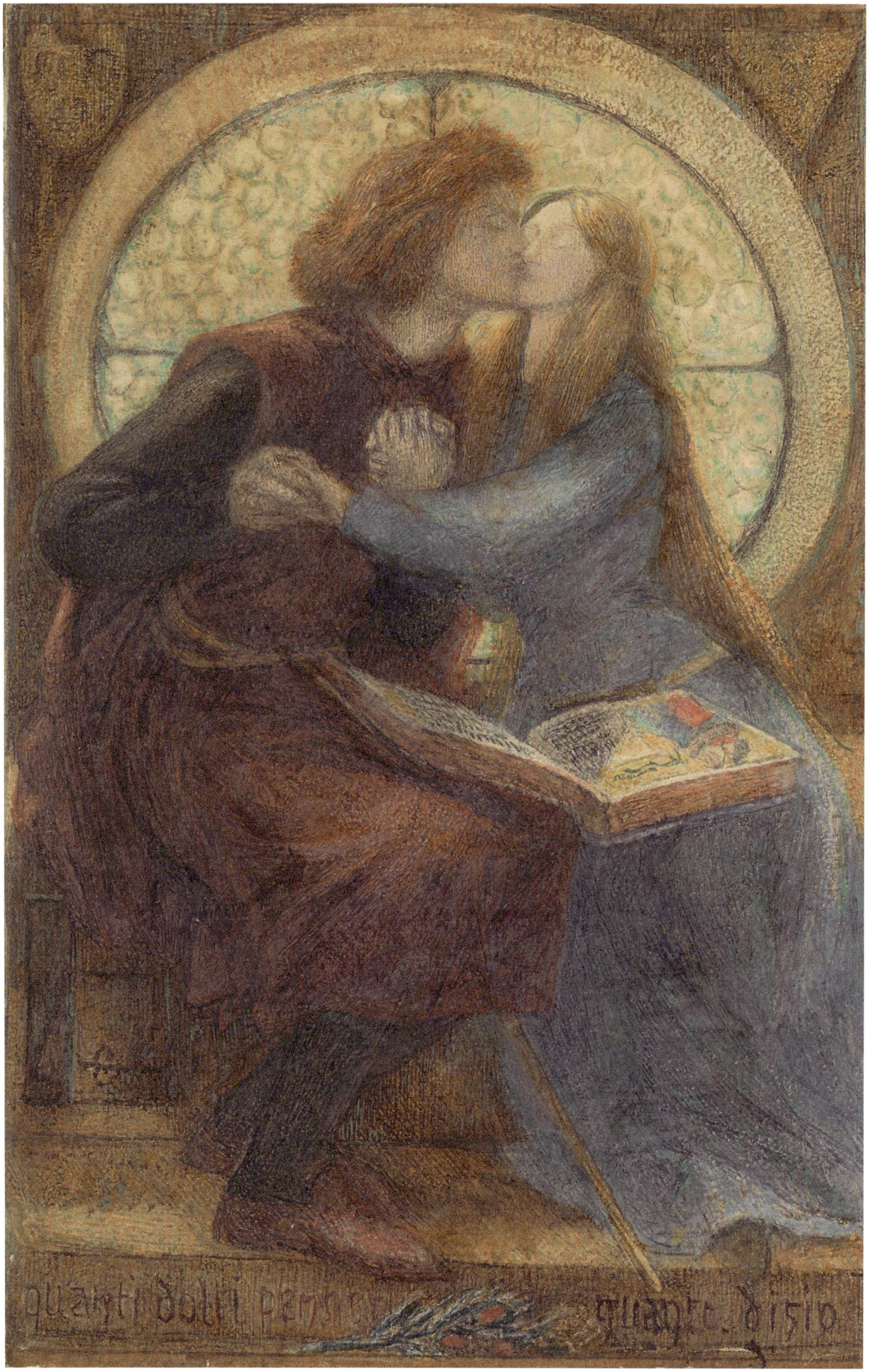
quanti dolci pensier
quanto disio

With contributions by James Finch, Margaretta Frederick,
Carol Jacobi, Jan Marsh, Chiedza Mhondoro,
Gursimran Oberoi, Wendy Parkins, Elizabeth Prettejohn,
Dinah Roe and Glenda Youde

The Rossettis

Edited by Carol Jacobi
and James Finch

TATE

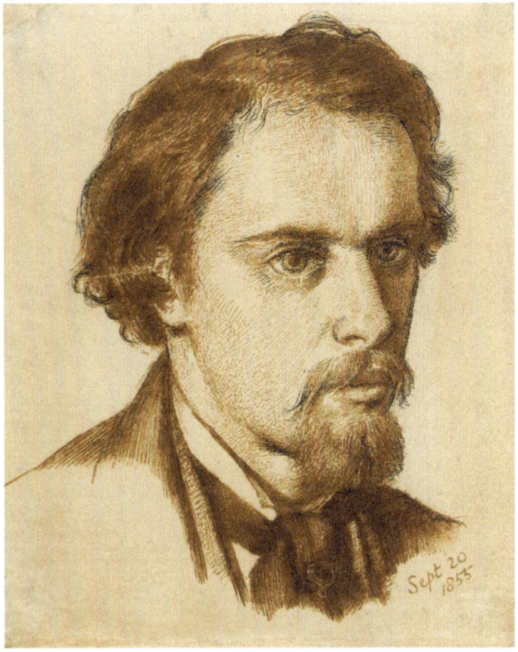
Sept 20
1855

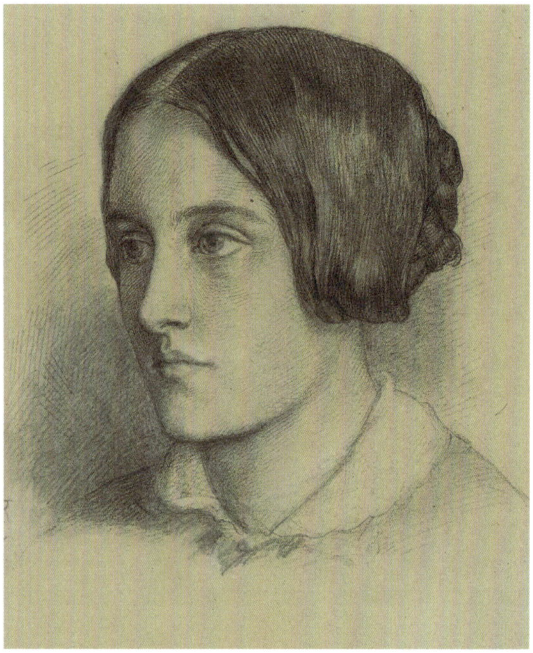

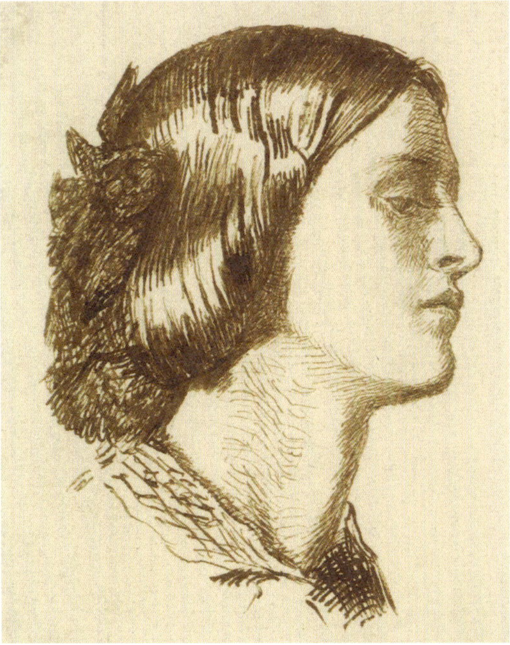

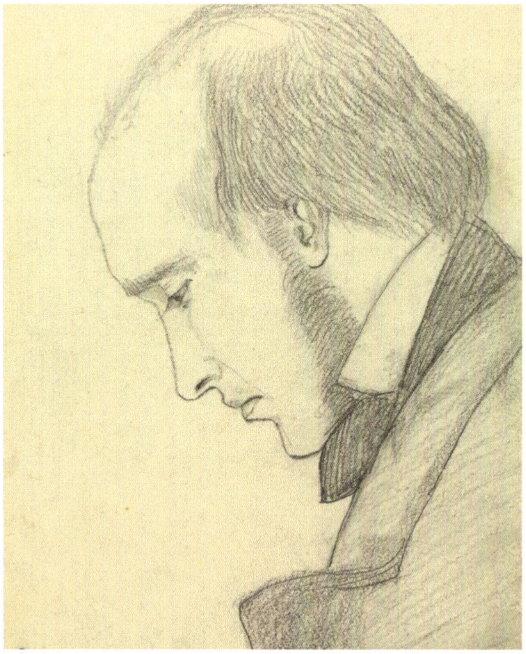

PAGE 2
NO.1 Dante Gabriel Rossetti, *Paolo and Francesca da Rimini* 1855 (detail), watercolour on paper, 25.4 × 44.9

OPPOSITE, CLOCKWISE FROM TOP LEFT

NO.2 Dante Gabriel Rossetti, *Self-Portrait* 1855, pen and Indian ink and brown ink on paper, 12.9 × 11.5

NO.3 Dante Gabriel Rossetti, *Christina Rossetti* 1848, chalk on paper, 28.8 × 21.5

NO.4 Christina Rossetti, *Portrait of William Michael Rossetti* c.1853, graphite on paper, 18.1 × 12.7

NO.5 Dante Gabriel Rossetti, *Portrait of Elizabeth Siddal* 1850, ink on paper, 10.5 × 10.2

Director's Foreword

The Rossettis were one of the most remarkable artistic families of the nineteenth century. The children of parents rooted in the struggle for Italian independence, Gabriel, Christina, William Michael and Maria all went on to significant cultural achievements, while through marriage, two more talented artists, Elizabeth (born Siddall, later Siddal) and Lucy (born Madox Brown), entered the family. In spite of holding one of the prime collections of the work of Dante Gabriel Rossetti, Tate has never held a Rossetti exhibition before now. The present survey highlights the synergies and overlaps between Gabriel and other, just as radical artists and writers of the Rossetti family.

Gabriel, Christina and Elizabeth, the three protagonists of the exhibition, are all widely known, although in all cases there is something fugitive and unsatisfying about their reputations. Gabriel is known as the young Pre-Raphaelite tyro (in truth, a very brief period of his life) and for his later 'poetic portraits' of women in mythological or allegorical settings. While revered by artists, he exhibited little during his lifetime, and worked for patrons such as Frederick Leyland more than for the vicissitudes of the gallery wall. Christina, a formidable poet whose international reputation exceeds that of her brother, is similarly known through thousands of musical settings of her works, and poems such as 'In the bleak mid-winter'. Elizabeth, meanwhile, in spite of the attention paid her through exhibitions such as *Pre-Raphaelite Sisters* at the National Portrait Gallery, and a 2019 exhibition at Wightwick Manor, is still rarely visible on gallery walls, due in part to most of her surviving works being on paper.

Surveying the Rossettis in concert draws out the common ground between their work: they modelled for each other, illustrated each other's poems, wrote about each other's work, and pursued shared themes, particularly that of love in all its forms. The relationship between art and poetry, intrinsic to Gabriel's practice as a 'painter-poet', is central to the exhibition as a whole. It opens with Gabriel's early masterpiece *Ecce Ancilla Domini! (The Annunciation)*, for which Christina and William Michael modelled for the Virgin and the angel, sharing space with extracts of Christina's poetry experienced in both written and spoken forms. Throughout, care has been taken to reanimate the Rossettis' process of creation: works by Gabriel and Elizabeth are paired to draw out their mutual influence; a wallpaper design by Gabriel is transformed from a sketch into a full-scale design in the galleries; and two of Gabriel's most enigmatic works, *The Beloved* and the unfinished *Found*, receive sustained study. In preparation for the exhibition, Tate conservators have conducted technical research into Rossetti paintings in the Tate collection, yielding fascinating results into Gabriel's painstaking method of revision and retouching.

Ever since their astonishing paintings were first exhibited in 1849, the Pre-Raphaelites, and perhaps Rossetti above all, have retained associations of radicalism and reinvention befitting their status as the first avant-garde movement in British art. A recent example of the continuing resonance of the movement is Sunil Gupta's series of photographs *The New Pre-Raphaelites*, commissioned by Autograph in 2008, one of which closes the exhibition. In these photographs, which take as their starting point works by Dante Gabriel Rossetti and other Pre-Raphaelite artists, Gupta responded to Section 377 of the Indian Penal Code, a law criminalising homosexuality, which was instituted by the British in 1861 and not overturned until 2018. Gupta has said of his sources: 'I've updated them to reflect contemporary queer culture in India.' The photograph included in the exhibition, *Untitled #02*, draws upon Gabriel's watercolour *Paolo and Francesca da Rimini* of 1855 in the Tate collection, itself a key work in the exhibition. Gupta updates this work in a celebration of both its enduring power and message of transcendent love.

The Rossettis were Victorian artists, however much their experimentation in art and life departs from the common associations of that word, and the careers of Gabriel, Elizabeth and Christina fall squarely within the reign of Queen Victoria. The work of the Rossettis was by turns complicit with, and critical of, the values and ideology of the

Britain at the height of Empire, with its hierarchies and discriminations structured on race, ethnicity, class, gender and sexuality. Orientalist tropes are present in many of Gabriel's best-known later paintings, while his major patron Frederick Leyland profited from the import of cotton from the American South, where the labour of Black people continued to be exploited after the abolition of slavery in the southern states. At the same time, the Pre-Raphaelite milieu was receptive to female and working-class artists, and subject matter such as the buying and selling of sex, largely considered taboo in the mainstream culture of the time. The work of Christina and Elizabeth is especially illuminating in this regard.

We are particularly pleased, in this exhibition, to assemble the largest collection of drawings and watercolours by Elizabeth Siddal since Jan Marsh's landmark exhibition at the Ruskin Gallery in Sheffield, in 1991. Elizabeth's own artistic achievement has continued to be overshadowed by a (gendered) fascination with her biography, particularly her role as a model for iconic works such as John Everett Millais's *Ophelia*, and the circumstances of her early death. The art and poetry produced during her brief career has too often been dismissed as derivative of that of Gabriel. New research by Glenda Youde, published in this catalogue, makes clear the extent to which Gabriel and Elizabeth embarked on a parallel project to find new significance in the medieval narratives that informed their works of the 1850s - as did other artists associated with the Pre-Raphaelite Brotherhood - and offered alternatives to the prevailing modes of realism which formed the mainstream of British art at this time. We are delighted that Jan Marsh has also contributed to the catalogue an essay dispelling the prevailing myths around Elizabeth Siddal, and that we are able to restore the visibility of her own artistic achievement, through exhibiting a superlative selection of her extant works.

The Rossettis have long been an inspiration to practitioners in a range of art forms: Debussy's setting of Gabriel's early poem 'The Blessed Damozel' (*La Damoiselle élue*) and Samuel Coleridge-Taylor's *Sorrow Songs* on texts by Christina Rossetti are among the many adaptations of their poetry, while the Pre-Raphaelite circle, of which the Rossettis were an integral part, provided the template followed by subsequent radical artistic movements in British Modern art.

The exhibition was developed and curated by Carol Jacobi, Curator, British Art 1850–1915, and James Finch, Assistant Curator, 19th Century British Art, working alongside Kiko Noda, Exhibitions Registrar. I join the curators in thanking the numerous colleagues at Tate, and the many curators, conservators and scholars, who contributed to the making of this exhibition and catalogue.

I would also like to thank all of the lenders, private and institutional, whose generosity has made the exhibition possible, in particular our tour partner. The Delaware Art Museum is a natural fit for the American venue of this exhibition. Home to the largest collection of Pre-Raphaelite art outside of Britain, Delaware also holds the most significant collection of Rossettis in the United States. This is thanks to Samuel P. Bancroft, Jr., who assembled the first Pre-Raphaelite collection in America during the last decade of the nineteenth century and the first decade of the twentieth. While Bancroft collected paintings by all the founding members of the Pre-Raphaelite Brotherhood, as well as their followers, he was drawn most intensely to 'Rossettianism', the style of painting Dante Gabriel Rossetti pioneered in the 1870s, with larger-than-life women from myth and legend pressed up against the picture plane. One of Bancroft's proudest achievements was locating Fanny Schott (Cornforth) in London in 1892, purchasing objects, photographs, letters and memorabilia from her that are now housed in the manuscript collection at Delaware Art Museum's Helen Farr Sloan Library & Archives. Given his mutually beneficial relationship with Fanny, Bancroft was especially pleased to acquire Rossetti's *Found*, the first painting for which Fanny posed. We thank all of our colleagues in Delaware for their support of the exhibition and contributions to its realization, particularly Molly Giordano, Executive Director; Sophie Lynford, Annette Woolard-Provine Curator of the Bancroft Collection of Pre-Raphaelite Art; and Margaretta Frederick, Curator Emerita, Bancroft Collection, Delaware Art Museum.

The Rossettis at Tate Britain has been made possible by the provision of insurance through the Government Indemnity Scheme, and we thank HM Government for providing this, and the Department for Digital, Culture, Media and Sport and Arts Council England for arranging this indemnity. We are very grateful to the Tavolozza Foundation, The Rossettis Exhibition Supporters Circle and Tate Members for their additional support of the exhibition.

Alex Farquharson
Director, Tate Britain

Curators' Acknowledgements

We are indebted to Alex Farquharson for his support of the exhibition, together with that of Carolyn Kerr, Head of Programme Management, and Andrea Schlieker, Director of Exhibitions and Displays. We would like to express our gratitude to Tate colleagues: Kiko Noda, Exhibitions Registrar, and Wendy Lothian, Senior Programme Manager, for their professionalism and expertise; Gillian Wilson and Elliott Higgs for their work on the exhibition Interpretation, and the project editor of this book, Alice Chasey. Thanks too to Lorenz Klingebiel for his elegant design of the book, and to Emma O'Neill and Bill Jones for their picture research and production work. Thanks to Jenny Wilson for her impeccable copy-editing and proofreading. Taryn Power, curatorial intern from the Courtauld Institute, has judiciously compiled the chronology. The Conservation department have handled the range of objects and Joyce Townsend, Amy Griffin and Gabriella Macaro developed important new research into Dante Gabriel Rossetti's oil paintings. Many thanks to Alessia Arcuri, Bethan Bowers and Soraya Chumroo for design elements of the exhibition. Thanks also to Andy Shiel, Liam Tebbs and the exceptional Installation team. The expertise of Gareth Fox made the audio components possible. Finally, we thank all our colleagues in Visitor Experience, Press, Marketing, Development, and Tate Library and Archive, for their invaluable input.

A special thanks to our colleagues at the Delaware Art Museum, with whom it has been our privilege to work on this project: Molly Giordano, Executive Director; Margaretta Frederick, Curator Emerita, Bancroft Collection, Delaware Art Museum; Sophie Lynford, Annette Woolard-Provine Curator of the Bancroft Collection of Pre-Raphaelite Art; Benét Burton, Rachael DiEleuterio, John Gibbons, Josh Harding, Candice Kearns, Erin Robin, Saralyn Rosenfield, Jonathan Schoff, Meg Thomas, Amelia Wiggins, Margaret Winslow and Shannon Woodloe.

We are indebted to the contributors to this catalogue for their insightful essays. We sincerely thank Margaretta Frederick, Jan Marsh, Chiedza Mhondoro, Gursimran Oberoi, Wendy Parkins, Elizabeth Prettejohn, Dinah Roe and Glenda Youde for sharing their expertise.

We thank all lenders for their generous support: Colin Harrison and Katherine Wodehouse at the Ashmolean Museum; Matthew Watson at Bolton Museum; Pamela Keeton and James

Steward at Bradford Museums & Galleries; Alexandra Ault at the British Library; Hartwig Fischer at the British Museum; Maude Brezinski and Elizabeth Mitchell at the Cantor Arts Center at Stanford University; Luke Syson and Jane Munro at the Fitzwilliam Museum; Elizabeth Scott at the Guildhall Art Gallery; Stuart Morrison at Hales Gallery; Matthew Teitelbaum at the Museum of Fine Arts, Boston; Caroline Campbell at the National Gallery of Ireland; Sandra Penketh at National Museums Liverpool; Nicholas Cullinan and Alison Smith at the National Portrait Gallery; Helen Bratt-Wyton at the National Trust, Wightwick Manor; Dunia Maria Garcia-Ontiveros at the Society of Antiquaries; Lori Birrell at the University of Delaware Library; and Tristram Hunt, Rosalind McKeever and Max Donnelly at the Victoria and Albert Museum.

We are equally indebted to private lenders for their support. Our heartfelt thanks go to Stephen Calloway, Jane Cohen, Mark Samuels Lasner, Lowell Libson and Jonny Yarker, the Maas Gallery, Geoffrey Munn, Peter and Renate Nahum, the Ramsbury Manor Foundation, David Smith, and private lenders who wish to remain anonymous.

This exhibition could not have been developed without wonderful conversations with scholars and descendants of the Rossetti family. We are grateful to Jan Marsh for sharing her huge knowledge and to Hope Kingsley for her knowledge of nineteenth-century photography. We also thank Martin Beisly, Peter Brown, Annabel Kishor, Rupert Maas, Christopher Riopelle and Simon Toll. We warmly thank Sunil Gupta and Diana Quick for their receptiveness to being involved in the exhibition. Ilyanna Kerr's beautiful realisation of Dante Gabriel Rossetti's wallpaper design has proved revelatory and perfectly encapsulates our aspirations for the project.

Carol Jacobi
Curator, British Art 1850–1915, Tate

James Finch
Assistant Curator,
19th Century British Art, Tate

Carol Jacobi

The Rossettis: Dreaming with Eyes Open

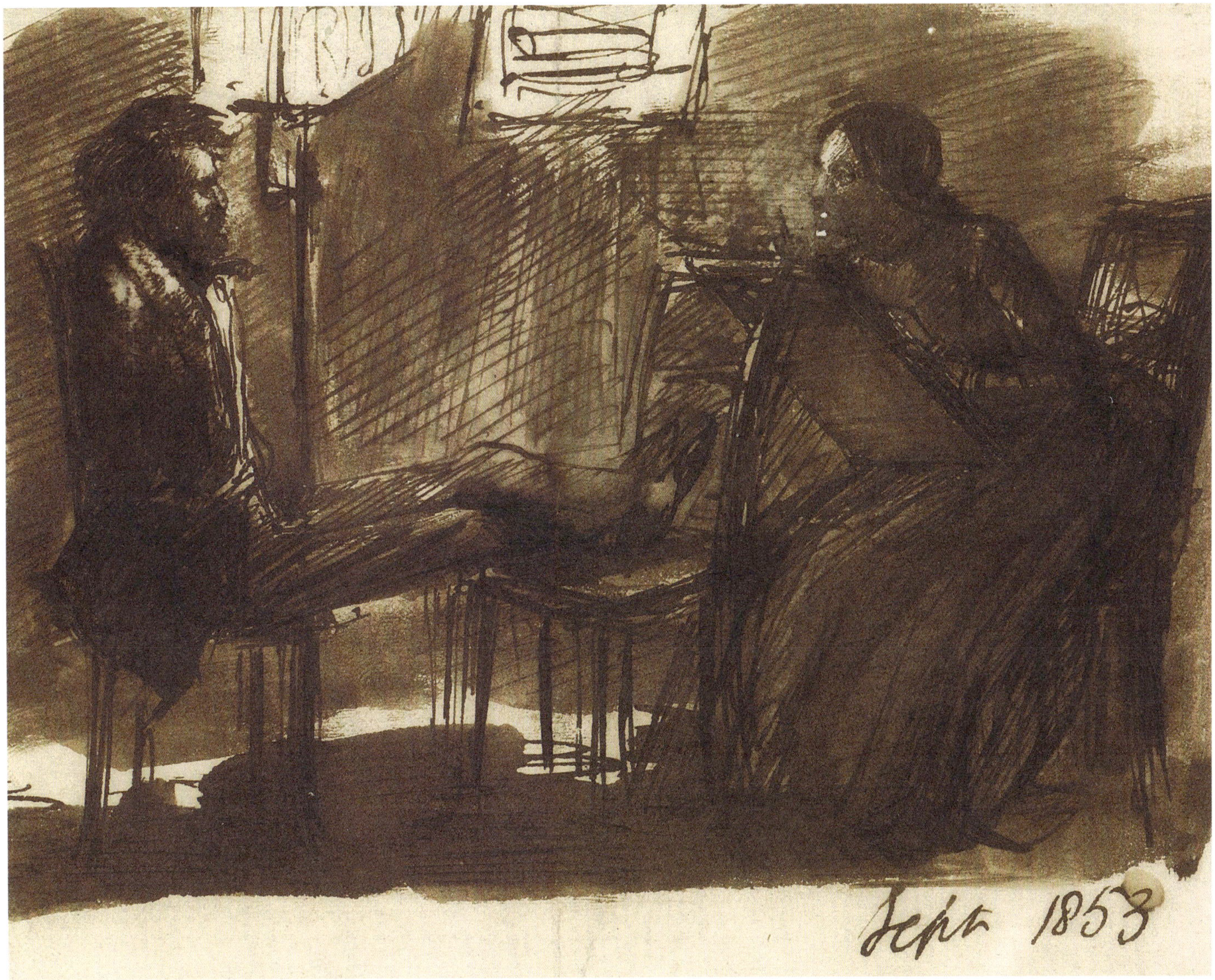
Sept 1853

PAGE 11
NO.6 Dante Gabriel Rossetti, *Rossetti Sitting to Elizabeth Siddal* 1853 (detail), ink on paper, 12.9 × 17.5

BELOW
NO.7 Dante Gabriel Rossetti, *Self-portrait with William Michael Rossetti* c.1853, pen and brown ink with brown wash on laid paper, 17 × 19.5

The year 1847 saw a small private printing of *Verses*, forty-two poems by Christina Rossetti. She was sixteen years old, the youngest of four siblings, but the first of that radical Rossetti generation – Maria, Gabriel, William Michael and herself, Gabriel's future wife Elizabeth (born Siddall, later Siddal), and William Michael's wife Lucy (born Madox Brown) – to bring work to public attention. One edition was illustrated by a teenage Gabriel, himself already a poet and accomplished and irreverent draughtsman. Born in the last few years of the Georgian era, the Rossettis were Victorians, but they challenge our perceptions of Victorian men and women. In their teens and twenties, they were marginal or controversial figures, but they created international careers and extended their artistic influence to their wider circle and into the present. Responding to their fast-changing modern world, they experimented with everything – beliefs and values, work and love. Gabriel, Christina and Elizabeth reinvented poetry and painting, enriched by personal lived experience, and their daring stories remain relevant today.

The Rossetti children were first-generation Londoners. Their father Gabriele was a poet, revolutionary and political refugee from Italy, who made a living as a teacher and translator of Italian medieval poetry; their mother Frances (born Polidori) was also a scholar from an Italian family, who home-educated her children in Italian and English; Elizabeth Siddal's family were cutlers, economic migrants from Sheffield; and Lucy Madox Brown, the daughter of an artist, was born in Paris. During their lifetimes, the population of cosmopolitan London would double to four million. The Rossetti revolution began when there was a single London train station and the streets were dark at night, but changes soon followed: a rail and underground system; homes, streets and factories lit up with gas, and then electricity; the telegraph; a water supply and sewers. Notably, the Rossettis' careers were shaped by advances in printing and the exponential expansion of a reading public.

These transformations were generated by market capitalism at full tilt: technological changes, resources from Imperial occupation and trade networks, and mass workforces of cheap, indentured or enslaved labour at home and overseas. As incomers arrived from across the UK and the wider Empire, a vast working class condensed into service industries, factories and other occupations. The people that we see in Gabriel's most famous paintings were among these. They came across each other in the city spaces where classes mixed: Elizabeth Siddal most likely in the shop where she was employed; Annie Miller in a pub; Fanny Cornforth at a party in a park; Jane Morris at the theatre; and Alexa Wilding in the street, walking to work. Fanny Eaton, who had travelled from the Caribbean, and Ellen Smith were domestic servants.

The affluent minority used their wealth and power to secure distinct positions in the growing population, signalled by carefully monitored behaviours and conspicuous consumption. Middle-class men were expected to take commanding roles in the worlds of commerce and manufacture, wearing their uniform of top hats and sober black. Women were encouraged to marry and remain modestly in a domestic 'separate sphere'. The Rossetti generation benefitted from patrons enriched by industry, trade and banking; John Ruskin,

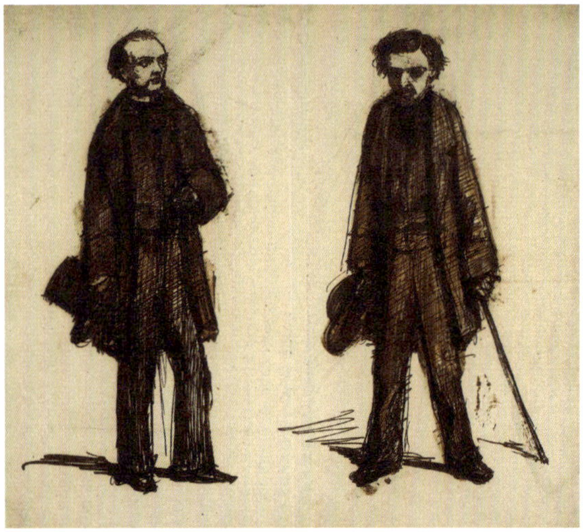

for example, the son of a wealthy sherry importer, was their most important defender and bought a great deal of work by Elizabeth and Gabriel. They tested the social order, however; engaged with – and tried to change – their world. The Rossetti parents' household at 38 Charlotte Street was noisy with dissidents and intellectuals. The children supported each other's careers and aligned themselves with social causes. They were susceptible to the prejudices of their age, but they addressed social issues from first principles.

In their different ways, the Rossettis questioned gender and class categories. Histories have cast working-class women such as Elizabeth Siddal, Fanny Cornforth and Jane Morris as 'muses', protagonists of rags-to-riches romances propelled by their appearance, but the reality was more reciprocal. They collaborated in less conventional and more authentic relations with Gabriel, expressed in freer lifestyles (see NO.8) or in looser fashions that became associated with emancipation. They all read and wrote as children, and went on to independent careers. Elizabeth had the support of her family in challenging class expectations to become a poet and a professional artist. Jane Morris was no less of a stableman's daughter for running a large household and contributing to Morris & Co.

Maria and Christina departed from expected norms by never marrying. Like their mother, they entered the world of work in their early teens, as carers, then governesses, teachers or social workers, and their writing brought them into the public eye. Their religious faith has often been described as at odds with fulfilling lives and thought, but it was a means to original emotional, intellectual and professional lives. High Church Anglicanism and involvement in new women's orders also provided an alternative to subordinate married roles. The year 1847 which saw *Verses*, *Jane Eyre* and *Wuthering Heights* also produced Alfred Tennyson's exploration of women's equality, *The Princess*, and Christina was quickly nicknamed after its eponymous feminist heroine, Ida. Unlike Ida, she retained her independence. By her forties she was famous for works such as 'Goblin Market' and 'A Christmas Carol' ('In the bleak mid-winter'). She published nine hundred of her poems, and at her death left the equivalent of half a million pounds. This was three times as much as Gabriel, and her international fame continues to outstrip that of her siblings.

The Rossetti brothers were educated inside and outside the home. They made their way as writers and translators – and, in Gabriel's case, as a painter and poet. Where Christina negotiated the difficult task of performing without appearing performative, Gabriel struck a charismatic pose in shabby evening dress. William Michael, though the most uncompromisingly radical in his politics, brought some security to the family as a civil servant, as an art critic and, after the deaths of the others, as their historian. The men married in their thirties and forties, to fellow professionals, Gabriel extending his long-standing relationship with artist and poet Elizabeth Siddal for only two years until her death at thirty-two. William Michael and the writer and artist Lucy Madox Brown were married for twenty years and had five children late in life. Glimpses of their parenting – 'to make [the children] feel constantly that they were cared for and loved, and their future kept well in view, was the chief incentive applied to their dawning facilities'[1] – provide a sense

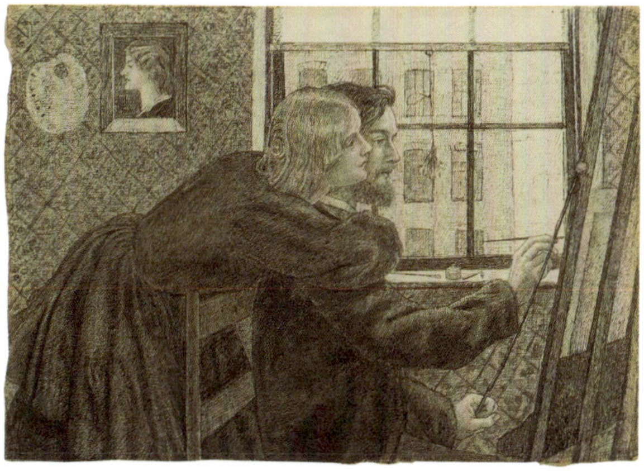

NO.8 Dante Gabriel Rossetti, *George Price Boyce with Fanny Cornforth in Rossetti's Studio, Chatham Place* c.1858, ink on paper, 22.2 × 31.8

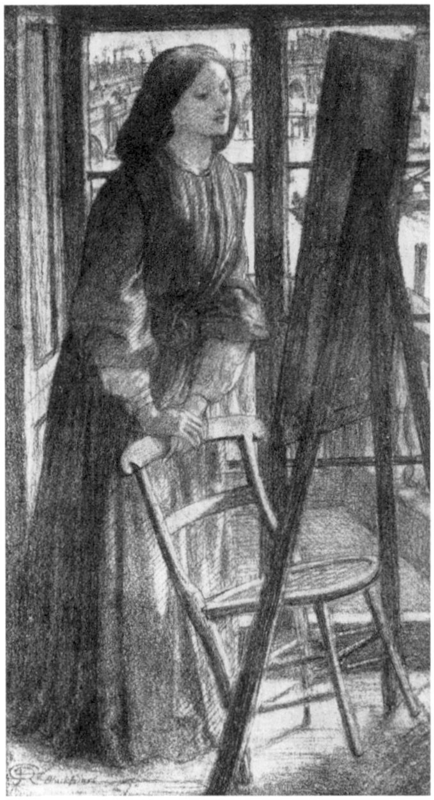

ABOVE
NO.9 Dante Gabriel Rossetti, *Elizabeth Siddal* c.1855, graphite on paper, 31.8 × 18.1

OPPOSITE
NO.10 Dante Gabriel Rossetti, *Beata Beatrix* c.1864–70, oil paint on canvas, 86.4 × 66

of the special environment of the Rossettis' own childhood and the encouragement they received to challenge the world on their own terms.

The dramatic back-story of the freedom-fighter Gabriele and the Polidori family, as well as the vivid characters who called at Charlotte Street, perhaps stimulated the Rossetti children's fascination with counter-cultural figures. They were drawn to old ballads and medieval writers and artists, with their life-or-death tales of violence and romance. Gabriele was a scholar of Dante Alighieri; the exiled medieval poet was practically a member of the family, with Dante Gabriel famously taking his name. All the Rossetti siblings followed their father in publishing critical and popular translations of the poet, and the latter's tragic romance with Beatrice was interpreted in many of Gabriel's most poignant poems and paintings (see NO.10).

The Rossettis were also excited by romantic writers who were then somewhat out of fashion, such as William Blake, John Keats and the Shelleys (Lucy published a biography of Mary Shelley, and William Michael of Percy Bysshe Shelley). They sought out mould-breaking modern writers, including Charles Baudelaire and Edgar Allan Poe, and forged friendships with Tennyson, William Bell Scott, and Elizabeth and Robert Browning. William Michael corresponded with Walt Whitman and championed him in Britain with an early edition of his poems. He also edited collections by Christina, Gabriel and Elizabeth.

Gabriel inspired rebellion against the Academy's dominance over artistic style, content and market – most notably through his leading involvement with the first British avant-garde, the Pre-Raphaelite Brotherhood, and, later, with the Aesthetic and Arts and Crafts movements. He and Elizabeth built careers without exhibiting at the Royal Academy. The success of this alternative model pre-empted the individualism that made possible the innovations of later nineteenth-century artists. Travelling exhibitions and the world trade in printed material made Gabriel one of the first painters to gain global celebrity. Artists inspired by him over the last two centuries include: photographers from Pictorialists such as Zaida Ben-Yusuf to Sunil Gupta, painters Vincent van Gogh, Pablo Picasso and Paula Modersohn-Becker, animators Hayao Miyazaki and Barry Windsor-Smith, and many others around the world.

Elizabeth Siddal was before her time in exemplifying the largely self-trained, socially non-aligned, individualist artist – a model which, by the early twentieth century, would become mainstream as a signifier of avant-garde authenticity or 'genius' (a term Ruskin applied to Elizabeth in her lifetime). Her legacy was – and is – fragile, buffeted by gendered expectations and poor survival of her work. She is often characterised through her mental and physical ill health. However, this was not unusual in nineteenth-century lives before improvements in modern medical care, and also hindered Christina and Gabriel. From the time of the Romantic poets, narratives of illness and addiction were a sensational feature of artistic biographies, but the reputation of Elizabeth – reduced to a 'muse' by her modelling work – has been especially distorted by sacrificial readings of her posing in a bath for John Everett Millais's drowning Ophelia, and her own early death. Like many working-class artists and women artists, her ten-year career was disrupted by limited

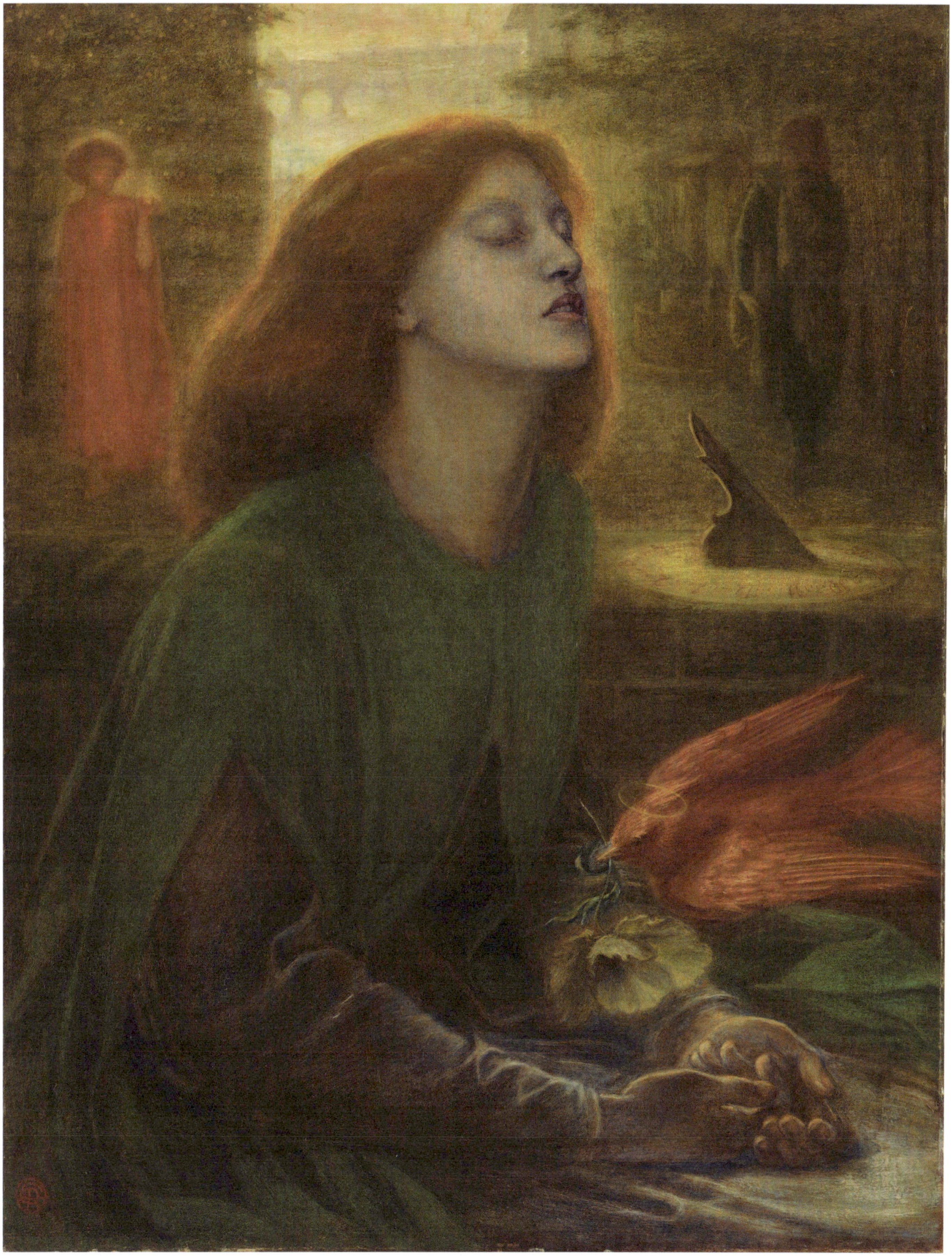

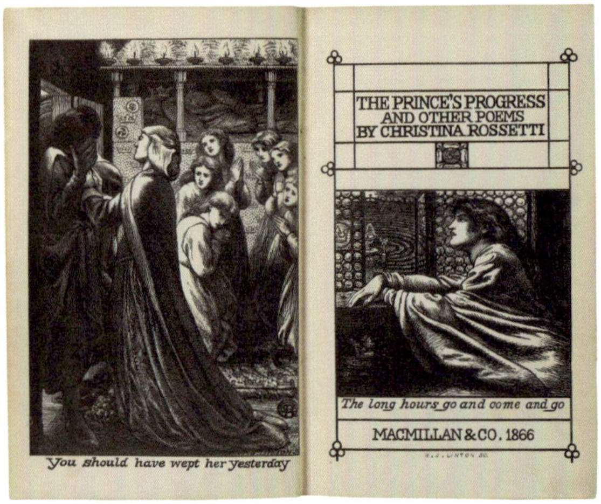

ABOVE
NO.11 Christina Rossetti, *The Prince's Progress and Other Poems* 1866, book, open at frontispiece, 17.8 × 11.4

OPPOSITE
NO.12 Elizabeth Siddal, *Lady Clare* 1854–7, watercolour on paper, 33.8 × 25.4

training and studio access, difficult personal circumstances and, at the end, pregnancy; she died after the stillbirth of a child and while expecting a second. Sixty of her works are known, many only from a photographic record made by Gabriel. A small number were exhibited just once in a Pre-Raphaelite show in London and New York, and the album remained private. It is an astonishing thirty years since her work was last brought together in a retrospective. Her influence on Gabriel and others in the circle, evident in this exhibition, has only very recently come to light.

Viewed for the first time through a set of shared spaces, the art of the Rossettis reveals itself to be essentially existential; a call-and-response around the conflicts and meaning of individual lives, overwhelmingly realised as dramas of love. Love is explored in all its forms: romance and sex, devotion and sacrifice, temptation and addiction, enchantment and betrayal; brotherly and sisterly love; love across classes; love between parent and child; love from conception to death, and beyond the grave.

The Rossettis searched literature for stories of lovers, or wrote their own. Gabriel and William Michael were life-long atheists, but, like their sisters, they appreciated the artistic and poetic potential of religious imagery such as natural symbols. Pre-Raphaelite paintings and writings, including Christina's contributions to the Pre-Raphaelite journal, *The Germ*, interpreted Biblical and literary subjects in personal, domestic terms. The viewer has the strange sensation of the past being intimately in the present. Gabriel's *Ecce Ancilla Domini! (The Annunciation)* (see NO.73) was modelled by Christina and William Michael. William Michael recalled his brother envisaging the scene as '"The Virgin ... in bed, but without any bedclothes on"'.[2] She is daringly turned to face the viewer, and her thin limbs revealed through crumpled cotton are worlds away from the traditional draped figure. The psychological closeness of *The Annunciation* – the atmosphere flavoured by colour; the use of intimates as sitters – looks forward to the chambers of Gabriel's and Elizabeth's watercolours, and the bowers of his famous later work.

The Rossettis energised the past with the present, dreaming with open eyes. In their twenties, Gabriel's and Elizabeth's watercolours set modern dilemmas in imagined medieval fantasy spaces. Inventively interlocked figures are strung across tense compositions. The couples are modelled on each other; they stand in for Paolo and Francesca, Lancelot and Guinevere, Macbeth and Lady Macbeth, struggling with transgressive love. After Elizabeth's death, Gabriel turned to love and mysterious female power, the intermingled enchantments of beauty and art, of the fathomless gaze, sumptuous colour, surface, scent and song. Fanny Cornforth, Jane Morris, Alexa Wilding and others brood in the guise of poetic or literary figures, such as Lilith, subtly contradicted by accompanying poems in 'double works of art'. An obsessive series of likenesses of Jane Morris was dominated by eight versions of *Proserpine* (three of which are in the exhibition), on which Gabriel was still working at his death.

The perennial fascination of the Rossettis' art lies in its framing of questions still current today – conflicts between love and loyalty; duty to family or country; love satiated, unrequited and lost; the meaning of modern beauty – and all the more potent because they remain unresolved

1 William Michael Rossetti, *Some Reminiscences of William Michael Rossetti*, 2 vols., London 1906, vol.1, p.448.

2 William Michael Rossetti, *Dante Gabriel Rossetti: His Family-Letters with a Memoir*, 2 vols., London 1895, vol.1, p.160.

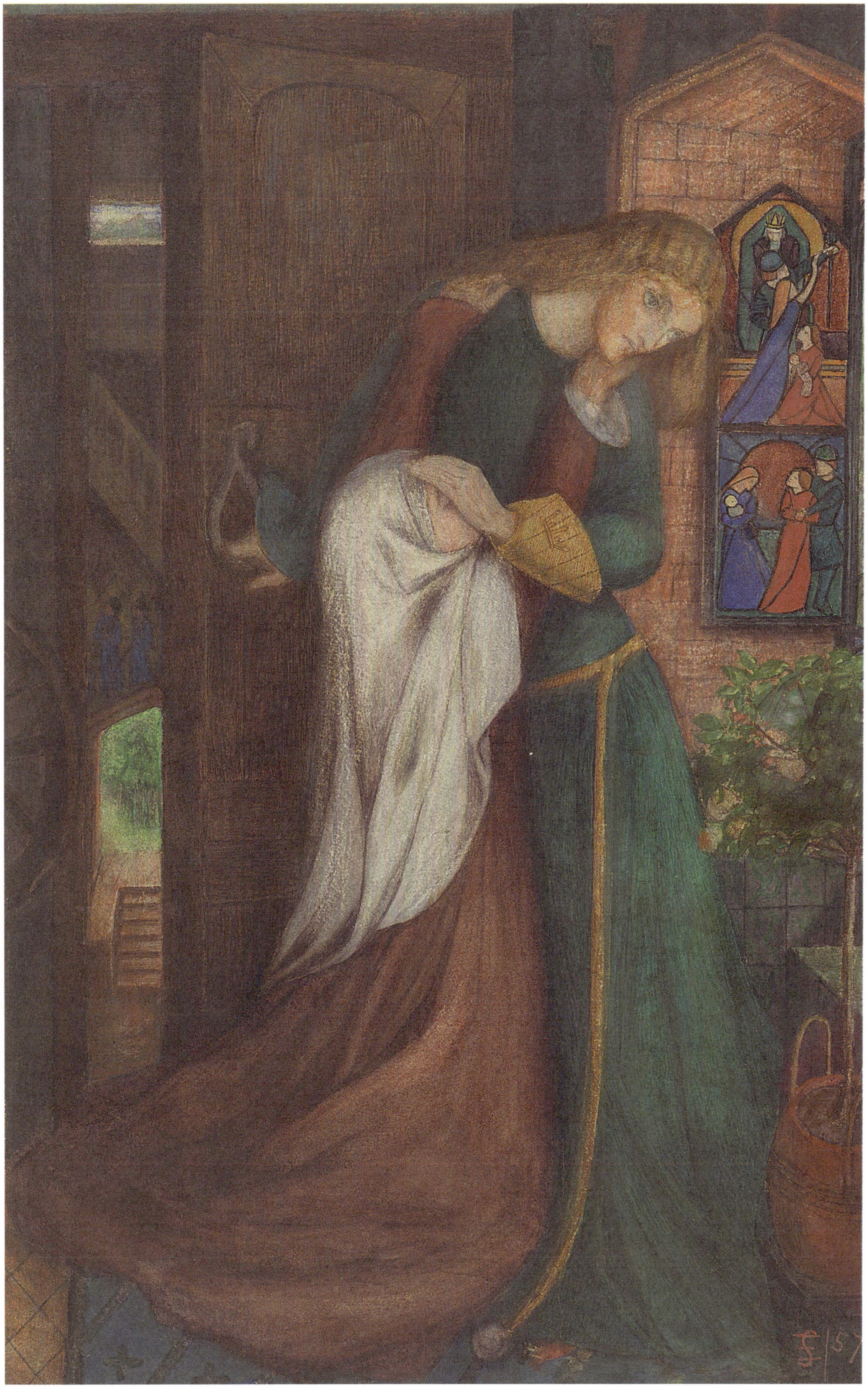

James Finch

Teenagers: The Young Rossettis

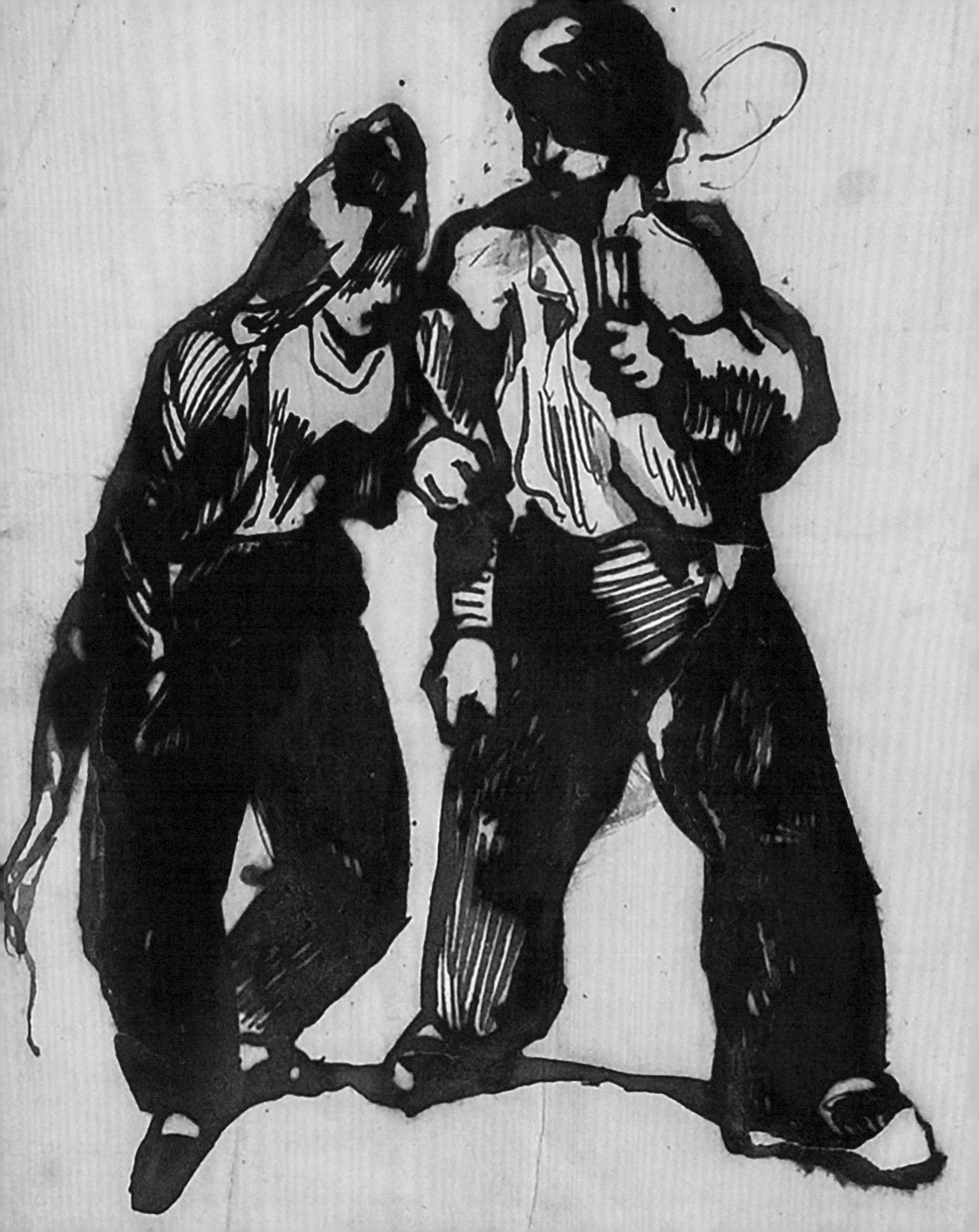

In 1824 Gabriele Rossetti, an Italian poet, scholar and political activist, arrived in England. Having been prominently involved in the 1820 revolution which agitated for a constitution for the Kingdom of Naples, Gabriele had fled Italy during Ferdinand I's crackdown on dissidents the following year. After spending three years in Malta, Gabriele made his way to London, where he became a central figure in the city's Italian community, his Charlotte Street home a meeting place for Italian exiles and radical cultural figures. Among his many notable acquaintances were the Romantic poet Samuel Taylor Coleridge, the history painter Benjamin Robert Haydon, and the violin virtuoso Niccolò Paganini.

In 1826 Gabriele married Frances Mary Lavinia Polidori, the daughter of another Italian émigré, Gaetano Polidori. The couple then had four children in quick succession: Maria Francesca was born in 1827, followed by Gabriel Charles (who later adopted the first name Dante) in 1828, William Michael in 1829, and Christina Georgina in 1830.[1] The Rossetti children were raised to value the intellectual pursuits beloved of their parents and were encouraged in their literary efforts from an early age. They would all, for instance, emulate their father, a Dante specialist, by publishing books on the Italian poet, while Gabriel went as far as to assume the name Dante from 1849 onwards.[2] They collaborated on stories, illustrated each other's works, and worked together on family magazines with titles such as *Hodge-Podge* (1843).[3]

A key figure in the creative development of the Rossetti siblings was their grandfather Gaetano Polidori, also a writer. Gaetano owned a printing press and, besides publishing his own works, he printed the first publications of both Gabriel (*Sir Hugh the Heron: A Legendary Tale, in Four Parts*, in 1843) and Christina (*Verses*, her first book of poems, in 1847; see NO.49). As a result, at an early age the Rossetti children crossed the threshold between private juvenilia and public literary production. Looking forward towards the subsequent generations of the family, moreover, there are clear echoes of this independent publishing spirit to be found in both the Pre-Raphaelite journal *The Germ* (see NOS.70, 71) and the anarchist journal founded by William Michael's children Olivia and Helen nearly fifty years later, *The Torch*.

The siblings worked closely together, particularly William Michael and Gabriel: the former wrote of their relationship that '[w]e read the same authors, coloured prints in the same book, collected woodcuts for the same scrapbook', and that ownership of their books was simply indicated by the single word 'Rossetti'.[4] The collecting and sharing of images was another communal family activity. At the age of fifteen Gabriel spent time staying in Boulogne

PAGE 19
NO.13 Dante Gabriel Rossetti, *Homeward Bound* 1844 (detail), ink on paper, 18.7 × 15

OPPOSITE, CLOCKWISE FROM TOP LEFT

NO.14 Filippo Pistrucci, *A Portrait of Maria Francesca Rossetti* 1839–40, graphite and watercolour on card, 16.2 × 12.4

NO.15 Filippo Pistrucci, *A Portrait of Dante Gabriel Rossetti* 1839–40, graphite and watercolour on card, 16.2 × 12.4

NO.16 Filippo Pistrucci, *A Portrait of Christina Georgina Rossetti* 1839–40, graphite and watercolour on card, 16.2 × 12.4

NO.17 Filippo Pistrucci, *A Portrait of William Michael Rossetti* 1839–40, graphite and watercolour on card, 16.2 × 12.4

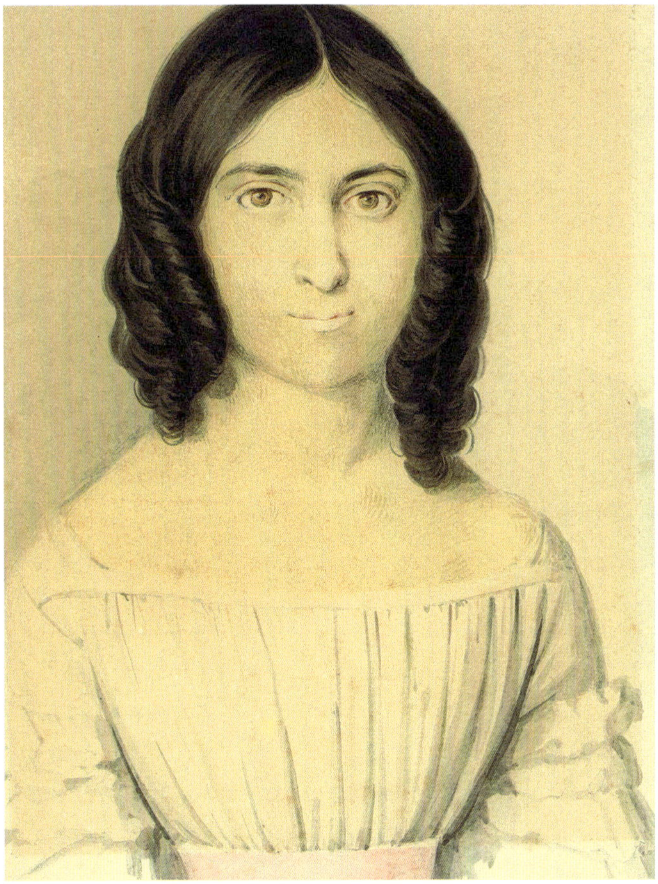
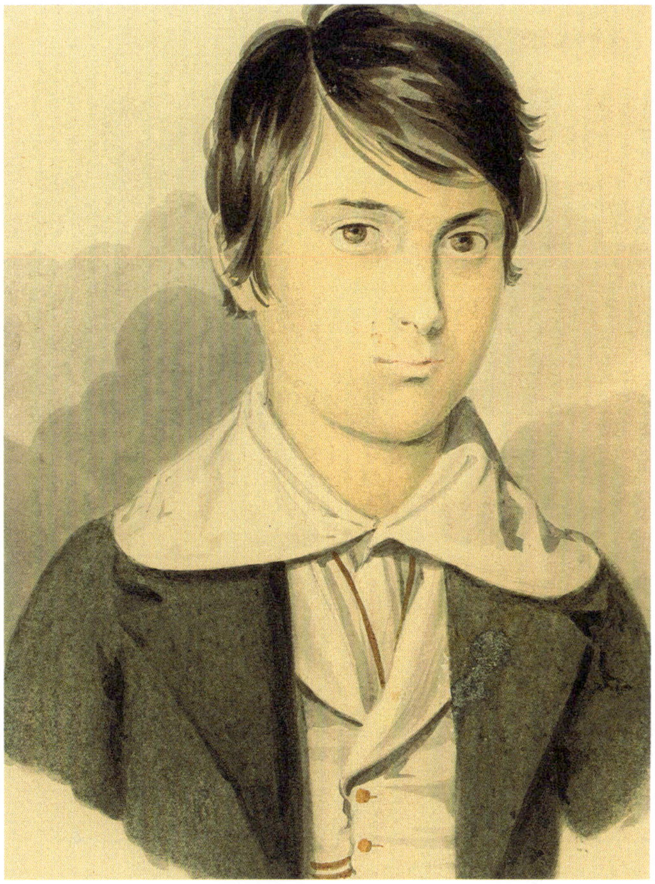
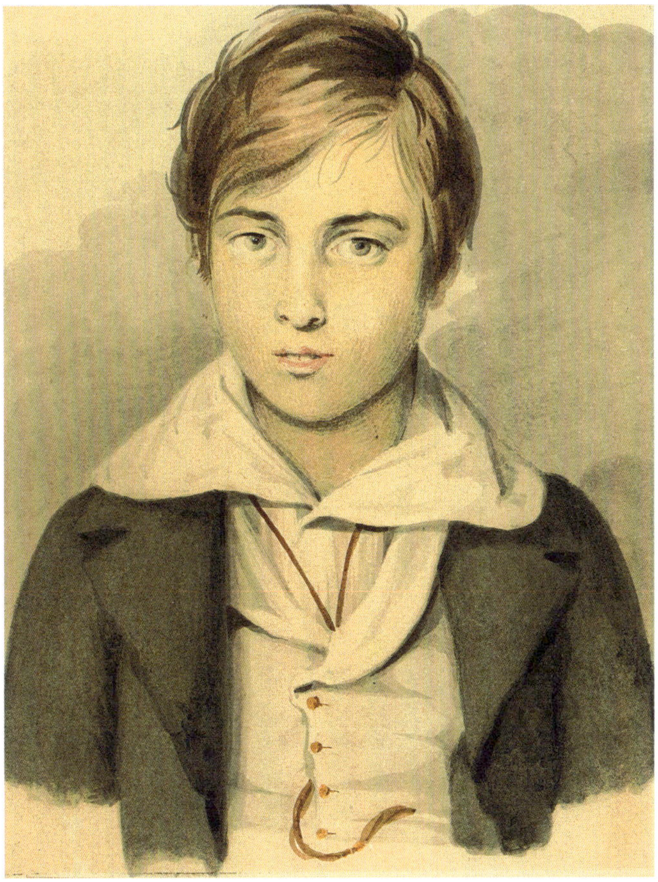
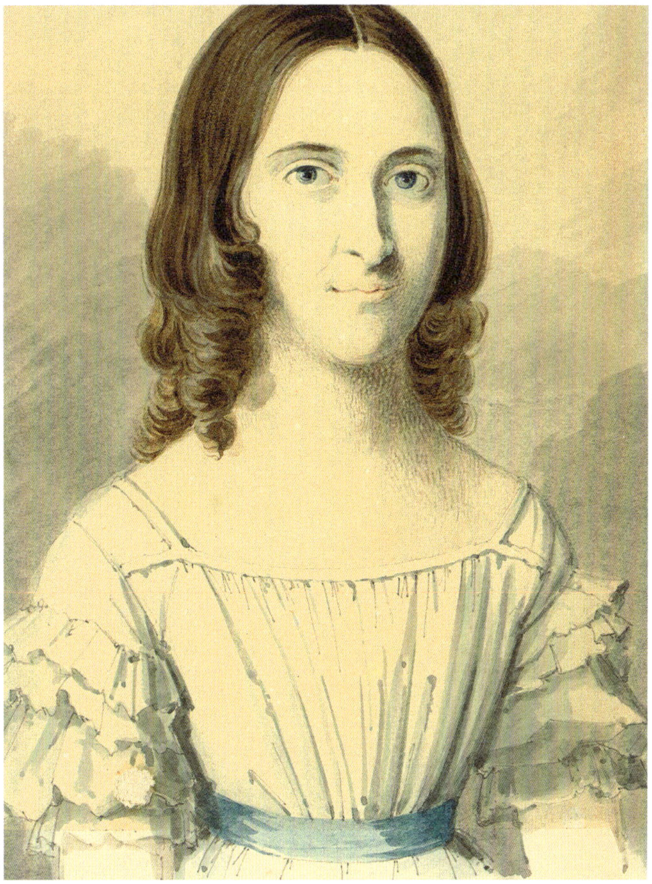

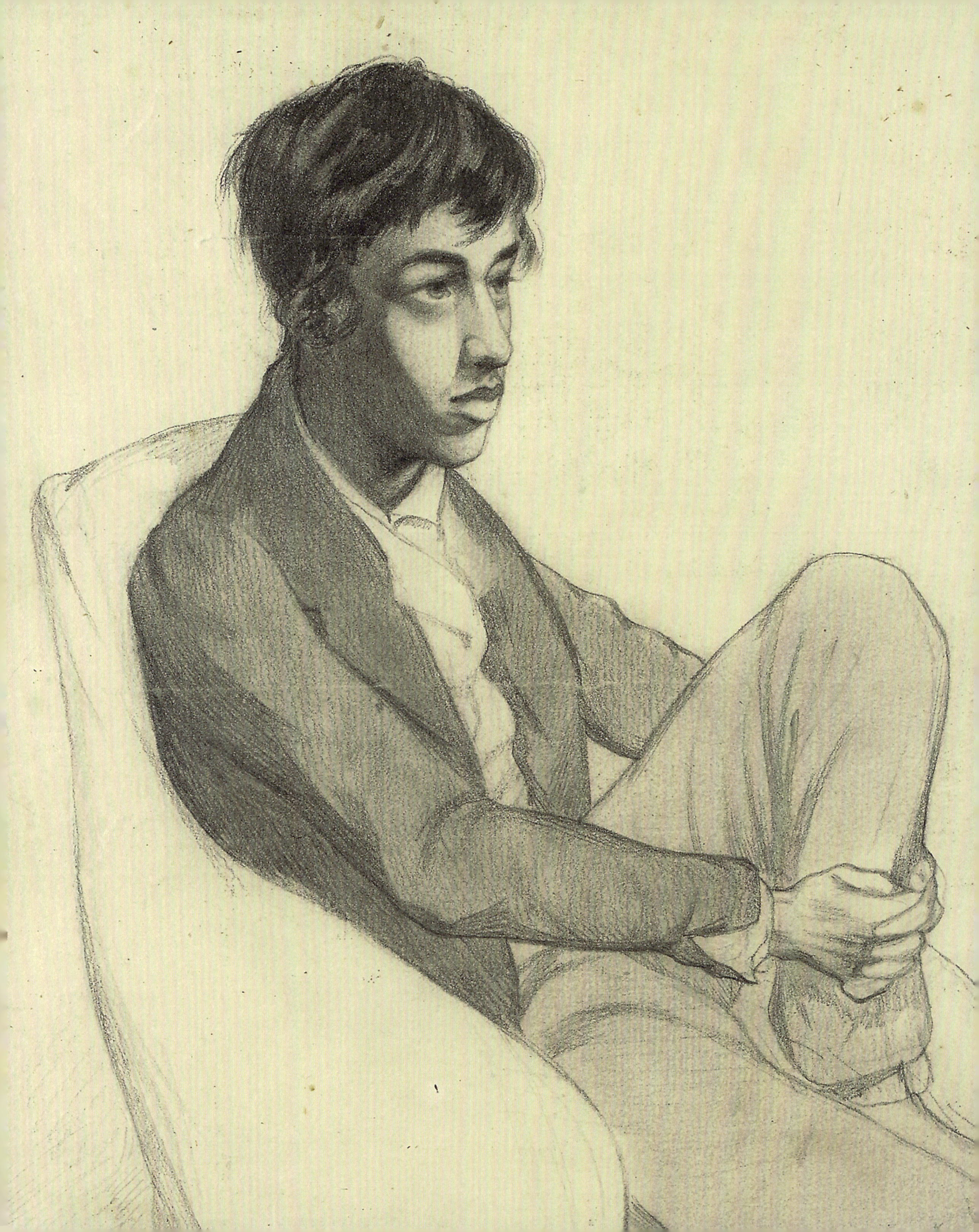

'We read the same authors, coloured prints in the same book, collected woodcuts for the same scrapbook'

William Michael Rossetti

OPPOSITE
NO.18 Filippo Maenza, *Portrait of the young Dante Gabriel Rossetti, seated in an arm-chair* 1843, graphite on paper, 22.2 × 19

with acquaintances of his father, the Maenzas. He was there to recuperate from illness, as can be understood from his portrait made at that time by Filippo 'Peppino' Maenza (NO.18), but he nonetheless wrote enthusiastically to William Michael of his recent purchases:

> I have bought several things here. Among others I picked up yesterday for 15 sous (7d-1/2 English) no less than *5 coloured Gavarnis*, being 3 "Enfants Terribles"; 1 "Fourberies de Femmes," & 1 "Etudiants de Paris," all splendid specimens, and which usually sell at a franc apiece. I have likewise got six Nos. of Johannot's Don Quixote, which is actually being reissued at 4 sous the number!!![5]

The influence of these artists on Gabriel's own artistic development would soon become apparent. In 1846, meanwhile, Christina wrote to William Michael to complain that 'Gabriel receives my woody gleanings with such scorn', referring to woodcuts she had proffered for a scrapbook the two brothers were assembling.[6]

While the four siblings harboured shared literary aspirations, they were not afforded equal access to educational opportunities. Gabriel and William Michael attended King's College School, enabled to do so by the large reduction in fees resulting from Gabriele's position as Professor of Italian at the school.[7] Christina and Maria, meanwhile, were home-schooled by their mother. Furthermore, the children's teenage years were marked by financial instability and ill health. From 1842 onwards Gabriele, whose final book *La Beatrice di Dante* had recently been published to mocking reviews, suffered poor health and partial blindness, reducing his teaching and forcing the family to find alternative sources of income.[8] Frances and Maria took up jobs as governesses, and William Michael entered professional life by joining the Excise Office (later the Inland Revenue Board), where he would work until his retirement in 1894. Christina, meanwhile, took over Gabriele's daily care while scarcely a teenager. The breakdown which Christina suffered in 1845 can surely in part be attributed to the weight of the caring responsibilities that she had assumed, although other circumstances were no doubt involved.[9]

Sappho

Christina Rossetti

I sigh at day-dawn, and I sigh
When the dull day is passing by.
I sigh at evening, and again
I sigh when night brings sleep to men.
Oh! It were better far to die
Than thus for ever mourn and sigh,
And in death's dreamless sleep to be
Unconscious that none weep for me;
Eased from my weight of heaviness,
Forgetful of forgetfulness,
Resting from pain and care and sorrow
Thro' the long night that knows no morrow;
Living unloved, to die unknown,
Unwept, untended and alone. [1847]

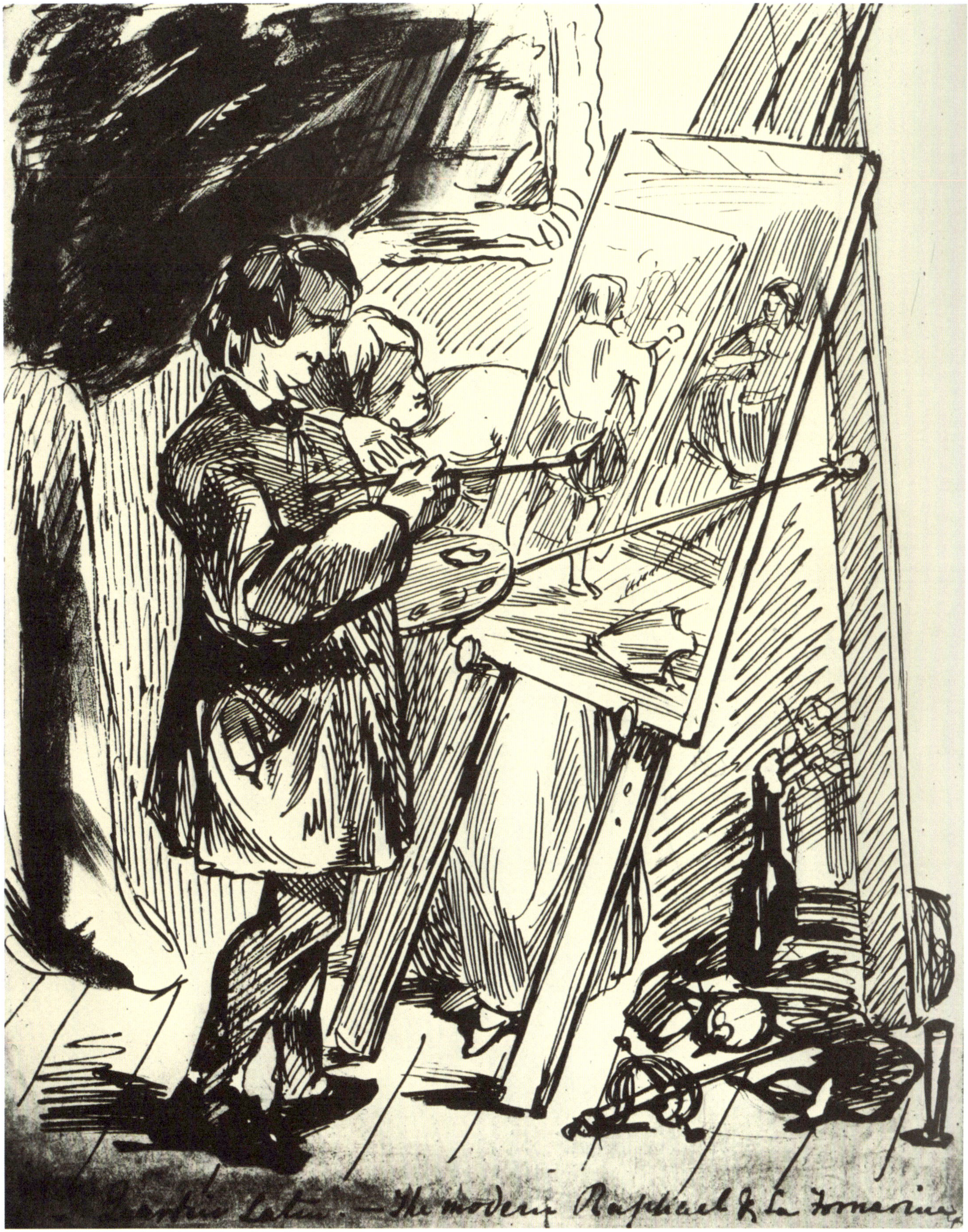
— The modern Raphael & La Fornarina

Christina's poems of this period, such as 'Sappho' and 'Hope in Grief', are weighed down by melancholy, albeit tempered by the anticipation of consolation in the afterlife:

> Our present life is as the night,
> Our future as the morning light:
> Surely the night will pass away,
> And surely will uprise the day.[10]

The religious feeling in the family (among its female members, at least) intensified around 1843, when they became strongly attached to the Tractarian movement, a muscular and worldly form of Christianity which argued for the reinstatement of earlier Christian traditions of faith. The services of the charismatic William Dodsworth at Christ Church, Albany Street, were particularly influential.[11]

Gabriel alone was able to continue his education, occupying a position whereby, in William Michael's words, he 'cost something and earned nothing'.[12] After attending Henry Sass's art school in Bloomsbury, where his fellow students included the artists Anna Mary Howitt and Walter Deverell, Gabriel finally (after several failed applications) progressed to the Antique School of the Royal Academy. One wonders how Gabriel was affected by his position in relation to the rest of his family, and their straitened circumstances. It is hard to find more than traces in his art of this time. His experiments with lithography at this period, including an illustration to Frédéric Soulié's novel *Les Mémoires du diable* and an incomplete set of playing card designs, have been posited as intended for commercial publication, perhaps as a way of contributing to family income.[13] Perhaps his only drawing to reflect on financial hardship dates from September 1846, and shows a well-meaning young woman attending to a beggar, in front of whom the words 'I AM STARVING' are written on the pavement. The inscription below the drawing, 'A Feeling for Art', however, feels sharply ambivalent (NO.26). Nonetheless, awareness of the difficulties faced by the Rossetti family does cast new light on Gabriel's reputed bohemian pose of his student days. William Holman Hunt, for instance, recalled Gabriel as being 'careless in his dress' and '[s]o indifferent ... to the accepted requirements of society, that he would allow spots of mud to remain dry on his clothes for several days'.[14] This may have been a matter of necessity rather than indifference.

PAGE 25
NO.19 Dante Gabriel Rossetti, *Quartier Latin: The Modern Raphael and La Fornarina*, ink on paper, 22.8 × 18.8

OPPOSITE
NO.20 Dante Gabriel Rossetti, *Self-Portrait* 1847, graphite and chalk on paper, 20.7 × 16.8

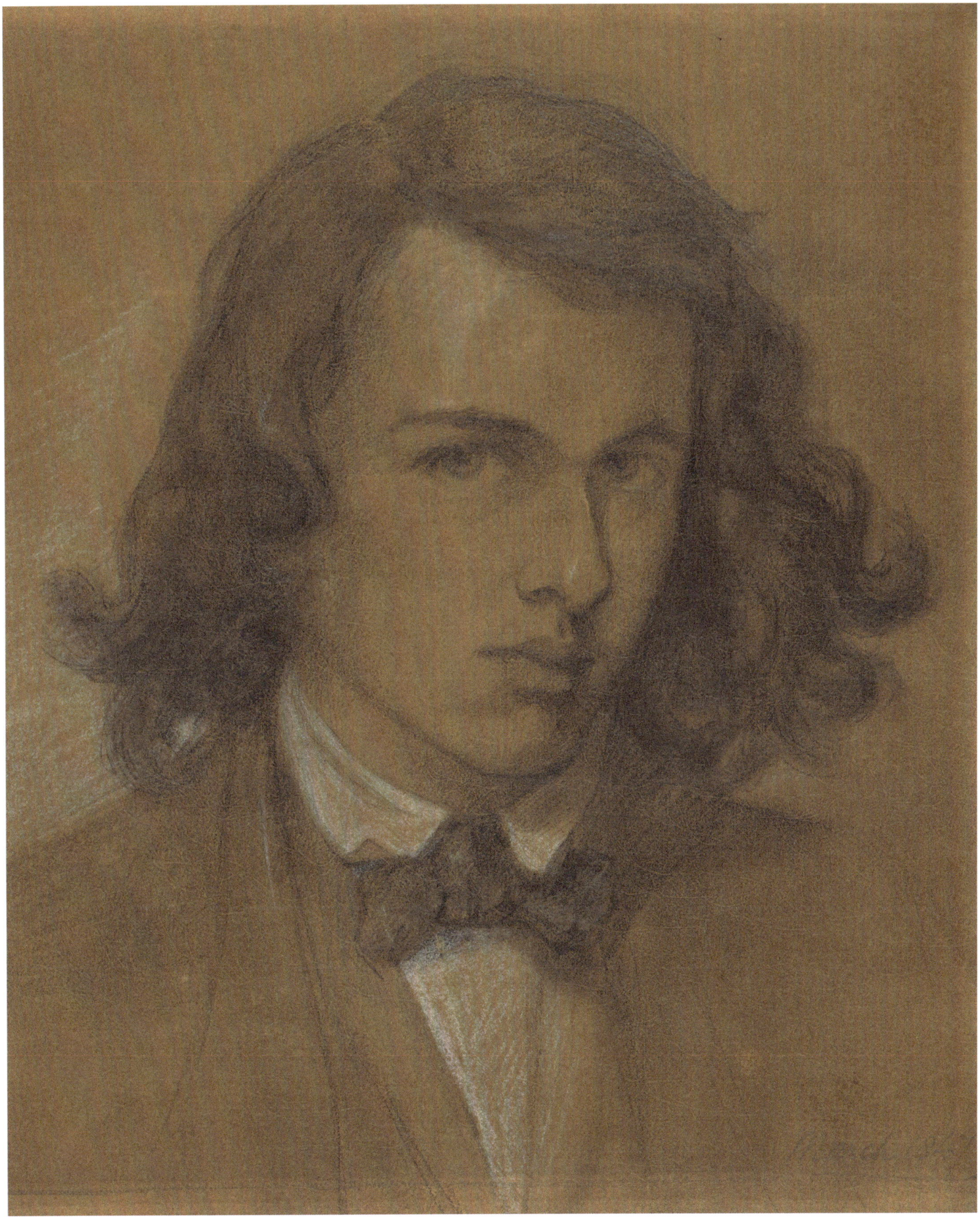

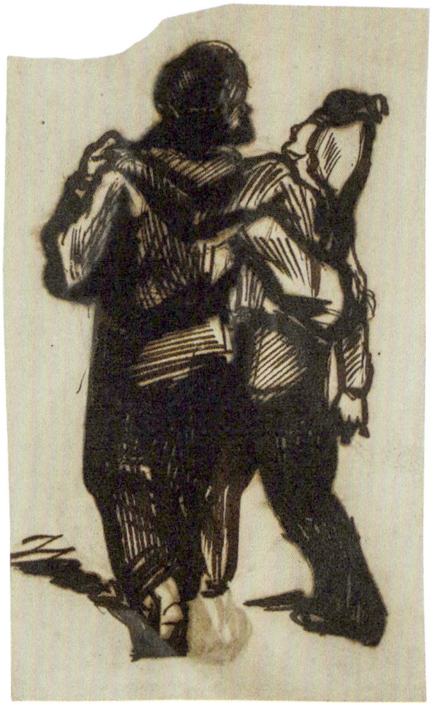

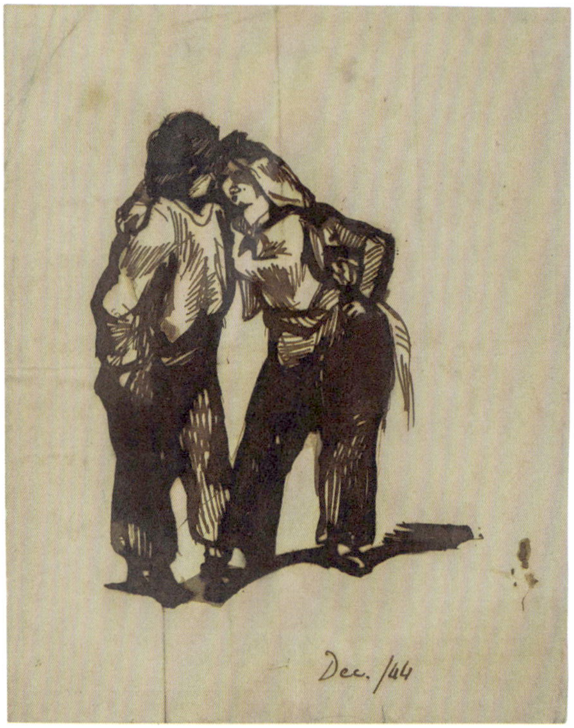
Dec. /44

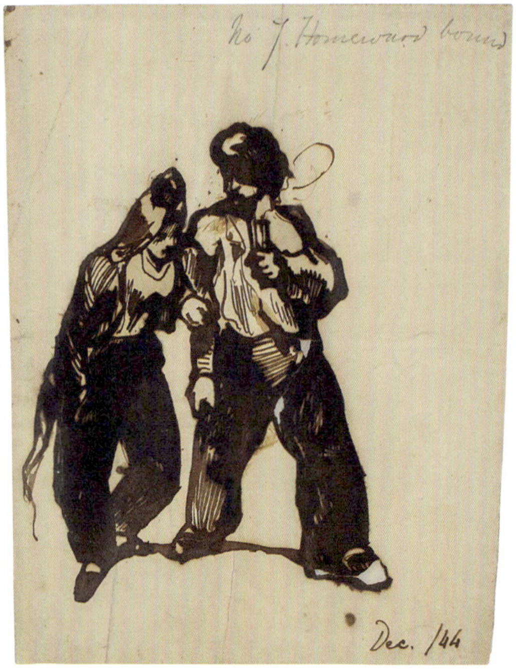
No 7. Homeward bound
Dec. /44

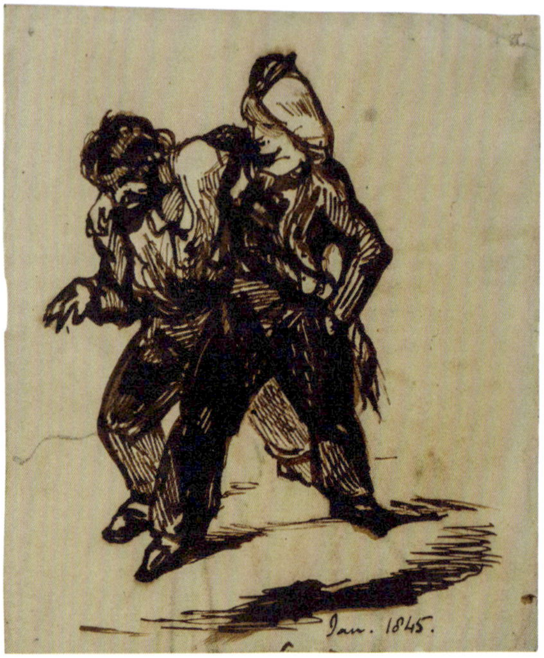
Jan. 1845.

RIGHT
NO.25 Paul Jonnard after John Hancock, *Dante Gabriel Rossetti* 1889, line engraving on paper, 12 × 11.5

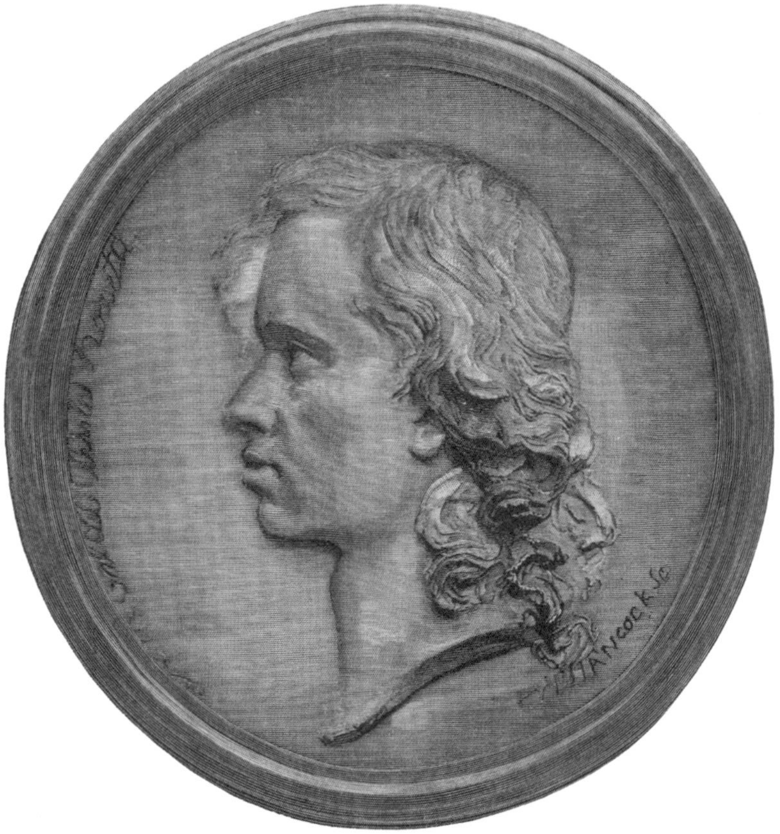

OPPOSITE, CLOCKWISE FROM TOP LEFT

NO.21 Dante Gabriel Rossetti, *Back View of Man and Woman* 1844, ink on paper, 16 × 10

NO.22 Dante Gabriel Rossetti, *Man with Woman Wearing Trousers* 1844, ink on paper, 19 × 16

NO.23 Dante Gabriel Rossetti, *Man Dancing with Woman Wearing Trousers* 1845, ink on paper, 15.5 × 13

NO.24 Dante Gabriel Rossetti, *Homeward Bound* 1844, ink on paper, 18.7 × 15

At any rate, unlike his future Pre-Raphaelite Brother John Everett Millais, Gabriel was no model student. His attendance was irregular, and he rebelled against accepted norms. Similarly, he chafed against the rigorous discipline of the RA Schools, which mandated the diligent copying from the academy's collection of casts of classical sculpture. Instead, art critic and Pre-Raphaelite Brother F.G. Stephens recalled, he acquired a reputation as a 'clever sketcher of chivalric and satiric subjects', a description which aptly characterises his many figure studies and modern life subjects of this period.[15] *The Bivouac after the Ball* (NO.28), *The Ladies of Marlboro' Street* (see NO.97) and *Quartier Latin: The Modern Raphael and La Fornarina* (NO.19) are vivid translations of the illustrations of Paul Gavarni (see NO.27), George Cruikshank, and other contemporary graphic artists whom Gabriel admired and collected, while several pairs of figures showing men and women dancing or walking clumsily are full of humour. *The Bivouac after the Ball*, in particular, has the wit and economy of Gabriel's models at this time. Two figures smoke on a street corner, bottles at their feet, while nearby, outside the titular 'BAL' (the French spelling is used), another group of revellers stagger and sway. Above the rooftops, a full moon is partially visible in the cloudy sky, illuminating the scene.

Equally, Gabriel's wide-ranging literary influences are clearly visible in his drawings of this period, whose subjects included the European canon (Dante and Shakespeare), recent literature (Adelbert von Chamisso's 1814 novella *Peter Schlemihl*), and popular ballads (Bishop Thomas Percy's *Reliques of Ancient English Poetry*).

BELOW
NO.26 Dante Gabriel Rossetti, *Beggar and Woman* 1846, ink on paper, 24.1 × 15.2

BOTTOM
NO.27 Paul Gavarni, *Les gens de Paris: petit commerce* 1846, lithograph on paper, 26.3 × 17

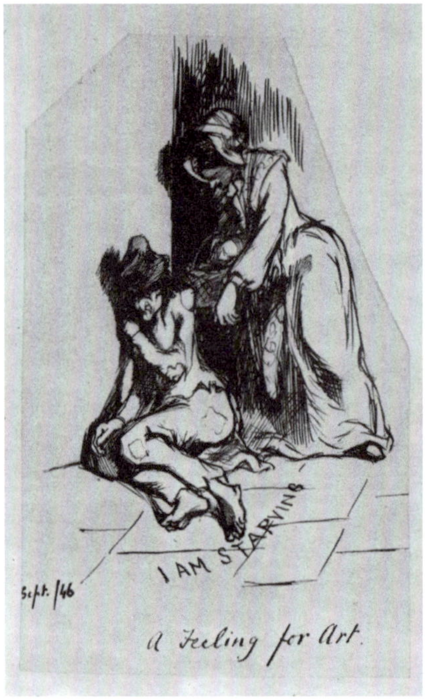

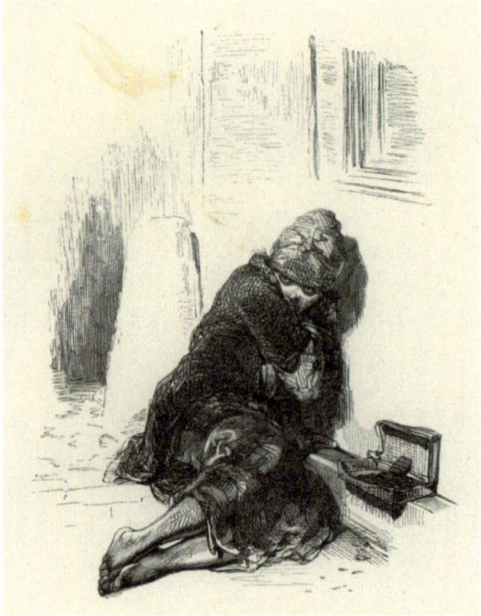

Two sources in particular captivated him, however: Goethe's *Faust*, and the works of Edgar Allan Poe. Such interest in these sources is unsurprising considering that Gabriel's uncle, John William Polidori, had written *The Vampyre*, which established the prototype for subsequent novels such as Bram Stoker's *Dracula*.[16]

Gabriel was also known for his interest in the macabre and diabolic while at the RA Schools. An American friend, Charley Ware, painted a picture of himself, Gabriel and others 'either playing whist … or enjoying a light symposium' – with the Devil.[17] It was probably through Ware and a compatriot, Thomas Doughty, that Gabriel was introduced to Poe's writings, which inspired a number of important drawings at this period.[18] Indeed, Gabriel is believed to have been the first artist to illustrate Poe's narrative poem 'The Raven'. This was first published in the New York *Evening Mirror* on 29 January 1845, while Gabriel's earliest dated illustration to it is dated June 1846. He was similarly quick to illustrate Poe's 'Ulalume' after it was published in 1847.[19] William Michael described Poe as being 'a deep well of delight' to Gabriel during these years, and the artist's admiration for the writer is evident in the way that he praised Theodor von Holst as 'in some sort, the Edgar Poe of painters'.[20] This taste for the macabre was shared, at least in part, by Christina. It was demonstrated in the first poem in her 1847 *Verses*, 'The Dead City', in which a feast taking place in a splendid city is revealed to comprise of the dead:

> Here a dead man sat to sup,
> In his hand a drinking cup;
> Wine cup of the heavy gold,
> Human hand stony and cold,
> And no life breath struggling up.[21]

'The Raven' and *Faust* helped Gabriel to move beyond the isolated figures of his earliest drawings, and to create scenes that depicted decisive narrative events within a fully realised interior. They also provided a means to explore some of the emerging central themes in his work: the uncanny, the doppelgänger, and the permeability of life and death. In a drawing of the final scene of *Faust*, the heroine Margaret (Gretchen) prays for strength to resist the Devil (NO.36); while the narrator of 'The Raven' feels the presence of angels while seated in his drawing room (NOS.33, 34). From Gabriel's response to Poe, the poem 'The Blessed Damozel',[22] to works such as *How They Met Themselves*, Gabriel's later work is permeated with the themes of the uncanny that are explored in these drawings. Love, the central theme of Gabriel's art, is already an animating force in many of the drawings.

The Shadowless Man c.1846, an illustration to Chamisso's *Peter Schlemihl* (in which the protagonist trades his shadow in exchange for an endless supply of gold), is one of the most fascinating of Gabriel's drawings from this period (NO.30). It shows the decisive moment in which Schlemihl's companion realises he casts no shadow, which disrupts their relationship and introduces consequences for the loss of the shadow. Beyond the evident appeal of such gothic literature at this moment in Gabriel's career, this subject is interesting given the use of long, raking shadows in so many of his

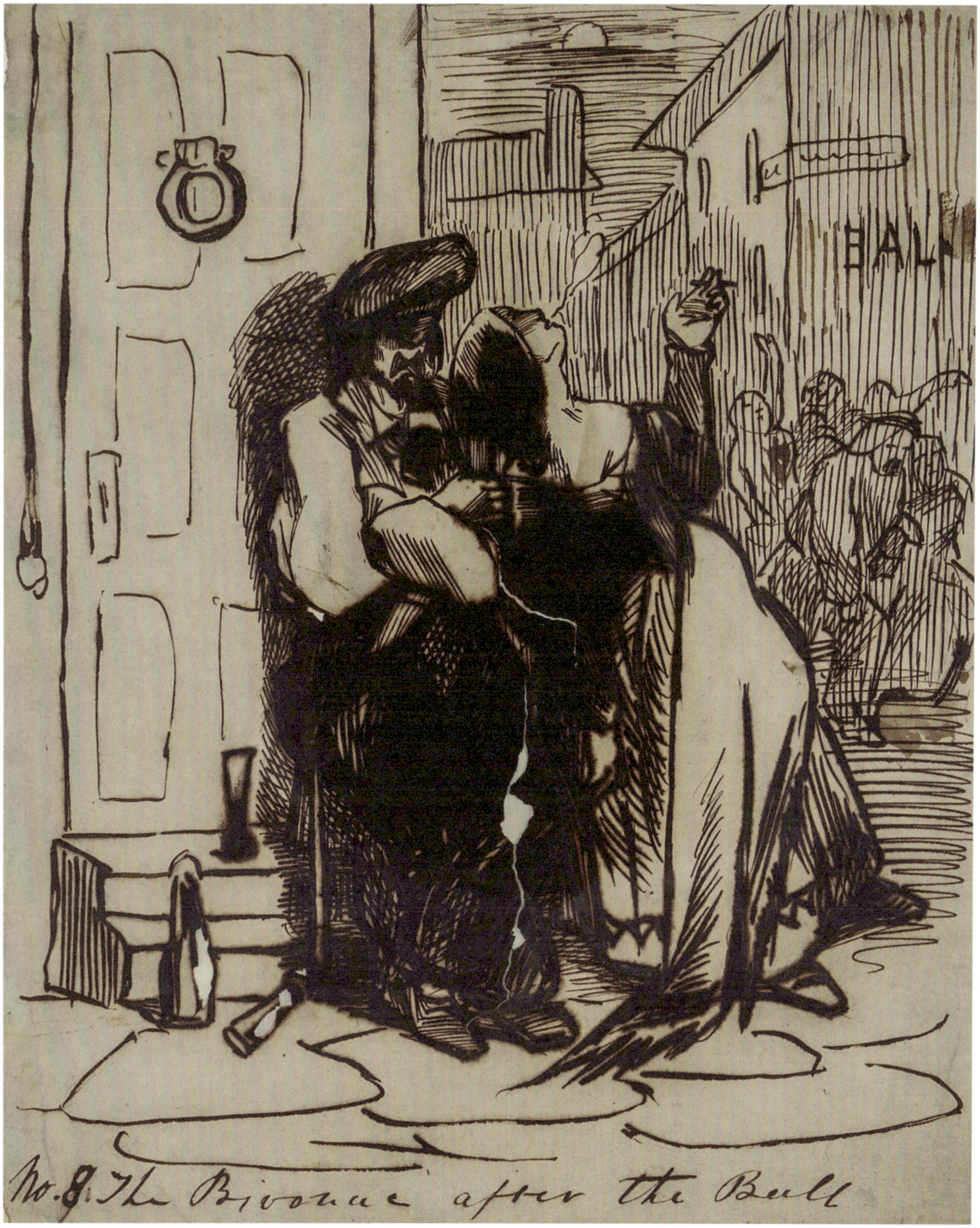

NO.28 Dante Gabriel Rossetti, *The Bivouac after the Ball* 1845, ink and graphite on paper, 22.5 × 18.5

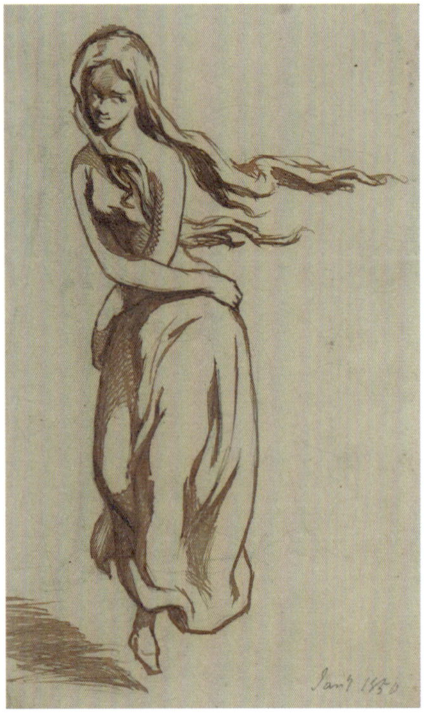

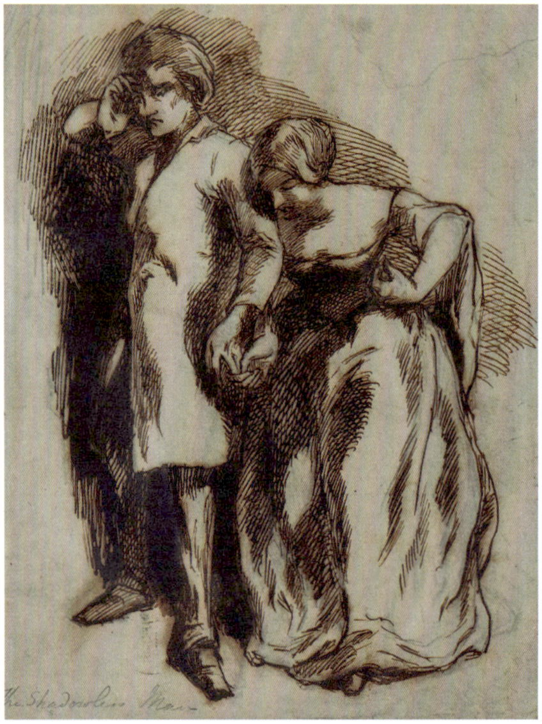

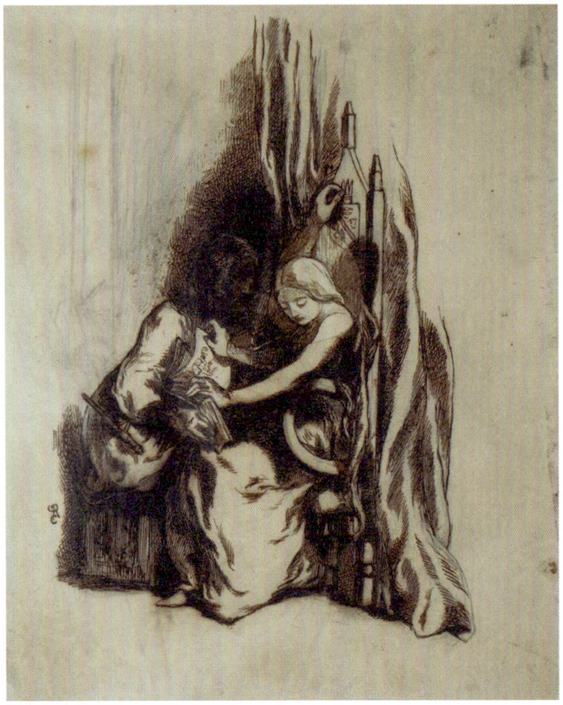

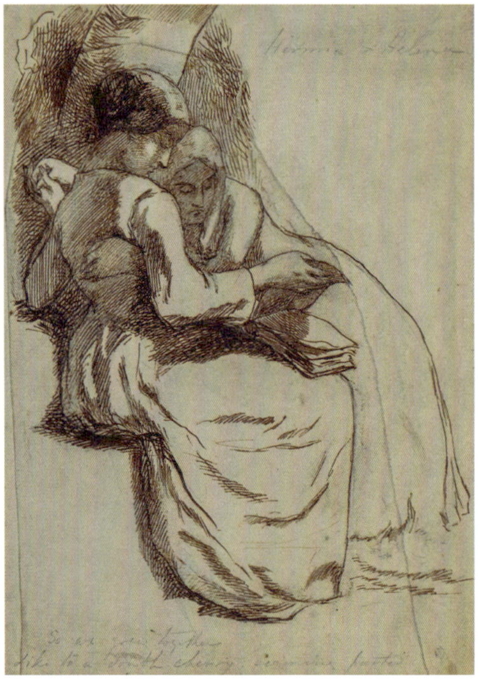

drawings around this time. The decision to draw a man who literally cast no shadow, beyond its literary function, might even point towards the shallow space of Gabriel's Pre-Raphaelite works.

This vein of exuberant fantasias on literary themes might appear to have little in common with the meticulous renderings of Biblical subjects that characterised Gabriel's work after 1848. However, several drawings pre-dating the Pre-Raphaelite Brotherhood show him to have been moving through a transitional stage. As art historian Alastair Grieve has shown, *The Sleeper* of 1846–7 anticipates *The Girlhood of Mary Virgin* 1848–9 in its organisation of space, with the 'pale sheeted ghosts' of Poe's poem in the drawing viewed through a window similarly to Joachim in the later painting (see NOS.35, 53).[23] Similarly, *Faust: Margaret in the Church* 1848 shows the kneeling figure in a markedly similar position to that of the Virgin in *Ecce Ancilla Domini! (The Annunciation)* of 1849–50 (see NOS.36, 73). In both cases, the episodes from Poe's 'The Sleeper' and Goethe's *Faust* that Gabriel selects, and the way in which they are depicted, clearly anticipate his Pre-Raphaelite paintings.

Gabriel's abortive first oil painting, *Retro Me, Sathana!* (meaning 'Get thee behind me, Satan!') of 1847, was also part of this transition. The work, featuring Mephistopheles lurking behind a priest, accompanied an early poem, by Gabriel, related to Faust. The painting was abandoned following disapproving comments from Charles Eastlake, then Keeper of the National Gallery, and an ally of the artist since he first saw Gabriel's sketches in June 1846. The following year, Gabriel made a drawing of the same subject (NO.40).[24] This shows him to have been working with a Biblical subject which – similarly to subjects favoured by artists, such as the Temptation of St Anthony – gave licence for the artistic depiction of the grotesquerie which was so much a part of Gabriel's early work. At the same time, its precision and flat, frieze-like composition anticipate *The Girlhood of Mary Virgin* and other works of the following years.

There was also another reason for Gabriel to abandon *Retro Me, Sathana!* in favour of more conventional Biblical subjects. His religious mother and sisters would not have wanted to sit for

OPPOSITE, CLOCKWISE FROM TOP LEFT

NO.29 Dante Gabriel Rossetti, *Girl Walking or Flying* 1846–50, ink on paper, 22 × 16.5

NO.30 Dante Gabriel Rossetti, *The Shadowless Man* c.1846, ink on paper, 17 × 12.5

NO.31 Dante Gabriel Rossetti, *Hermia and Helena* c.1846, ink on paper, 21 × 15.5

NO.32 Dante Gabriel Rossetti, *Paolo and Francesca da Rimini* 1846–8, ink and graphite on paper, 28 × 23

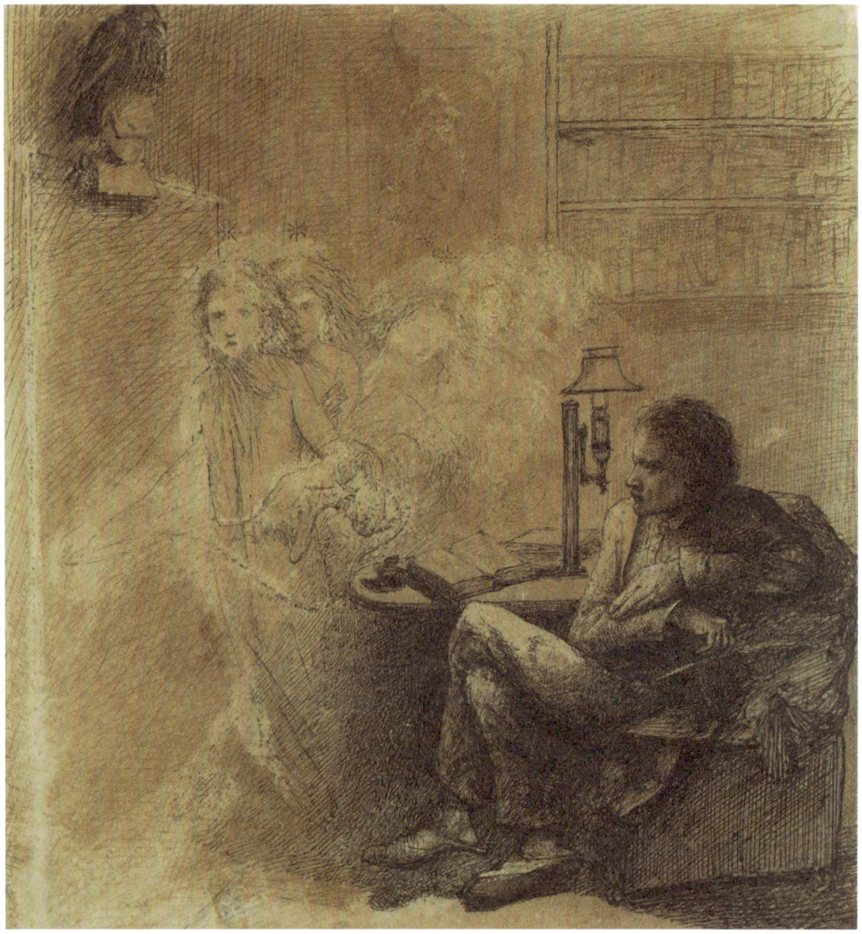

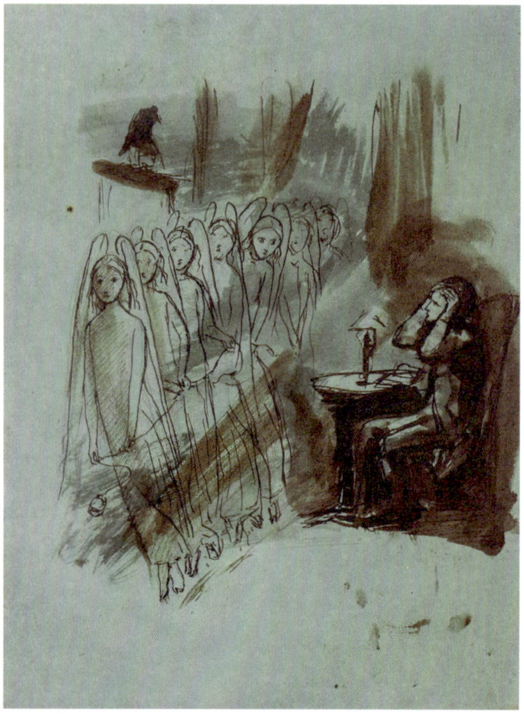

ABOVE
NO.33 Dante Gabriel Rossetti, *The Raven: Angel Footfalls* c.1848, pen and brown ink on light brown paper, 22.9 × 21.6

RIGHT
NO.34 Dante Gabriel Rossetti, *The Raven: Angel Footfalls* 1846, ink on paper, 28.5 × 22

NO.35 Dante Gabriel Rossetti, *The Sleeper* 1846–7, ink and wash on paper, 26.6 × 17.4

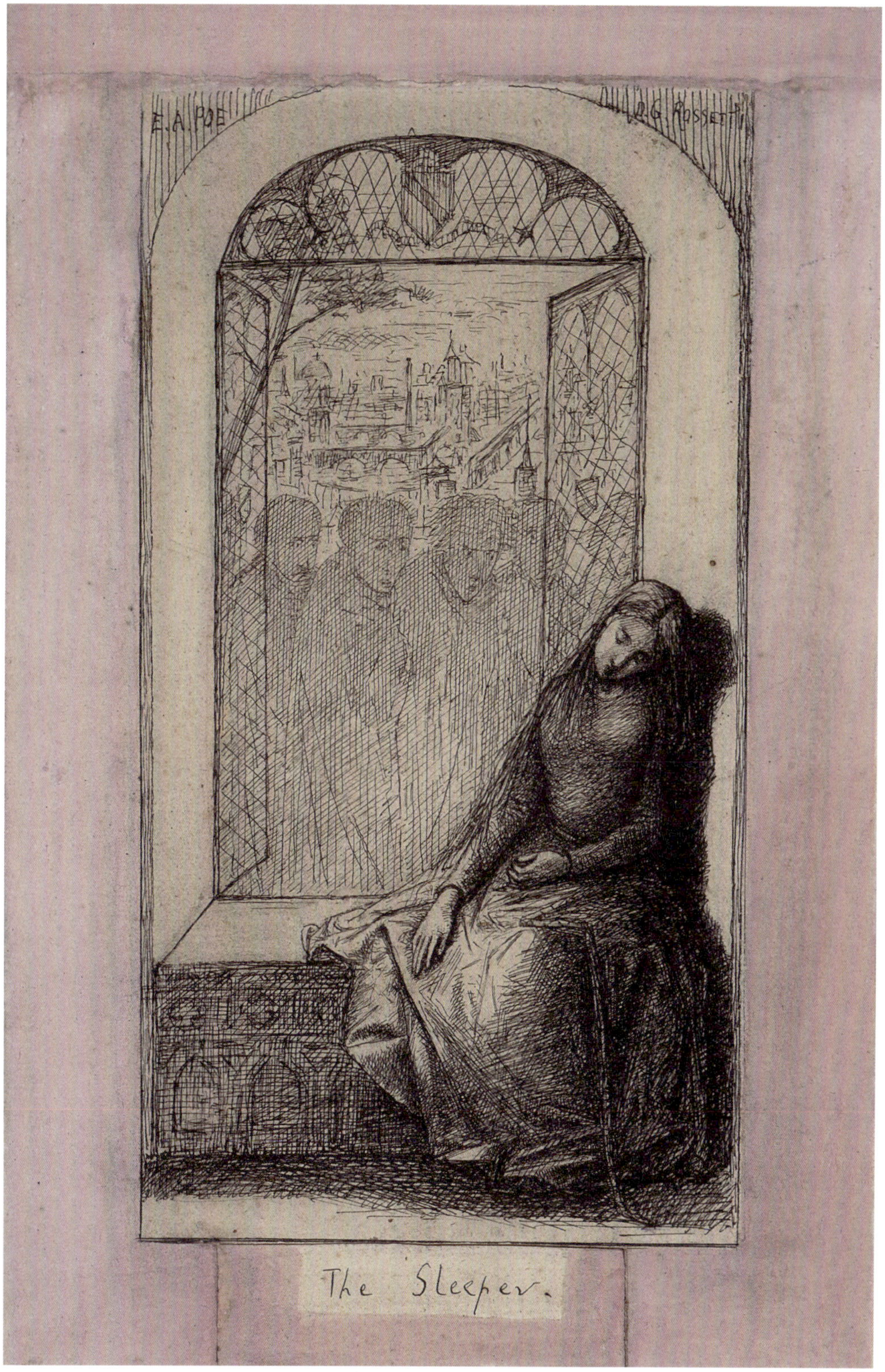

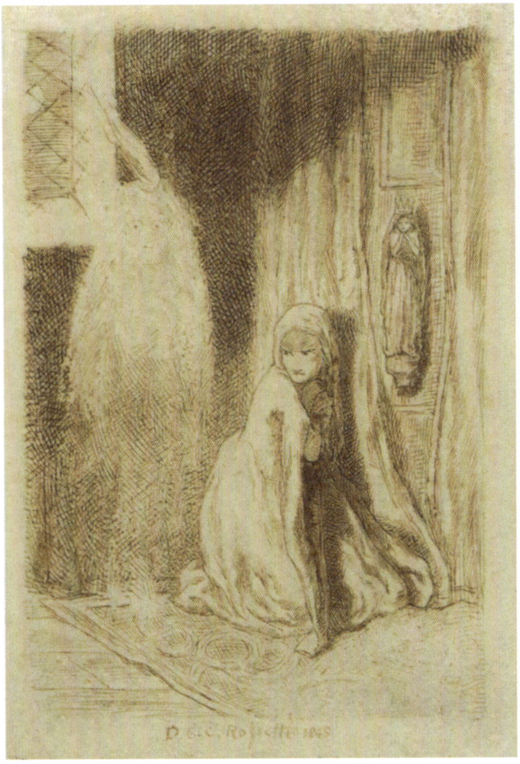

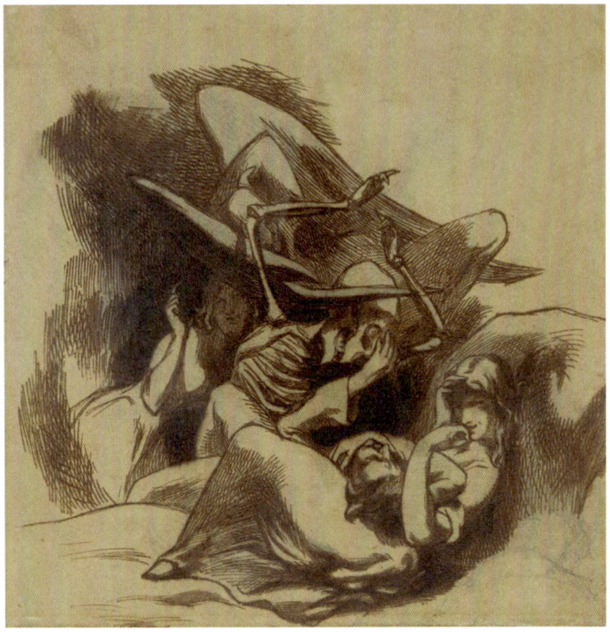

ABOVE LEFT
NO.36 Dante Gabriel Rossetti, *Faust: Margaret in the Church* 1848, ink on paper, 17.8 × 12.1

ABOVE RIGHT
NO.37 Dante Gabriel Rossetti, *Faust* 1846, ink on paper, 24 × 23.5

OPPOSITE
NO.38 William Blake, *The Notebook of William Blake ('the Rossetti Manuscript')* 1787–1847, graphite and ink on paper, 19.7 × 15.9

anything irreligious, and Gabriel similarly would not have wished to alienate his family. Christina, in particular, was perhaps his most regular model in the late 1840s, and according to William Michael, it was an 1848 portrait of her which was Gabriel's first completed oil painting.[25] Gabriel also advocated for her presence within the Pre-Raphaelite Brotherhood. William Michael, meanwhile, would become a crucial chronicler of the Brotherhood.[26]

At the same time that Gabriel's visual language was being refined, he was also wavering between art and poetry. He was, like his future Pre-Raphaelite colleagues, an enthusiast, spurred on by the desire to emulate his heroes (as demonstrated by the list of 'Immortals' compiled by the Brotherhood in 1848), and in 1847 he wrote to two of his literary inspirations to congratulate them and solicit advice. First he instigated correspondence with the poet Robert Browning, whose *Pippa Passes* (1841) and *Sordello* (1840) would inspire works by both Gabriel and Elizabeth Siddal, his future collaborator and later wife. He then contacted Leigh Hunt, sending samples of his work and enquiring about the relative wisdom of pursuing painting or poetry as a career. Hunt, while admiring Gabriel's original poetry, counselled him that 'poetry, even the very best ... is not a thing for a man to live upon while he is in the flesh, however immortal it may render him in spirit'.[27]

Perhaps most significant in shaping the contours of Gabriel's career, however, was his purchase of a notebook by William Blake in April 1847 (NO.38). William Michael loaned Gabriel ten shillings to purchase a notebook of Blake's designs from an attendant at the British Museum who was related to the artist Samuel Palmer, who

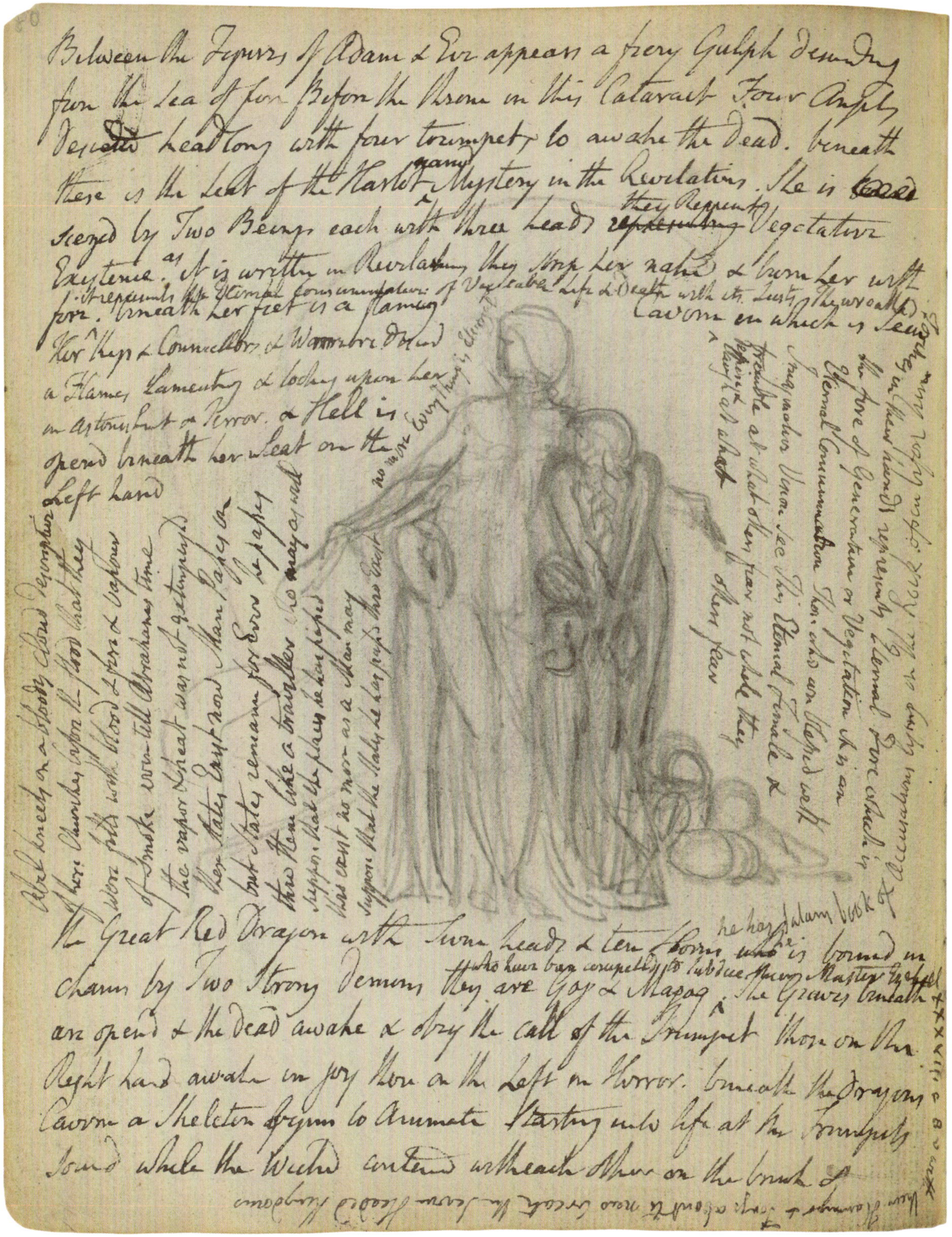

Between the Figures of Adam & Eve appears a fiery Gulph descending from the sea of fire Before the Throne in this Cataract Four Angels descend headlong with four trumpets to awake the dead. beneath these is the Seat of the Harlot named Mystery in the Revelations. She is seized by Two Beings each with three heads they Represent Vegetative Existence. as it is written in Revelations they strip her naked & burn her with fire. it represents the Eternal Consummation of Vegetable Life & Death with its Lusts. The wreathed Torches in their hands represents Eternal Fire which is the fire of Generation or Vegetation it is an Eternal Consummation Those who are blessed with Imaginative Vision see This Eternal Female & tremble at what others fear not while they despise & laugh at what others fear. beneath her feet is a flaming Cavern in which is seen Her Kings & Councellors & Warriors descend in Flames Lamenting & looking upon her in astonishment & Terror. & Hell is opend beneath her Seat on the Left hand

Abel kneels on a bloody cloud descriptive of those Churches before the flood that they were filld with blood & fire & vapour of smoke even till Abrahams time the vapor & heat was not extinguishd These States Exist now Man Passes on but States remain for Ever he passes thro them like a traveller who may as well suppose that the places he has passed thro exist no more as a Man may suppose that the States he has passd thro exist no more Every Thing is Eternal

The Great Red Dragon with Seven heads & ten Horns who is bound in chains by Two strong demons they are Gog & Magog who have been compelled to subdue their Master Ezekiel XXXVIII c 8 v he has Satanic book of Laws with their Hammer & Tongs about to new Create the Seven Headed Kingdoms. The Graves beneath are opend & the dead awake & obey the call of the Trumpet those on the Right hand awake in joy those on the Left in Horror. beneath the Dragons Cavern a Skeleton begins to Animate starting into life at the Trumpets sound while the Wicked contend with each other on the brink of

BELOW
NO.39 Dante Gabriel Rossetti, *Lady Anne Bothwell's Lament* 1846–7, graphite, brown ink and wash on paper, 29.2 × 23.2

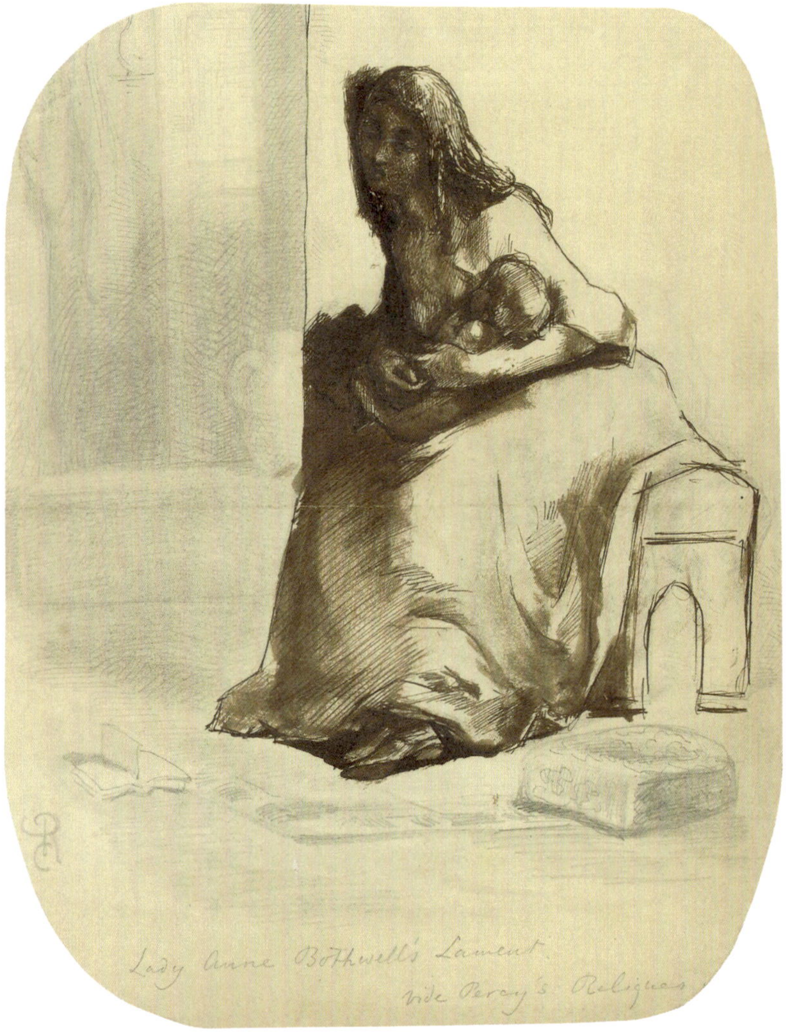

OPPOSITE
NO.40 Dante Gabriel Rossetti, *Retro me Sathana – Get thee behind me Satan* 1848, ink on paper, 24.1 × 17.5

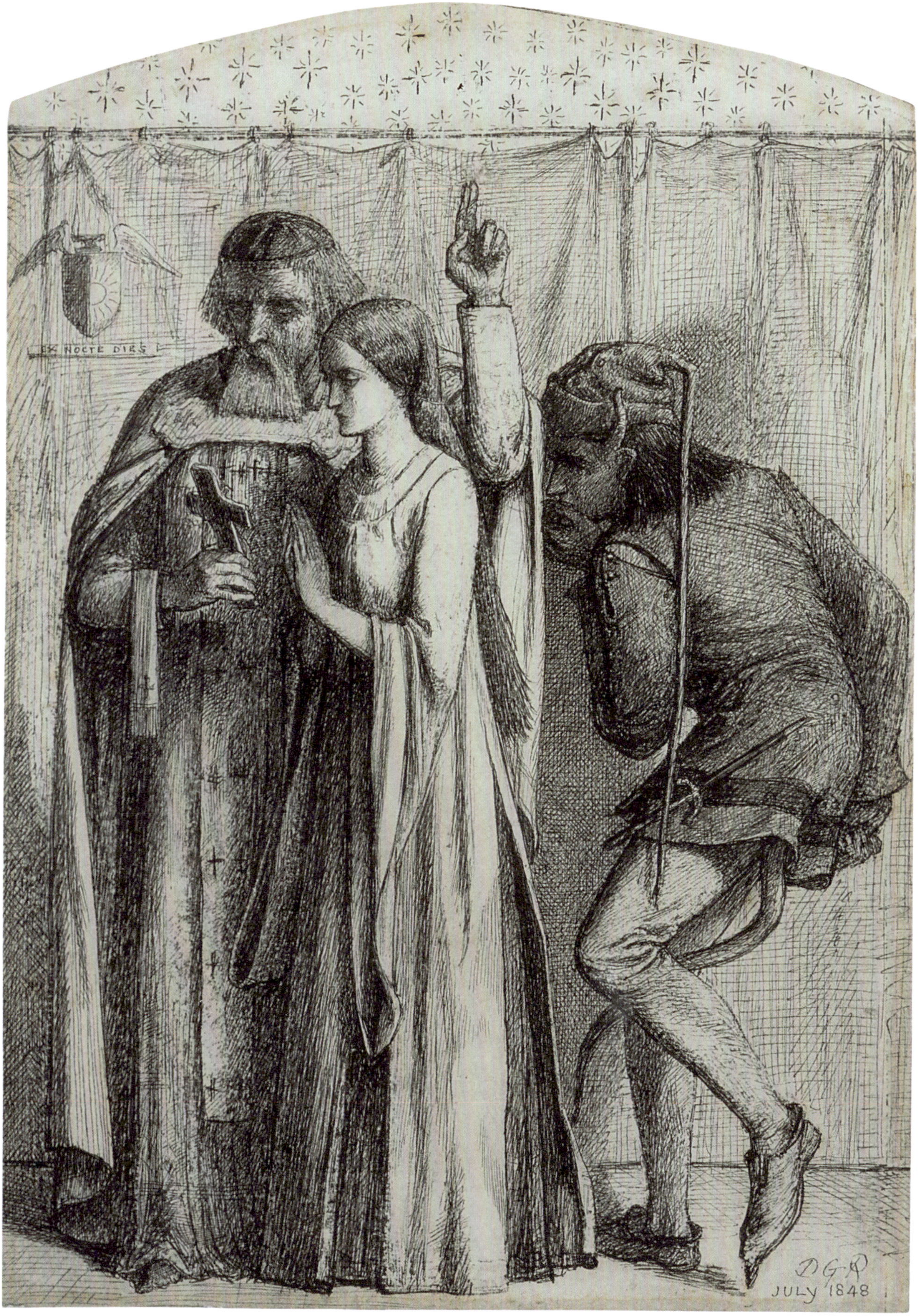
EX NOCTE DIES
DGR
JULY 1848

'"I wish that he were come to me,
For he will come," she said'

Dante Gabriel Rossetti, 'The Blessed Damozel', 1847

had known and been profoundly influenced by Blake.[28] Gabriel was born just after Blake's death, at a time when Blake's critical reputation was at a low ebb, but in time, Gabriel would go on to become the chief inheritor, in British art, of Blake's legacy as a poet-painter. There are certainly resemblances between Blake's designs in the book and some drawings by Gabriel and Elizabeth Siddal, but more fundamentally Blake was the foremost exemplar for the innovative and pioneering ways that the Rossettis would combine these aspects of his work, anticipating Gabriel's dual works of art and Siddal's own parallel practice as artist and poet.

It was also in 1847 that Christina's *Verses* were published in a small edition by Gaetano Polidori, comprising poems written by her between the ages of twelve and sixteen. Polidori had pronounced that Christina '[a]*vrà più spirito di tutti*' (would have more wit - or cleverness - than any of the others) and this promise was now being borne out, marking a new stage of her career following the difficulties of 1845.[29] In a copy of the book passed down through the family, Gabriel drew a series of elegant illustrations to his sister's poems, continuing the collaborations of their childhood (see NOS.50–2). These responded to some of the most melancholy poems in the volume: the wanderer dying upon reaching 'The Ruined Cross'; the recollections of a former lover in 'The Dream'; Leonora d'Este's visit to the incarcerated Torquato Tasso in 'Tasso and Leonora'. Moreover, during the formation of the Pre-Raphaelite Brotherhood, Gabriel showed his respect for Christina's poetry by soliciting her involvement, although this came to nothing, owing to her reticence about sharing her work.[30] By the end of the 1840s, all four of the Rossetti siblings had begun their careers as writers. Maria's first book *The Rivulets* was printed privately by Alfred Dod in 1846, while William Michael played a crucial role in *The Germ* (including authoring the sonnet that appeared on its cover). As they crossed the threshold into adulthood, the Rossetti teenagers had all taken the first steps towards their future as a literary family of rare distinction

1 Alison Chapman and Joanna Meacock, *A Rossetti Family Chronology*, Basingstoke and New York 2007, p.43.

2 Christina Rossetti observed this common family involvement with Dante in her article 'Dante, The Poet Illustrated out of the Poem', *The Century*, Feb. 1884, pp.566–73 (p.566).

3 Chapman and Meacock 2007, p.18.

4 William Michael Rossetti, *Some Reminiscences of William Michael Rossetti*, 2 vols., London 1906, vol.1, p.57.

5 Dante Gabriel Rossetti to William Michael Rossetti, 1 December 1844, in William E. Fredeman (ed.), *The Correspondence of Dante Gabriel Rossetti*, 10 vols., Cambridge, Woodbridge and Rochester, NY 2002–15, vol.1, p.33.

6 Antony H. Harrison (ed.), *The Letters of Christina Rossetti*, 4 vols., Charlottesville, VA 1997–2004, vol.1, pp.6–7.

7 There they studied with the artist John Sell Cotman, who set his students to copy medieval figures in armour, possibly contributing to the importance of medieval subject matter for Gabriel. See Alastair Grieve, *The Best Years of Rossetti's Art: 1846–1862*, Norwich 2017, p.22, and Frances Thomas, *Christina Rossetti: A Biography*, London 1994, p.40.

8 See Jan Marsh, *Dante Gabriel Rossetti: Painter and Poet*, London 1999, p.13.

9 A doctor's report at the time referred to a 'kind of religious mania'. See Jan Marsh, *Christina Rossetti: A Literary Biography*, London 1994, p.52.

10 Christina Rossetti, 'Hope in Grief' (ll.27–30), in *Christina Rossetti: Selected Poems*, ed. Dinah Roe, London 2008, p.4.

11 Dinah Roe, *The Rossettis in Wonderland*, London 2011, p.66.

12 William Michael Rossetti 1906, 1, p.39.

13 William Michael asserted that Gabriel intended to complete the cards for publication: Chapman and Meacock 2007, p.31.

14 William Holman Hunt, *Pre-Raphaelitism and the Pre-Raphaelite Brotherhood*, 2 vols., London 1905–6, vol.1, p.145.

15 F.G. Stephens, *Dante Gabriel Rossetti*, London 1894, p.10.

16 *The Vampyre* was first published under the name of Lord Byron and Goethe, not knowing the true identity of its author, acclaimed the story as Byron's masterpiece. See Nigel Leask, 'Polidori, John William (1795–1821)', *Oxford Dictionary of National Biography* (online), accessed 13 October 2022.

17 William Michael Rossetti, *Dante Gabriel Rossetti: His Family-Letters with a Memoir*, 2 vols., London 1895, vol.1, p.108.

18 Marsh 1999, p.22.

19 Grieve 2017, p.37.

20 Marsh 1999, p.28.

21 Christina Rossetti, 'The Dead City' (ll.241–5), in *Verses*, London 1847, p.9.

22 T. Hall Caine, *Recollections of Dante Gabriel Rossetti*, London 1882, p.284.

23 Grieve 2017, p.83.

24 Chapman and Meacock 2007, p.29.

25 William Michael [W.M.] Rossetti, 'List of Works of Art', 1908, no.56.

26 Fredeman 2002–15, 1, pp.64–7.

27 Leigh Hunt to Dante Gabriel Rossetti, 31 March 1848, in Fredeman 2002–15, 1, p.52.

28 Chapman and Meacock 2007, p.32.

29 William Michael Rossetti 1906, p.21.

30 Fredeman 2002–15, 1, p.66.

Dinah Roe

Christina Rossetti's Secret

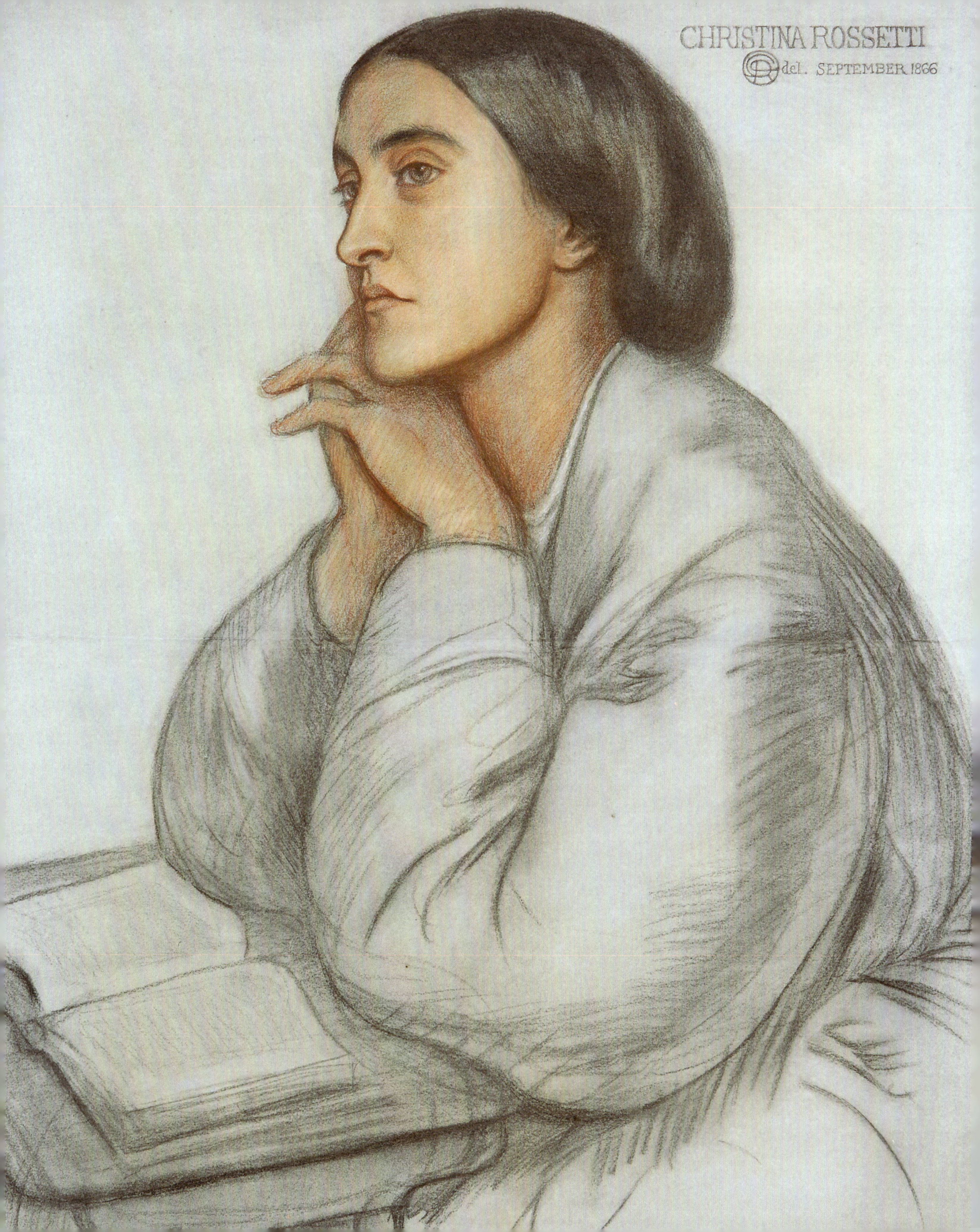
CHRISTINA ROSSETTI
del. SEPTEMBER 1866

PAGE 43
NO.41 Dante Gabriel Rossetti, *Portrait of Christina Rossetti* 1866, chalk on paper, 79 × 63.5

OPPOSITE
NO.42 Dante Gabriel Rossetti, *Portrait of Christina Rossetti* c.1848–50, graphite on paper, 14.9 × 11.4

Who was Christina Rossetti? What did she do? Why does her work still appeal to us? If we could travel back in time and ask Christina herself, she probably would not tell us. A poem like 'The Heart Knoweth Its Own Bitterness' might invite us to 'pierce, nay probe, nay dig within', but the author herself insists on remaining 'A fountain sealed' (ll.35, 44). Another poem, 'Winter: My Secret', teases with imminent disclosures, then denies us in the end: 'Only, my secret's mine, and I won't tell' (l.6). No wonder Christina Rossetti has long tormented readers and biographers alike. Heartbreak, sexual abuse, mental illness, repressed homosexuality and religious crisis have all been proposed as hidden causes of her notoriously melancholy and guarded temperament. With little conclusive evidence, the truth is that we will never know for sure. What we can investigate is the poet's own attraction to secrecy itself, which is apparent in her fascination with riddles, puzzles, word games, and the interplay of the seen and the unseen in the world.

It is typical that Christina Rossetti today hides among us in plain sight. Many of us meet her regularly at Christmas when we hear 'In the Bleak Mid-winter' sung at carol services. Her poem 'Remember' ['Remember me when I am gone away'], with its ironically unforgettable final lines 'Better by far you should forget and smile / Than that you should remember and be sad', is a staple of funerals and memorials, as is 'Song' ['When I am dead my dearest']. We come across her in childhood, in nursery classics like 'Who Has Seen the Wind?' and 'What is Pink?' She can also appear in less likely places like the television series *Peaky Blinders* where gangsters ritually murmur 'In the bleak mid-winter' to mark moments of violence, loss and grace. Her poems have featured in *Boardwalk Empire*, *The Crown*, *Downton Abbey* and the sitcom *Ghosts*, and have been set to music over one thousand times, most recently by Japanese folk artist Rima Kato.

If Christina Rossetti herself sometimes disappears in these contexts, that is probably how she would have wanted it. Reserved, modest and self-critical, she was the opposite of her extroverted brother, the painter-poet Gabriel. She took great pride in her work, but was wary of public attention and celebrity. This is partly the result of Victorian gender conventions, which encouraged women to be diffident and demure. Propriety is the ostensible reason that she refused to join the Pre-Raphaelite Brotherhood. As Gabriel explained, his sister felt that membership 'would seem like display, I believe, – a sort of thing she abhors'.[1] His pencil drawing of c.1848–50 sensitively portrays his young sister's reserved demeanour and quiet beauty (NO.42). For Christina, humility was a religious necessity as well as a social obligation. The heroine of her autobiographical short story 'Maude' (1850) declares herself 'sick of display, and poetry and acting'.[2] Christina, too, worried that artistic creativity could encourage spiritual inauthenticity and an unhealthy focus on the self.

Consequently, her poems are seldom showy affairs. Their language is plain and simple, and their locations distinctly unglamorous. Yet some of her most memorable verses truck with the exotic. In 'My Dream', a giant crocodile king feasts on his smaller jewel-encrusted subjects while shedding 'appropriate tears' (l.48).

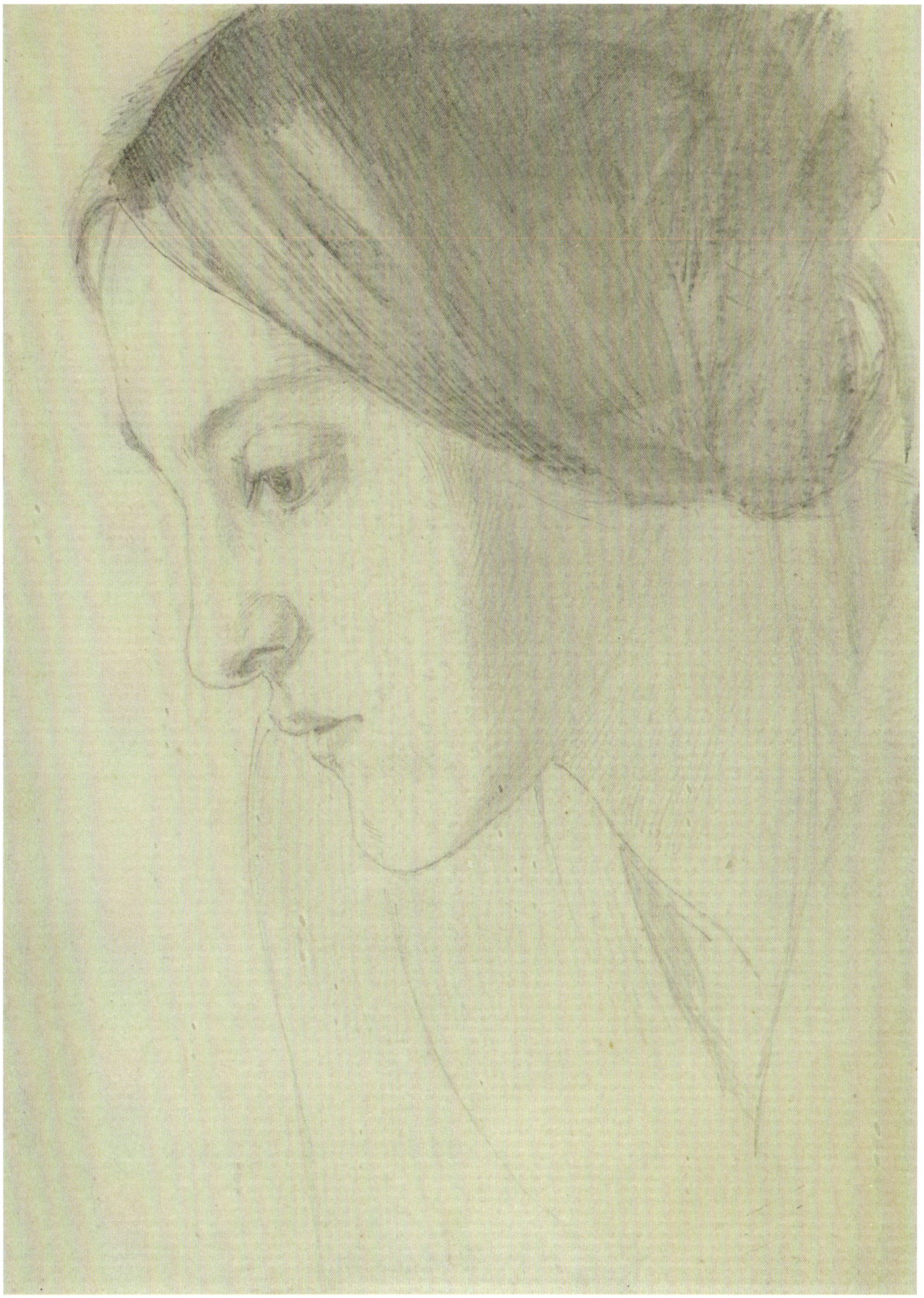

'Better by far you should forget and smile /
Than that you should remember and be sad'

Christina Rossetti

A Christmas Carol

Christina Rossetti

In the bleak mid-winter
   Frosty wind made moan
Earth stood hard as iron,
   Water like a stone;
Snow had fallen, snow on snow,
   Snow on snow,
In the bleak mid-winter
   Long ago. ...

Enough for Him, whom cherubim
   Worship night and day,
A breastful of milk
   And a mangerful of hay;
Enough for Him whom angels
   Fall down before,
The ox and ass and camel
   Which adore. ...

What can I give Him,
   Poor as I am? –
If I were a shepherd
   I would bring a lamb;
If I were a wise man
   I would do my part, –
Yet what I can I give Him,
   Give my heart. [1872]

'A Birthday' celebrates its titular occasion on a silky purple dais festooned with doves, pomegranates and peacocks 'with a hundred eyes' (l.12). More often, though, Christina explores native hedgerows rather than far-flung lands, and favours private domestic settings to grand palaces. Her most famous poems are short, tightly wrought, emotional lyrics that explore love in all its guises: romantic, familial, ecological, creative and spiritual. Fittingly, the human heart is one of Christina's favourite motifs, but it is not the sentimental symbol of Victorian romance. As often barred shut and bleeding as it is 'Brimful of love', the Rossettian heart represents the pleasures and pains of experiencing love in a fallen world.[3] Love in Christina's poems is gentle and kind, but also radical and transformative, resisting the conventions of her time while operating within them. Christina was very protective of her own heart, and was keen to keep her private life and creative identity in separate compartments. Her horror of her poems being misinterpreted as 'outpourings of a wounded spirit' or biographical 'love personals' never left her.[4]

Given her extreme aversion to display, we might well wonder what Christina would have made of her appearance in this exhibition. She was certainly no stranger to London exhibitions, museums and modelling for artists. As a child, she had been taken to the National Gallery and the British Museum by her mother Frances, who wanted to make sure her children experienced London's public institutions as 'a stream of pure enjoyment flowing to the mind'.[5] Although Christina confessed that she preferred 'nature treasures' to 'art treasures', she attended exhibitions throughout her life, particularly those featuring Pre-Raphaelite work.[6] She sat for several important Pre-Raphaelite pictures, including Gabriel's *Ecce Ancilla Domini! (The Annunciation)* and *The Girlhood of Mary Virgin* (see NOS.53, 73), her fiancé James Collinson's *St Elizabeth of Hungary* (1850) and William Holman Hunt's *The Light of the World*.

In the early 1850s, Christina even flirted with becoming an artist herself, enrolling in classes at the North London School of Drawing and Modelling in Camden Town, where she was taught by Ford Madox Brown. She drew pencil portraits of her mother and brother William Michael which are notable for their realism, even if they do not indicate a native talent (see NO.4). Christina's drawings, like her poems, are not inclined to prettify. Where her brother Gabriel smoothes flaws in family profiles, Christina tentatively and tenderly includes her mother's double chin and William Michael's prematurely receding hairline. Although she quickly abandoned any attempt to become a serious artist, Christina continued to draw amateur pencil pictures, including illustrations for her own poems. She produced over one hundred sketches for her 1872 nursery rhyme collection, *Sing-Song*, which provided a blueprint for the volume's official illustrator, Arthur Hughes (see NOS.44, 45).

Christina might seem an odd woman out among the raucous Pre-Raphaelite Brotherhood, who joked that their initials stood for 'Penis Rather Better'. However, the group gave her space in their art magazine, *The Germ* (1850; see also NOS.70, 71), and she lent them much-needed literary credibility in return. Pre-Raphaelite poems

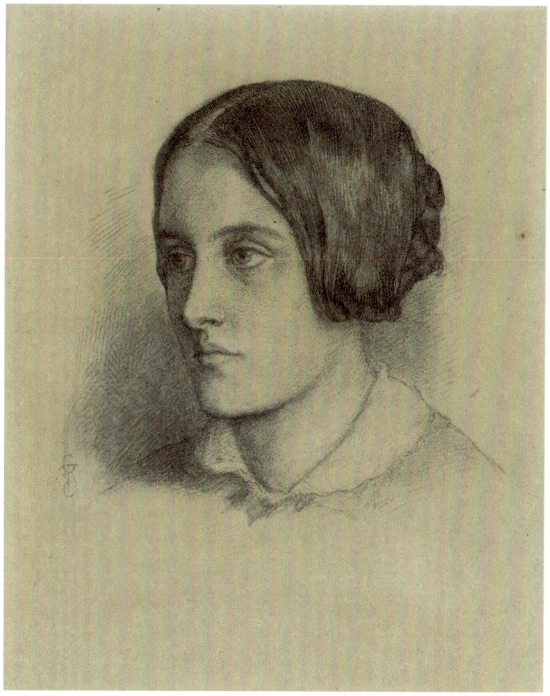

NO.43 Dante Gabriel Rossetti, *Christina Rossetti* 1848, chalk on paper, 28.8 × 21.5

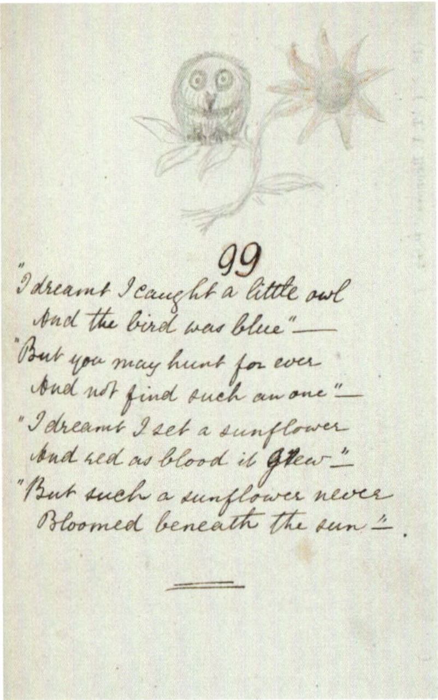

99

"I dreamt I caught a little owl
And the bird was blue"—
"But you may hunt for ever
And not find such an one"—
"I dreamt I set a sunflower
And red as blood it grew"—
"But such a sunflower never
Bloomed beneath the sun"—

NO.44 Christina Rossetti, 'I dreamt I caught a little owl', manuscript 1868–70

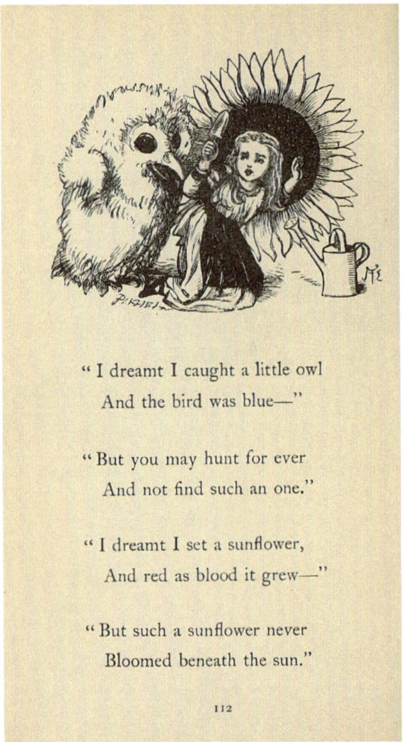

"I dreamt I caught a little owl
And the bird was blue—"

"But you may hunt for ever
And not find such an one."

"I dreamt I set a sunflower,
And red as blood it grew—"

"But such a sunflower never
Bloomed beneath the sun."

112

NO.45 Arthur Hughes, 'I dreamt I caught a little owl', illustration in Christina Rossetti's *Sing-Song* 1872

were roundly ignored, mocked or dismissed until 1862, when critics lauded Christina's first widely distributed collection, *Goblin Market and Other Poems* (see NO.46). The poet Algernon Charles Swinburne declared her 'the Jael who led' the Pre-Raphaelites 'to victory'.[7] The volume also makes illustrated book history: it was normal practice to bring out illustrated editions of poems that had already been commercially successful, but this first edition includes genre-defining illustrations by Dante Gabriel Rossetti.

Despite this success, Christina's feelings about the art world remained decidedly mixed. Her sonnet 'In an Artist's Studio', widely regarded to be about Elizabeth Siddal and Dante Gabriel Rossetti's unhappy relationship, portrays a painter's space as one of claustrophobic self-absorption. Christina's letters give few clues about her feelings towards her sister-in-law; the pair appear to have maintained a frosty detente that thawed somewhat following the stillbirth of Elizabeth's baby. But Christina's encounter with her at a distance bequeaths us a stinging critique of Pre-Raphaelite art:

One face looks out from all his canvasses,
One selfsame figure sits or walks or leans:
We found her hidden just behind those screens,
That mirror gave back all her loveliness.
A queen in opal or in ruby dress,
A nameless girl in freshest summer greens,
A saint, an angel; – every canvass means
The same one meaning, neither more nor less.
He feeds upon her face by day and night,
And she with true kind eyes looks back on him
Fair as the moon and joyful as the light:
Not wan with waiting, not with sorrow dim;
Not as she is, but was when hope shone bright;
Not as she is, but as she fills his dream.

Hidden by screens and reflected in a mirror, these obsessive pictures reveal more about the artist than they do his model. He is a vampiric figure who 'feeds upon' his model's face, both in an erotic and an economic sense; after all, she helps him earn his living. While the model's 'true kind eyes' at first appear to 'look back on him', in fact they are blanks. These unseeing painted 'eyes' represent the artist's 'dream' rather than his model's sorrowful reality.

While it is tempting to read this poem simply as a feminist critique about the power imbalance between model and artist, we must remember that the problem with art, for Christina, is as much a religious as a social one. The clue is in the studio's mirror. In the Anglo-Catholic faith, the world is not real. It is simply an illusion, a mirror that reflects the 'real' world of heaven. An artist who paints the world is effectively trying to paint a reflection, and can only produce a poor reproduction (a picture) of a poor reproduction (earth). In this sense, art, or 'any likeness of any thing' (as the Second Commandment has it), is a double distortion, and not to be trusted.

Would Christina have disapproved, then, of us looking at her pictures and poems in a gallery? The answer is no, just so long as we understand a human life can only be represented, not faithfully reproduced. '[A]n artist may paint a lifelike picture, but he cannot

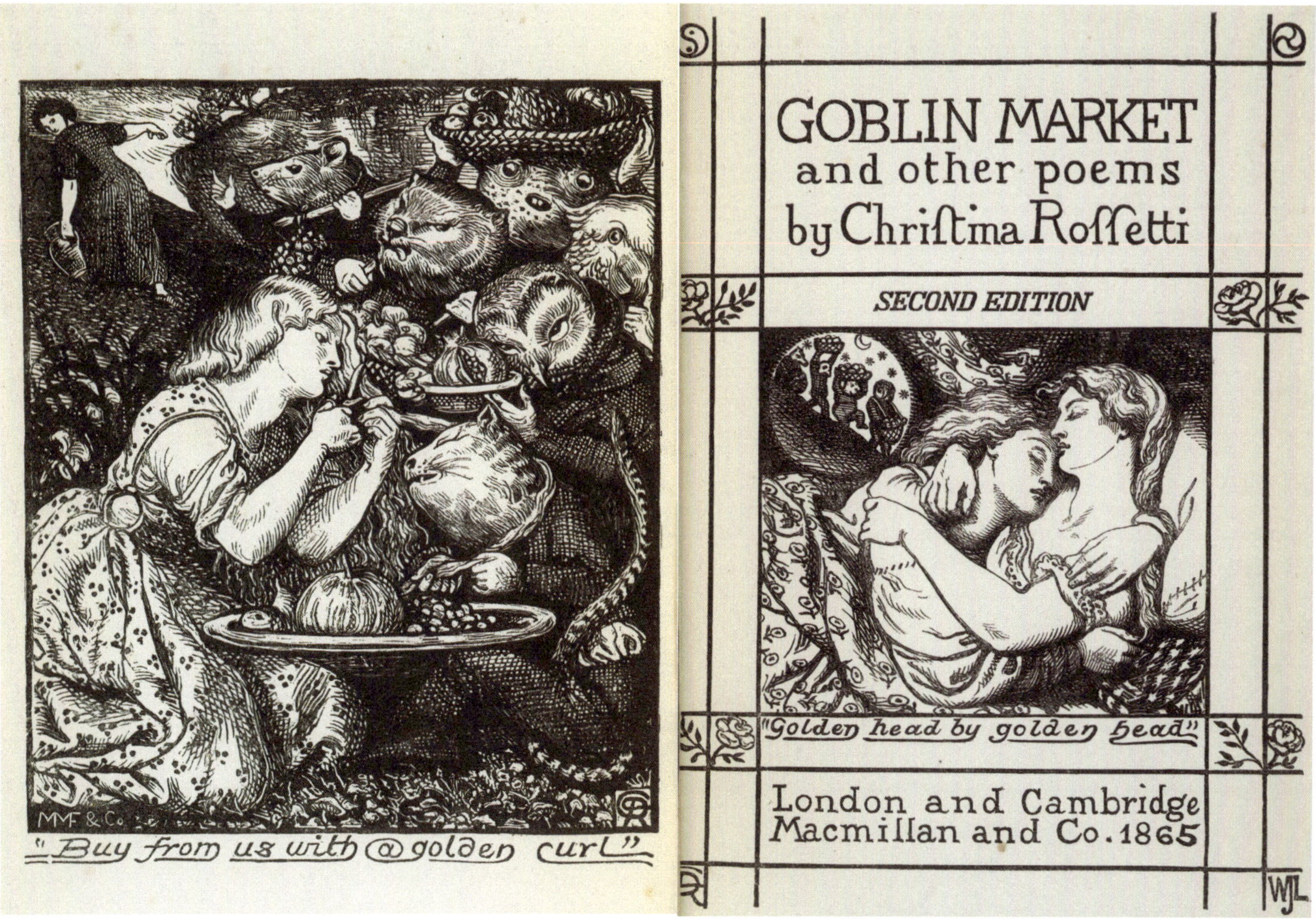

NO.46 Christina Rossetti, *Goblin Market and Other Poems* 1865 (second edition), book, open at frontispiece, 22.9 × 15.2

endow it with life like his own', she writes in *Seek and Find*.[8] Even so, we can cautiously engage with 'earthly things', because they 'teach some lesson to the teachable'. We should 'study the shadows' cast by heaven on the earth because they are trying to communicate with us.[9] 'Mirrors of Life and Death' (ll.1–5) describes this mysterious process:

> The mystery of Life, the mystery
> Of Death, I see
> Darkly as in a glass;
> Their shadows pass,
> And talk with me.

Christina's perspective was not without its detractors. Her agnostic brother William Michael worried that treating the world as heaven's mirror allowed his sister to ignore the pressing social realities of her day: he felt her poems were not sufficiently 'concerned' with 'rising currents of thought'.[10] There is some truth in what he says. Christina seldom addresses current affairs, and her religious conservatism prevents her from supporting important

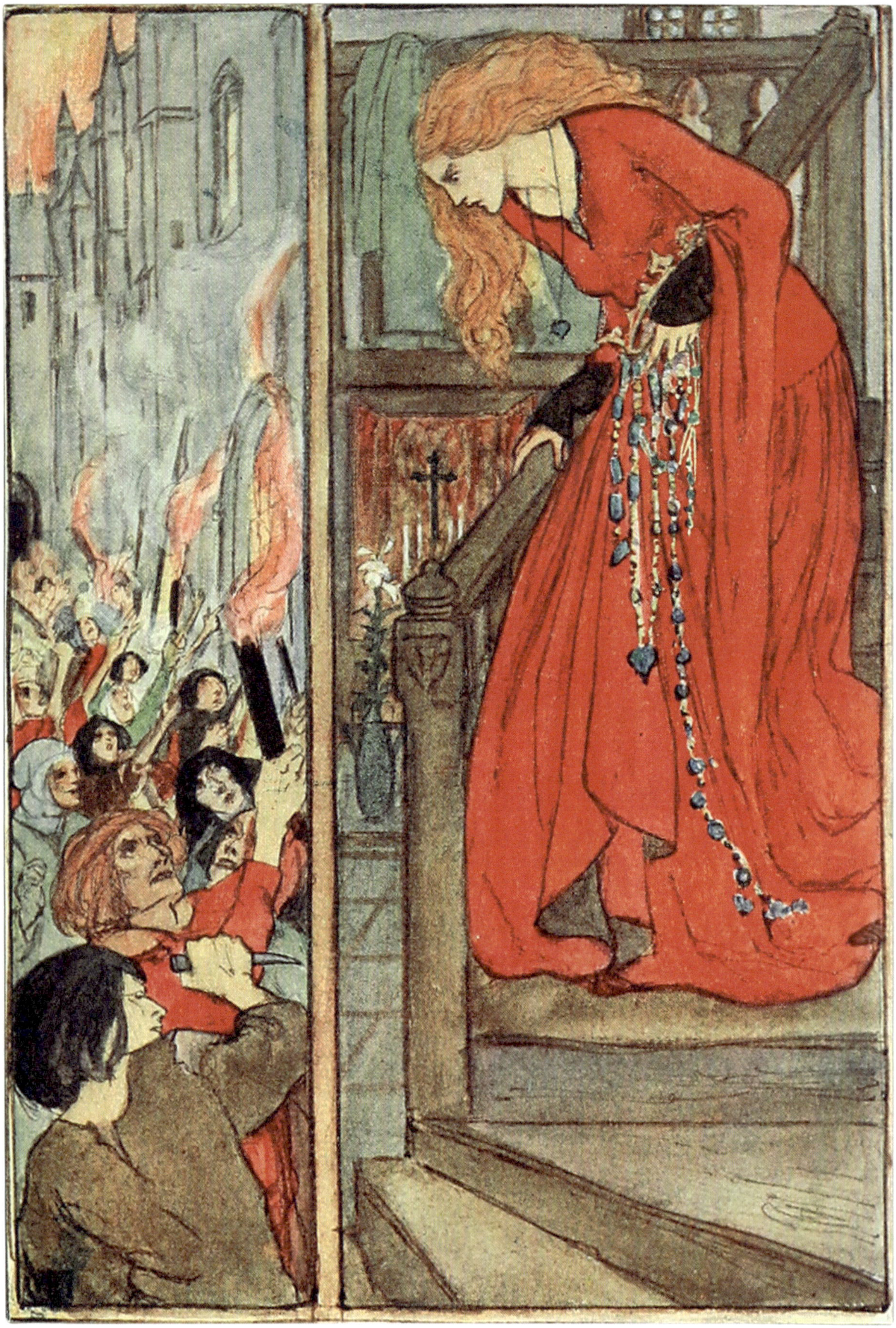

social movements of her age. On the other hand, her Christian belief that the world is only a mirror means that she can treat its conventions as distortions to be challenged, including rules that keep the oppressed and vulnerable in their places: women, children, the poor, nature and its creatures.

Endorsed and protected by her faith, Christina could critique inequalities that may have been invisible to William Michael. She came of age at a time when a woman's control over her money, property and bodily autonomy were severely restricted by law as well as social and religious custom. Women could not vote, hold political office, file for divorce or pursue most professions. They could, however, be active in their communities. Christina was a district visitor in her local parish, an animal rights activist who campaigned for the anti-vivisection movement, and a vocal opponent of pew rents, whereby the wealthy could reserve the best seats in church for themselves. She volunteered for over a decade at the St Mary Magdalene Penitentiary, an Anglican-run home for the rehabilitation of prostitutes. Recent research has revealed that some of the residents were as young as ten years old.

Christina's first-hand engagement with the disadvantaged in her community shaped a social consciousness expressed in poems like 'Behold, I Stand at the Door and Knock'. Here, Christ is repeatedly turned away from a wealthy household because he appears disguised as a contemporary widow, a homeless man, and an abused child. The second-class citizenship of women is also a frequent subject. 'An Immurata Sister' complains that 'Men work and think, but women feel' (l.5), while the speaker of 'From the Antique' longs to escape her gender: 'Doubly blank in a woman's lot: / I wish and I wish I were a man' (ll.2–3).

'A Royal Princess' explores the disorientating effect of sheltering women from social realities. Completely unaware of the grave injustices which support her royal privilege, a princess feels alienated from herself and others (ll.10–12):

> All my walls are lost in mirrors, whereupon I trace
> Self to right hand, self to left hand, self in every place,
> Self-same solitary figure, self-same seeking face.

When she learns of her family's complicity in famine and poverty, the princess decides to deliver all her treasures to the revolutionaries who are storming her father's castle. Though the confrontation may mean her death, standing 'face to face' with members of an angry mob is preferable to being trapped by her own ignorance (l.101). In shifting from black and white to colour, Florence Harrison's 1910 illustrations convey the transformative power of the princess's decision to face the world (see NOS.47, 48).

'A Royal Princess' itself faced the world when it was published in a poetry volume to raise funds for Lancashire workers affected by the 'cotton famine' caused by Northern blockades of Southern cotton during the American Civil War. Christina's endorsement of this cause doubles as public support for abolition; the Lancashire workers were famous advocates for the North precisely because they opposed slavery.

OPPOSITE
NO.47 Florence Harrison, untitled colour illustration for 'A Royal Princess', in Christina Rossetti's *Poems* 1910

'An artist may paint a lifelike picture, but he cannot endow it with life like his own'

Christina Rossetti

But just as these poems seem to reveal Christina as a developing socialist or proto-feminist, she takes evasive action. In 1878, she refused to sign a petition in support of women's suffrage, and ten years later, she put her name to a petition against it. Here is the contradictory Rossetti that has so tantalised her readers, her biographers, and even her brother William Michael. As ever, she offers no easy answers. Commissioned to write an anti-suffrage poem, she produces 'A Helpmeet For Him'. The first line's declaration of male superiority, 'Woman was made for man's delight', sounds increasingly less confident as the poem proceeds. 'Woman' may be a 'World-wide champion of truth and right' but she must ensure that 'Her strength with weakness is overlaid' and that 'Meek compliances veil her might' (ll.1, 8, 5, 6). What is Christina saying here? Is male superiority a given, or an illusion only made possible by women pretending to be inferior?

Like so much else in her life, Christina's conception of marriage is informed by her Anglo-Catholic belief in a mirror world. For her, marriage between a man and a woman mirrors the relationship of Christ ('the bridegroom') to His Church ('the bride'), and thus husbands outrank wives. Instead of critiquing this hierarchy directly, Christina reminds us that romantic love is an illusion, and forgetting this can lead to exploitation, violence and a catastrophic loss of self.

The women portrayed in Christina's poem 'A Triad' are destroyed by romantic love, left 'famished', 'shamed', 'sluggish' and 'short of life' (ll.11, 9, 10, 14). Romance also saps female creativity. In the sonnet sequence *Monna Innominata*, Christina imagines the poems a medieval muse might have been able to write had she 'spoken for herself' (prefatory note). This ambitious muse-turned-poet envisions a relationship of 'happy equals' (sonnet no.7, l.3). Ultimately, however, she is abandoned by her lover, and left alone with a 'silent heart' that 'cannot sing again' (sonnet no.14, ll.11, 14). Enduring inequality ensures that romance remains a losing proposition for women, particularly creative ones.

Christina herself never married, although she turned down two proposals. The first was made by James Collinson, a Pre-Raphaelite artist (see NO.72) who initially converted from Roman Catholicism to marry the Anglo-Catholic Christina. She dissolved their engagement in 1850 when Collinson forced her hand by converting back to Roman Catholicism. In 1866 the scholar and translator Charles Cayley proposed, and was refused because of his agnosticism. The two remained close, however.

The broken engagement to Collinson shattered Christina in ways only first love can. Her brother William Michael called it a 'staggering blow', one 'from which she did not fully recover for years'.[11] Christina's extreme reaction hints at her own underlying emotional turmoil. Her mental health had been fragile from the age of fourteen, when she became what we would now call a young carer for her father Gabriele. After the Italian scholar suffered a severe physical and psychological breakdown, Christina stayed home to look after him while the rest of the family went out to work. She was overcome with what we might identify as depression and anxiety, which sometimes manifested in episodes of self-harm. Poetry helped her survive this crisis; going against the medical conventions of the day, her doctor appears to have recommended that she keep writing. Her health improved considerably when her grandfather privately printed her *Verses* (1847) for which her brother Gabriel provided illustrations (see NOS.49–52), and again when *The Athenaeum* published two of her poems in 1848.

If Christina's women suffer heartbreak in romance, they find safety and fulfilment in maternal love. The dedicatory sonnet to *A Pageant and Other Poems* characterises this 'first Love' as supportive rather than exploitative. Mothers teach a 'love-lore that is not troublesome', and that 'transcends the laws / Of time and change and mortal life and death' (['Sonnets are full of love, and this my tome'], ll.5, 6, 13–14). Mothers can also be a radical source for change. Christina writes that 'mighty maternal love' might one day 'sweep away the barrier of sex, and make the female not a giantess or a heroine but at once and full grown a hero and a giant'.[12] This fairy-tale comparison anticipates nothing less than a gender revolution that transforms society, language and women alike.

Perhaps Christina was thinking of her own celebrated poem, 'Goblin Market', whose hero is not a prince, but a young woman. In this fantasy, Lizzie saves her sister Laura from a soul-destroying addiction to magical fruit sold by 'goblin merchant men' (l.474). If this sounds unconventional, the means of salvation are even more so. Covered in enchanted fruit juice and pulp, Lizzie instructs Laura: 'Hug me, kiss me, suck my juices', asking her to 'Eat me, drink me, love me' (ll.468, 471). This startling mix of eroticism and sisterhood is straight out of the Bible: her words echo Christ in John 6:56, 'He that eateth my flesh, and drinketh my blood, dwelleth in me, and I in him'.

The poem's ending, where the sisters become wives and mothers, has been interpreted as a disappointing retreat from the poem's celebration of lesbian sexuality and female resistance. But this ignores Christina's re-imagining of the domestic sphere. Far from forgetting their experiences, the sisters commemorate their heroics in verse, which they pass on to their children. The 'little ones' chant an instructive ditty about the active power of female friendship, mutual dependence, care and community: 'there is no friend like a sister' because sisters 'cheer', 'fetch', 'lift' and 'strengthen' each other (ll.548, 562, 564–7).

After spending her final years as a carer for her mother and two elderly aunts, Christina died of complications from breast cancer in 1894. She chose to be buried in a biodegradable 'green' coffin made of wicker and flowers, demonstrating her acceptance of her role in the natural cycle, and her hope of resurrection.[13] This brings us to the final kind of love Christina celebrates: our relationship with the natural world. The world may only be a mirror of heaven, but it remains our human duty to love the earth because it is a gift from God. Christina's poems combine a Pre-Raphaelite appreciation for nature's details with a firm faith in their devotional significance. Her nursery rhymes invite children to look after all of God's creatures, especially the most humble: ladybirds, frogs, moths, moles, crickets, beetles and worms. For Christina, animal conservation is inseparable from ecological sustainability: 'Why should we grudge a hidden water stream / To birds and squirrels while we have enough?'[14] The price of such disregard is nothing less than Apocalypse. Christina

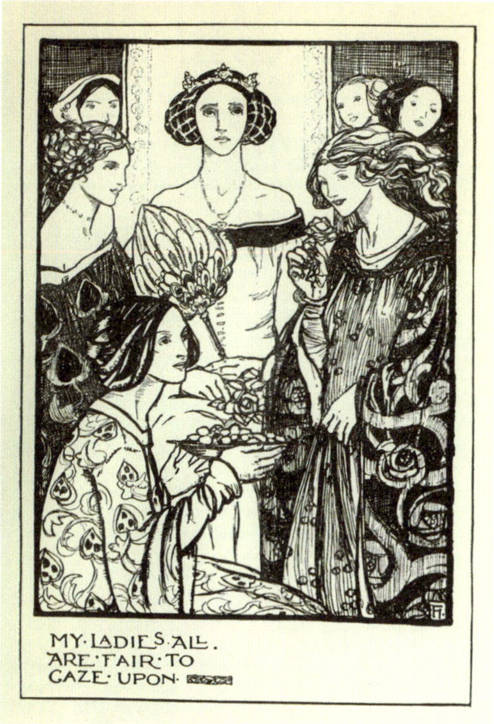

NO.48 Florence Harrison, 'My Ladies All Are Fair To Gaze Upon', illustration in Christina Rossetti's *Poems* 1910

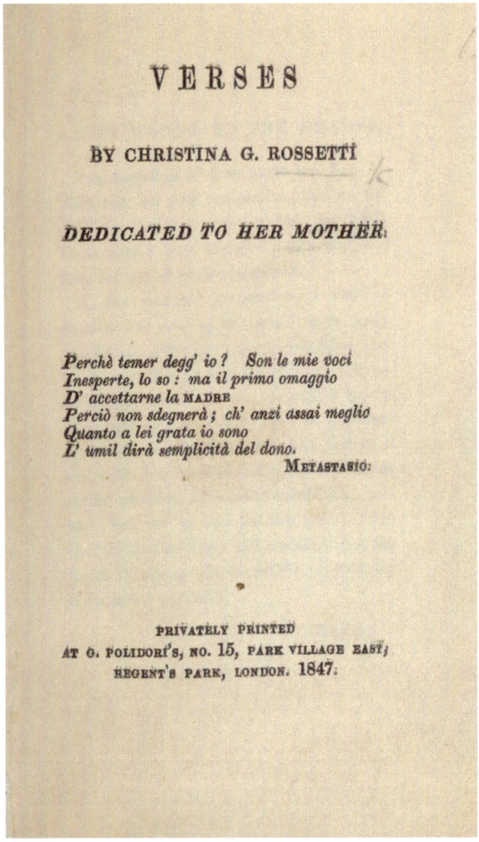

VERSES

BY CHRISTINA G. ROSSETTI

DEDICATED TO HER MOTHER.

Perchè temer degg' io? Son le mie voci
Inesperte, lo so: ma il primo omaggio
D' accettarne la MADRE
Perciò non sdegnerà; ch' anzi assai meglio
Quanto a lei grata io sono
L' umil dirà semplicità del dono.
METASTASIO.

PRIVATELY PRINTED
AT G. POLIDORI'S, NO. 15, PARK VILLAGE EAST,
REGENT'S PARK, LONDON. 1847.

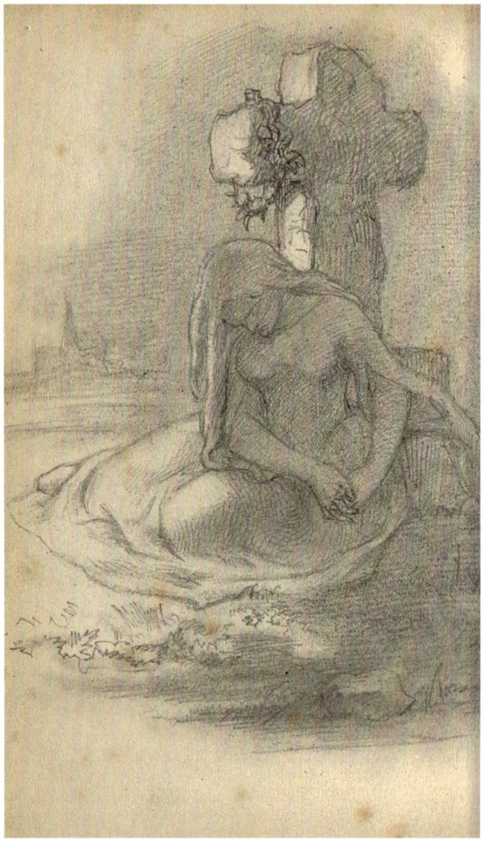

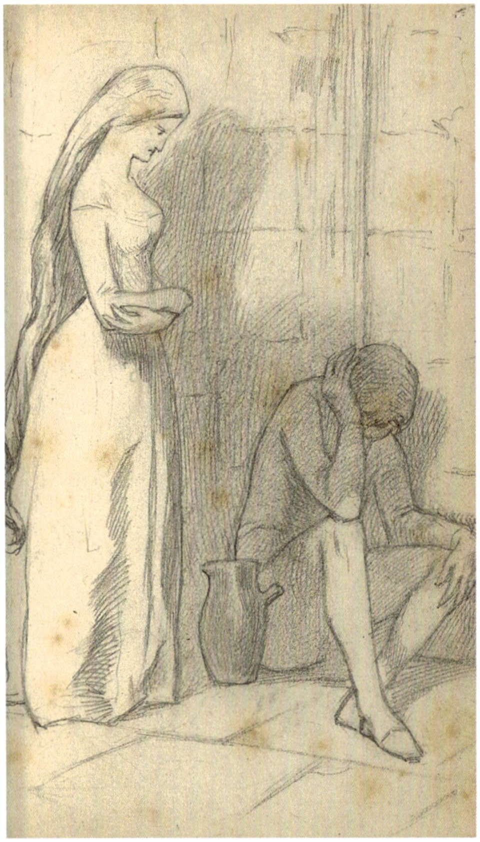

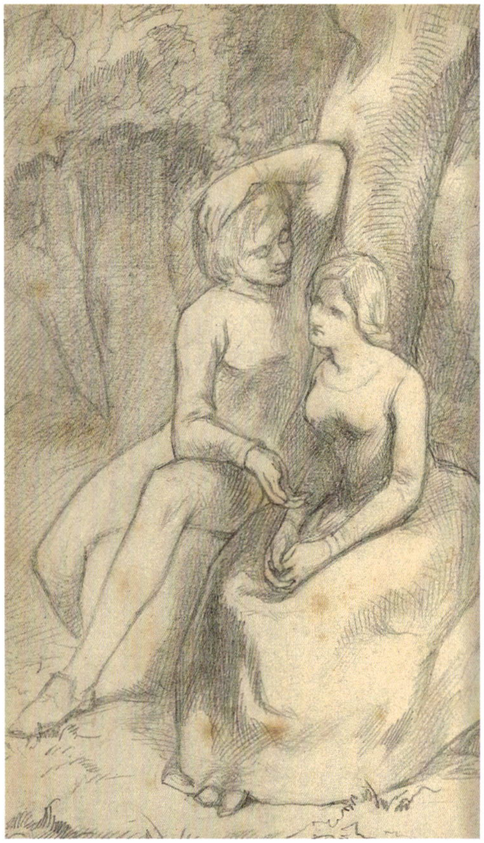

warns of a time 'when even the smallest, weakest, most grotesque, *wronged* creature' might 'rise up in the Judgment with us to condemn us'.[15] God can be found in the rhythms of the natural world, even if we cannot encounter Him directly. 'Who Has Seen the Wind' alludes to this idea, pointing out that while the wind is invisible to the human eye, we can perceive it by its effects: 'when the trees bow down their heads, / The wind is passing by' (ll.7–8).

In this way, nature works like poetry, communicating with us indirectly through analogy and metaphor. Perhaps this is why Christina chose to be a poet rather than a painter; not, as Gabriel mischievously suggests, because 'art' might 'interfere with the legitimate exercise of anguish'.[16] Her goal as a writer, she explains, is to 'gather simples and try to spell out their lessons'.[17] But this does not mean that her lessons are simple. Christina generally does not tell us what we want to hear, and she seldom offers comforting platitudes. 'From House to Home', for example, characterises human trauma and suffering as both inevitable and potentially fruitful (ll.221–4):

> Altho' today He prunes my twigs with pain,
> Yet doth His blood nourish and warm my root:
> Tomorrow I shall put forth buds again
> And clothe myself with fruit.

Her nursery rhymes, too, suggest that pain rather than pleasure inspires us:

> Stroke a flint, and there is nothing to admire:
> Strike a flint, and forthwith flash out sparks of fire.

The attraction of Christina's rather unsettling approach to pain and suffering is in her surprising directness and honesty, and her eagerness not to diminish the agony of human experience. Can we learn from trees and stones to make fruit and fire from our pain? Christina Rossetti speaks to us today because she is a writer who faces reality. Or, as she herself puts it: 'as a flint I set my face'.[18] Her poems, too, are flinty: sharp-edged and durable, they are meant to be used as tools or to start fires. Christina's enduring appeal proves that William Michael could not have been more wrong about his sister's refusal to engage with current events. For Christina, the human struggle to endure, to look after the natural world, to find ourselves in loving others, is eternally current

OPPOSITE, CLOCKWISE FROM TOP LEFT

NO.49 Christina Rossetti, *Verses* 1847, book, frontispiece, 17.1 × 10.8

NO.50 Dante Gabriel Rossetti, illustration, graphite on paper c.1847, for 'The Ruined Cross' by Christina Rossetti

NO.51 Dante Gabriel Rossetti, illustration, graphite on paper c.1847, for 'Life out of Death' by Christina Rossetti

NO.52 Dante Gabriel Rossetti, illustration, graphite on paper c.1847, for 'Tasso and Leonora' by Christina Rossetti

1 Dante Gabriel Rossetti to William Holman Hunt, September 1848, in *The Letters of Dante Gabriel Rossetti*, 4 vols., ed. Oswald Doughty and J.R. Wahl, Oxford 1965–7, vol.1, p.45.

2 Christina Rossetti, *Maude: A Story for Girls*, ed. William Michael Rossetti, London 1897, p.29.

3 Christina Rossetti, 'Later Life', sonnet no.28 (l.14).

4 Christina Rossetti to William Michael Rossetti, 28 April 1849, in *The Letters of Christina Rossetti*, 4 vols., ed. Antony H. Harrison, Charlottesville, VA 1997–2004, vol.1, p.16.

5 Frances Maria [*sic*] Lavinia Rossetti, 'Reflections', *Hodge-Podge*, 27 May 1843, Rossetti Family Correspondence and Papers, Bodleian Library Special Collections. Ms.facs.C95.

6 Christina Rossetti to Anne Gilchrist, Autumn 1865, in Harrison 1997–2004, 1, p.254.

7 Edmund Gosse, *The Life of Algernon Charles Swinburne*, London 1917, p.137.

8 Christina Rossetti, *Seek and Find: A Double Series of Short Studies of the Benedicite*, London 1879, p.14.

9 Christina Rossetti, *The Face of the Deep: A Devotional Commentary on the Apocalypse*, London 1892, p.438.

10 William Michael Rossetti (ed.), 'Preface', in *The Poetical Works of Christina Rossetti*, London 1904, p.lxviii.

11 Ibid., p.lii.

12 Christina Rossetti to Augusta Webster, c.1878, in Harrison 1997–2004, 2, p.158.

13 Emma Mason, *Christina Rossetti: Poetry, Ecology, Faith*, Oxford 2018, p.1.

14 Christina Rossetti, 'To What Purpose is This Waste?', ll.90–1.

15 Christina Rossetti, *Time Flies: A Reading Diary*, London 1885, p.129.

16 Dante Gabriel Rossetti to Christina Rossetti, 8 November 1853, in William Michael Rossetti, *Dante Gabriel Rossetti: His Family-Letters with a Memoir*, 2 vols., Boston 1895, vol.2, p.120.

17 Christina Rossetti, *Called To Be Saints: The Minor Festivals Devotionally Studied*, London 1881, p.xvi.

18 Christina Rossetti, 'From House to Home', l.206.

Elizabeth Prettejohn

Revolutionaries: The Rossettis and the Pre-Raphaelite Brotherhood

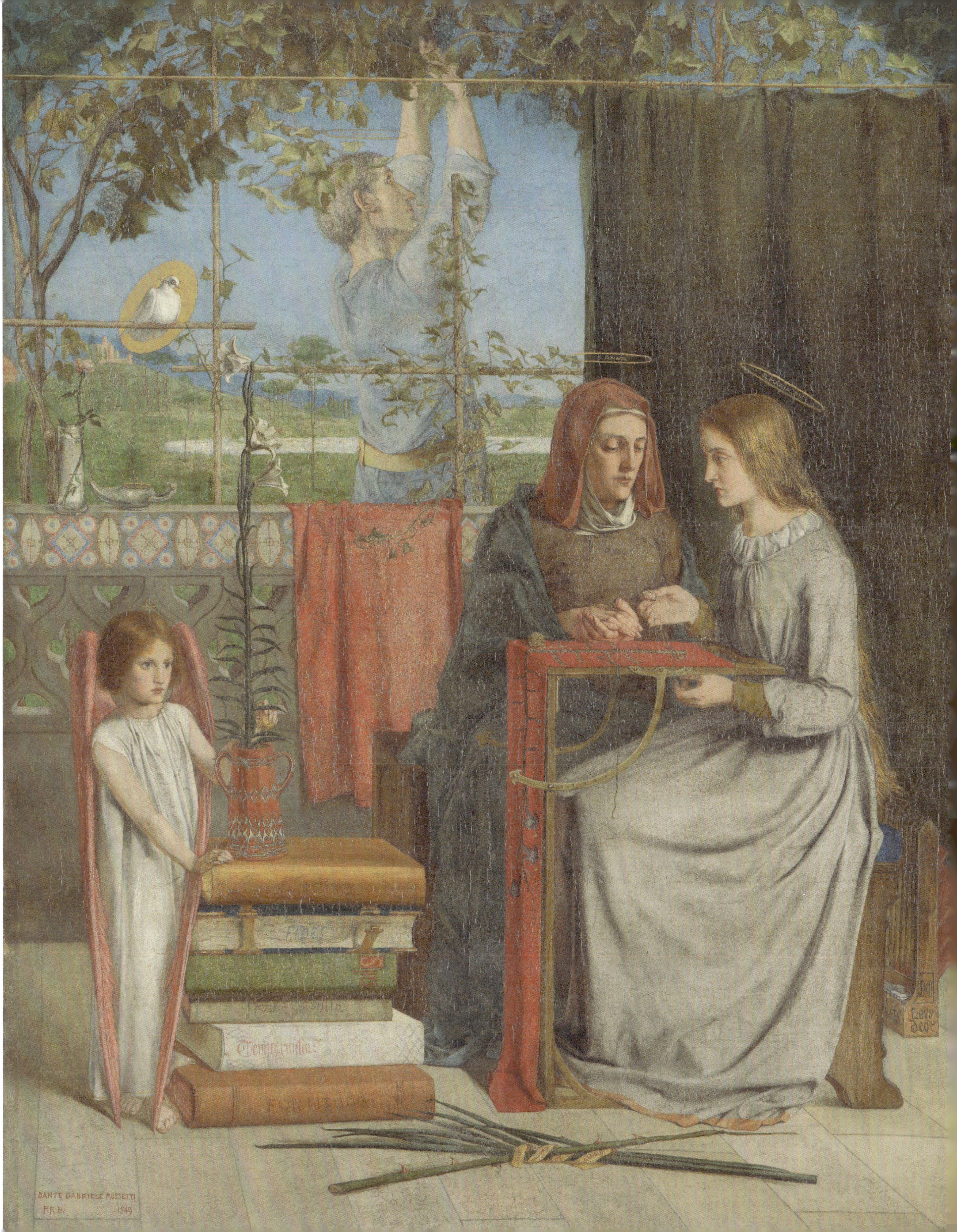
DANTE GABRIELE ROSSETTI
P.R.B. 1849

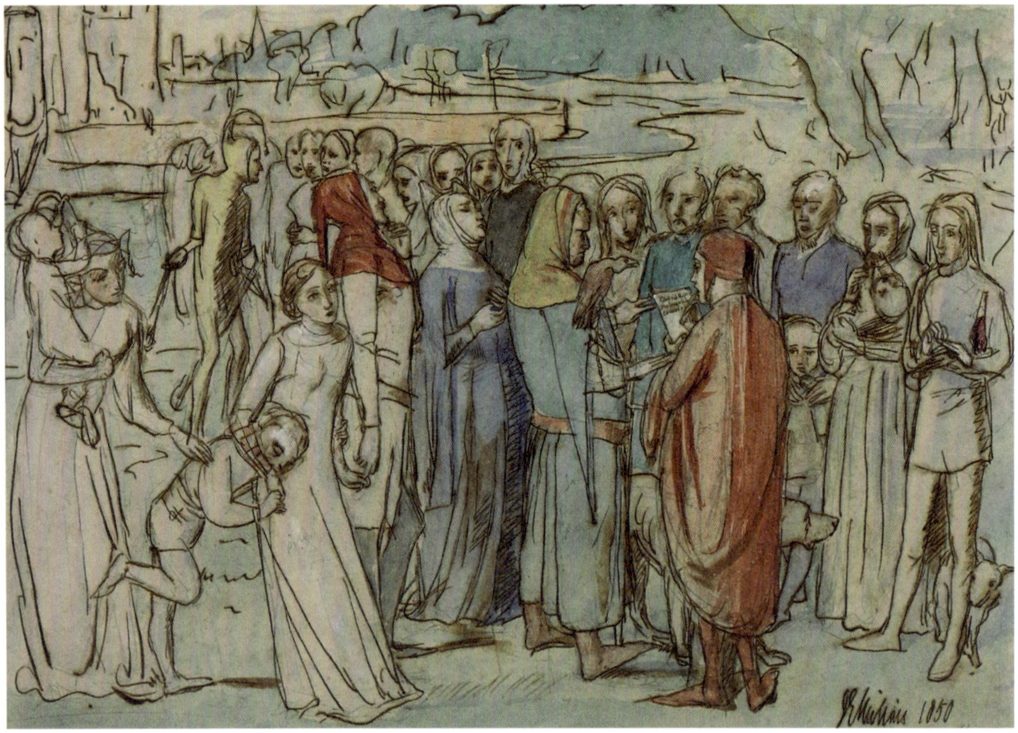

PAGE 57
NO.53 Dante Gabriel Rossetti, *The Girlhood of Mary Virgin* 1848–9, oil paint on canvas, 83.2 × 65.4

'The germ of a mighty revolution': a boy is cruelly slain; his roughly clad brother raises a fist in defiance as the noblemen depart on horseback, their lances and helmets gleaming silver in the Italian sunlight, heedless of the anguish they have caused to a humble family. *Rienzi Vowing to Obtain Justice for the Death of his Young Brother, Slain in a Skirmish between the Colonna and Orsini Factions* (NO.57) was William Holman Hunt's contribution to the Royal Academy in 1849, the first exhibition season after the formation of the Pre-Raphaelite Brotherhood – the germ of another revolution, at least in the hopes of the young artists who, for that year only, signed their paintings with the 'P.R.B.' initials (see NO.53).

Revolution was in the air when Hunt designed his picture, and when the seven young artists joined forces against the academic establishment. Their artistic brotherhood was at first secret, like the Carbonari in Naples, whose revolt of 1820–1 against Bourbon rule led to Gabriele (the father) Rossetti's political exile, and thus, indirectly, to the very existence of a Rossetti family in London.[1] In 1848, the year of European revolutions, Hunt and John Everett Millais witnessed the Chartist demonstration on Kennington Common, an event famous in later Pre-Raphaelite lore but deprecated at the time by the Rossetti brothers, nurtured on the sterner zeal of the 'escaped revolutionists from the Continent' who gathered around their father's fireside.[2] Gabriel's satirical poem 'The English Revolution of 1848' is subtitled '*(No connection with over the way)*'; this rather flippant juvenile effort was followed by a more powerful sonnet, 'On Refusal of Aid Between Nations', which laments the indifference of the major powers to the brutal suppression of revolutions against Austrian rule in Italy and Hungary.[3]

ABOVE
NO.54 Sir John Everett Millais, *A Baron Numbering his Vassals* 1850, graphite, ink and watercolour on paper, 29.2 × 40.6

RIGHT
NO.55 William Holman Hunt, *Portrait of Dante Gabriel Rossetti* 1848 ink on paper, 22.5 × 18.2

BELOW
NO.56 Dante Gabriel Rossetti, *William Michael Rossetti* 1853, graphite on paper, 28.2 × 21

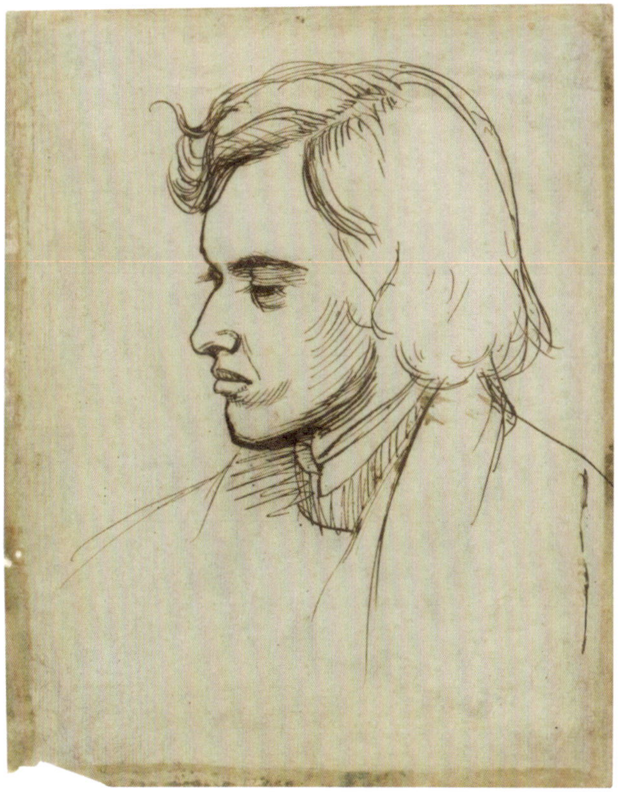

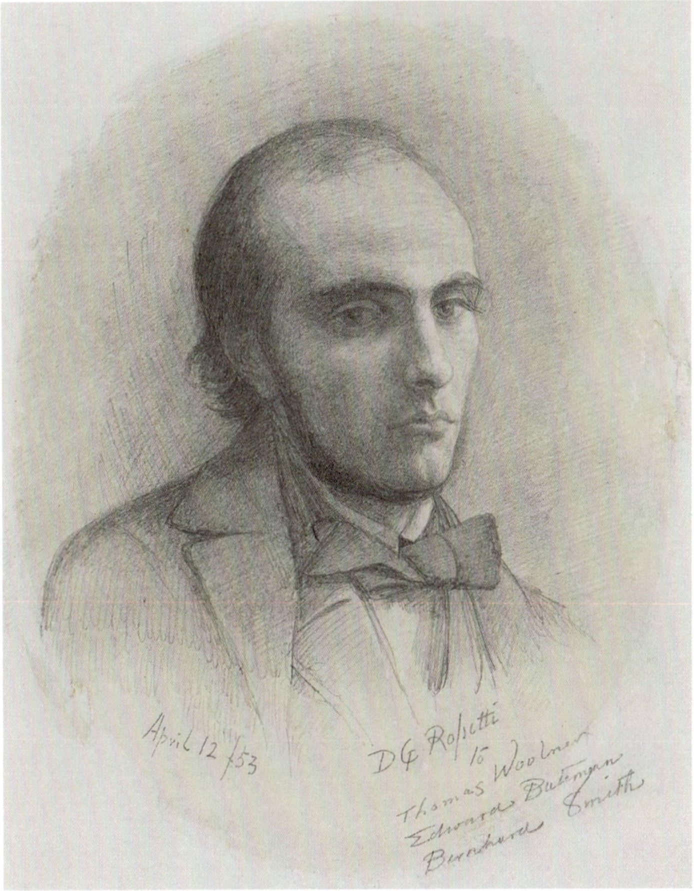

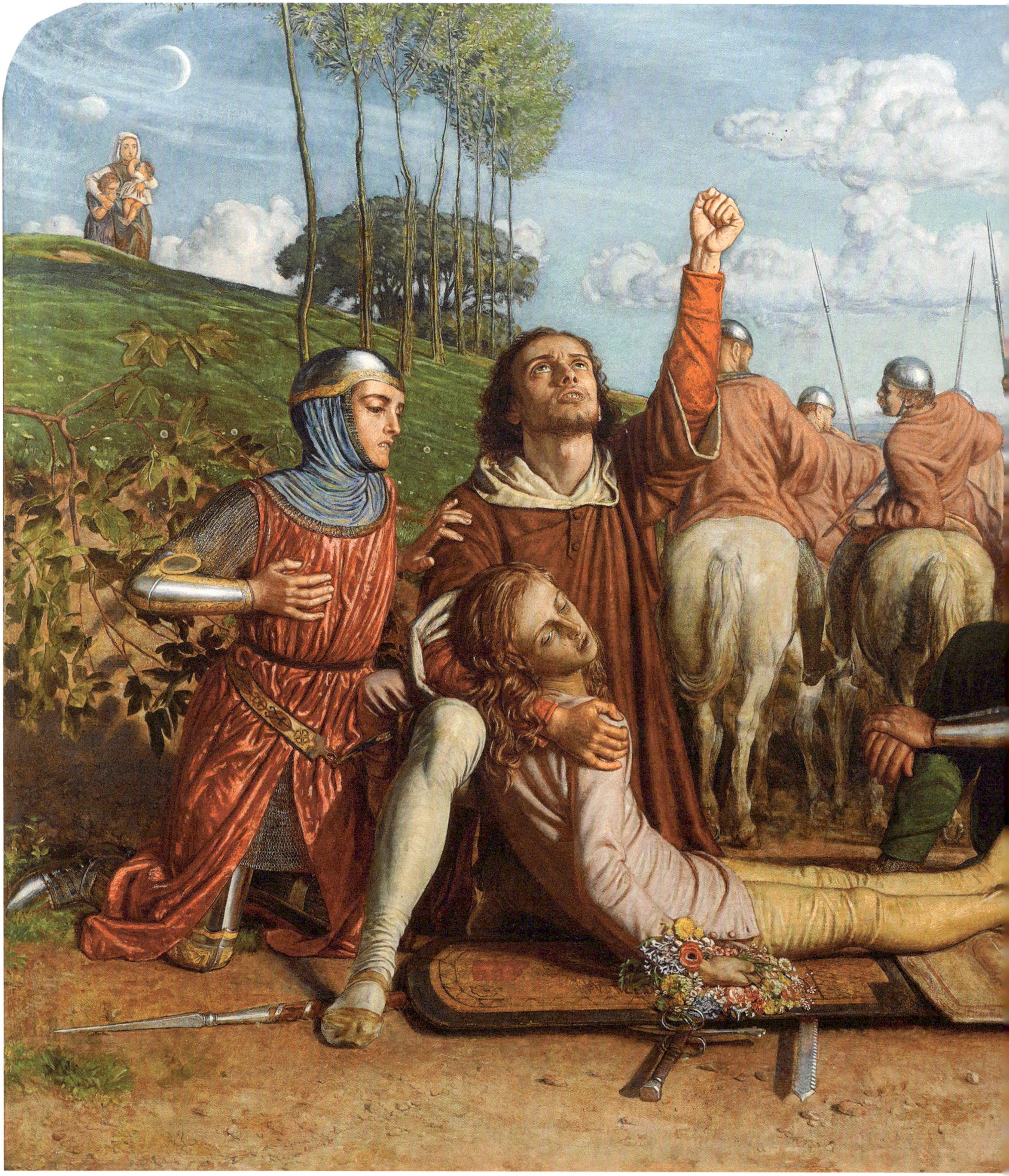

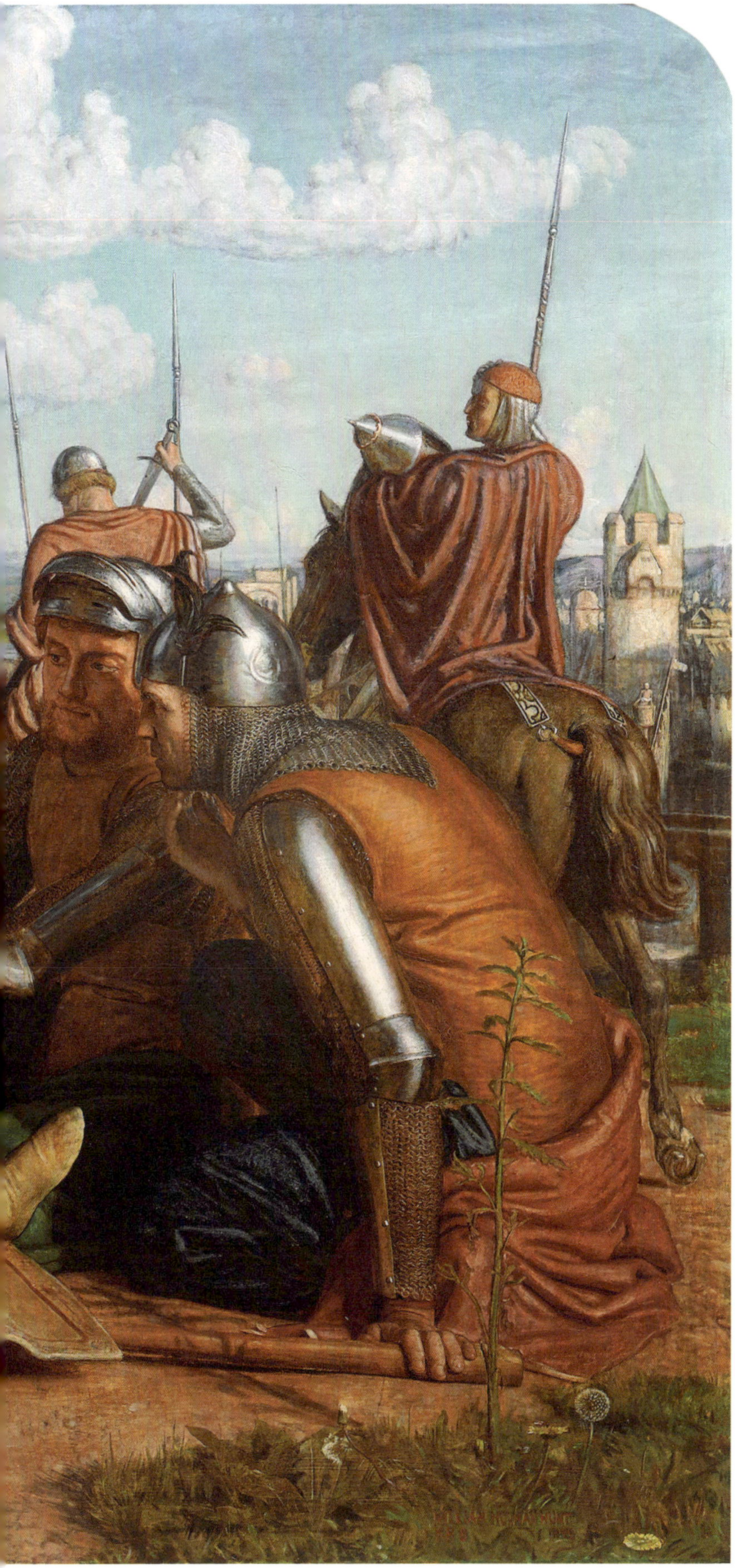

NO.57 William Holman Hunt, *Rienzi Vowing to Obtain Justice for the Death of his Young Brother, Slain in a Skirmish between the Colonna and Orsini Factions* 1848–9, oil paint on canvas, 86.4 × 121.9

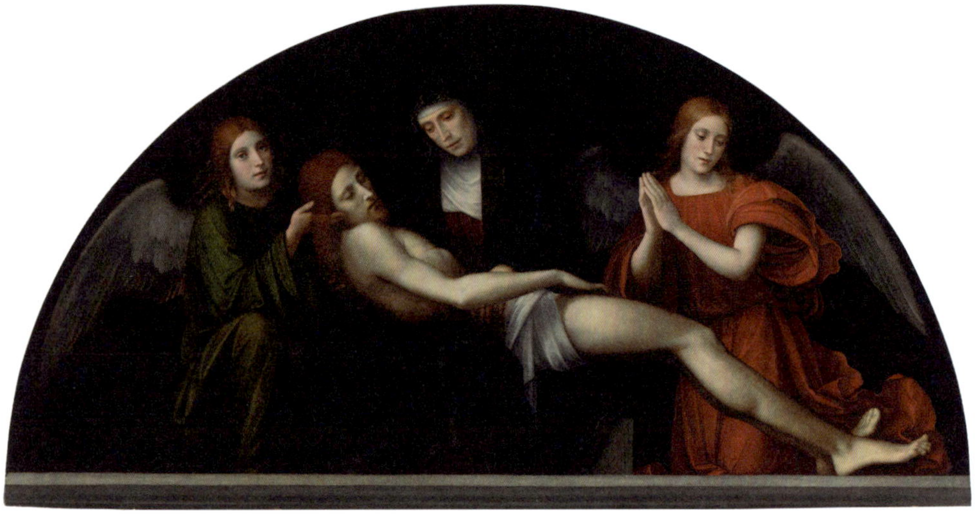

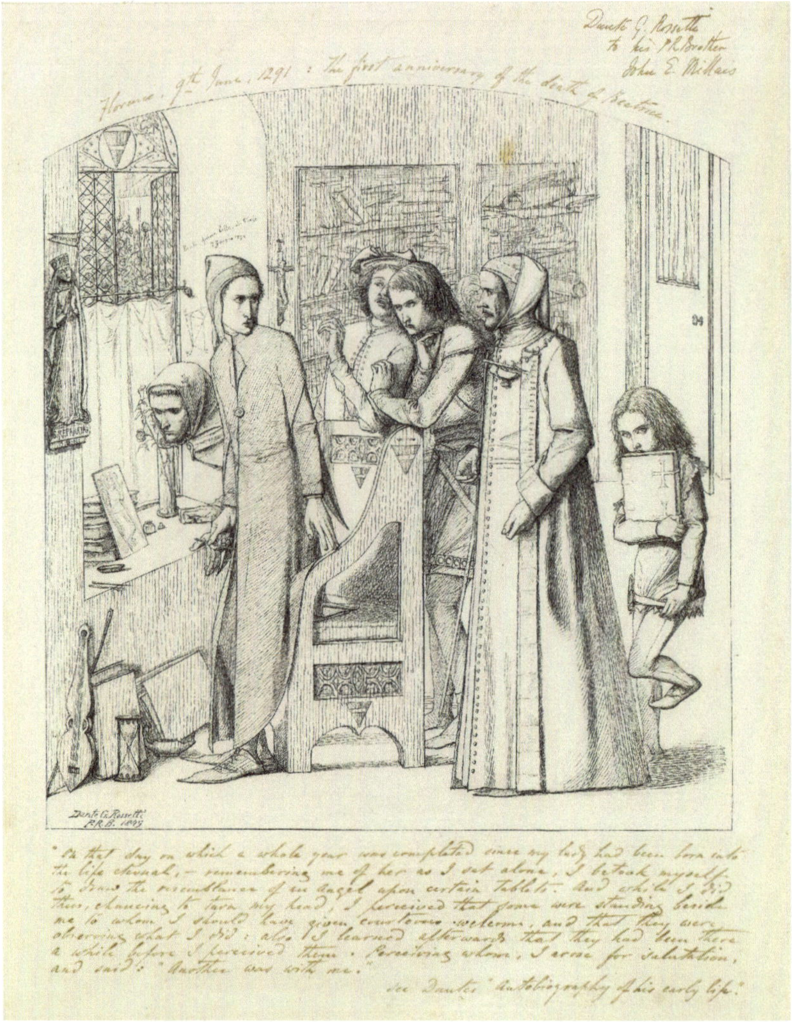

ABOVE
NO.58 Francesco Francia, *Pietà*
1510–12, oil paint on wood, 94 × 184.5

RIGHT
NO.59 Dante Gabriel Rossetti, *The First Anniversary of the Death of Beatrice*
1849, ink on paper, 40 × 32

It was also in 1848 that Edward Bulwer Lytton's novel of 1835, *Rienzi, the Last of the Roman Tribunes*, was republished with a new preface that made explicit the analogy between contemporary Italian politics and the fourteenth-century revolution of Cola di Rienzo against the Roman noble families. The novel had already inspired an opera by the young Richard Wagner (premiered in Dresden in 1842), and it was something like a stroke of genius for Hunt to take it up for painting at this moment. The subject is literally 'Pre-Raphaelite', drawn from Italian history before the period of Raphael (in art) and Machiavelli (in politics). In his much later (and notoriously one-sided) autobiography, Hunt emphasises the innovative realism of the painting: 'I was putting in practice the principle of rejection of conventional dogma, and pursuing that of direct application to Nature for each feature, however humble a part of foreground or background this might be'; this required 'painting the whole out of doors, direct on the canvas itself, with every detail I can see, and with the sunlight brightness of the day itself'.[4]

However, the painting also betrays evidence of that other side of the Pre-Raphaelite project, the reverent imitation of early Italian art which Hunt later wished to downplay. The pathos of the boyish limbs recalls the *Pietà* of Christ in the lunette of an altarpiece by Francesco Francia (NO.58), dated around 1510 and therefore not dramatically 'Pre-' the time of the 'Raphaelites', but nonetheless among the earliest Italian pictures available for Hunt to study in London at the time (it was acquired by the National Gallery in 1841).[5] Thus the visual look of the painting, as well as its subject matter, partakes of the retrospective or backward-looking aspect of the Pre-Raphaelite project – its readiness to draw profound inspiration from the past. Despite Hunt's later unease, this should not be seen as derogating from the vanguard or revolutionary character of the movement.[6] By styling himself 'tribune' of the Roman people, Rienzi himself declared the inspiration of his revolution by looking back, in his case to the Roman Republic.

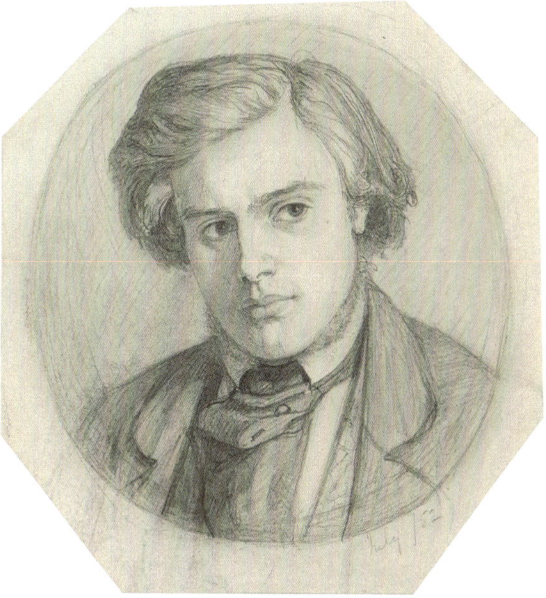

NO.60 Dante Gabriel Rossetti, *Thomas Woolner* 1852, graphite on paper, 15.5 × 14.6

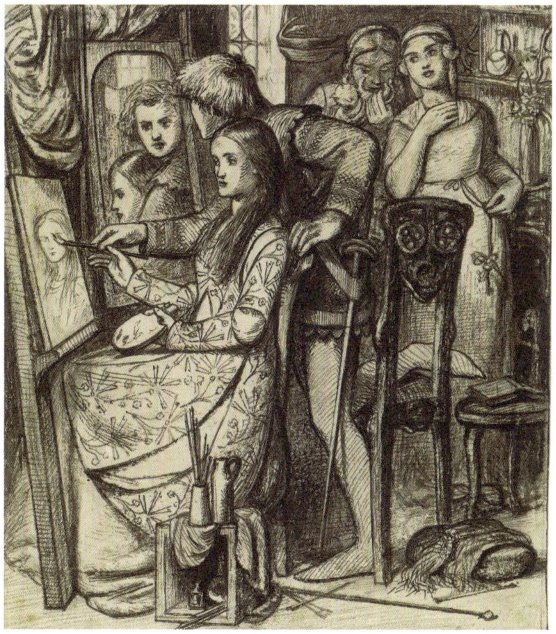

NO.61 Dante Gabriel Rossetti, *Love's Mirror or a Parable of Love* 1850–2, pen and ink over graphite with ink wash on paper, 17.5 × 19.5

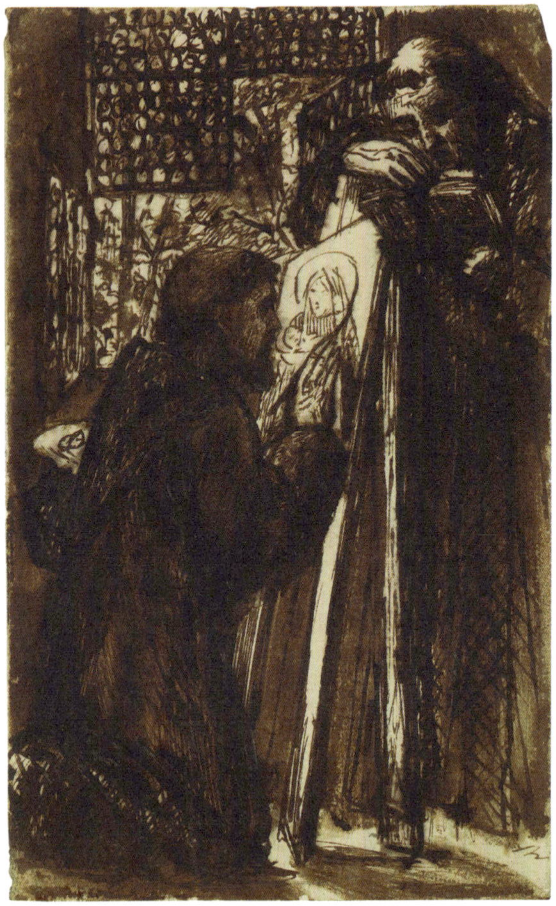

ABOVE
NO.62 Dante Gabriel Rossetti, *Fra Angelico Painting* 1853, pen and ink and wash on paper, 17.8 × 11.2

OPPOSITE
NO.63 Dante Gabriel Rossetti, *St Catherine* 1857, oil paint on canvas, 34.5 × 25

This complex amalgam of looking forwards and back is equally evident in the depiction of the main character, Rienzi, a portrait of the young Dante Gabriel Rossetti. As Hunt later recalled, he first used a fellow student as his model, 'but soon I became convinced that the racial character would be more satisfying if Gabriel would serve as my model'.[7] This obviously refers to Gabriel's Italian appearance, which made a forcible impression on everyone who met him in these early years. Equally remarked, though, were his 'unconventionalities', his contempt for authority, and the left political leanings of his family; these must have contributed to Hunt's sense of his appropriateness for the role of Rienzi.[8] Hunt's portrait in oil paint, realised just after Gabriel's death on the basis of a chalk drawing of him aged twenty-two, still preserves the intensity of gaze and expression that characterises the upturned face of Rienzi – 'Rossetti to the life', in the words of another of the Pre-Raphaelite Brothers, F.G. Stephens.[9] Rossetti the painter-poet merges with the character in Bulwer Lytton's novel, 'a dreamer, a scholar, a poet', galvanised by the events of the day into 'dark and stern thoughts, thoughts in which were the germ of a mighty revolution'.[10]

Hunt's *Rienzi* is a family picture in significant respects: the uprising is engendered by the death of a brother, and strikes against the most powerful families of the Roman establishment, the Colonna and Orsini. Just one of the Colonna clan, Adrian di Castello, clasps Rienzi's shoulder in sympathy. Appropriately, the figure of Adrian was modelled first by the Pre-Raphaelite Brother Millais, then by William Michael Rossetti, the real (as well as Pre-Raphaelite) brother of Rossetti-as-Rienzi.[11] Like the Pre-Raphaelite Brotherhood itself, these are all-male families, but in the summer after the picture's first exhibition Hunt added the figures of a mother and her two children approaching over the crest of the hill on the left. Perhaps these figures recall Rienzi's family in the novel: the mother whose 'fond vanity ... might be detected in the care with which the long and silky ringlets [of the younger brother] had been smoothed and

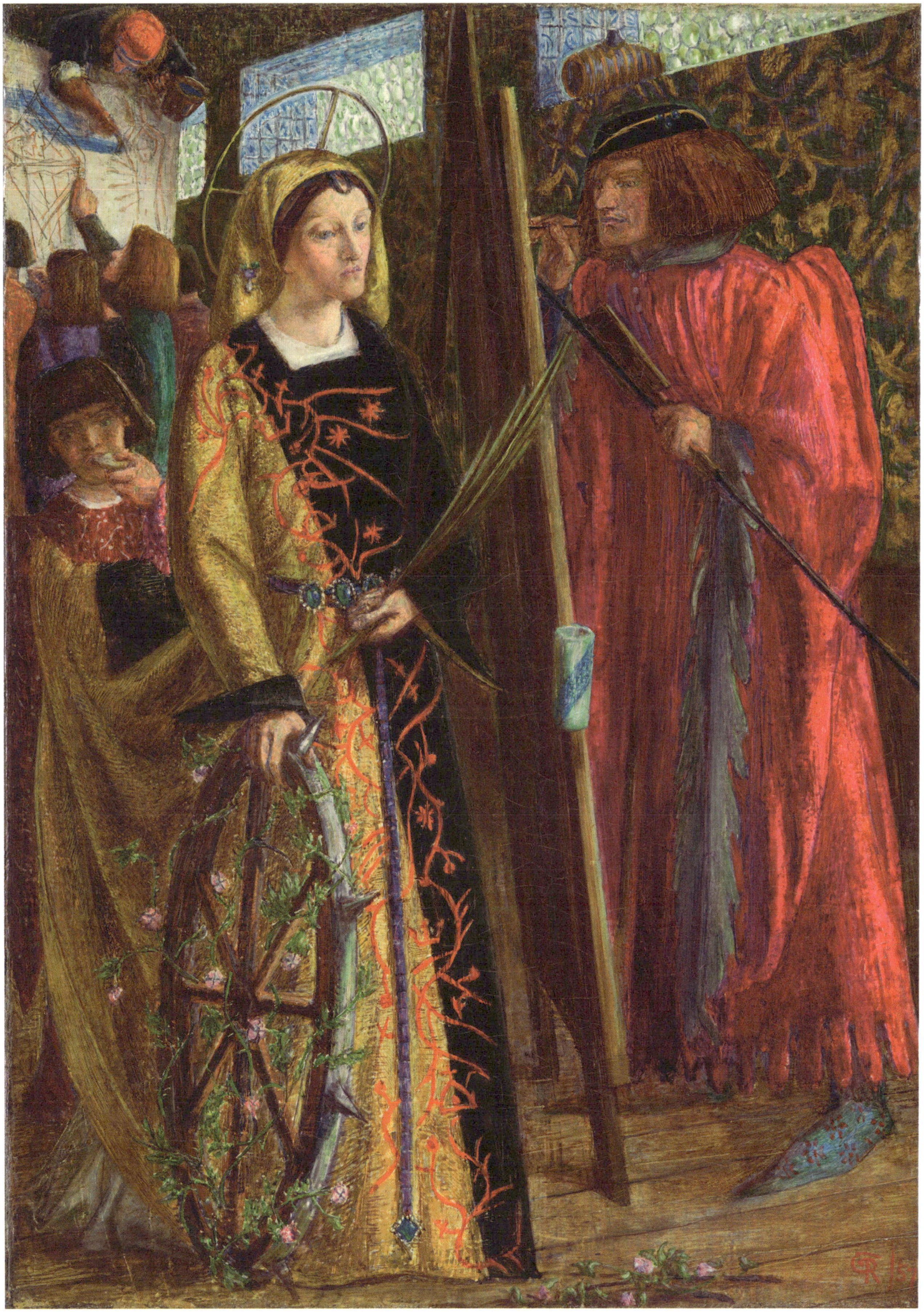

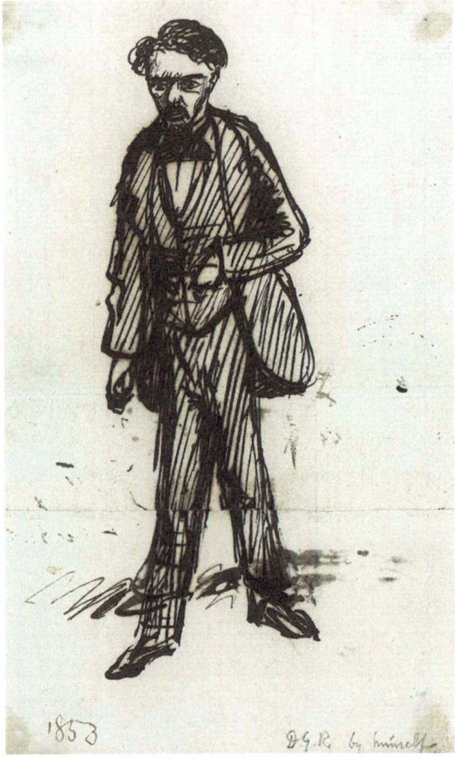
1853
D.G.R. by himself

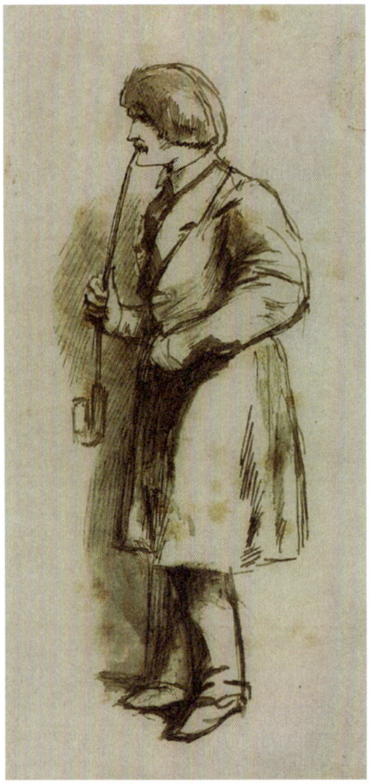

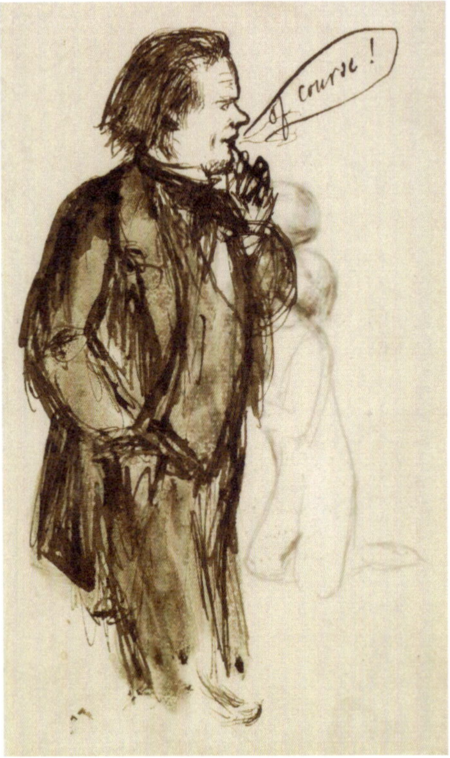
Of course!

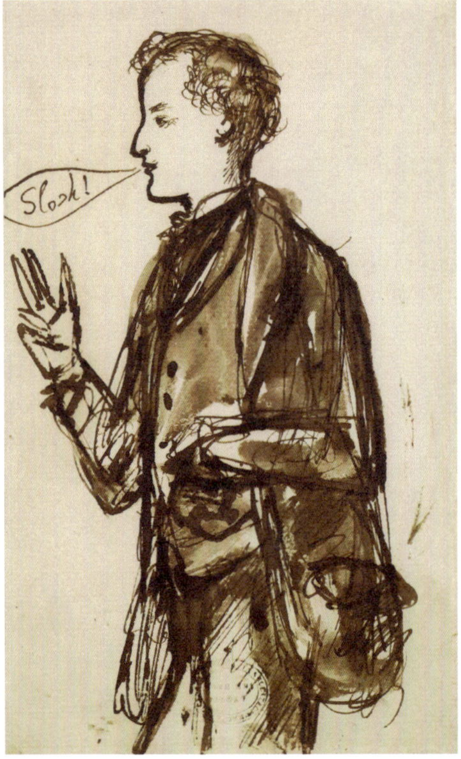
Slosh!

parted', and the 'little sister, Irene', for whom he has been making the garland of flowers that lies on his now inert hand.[12] Something is not quite resolved in the scale relations of the figures, and in the wide-angled perspective, which reminds us that Hunt, too, was a beginner in art, just twenty-two years old. Yet the very awkwardnesses of the painting – the insistent natural detail, the rumps of the departing horses – give compelling visual immediacy to this moment, the germ of a revolution both political and artistic.

Hunt's own family was solidly English, and lower-middle-class; his father was the manager of a warehouse in the City of London, not easily persuaded of the advisability of his son's pursuit of an artistic career. The reciprocal portrait drawings by Hunt and Millais (who came from a well-off Jersey family) show them in 1853 as neatly dressed, serious young men. By contrast, Dante Gabriel Rossetti's self-portrait drawing (NO.64), admittedly at a younger age, displays the more romantic, and more dishevelled, charm that contemporary descriptions invariably associate with his Italianness: the long hair with unruly curls, the full sensual lips, and the loose-fitting, slightly shabby clothing. In these descriptions there is more than a hint of a stereotype: what Millais's mother (according to the much later, not necessarily reliable, memory of Hunt) called the 'sly Italian'.[13] Indeed the traces of the stereotype persist, even today, for example in the charge that Gabriel was lazy – as frequent as it is nonsensical, with respect to the maker of such intricate drawings as *The First Anniversary of the Death of Beatrice* of 1849, among the first, pioneering works to experiment with creating a 'Pre-Raphaelite' drawing style (NO.59).

The stereotypical descriptions are signs, however, of the genuine unconventionality of the family. The Rossettis came across as foreign – Hunt makes special note of the 'maccaroni', which he acknowledges was delicious[14] – but also as defiant of normal bourgeois convention, and that is attributable not just to their Italianness but also to their commitment to a politics of the left, derived not

OPPOSITE, CLOCKWISE FROM TOP LEFT

NO.64 Dante Gabriel Rossetti, *Self-portrait* c.1853, ink and graphite on paper, 17.7 × 10.8

NO.65 Dante Gabriel Rossetti, *Study of a Man Smoking a Long Pipe* c.1849, ink and watercolour on paper, 19 × 9.2

NO.66 Dante Gabriel Rossetti, *Caricature of John Everett Millais* 1851–3, pen and ink and wash on paper, 17.9 × 11.1

NO.67 Dante Gabriel Rossetti, *Caricature of William Holman Hunt* 1851–3, pen and ink and wash on paper, 18 × 11.1

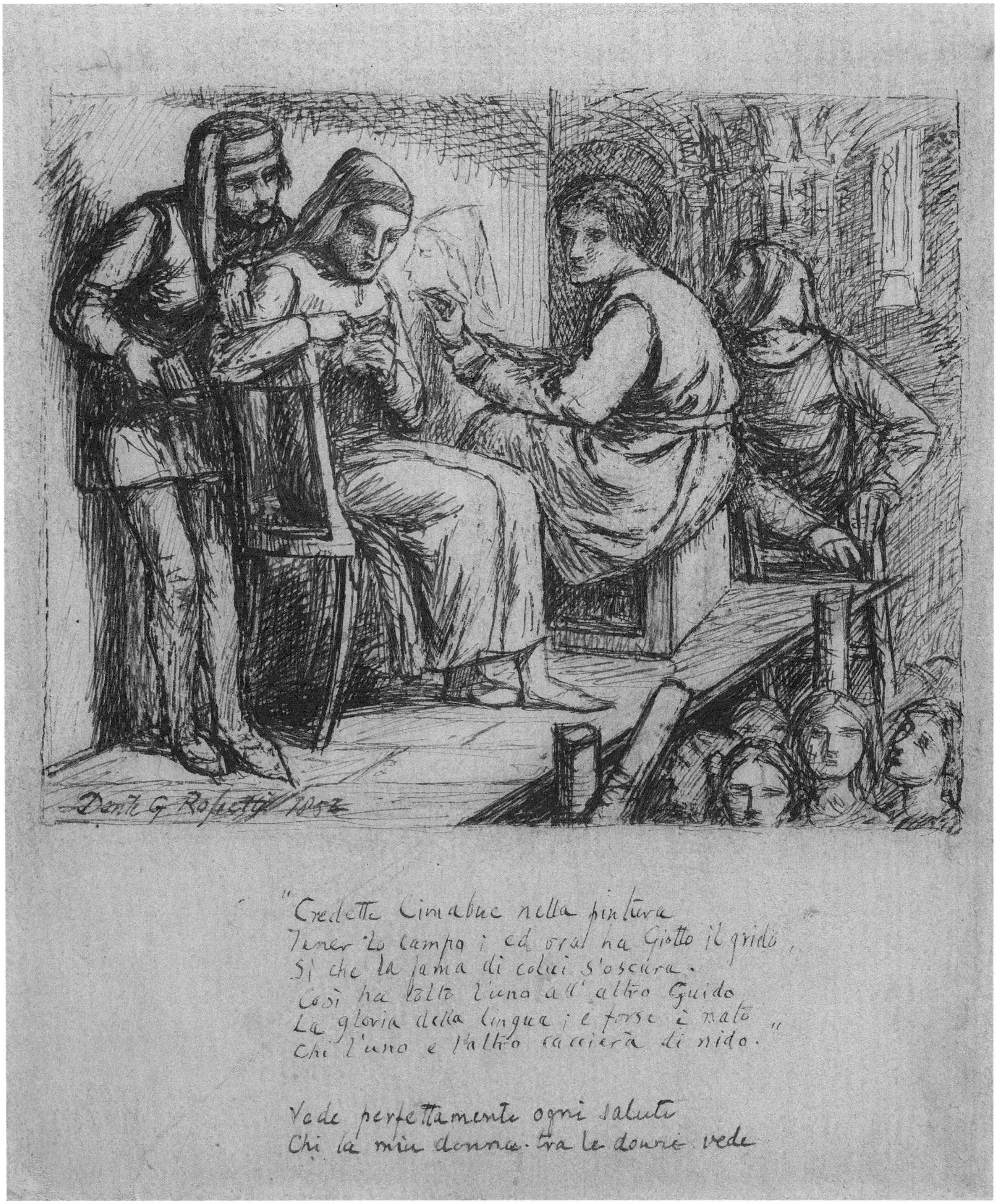
"Credette Cimabue nella pintura
Tener lo campo; ed ora ha Giotto il grido,
Sì che la fama di colui s'oscura.
Così ha tolto l'uno all'altro Guido
La gloria della lingua; e forse è nato
Chi l'uno e l'altro caccierà di nido."
Vede perfettamente ogni salute
Chi la mia donna tra le donne vede

OPPOSITE
NO.68 Dante Gabriel Rossetti, *Study for 'Giotto Painting the Portrait of Dante'* 1852, ink on paper, 19 × 16.8

BELOW
NO.69 Dante Gabriel Rossetti, *Rossetti Sitting to Elizabeth Siddal* 1853, ink on paper, 12.9 × 17.5

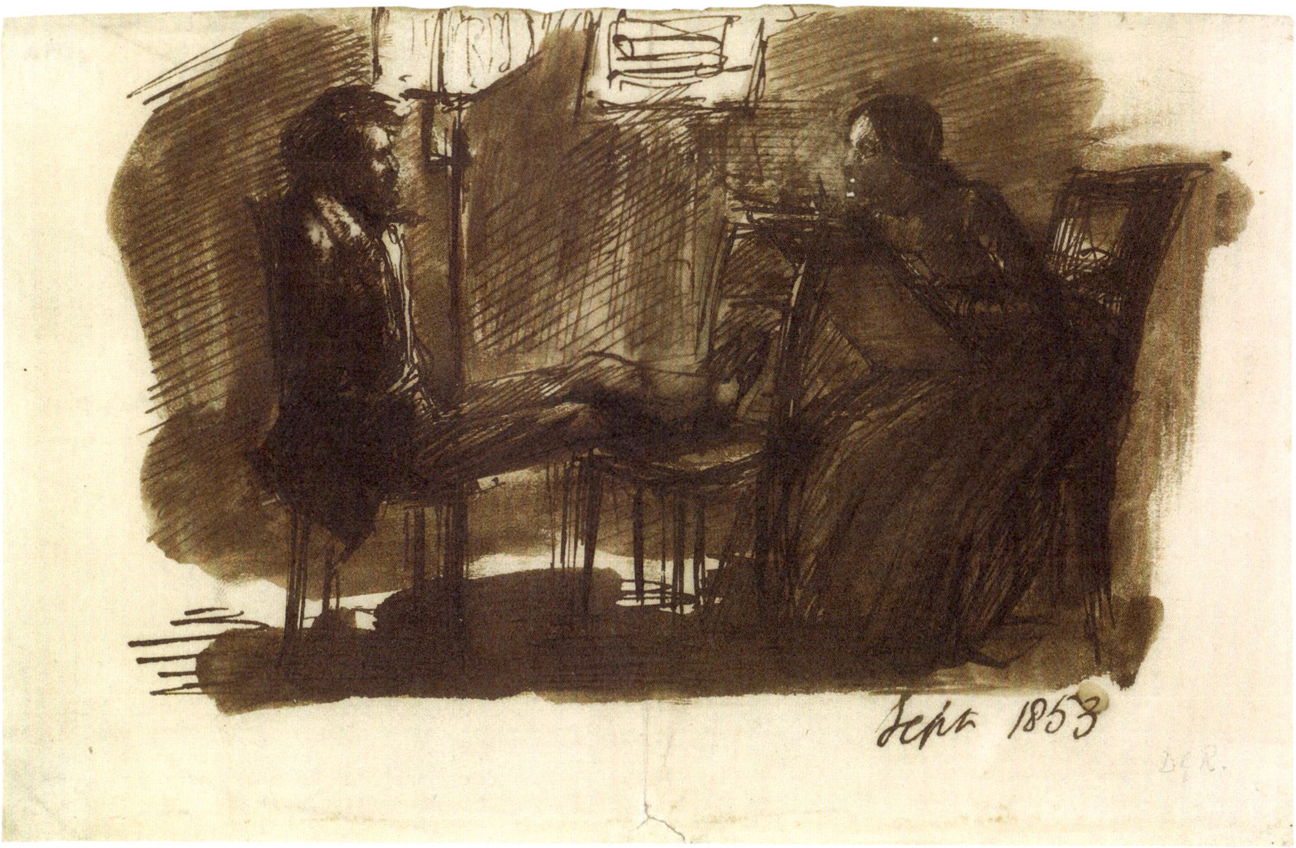

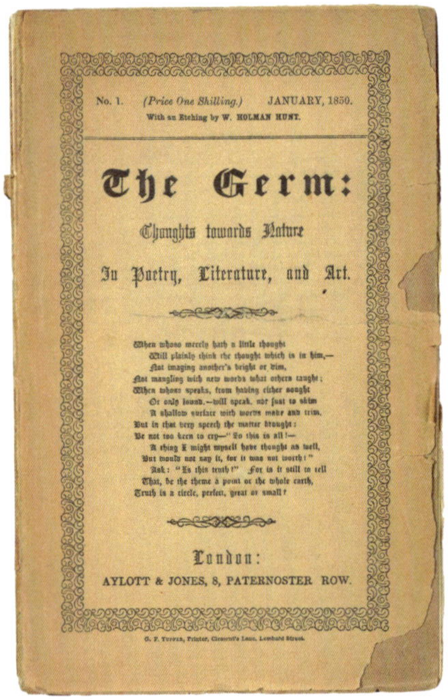

No. 1. (*Price One Shilling.*) JANUARY, 1850.
With an Etching by W. HOLMAN HUNT.

The Germ:
Thoughts towards Nature
In Poetry, Literature, and Art.

When whoso merely hath a little thought
Will plainly think the thought which is in him,—
Not imaging another's bright or dim,
Not mangling with new words what others taught;
When whoso speaks, from having either sought
Or only found,—will speak, not just to skim
A shallow surface with words made and trim,
But in that very speech the matter brought:
Be not too keen to cry—"So this is all!—
A thing I might myself have thought as well,
But would not say it, for it was not worth!"
Ask: "Is this truth?" For is it still to tell
That, be the theme a point or the whole earth,
Truth is a circle, perfect, great or small?

London:
AYLOTT & JONES, 8, PATERNOSTER ROW.

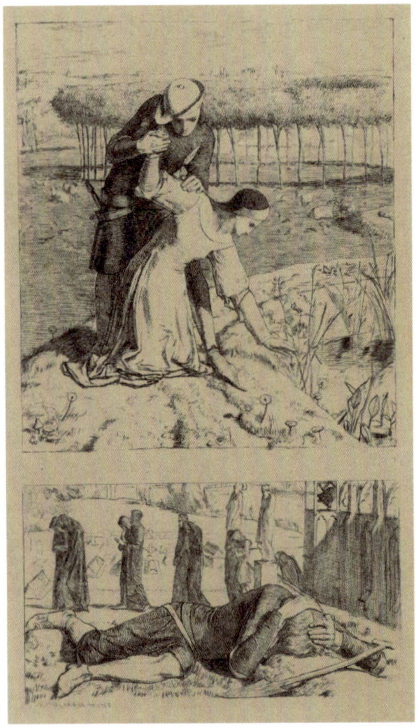

TOP
NO.70 *The Germ*, January 1850, title page of magazine, 21.6 × 14

ABOVE
NO.71 William Holman Hunt, frontispiece to *The Germ* 1850, etching on paper, 20.3 × 12.1

only from Gabriele Rossetti's Neapolitan exploits but also from the Polidori family into which he married.[15] The left-political orientation varied from mild to extreme, but it was characteristic of the family in all its branches. William Michael and his wife Lucy, daughter of the artist Ford Madox Brown, were the most overtly political of their generation - agnostics, feminists, and radical republicans with socialist convictions.[16] But the activism of other Rossettis should not be discounted. This includes the Rossetti women, Frances Mary Lavinia (born Polidori) and her daughters, whose fervent High Anglicanism meant not a retreat from politics, but rather a serious commitment to social justice.[17] Nor did the family's success and fame lead to conservatism in later generations. The novelist Ford Madox Hueffer (later known as Ford Madox Ford, grandson of Ford Madox Brown and nephew of William Michael and Lucy) recalled the politics of his Rossetti relatives as 'advanced in the extreme':

> Nay more, during that splendid youth of the world in the 'eighties and 'nineties the words 'the Social Revolution' were for ever on our lips. We spoke of it as if it were always just round the corner... In these young, splendid and stern days my cousins the Rossettis, aided ... by my energetic romantic aunt [Lucy], founded that celebrated anarchist organ known as the *Torch*.[18]

Writing shortly before the First World War, Hueffer is poking gentle fun at the idealism of his relatives, and the anarchist magazine is a children's game. But it also marks a family tradition of activism through writing and publication that goes all the way back to the private printing-press in the grandfather Gaetano Polidori's Regent's Park house, which issued the first poems of Christina and Dante Gabriel Rossetti in the 1840s, when they were still teenagers.

The Rossettis have the strongest claims of any nineteenth-century artists - with the possible exception of William Morris, their close associate - to be considered radicals in politics. But how does that relate to their artistic radicalism? Perhaps the question would have made little sense to them. Their printing and publishing ventures sometimes overtly advocated a revolutionary politics, but that was always within the context of belonging to a literary or artistic vanguard - as though the progressive idea could only achieve expression in a progressive art form. In this respect, the Pre-Raphaelite 'little magazine', *The Germ* (see NOS.70, 71), can be seen as an extension of Rossetti family practices, and it has often been observed that three Rossetti siblings (Christina, Gabriel and William Michael) contributed fully half of the total contents.[19] If it lasted just four issues before succumbing to financial failure, that is almost a badge of honour for a 'little magazine', too advanced to have a wide appeal. In its short run, however, it managed to publish poems of distinction (and enduring fame) by both Christina and Gabriel, as well as interesting experiments in critical and creative writing by members of the wider Pre-Raphaelite circle, and the group's first attempts at etching. Christina Rossetti had just turned nineteen when two of her poignant lyric poems, 'Dream Land' and 'An End', appeared in the first number, but they are among the most accomplished in what was, inevitably, an uneven collection of writings by inexperienced authors. Neither the miscellaneous contents nor the mission

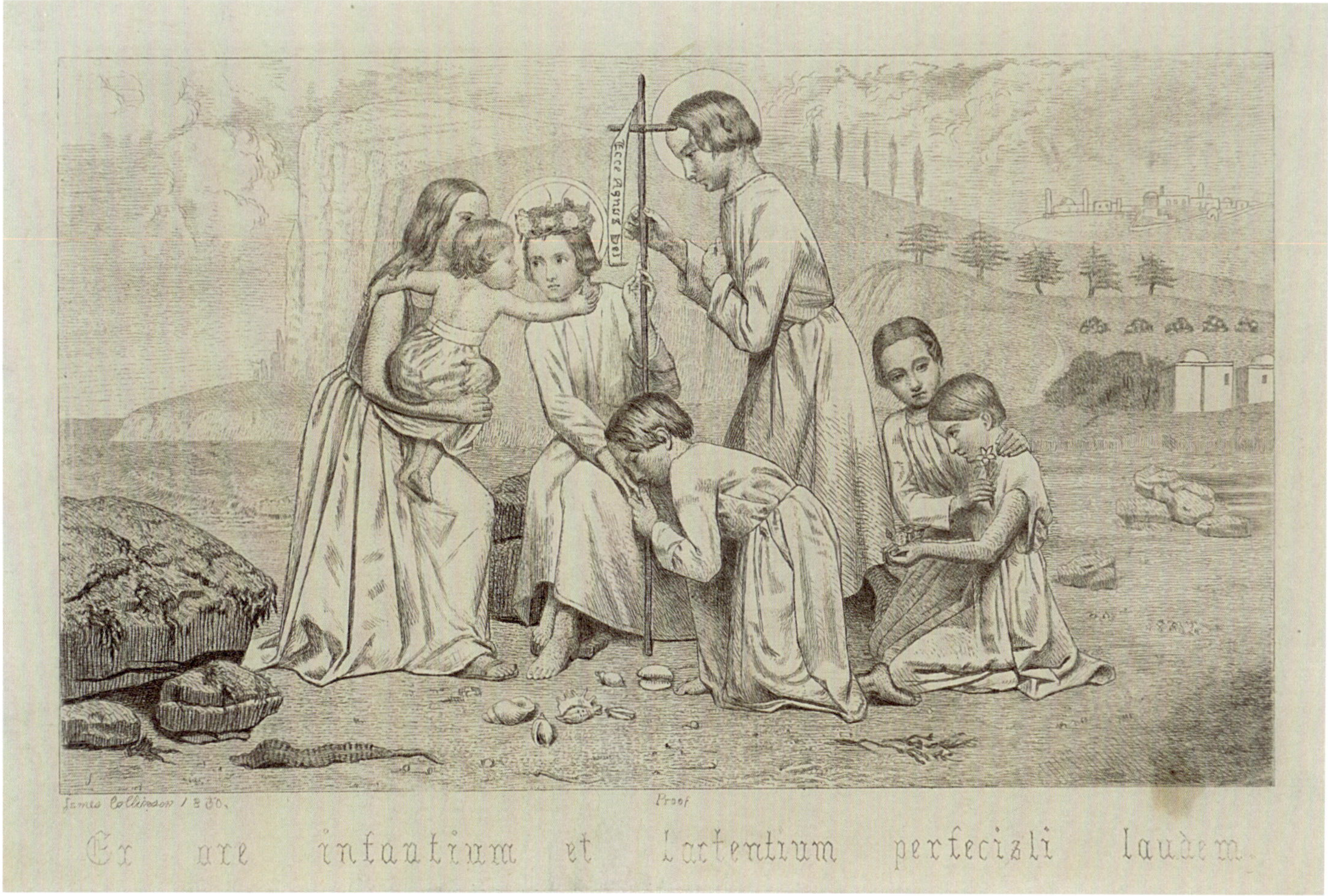

NO.72 James Collinson,
The Child Jesus 1850,
engraving on paper,
12 × 18.5

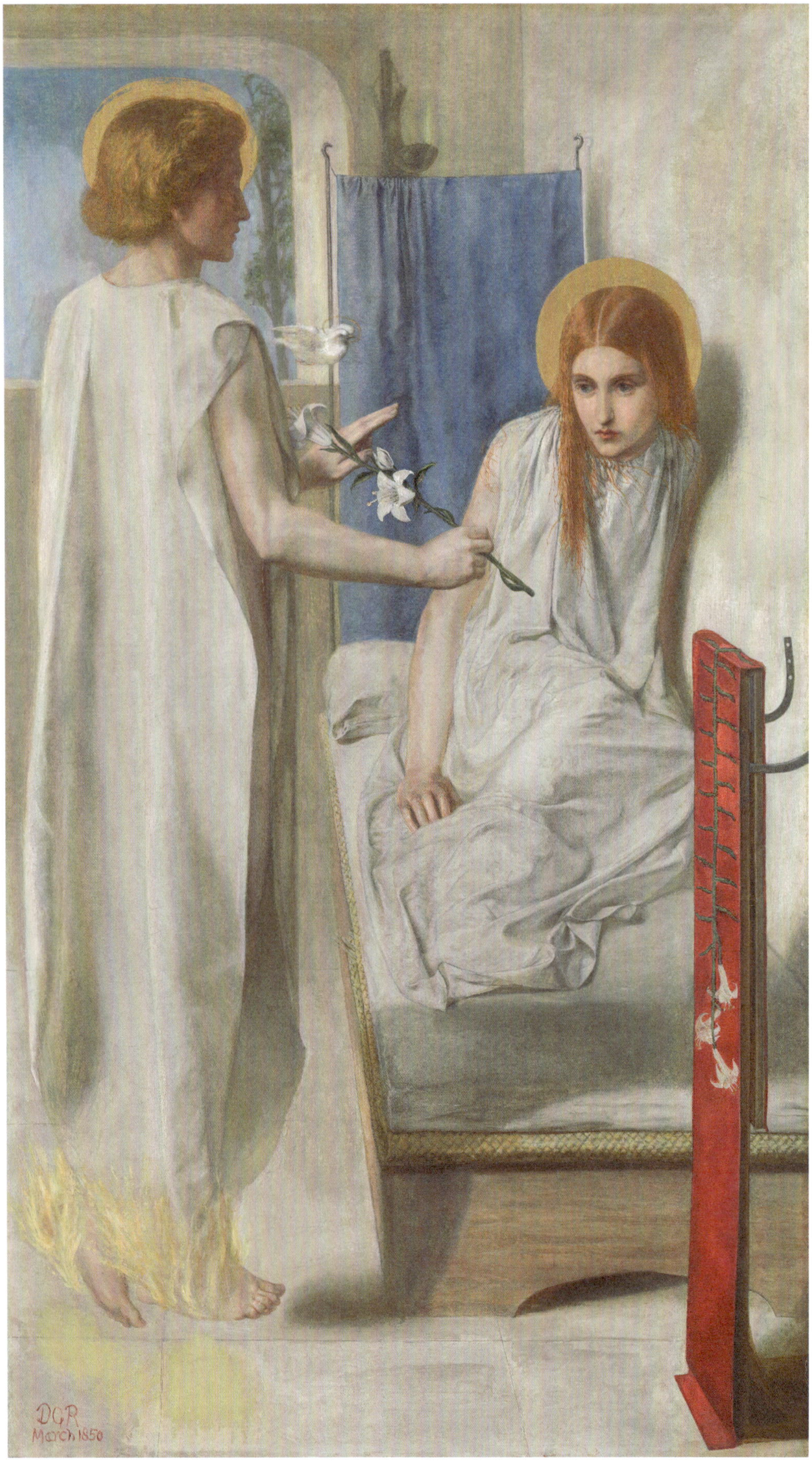

NO.73 Dante Gabriel Rossetti, *Ecce Ancilla Domini! (The Annunciation)* 1849–50, oil paint on canvas, 72.4 × 41.9

statements printed at the end of each issue quite amount to a manifesto for the Pre-Raphaelite movement, but that may be their strength. Like Rienzi's oath, they mark 'the germ' of a revolution that cannot be codified, since it is yet to come.

In comparison with Hunt's *Rienzi*, Dante Gabriel Rossetti's first oil paintings might seem less committed to the revolutionary spirit of the moment, but that would be a superficial view. *The Girlhood of Mary Virgin* (NO.53), exhibited simultaneously with *Rienzi* in 1849, and *Ecce Ancilla Domini! (The Annunciation)* of the next year (NO.73) are the artist's first completed paintings - the work of a beginner, more so than the first P.R.B. productions of Hunt and Millais, who had at least a few exhibited paintings behind them. Both of Gabriel's paintings have religious subjects of a traditional kind, centred on the Virgin Mary, and both emphasise feminine submission rather than the masculine activism of *Rienzi*. Yet for all its ingenuity, Hunt's picture is still readily comprehensible as a Victorian narrative painting in realist mode, with carefully researched antiquarian details from fourteenth-century Italy. Gabriel's paintings instead imagine a different world. It is a world deeply informed by the art of the Italian quattrocento (the classic 'Pre-Raphaelite' age of the fifteenth century), as critics immediately recognised, but also fully Pre-Raphaelite in the modern sense of observing the scene as though it were taking place before one's very eyes. One might call the pictures bilingual, in their combination of modern English realism with quattrocento Italian style.

The slight awkwardnesses of perspective and anatomy, in both of Gabriel's pictures, have often been taken as signs of the painter's immaturity. They might more productively be described as deliberate allusions to the art of the period before Raphael - before the codification of academic rules and conventions. On either view, they contribute to the distinctive expressiveness of the paintings. No subject has been more frequently depicted, in the art of the entire Western tradition, than the Annunciation to the Virgin. Yet Gabriel's painting, *Ecce Ancilla Domini!*, imagines the scene afresh. The title (in Latin, worrying to some critics for its Roman Catholic associations) presents the scene from the Virgin's perspective, in her own words, which mark her acquiescence to the angel's announcement that she will bear the son of God: 'Behold the handmaid of the Lord'. We believe that this Virgin is receiving a message so important that it terrifies her. Her shrinking pose may not quite be anatomically orthodox, but it is powerfully expressive, like the sharp diagonal perspective - 'wrong', but only according to the conventions of post-Raphaelite European art. At the same time the individual strands of her hair fall across her white garment, their disarray paradoxically captured with Pre-Raphaelite precision.

The characterisation of the Virgin is crucial to the mood and expressiveness of both paintings, and in both cases the model was Christina Rossetti, immediately recognisable even though her colouring has been altered to suit the conception (compare NO.53). Christina is typecast as a very young woman, but her quiet determination and intelligence also seem to pervade the paintings. Other family members served as models, too - William Michael as the angel of the Annunciation, and their mother as the Virgin's mother, St Anne, in the *Girlhood*. Of course an impecunious young artist

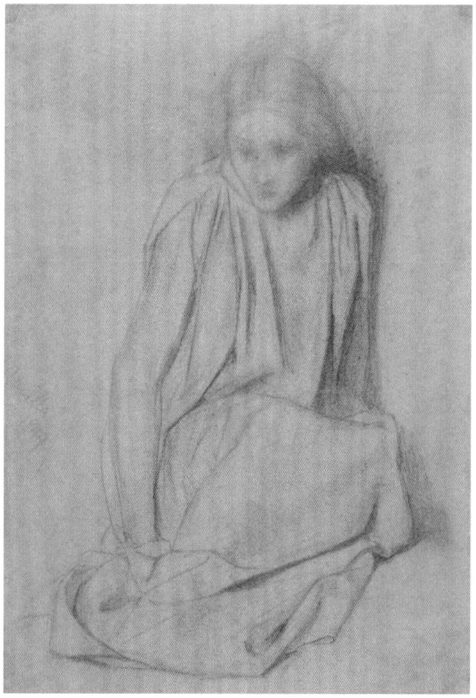

NO.74 Dante Gabriel Rossetti, *Study for 'Ecce Ancilla Domini! (The Annunciation)'* c.1849, graphite on paper, 19.4 × 13.7

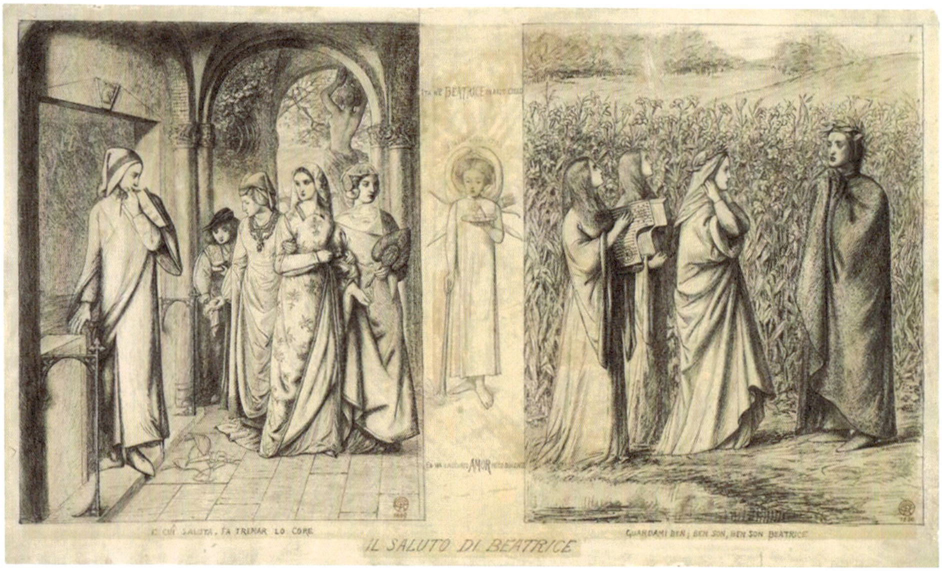

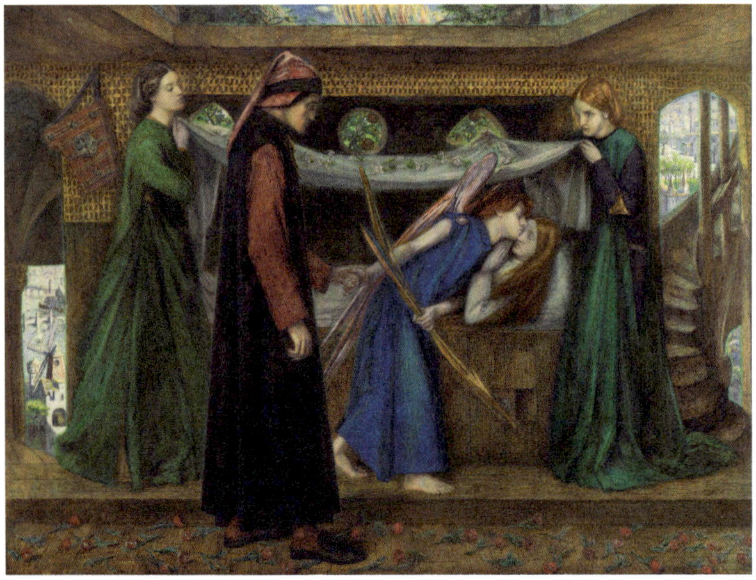

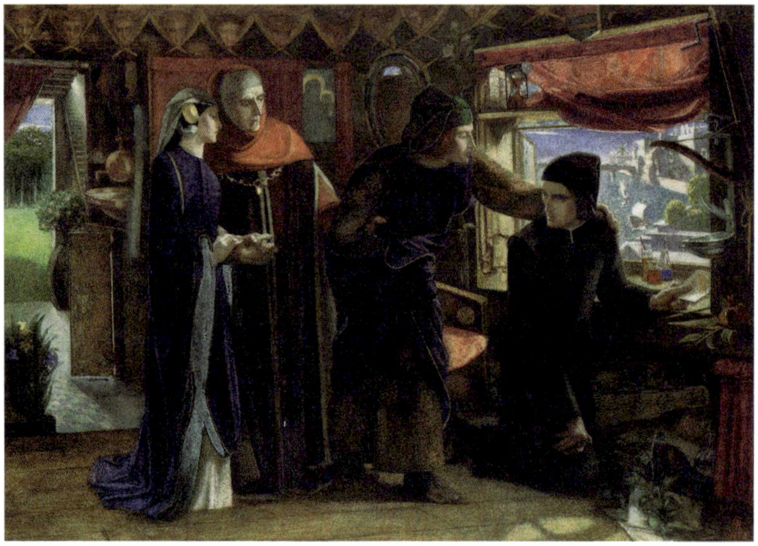

FROM TOP

NO.75 Dante Gabriel Rossetti, *The Salutation of Beatrice* 1849–50, ink, wash and chalk on paper, 39.5 × 67.7

NO.76 Dante Gabriel Rossetti, *Dante's Dream at the Time of the Death of Beatrice* 1856, watercolour on paper, 48.7 × 66.2

NO.77 Dante Gabriel Rossetti, *Dante Drawing an Angel on the Anniversary of Beatrice's Death* 1853, watercolour and bodycolour on paper, 42 × 61

might need to use family members rather than hired models. Nonetheless, the paintings seem rooted in the Rossetti family ethos, and perhaps their basic Pre-Raphaelite premise can be traced back to Gabriele Rossetti's studies of Dante, the great Italian poet of the late-medieval past whose political and artistic messages, in Gabriele's interpretation, remained vitally relevant to the present day.

It is remarkable enough, in a period of high infant mortality, that all four children of Gabriele and Frances Rossetti lived to maturity, and even more remarkable that they all achieved distinction in one or more art forms. A factor in the creativity of the Rossetti household must have been its Italianness, that sense of difference from the mundane realities of everyday English life – or, more precisely, the bilingual orientation that maintained an alternative perspective, a different and unconventional point of view, in every situation. Above all, it was the supportive family environment that enabled them to excel in their various pursuits – the spirit of the children's home-printed magazine, in which even the smallest child takes their part. In the family circle, everyone practised creative writing, and everyone, including Christina and William Michael, made drawings. For Gabriel, it was entirely conceivable that his own friends might be geniuses on a par with the greatest of the Old Masters, and this helps to explain his extraordinary influence on the people who surrounded him. His optimism may have been excessive, but it was infectious, and helped to spur his friends, including Elizabeth Siddal and the Pre-Raphaelite Brothers, to greater achievement than they might otherwise have attempted. This, it may be argued, is the most important legacy of the Rossetti family: the conviction that everyone is capable of making art, developed in subsequent generations through the Arts and Crafts movement, in twentieth-century philosophies of creativity, and still powerful today.

A good deal of ink has been spilt on the question of who was the moving spirit among the original Pre-Raphaelite Brothers – a pointless question, in one sense: Millais, Hunt, Dante Gabriel Rossetti, and several even of the lesser-known Pre-Raphaelite artists each have a claim to have originated something new and vital. Perhaps, though, it is true to say that it was the Rossetti family spirit that turned this association among a few rebellious art students into a world-changing movement – that is, a revolution

1 On the Rossetti antecedents, see William Michael Rossetti, 'Memoir of Dante Gabriel Rossetti', in *Dante Gabriel Rossetti: His Family-Letters with a Memoir*, 2 vols., London 1895, vol.1, pp.3–36.

2 William Holman Hunt, *Pre-Raphaelitism and the Pre-Raphaelite Brotherhood*, 2 vols., London 1905–6, vol.1, pp.101–2 (Chartist demonstration), 154–5 ('escaped revolutionists').

3 William Michael Rossetti (ed.), *The Works of Dante Gabriel Rossetti*, London 1911, pp.261–2, 175.

4 Hunt 1905–6, 1, pp.107, 91.

5 Malcolm Warner, 'The Pre-Raphaelites and the National Gallery', *Huntington Library Quarterly*, vol.55, no.1, Winter 1992, pp.1–11 (p.3 on Hunt and Francia).

6 Elizabeth Prettejohn, *Modern Painters, Old Masters: The Art of Imitation from the Pre-Raphaelites to the First World War*, New Haven, CT and London 2017, pp.99–110 and passim.

7 Hunt 1905–6, 1, p.142.

8 F.G. Stephens, *Dante Gabriel Rossetti*, London 1894, p.10 (quoting a fellow student at the Royal Academy in the later 1840s); Hunt 1905–6, 1, pp.144–5.

9 Stephens 1894, p.24.

10 Edward Bulwer Lytton, *Rienzi, the Last of the Roman Tribunes*, London 1848 (and often reprinted), Book I, chap.1.

11 For these and other details on the painting, see Judith Bronkhurst, *William Holman Hunt: A Catalogue Raisonné*, 2 vols., New Haven, CT and London 2006, vol.1, pp.131–3 (cat. no. 61).

12 Bulwer Lytton 1848, I, chap.1. After the first exhibition Hunt also repainted the robe of Rienzi, originally a sober grey as in Bulwer Lytton's novel.

13 Hunt 1905–6, 1, p.219.

14 Ibid., p.155.

15 See Jan Marsh, 'Sibling Cultures', in *Outsiders Looking In: The Rossettis Then and Now*, ed. David Clifford and Laurence Roussillon, London 2004, pp.9–28.

16 Angela Thirlwell, *William and Lucy: The Other Rossettis*, New Haven, CT and London 2003.

17 Mary Arseneau, 'Pews, Periodicals and Politics: The Rossetti Women as High Church Controversialists', in Clifford and Roussillon 2004, pp.97–113.

18 Ford Madox Hueffer, *Ancient Lights and Certain New Reflections: Being the Memories of a Young Man*, London 1911, p.116.

19 Andrew M. Stauffer, '*The Germ*', in *The Cambridge Companion to the Pre-Raphaelites*, ed. Elizabeth Prettejohn, Cambridge 2012, pp.76–85.

Jan Marsh

Mythbusting Elizabeth Siddal

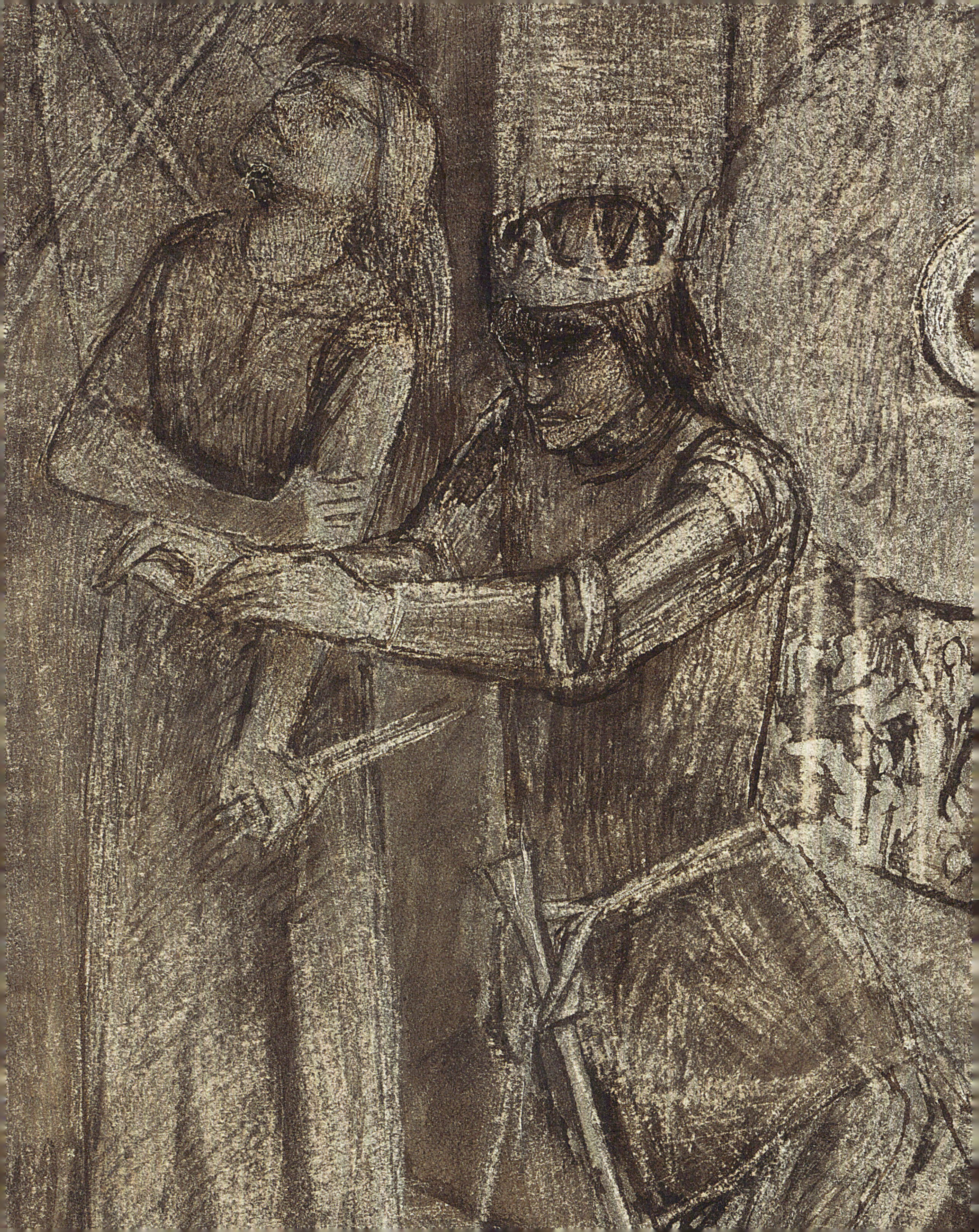

PAGE 77
NO.78 Elizabeth Siddal, *The Macbeths* 1850–62 (detail), ink with scratching out on paper, 21.4 × 13.5

BELOW
NO.79 Elizabeth Siddal, *Self-Portrait* 1853–4, oil paint on canvas, 22.9 (diameter)

OPPOSITE
NO.80 Dante Gabriel Rossetti, *Elizabeth Siddal* c.1854, graphite and watercolour on paper, 18.1 × 16.2

This landmark exhibition is the opportunity to correct the longstanding myth of Elizabeth Siddal as a 'meek, unconscious dove'[1] and sad victim of misogyny and drug addiction. She was not meek, nor invalid, but active and assertive, and her fatal opiate overdose was likely the result of post-natal psychosis after her daughter was born dead.

However, it is easy to see how the legends began and how they thrived in the 160 years after Elizabeth's death. In 1862, she was unknown, the wife of a not-yet famous artist, and the as-yet unnamed model for paintings by the short-lived Pre-Raphaelite Brotherhood, which was already fading from view. Twenty years later, in books and exhibitions following Dante Gabriel Rossetti's death, she was identified as the inspiration for his memorial picture of Dante Alighieri's *Beata Beatrix*, three versions of which were shown in 1883.

The consequent elevation of Gabriel to leadership of the Pre-Raphaelite Brotherhood prompted William Holman Hunt to assert a counter-claim. His earliest first-person account of the Brotherhood, published in the *Contemporary Review* in 1886, did not mention Elizabeth, but soon thereafter her name was established as a key feature of Brotherhood history; indeed, having known Miss Siddal emerged as an emblem of authenticity. In 1905, Hunt's enlarged account, *Pre-Raphaelitism and the Pre-Raphaelite Brotherhood*, dramatised the version that became one of the movement's foundation myths – her 'discovery' in a milliner's shop in Cranborne Alley, off London's Leicester Square. However, nothing corroborates this episode, with its conversations apparently recalled verbatim after fifty years, and it was unknown to William Michael Rossetti, Pre-Raphaelite Brother and archivist.

In recent decades, Elizabeth Siddal has moved from a marginal to a near-central position in Pre-Raphaelite histories. Whether as the model for the famed *Ophelia* and *Beata Beatrix* who was discovered in a bonnet shop, or as the frail drug addict who died from a laudanum overdose, or as the beautiful red-head whose coffin was exhumed to retrieve Gabriel's poetic manuscript, anecdotes about Elizabeth are now essential elements in accounts of the Pre-Raphaelite Brotherhood.

Lately, as in the present exhibition, attention has dwelt on her own career and artworks, rather than her image, elevating her into a practitioner. Each age, and indeed each commentator, presents Elizabeth Siddal in terms that reflect their own perspectives, interests and cultural positions, because while art history is grounded in observable and documented fact, opinion and interpretation are equally significant.

The first (and indeed only) obituary of Elizabeth Siddal in 1862 omits all mention of modelling for young artists in the Brotherhood circle. Instead, it describes a young woman with artistic aspirations, who as a dressmaker met the women of the Deverell family. She then showed her sketches – 'designs of her own leisure hours' – to Mr Deverell, principal of the London School of Design, who introduced her to his son Walter and his Pre-Raphaelite Brotherhood friends, who encouraged her practice. This was the start of her artistic career, according to William Ibbitt, the obituarist, who met Elizabeth in Sheffield in 1857 but knew no others in the London art world and must therefore have had his information from 'the amiable young artist' herself.[2]

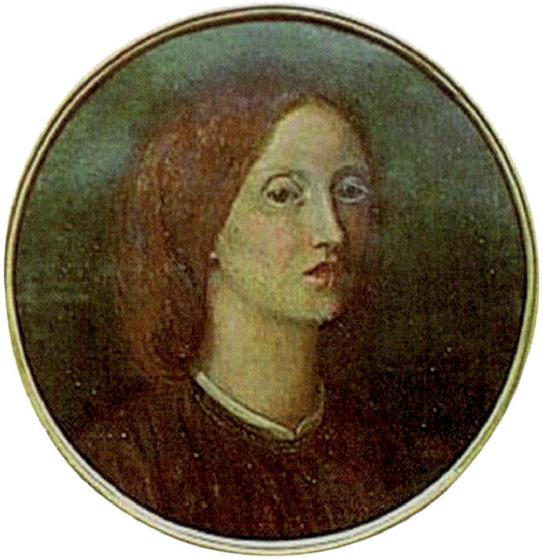

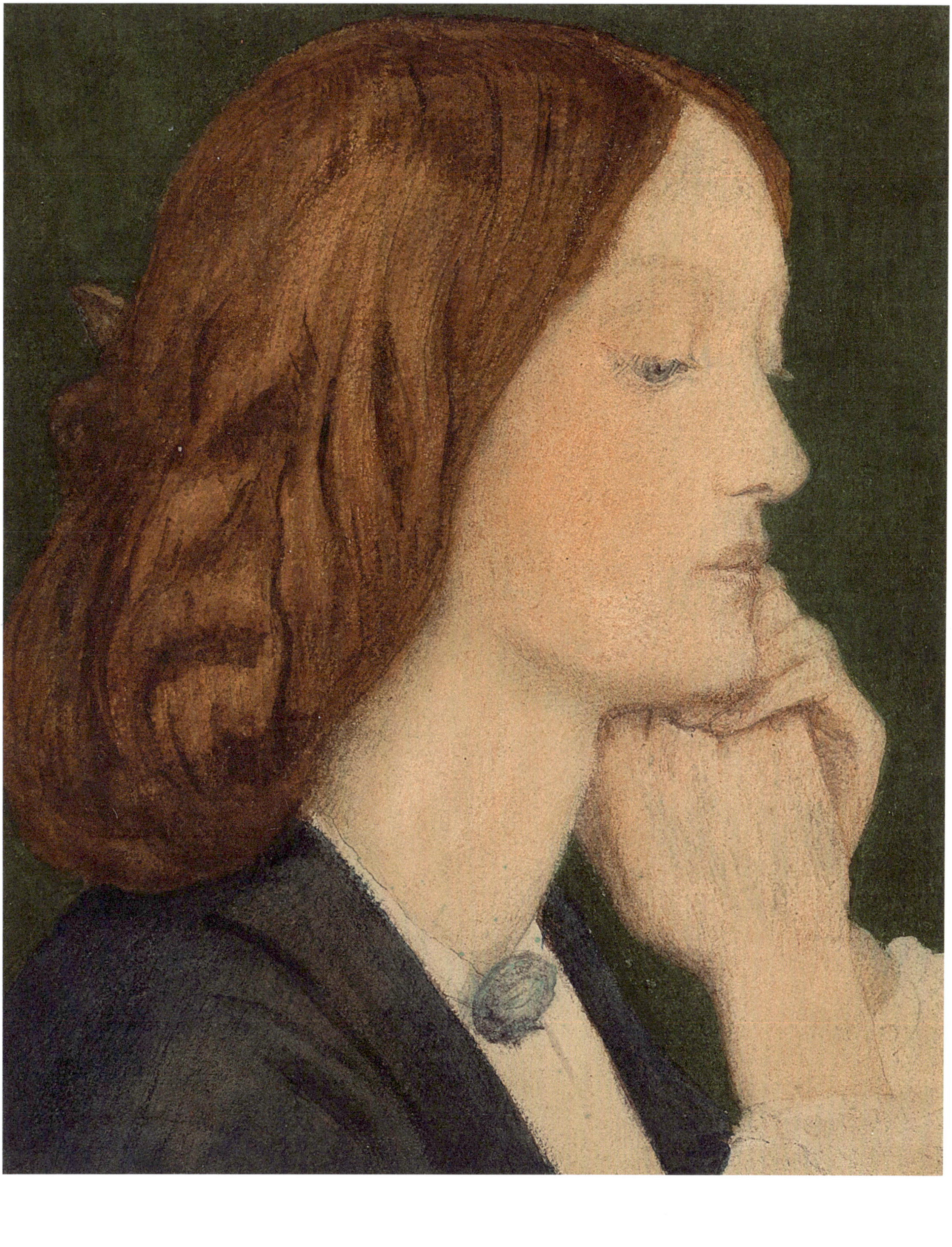

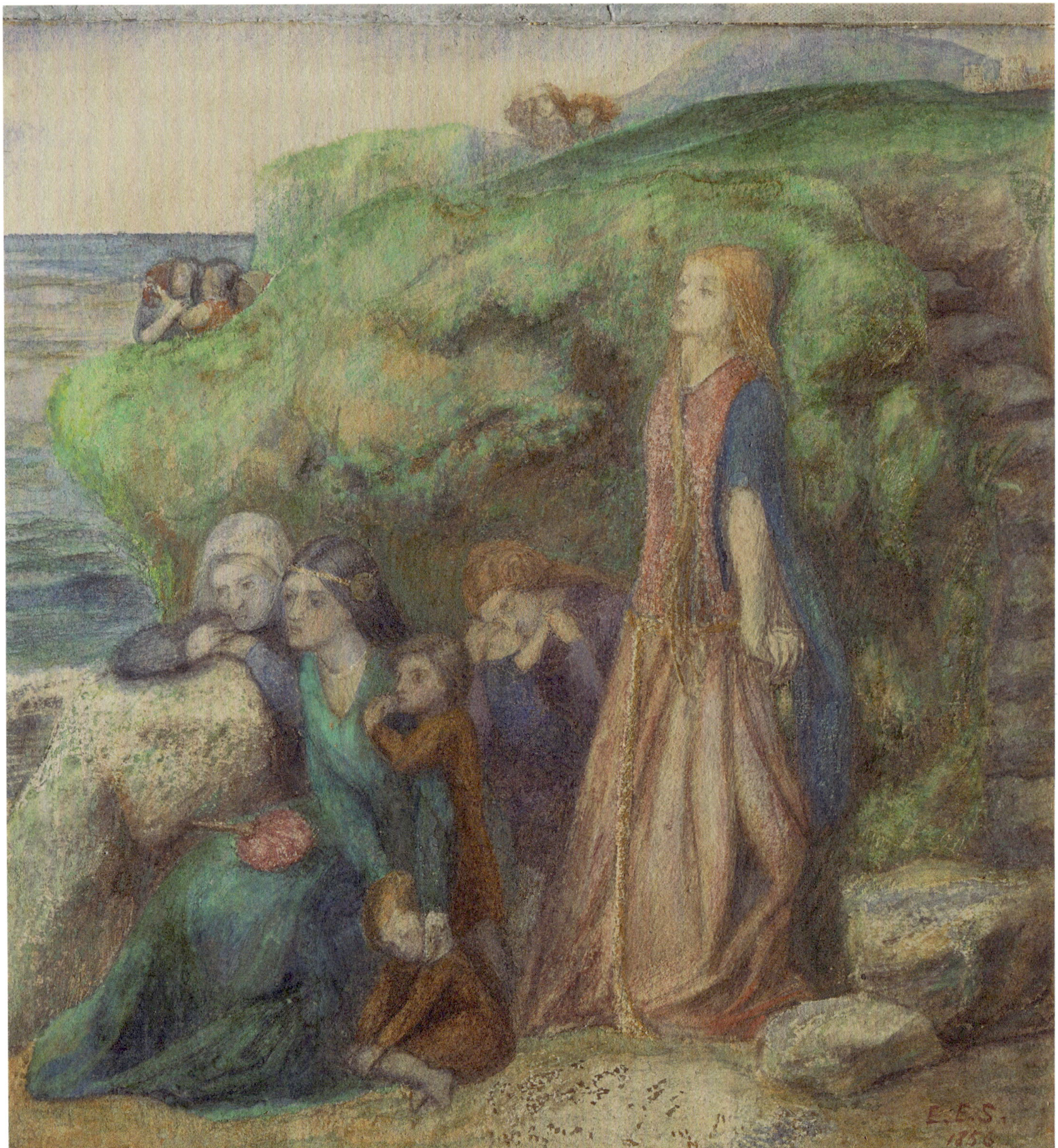
E.E.S.
1856

In view of Elizabeth's eager participation in art practice, it is easy to conceive of her as a teenager with drawings of her own. But harder to guess is what kind of drawings she could have shown to the Deverells. Were they sketches like the fashion plates published in illustrated magazines? Such would conform with the dressmaker's position, studying the new season's styles. Or were they imaginative illustrations to poems, as in keepsake annuals? Elizabeth was an admirer of Tennyson, and his early verse was immensely popular.

We cannot know. Although one very rough delineation of a millinery shop hints at such a sphere, no fashion sketches survive. The studies and watercolours that now comprise her oeuvre are all thought to post-date her meeting with Gabriel. Many of these share his literary tastes, for Shakespeare, Keats, Border ballads and Browning. But I wonder if her earliest finished design, for Tennyson's poem 'The Lady of Shalott' (NO.85), had its inception in the drawings shown to the Deverells?

The Cinderella from Cranborne Alley nevertheless became a key feature of the Pre-Raphaelite Brotherhood narrative. So too did the episode in John Everett Millais's studio, when as a willing model she lay in a bath tub of cooling water to simulate Ophelia's drowning. Even if perhaps embellished, this anecdote came from a reputable source – Millais's fellow artist, Arthur Hughes. Seldom repeated is the fact that soon afterwards Elizabeth told another painter that she modelled no longer, having now 'other occupation'.[3] The inference is that modelling – for Deverell, Hunt, Millais and others from 1849 to 1852 – was a way into the art world where her own creative ambitions lay.

By becoming Gabriel's student and sweetheart, she was committed to his view of artistic value – that of conception over practice. Had she trained with Ford Madox Brown, for example, she could have learned the basic skills of drawing as they then prevailed: observation, anatomy, perspective and composition. The writer and artist John Ruskin chided her imaginative fancies, urging her to draw from dull things, as students did endlessly. She preferred to depict scenes: from Tennyson ('The Lady of Shalott'), Browning ('Pippa Passes'), Wordsworth ('We are Seven') and Keats ('La Belle Dame Sans Merci'). Working on a small scale, she progressed to illustrations of Border ballads, including *Sir Patrick Spens* (NO.81), her source material being a volume that is neatly inscribed with her name.[4]

The next myth is that of ill health and frailty, which is undermined by Elizabeth's active life and aspiration. She had her own account with the artists' supplier Robersons in Long Acre, and the evidence of compositional sketches as well as finished drawings and watercolours shows she worked assiduously; Gabriel once joked about her 'scraping a hole' through the paper in her repeated attempts to amend an image.[5] She regularly travelled alone to Pre-Raphaelite Brotherhood studios across London, followed by extended visits in Britain and Europe, often undertaken solo. In 1855 she went on her own to Clevedon in Somerset and then spent the winter months on the Mediterranean, at Nice and Menton. In autumn 1856 she spent three months in Bath, and the following summer went with her sister to Sheffield.

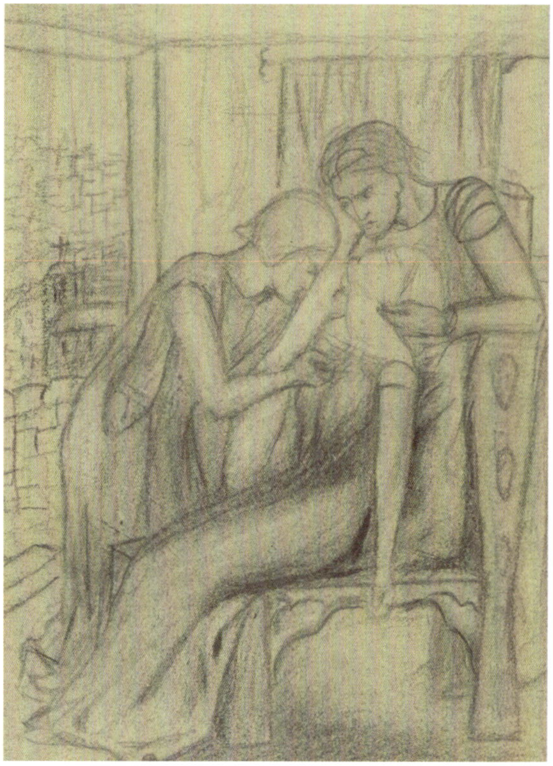

OPPOSITE
NO.81 Elizabeth Siddal, *Sir Patrick Spens* 1856, watercolour on paper, 24.1 × 22.9

ABOVE
NO.82 Elizabeth Siddal, *The Gay Goshawk* c.1854, graphite on paper, 10 × 7.5

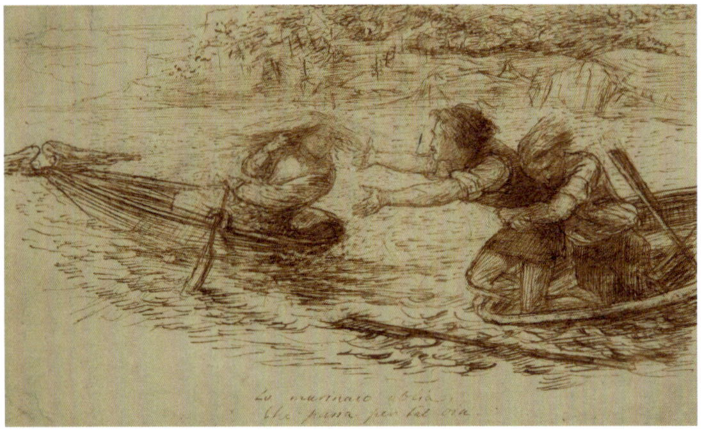

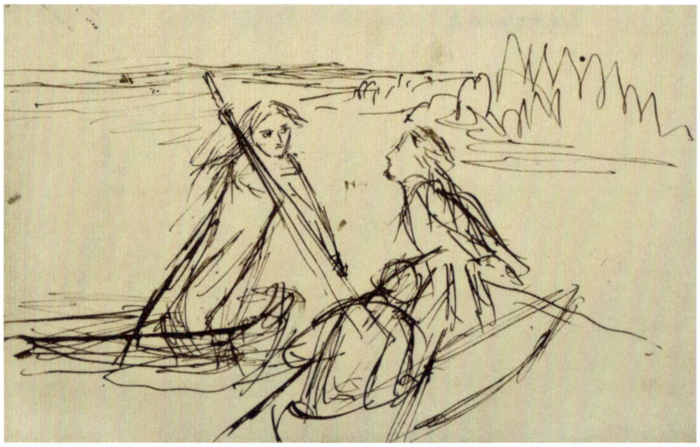

ABOVE LEFT
NO.83 Dante Gabriel Rossetti, *Boatmen and Siren* c.1853, ink on paper, 11.1 × 18.4

ABOVE RIGHT
NO.84 Elizabeth Siddal, *Two Men in a Boat and a Woman Punting* c.1850–62, ink on paper, 11.6 × 18.3

OPPOSITE
NO.85 Elizabeth Siddal, *The Lady of Shalott* 1853, ink on paper, 16.5 × 22.3

These movements, plus her repeated rejection of medical advice and remedies offered by others, indicate relative fitness for at least the first decade of her association with the Pre-Raphaelite circle. The winter in the south of France has prompted surprisingly little commentary, perhaps because it evidences independence rather than the pathos of emotional dependence on Gabriel which typically describes this period.

For the Victorian middle classes, physical weakness was a signifier of social refinement for 'ladies', and thus a useful reason to avoid disagreeable duties. Christina Rossetti 'rejoiced' that her health precluded working as a governess, although the medical fear of 'night air' also denied her evening parties and concerts. Elizabeth has been characterised as comparably sickly – usually from addiction to the opiate laudanum – but in these years no allusions to the drug are recorded, the first possible mention being her weak condition at the time of her marriage to Gabriel in 1860. Laudanum was the main painkiller available, used as both stimulant and sedative, and as widely consumed as later aspirin, codeine and paracetamol, so its use would not usually be remarked. We cannot know, but the accounts of Elizabeth as invalid addict morosely brooding on her wrongs are not supported by witnesses until after the stillbirth of her daughter in May 1861.

With a few exceptions, nor are descriptions of her 'matchless beauty'. As a historian, I dislike this topic, which endorses cultural judgements about appearance, but here the myth is instructive. Several women who sat for Pre-Raphaelite painters were not regarded as 'beauties' by contemporaries, only acquiring this accolade retrospectively, as fashions evolved, not least in response to the artworks. Elizabeth was tall for her time, which preferred petite women; she had red or reddish hair when this was thought ugly and unlucky; she had a distinctive overbite and slightly protruding eyeballs. And so she was not first choice as artist's model for saints and heroines; indeed, she suited Deverell and Hunt for the boyish

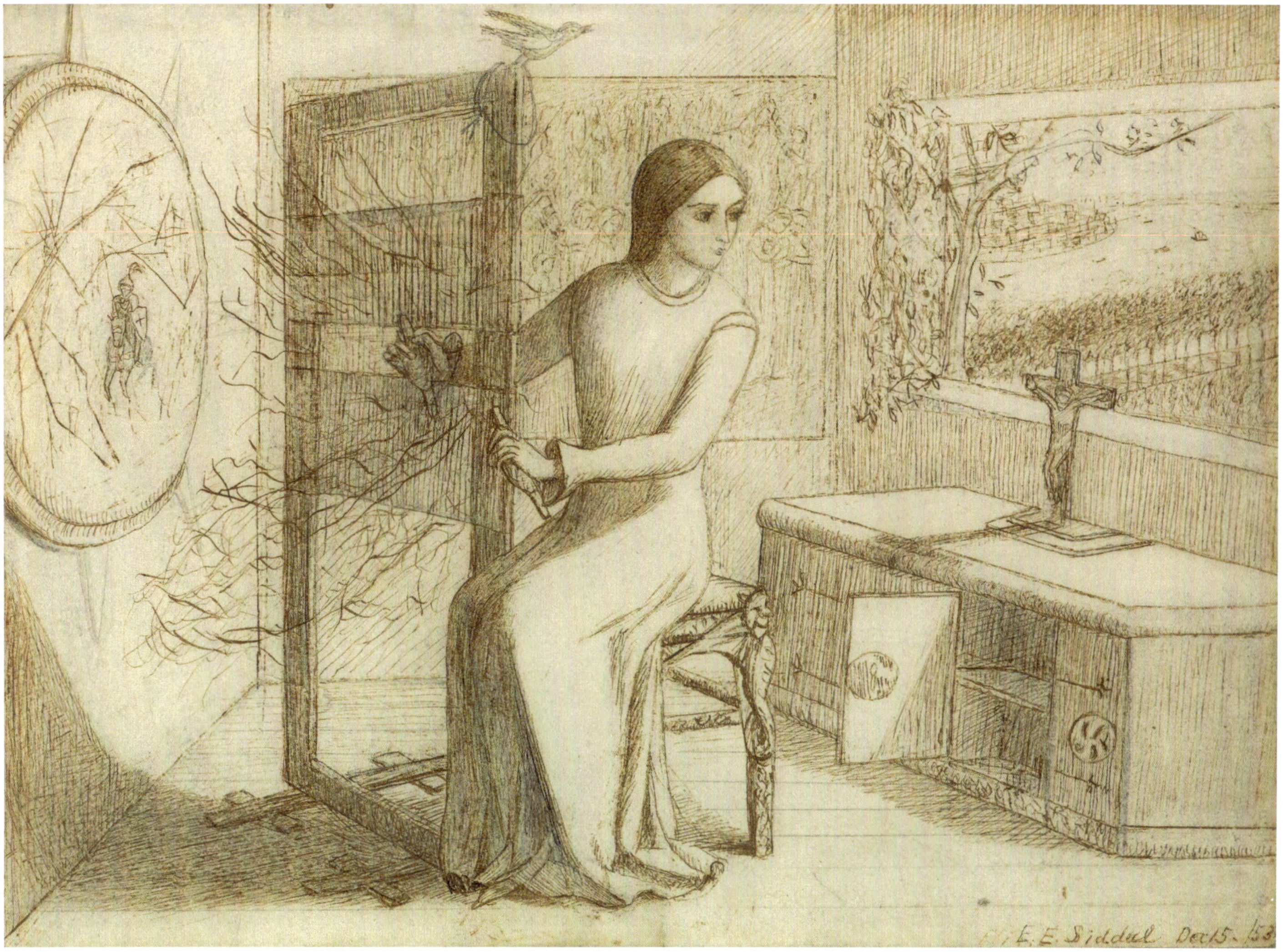

'She maintained an attitude of reserve, self-controlling and alien from approach ... along with a decided inclination to order her mode of life according to her own liking.'

William Michael Rossetti

RIGHT
NO.86 Elizabeth Siddal, *Study for the Nativity* 1860, graphite on paper, 19 × 18.6

BELOW
NO.87 Elizabeth Siddal, *Madonna and Child* 1850–62, watercolour over graphite on paper, 6.5 × 5.9

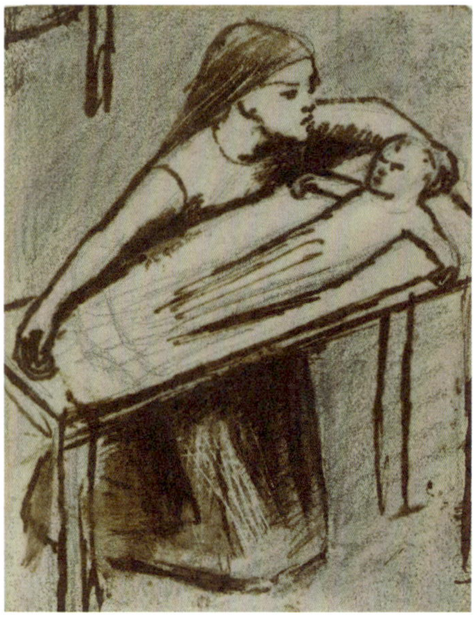

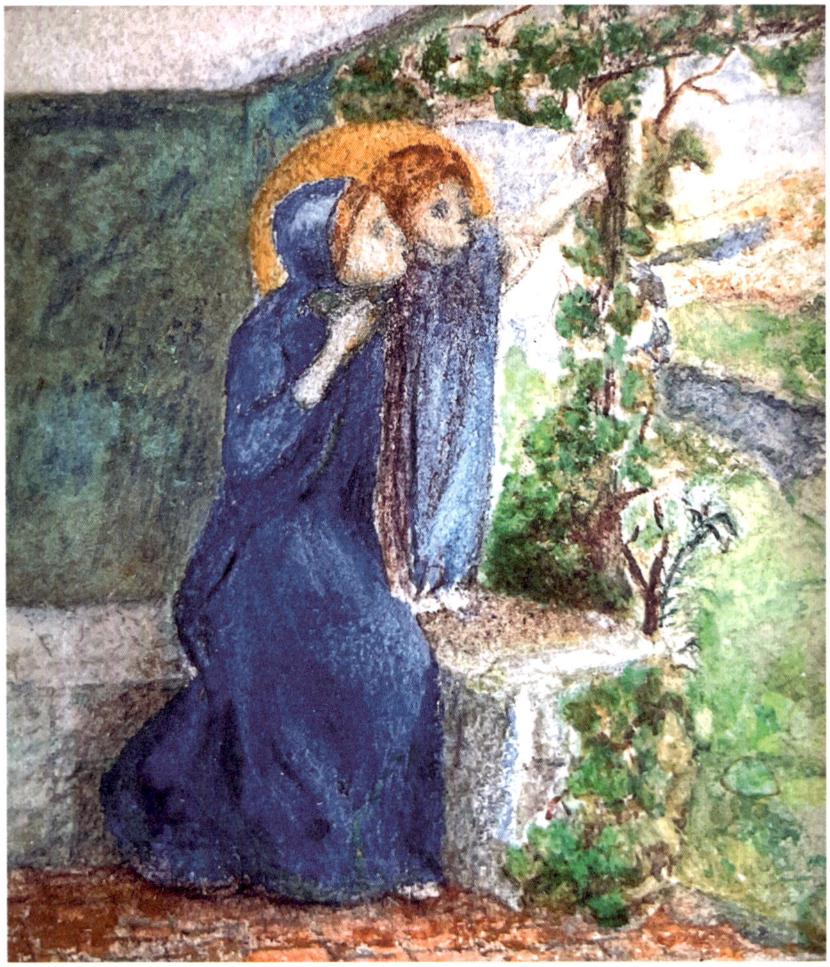

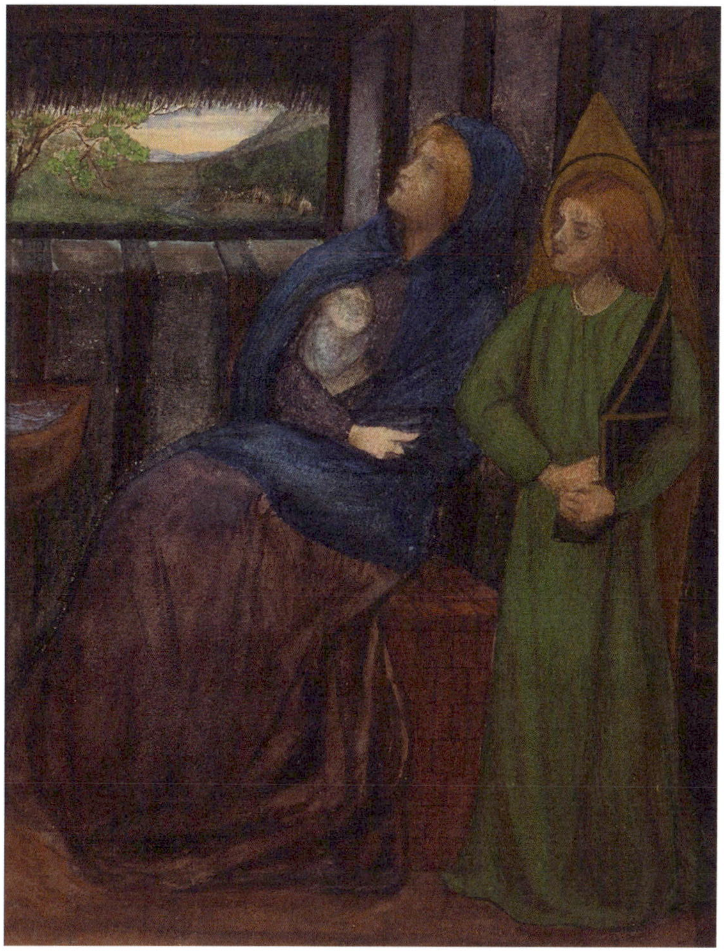

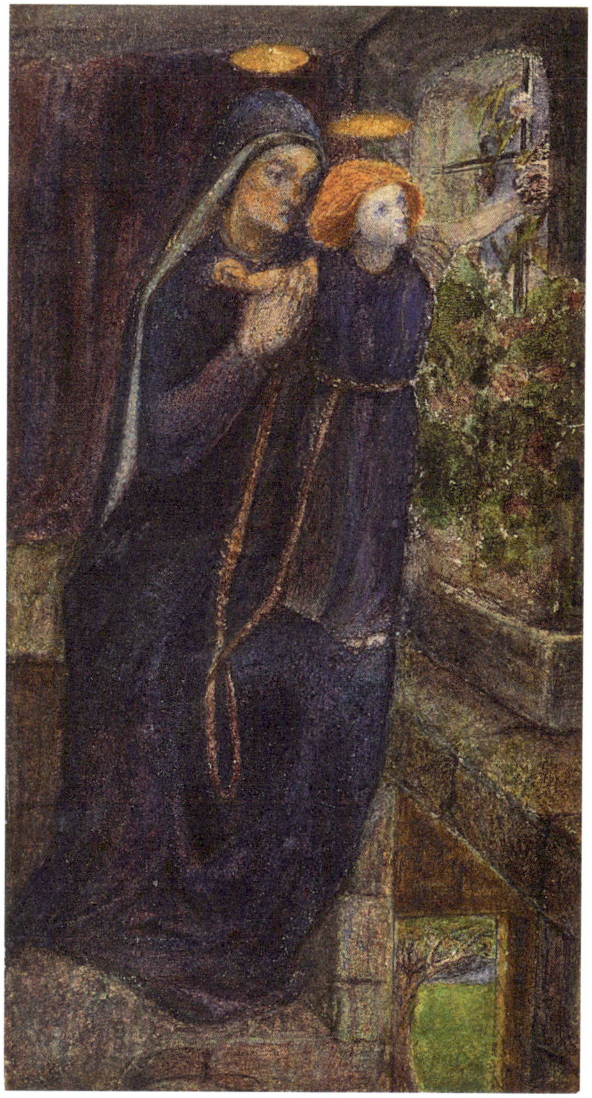

ABOVE
NO.88 Elizabeth Siddal, *Madonna and Child with Angel* c.1856, watercolour, gouache and metallic paint on paper, 19.7 × 15.2

RIGHT
NO.89 Elizabeth Siddal, *Madonna and Child* c.1850–62, watercolour on paper, 17.9 × 9.7

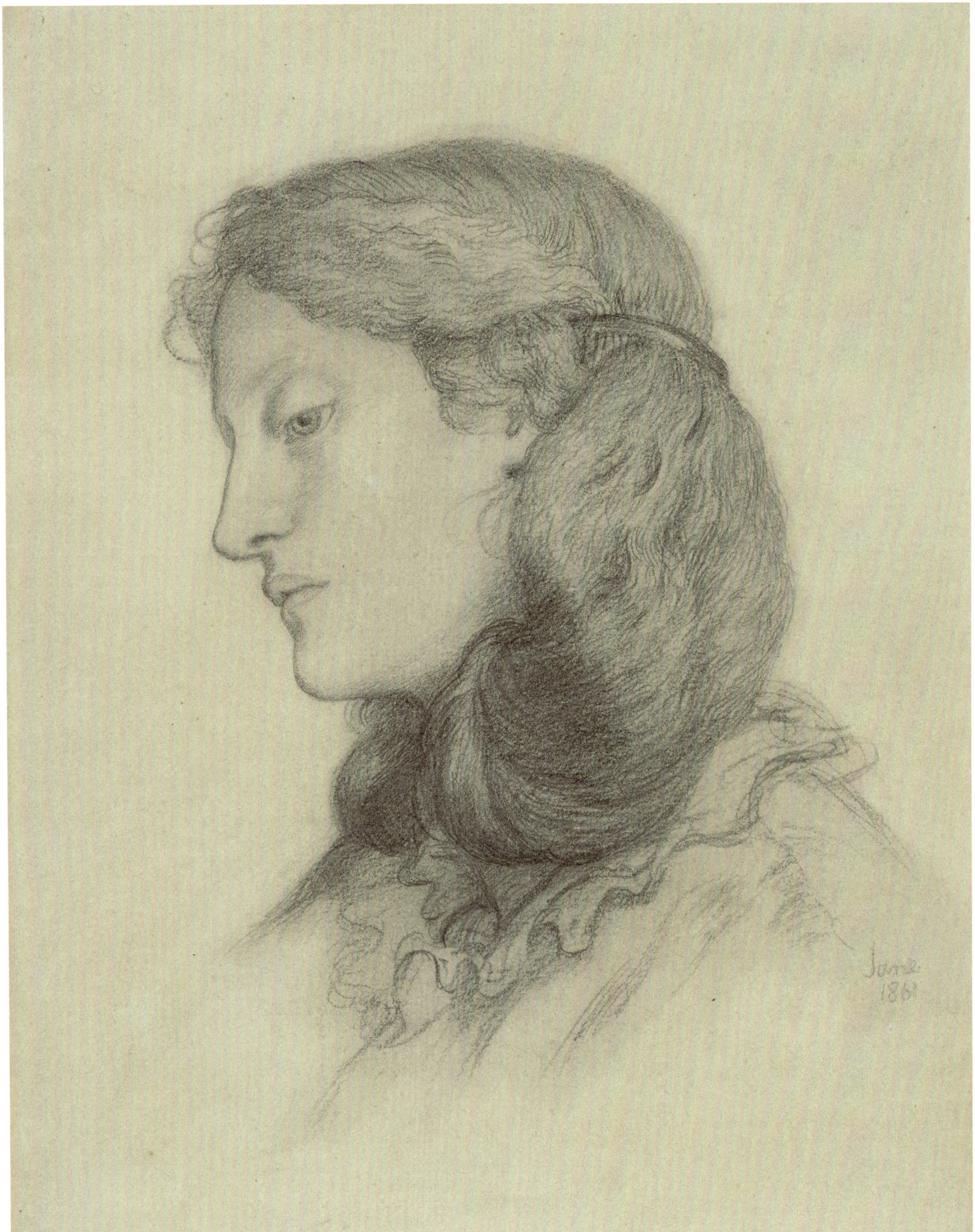
Jane
1861

cross-dressing roles of Viola and Julia. But because she modelled as Ophelia and Beatrice, and because she was beloved by the great Romantic Rossetti, posthumously she was endowed with beauty, and criteria shifted.

Her remarkable self-portrait – currently known only from a photograph – conveys a candidly unromanticised image. Elizabeth did not regard her features as conventionally beautiful, nor did she aim to trade on her appearance. Contemporary accounts, however, confirm that she dressed fashionably, in full-skirted dresses made by hand in cotton twill or silk, and stylishly trimmed bonnets. Her sister worked for a clothing wholesaler, perhaps the source of the new mantle (a full-length cloak to cover widening skirts) that Elizabeth purchased shortly before she died.[6]

Then what of her unhappy, even wretched relationship with Gabriel? Most accounts read back from her woeful death to the references to quarrels and resentments, to create a narrative of youthful romance soon turning sour over the vexed issue of marriage – Elizabeth pleading, Gabriel prevaricating. To an extent, the sources support this, though not the popular image of Elizabeth as the betrayed, abandoned Gretchen or Mariana of Romantic art, pining unto death, preferably from consumption. Witness accounts – mainly from Ford Madox Brown – portray instead a long-running, volatile relationship marked by angry ruptions and reconciliations. Elizabeth argued when Gabriel urged her to accept Ruskin's allowance rather than payment for work produced. She resisted the plan for a medical consultation with Dr Acland in Oxford. She agreed to winter at Menton because it included a substantial period of time in Paris.

Some versions of Elizabeth's life have her living unmarried with Gabriel at Chatham Place through the 1850s, an idea extrapolated from Gabriel's letter to his brother in summer 1853 when he was away from London. 'I want to tell you that Lizzy is painting at Blackfriars,' he wrote. 'Do not therefore encourage any one to go near the place. I have told her to keep the doors locked, and she will probably sleep there sometimes.'[7] This was undoubtedly bold, and if known would have been scandalous. When she was away over the winter of 1855–6, Gabriel composed a mournful Valentine, portraying the apartment in need of her presence, with unwound clock – 'No Lizzy there to help its stroke' – and unkempt artist:

> Come back, dear Liz, and, looking wise
> In that armchair which suits your size,
> Through some fresh drawing scrape a hole.
> Your Valentine and Orson's soul
> Is sad for those two friendly eyes.[8]

This sketches a conjugal scene, and Elizabeth certainly was at home there, with a key to the apartment, but evidence indicates that she did not move in, preferring her own lodgings, first in Weymouth Street, later in Hampstead. Between times and between travels, she must also have returned to the Siddal (or Siddall) home, across the Thames in Southwark. Messages and letters sent to Chatham Place reached her, but her reputation was not compromised. In May 1857, in the small catalogue accompanying the Pre-Raphaelite exhibition

OPPOSITE
NO.90 Dante Gabriel Rossetti, *Elizabeth Siddal* 1861, graphite on paper, 24.8 × 21

OPPOSITE
NO.91 Elizabeth Siddal, *Clerk Saunders* 1851, watercolour, bodycolour and coloured chalks on paper, laid on a stretcher, 28.4 × 18.1

in Russell Place, Fitzroy Square, her address is given as Eland House, half-way up to Hampstead village, where one evening when Gabriel called she was entertaining her mother and sister.

As regards the idea of sex during these unmarried years, the evidence is inferentially negative. The young Pre-Raphaelite Brothers were certainly concerned, even obsessed, with the idea – evident in the pictorial fascination with 'fallen women'. But they were deterred from the practice – by the moral injunctions against seduction, by the quasi-medical belief that sex depleted artistic energies, and by the practical cost. Widowed Ford Madox Brown's relationship with Emma Hill led to a daughter, then to marriage and more children, as Brown struggled to support all, including the child of his first wife. By contrast, James Hannay, a close friend of Gabriel's, 'paid off' the woman whose baby he fathered, so that he might seek a wealthier wife. For Elizabeth's part, even if from today's perspective the unchaperoned relationship, in London as well as shared lodgings in Brighton and Matlock, seems self-evidently sexual, she – and more probably Gabriel – is unlikely to have risked pregnancy, with its attendant shame. Moreover, conception followed within weeks of her marriage, which may not disprove but argues against pre-marital sex.

Long-deferred weddings were standard at this time, with broken engagements weighing heavier on women, who could sue for breach of promise but also be seen as 'damaged goods' in the marriage market. The Siddal-Rossetti stories are notable for her angry responses to his apparent actions, as when she berated him for discussing adjacent studios for married artists, or when she departed to Sheffield after he chose to spend the summer in Oxford, or when she (as it seems) summoned him north on hearing of his 'new model' Jane Burden.[9]

Equally notable is Gabriel's desire to join her, at Hastings, Clevedon and Matlock. One can infer that he enjoyed her company, her independent soul, her disrespect for convention, even her discourtesy to his family. Gabriel's friends knew that he himself was unpredictable. He was 'a queer fellow', Millais later told his son – 'so dogmatic and so irritable when opposed'.[10] Brown 'could narrate a hundred instances of the most noble and disinterested conduct towards his art-rivals, which places him far above [others] in his greatness of soul, and yet he will, on the most trivial occasion, hate and backbite any one who gives him offence'.[11] But even the apparent rupture in the Siddal-Rossetti romance – the months between summer 1858 and spring 1860, when none of the familiar sources reference Elizabeth's presence in Gabriel's life, and which biographers, including myself, have interpreted as the cause of her despair and drug addiction – has been challenged by the recent discovery of an evidently companionable visit to Warwickshire around Christmas 1859.[12]

When Elizabeth went to Sheffield in summer 1857, she made arrangements to work in the studios of the municipal art school – a common system among artists. Having sold her picture *Clerk Saunders* (NO.91), she was perhaps working up other watercolours, such as those featuring the Virgin Mary (Annunciation, Nativity, Christ Child, Deposition). Or she may have been composing chivalric scenes, such as the Knight and Lady preparing for a tournament title (see NO.118).

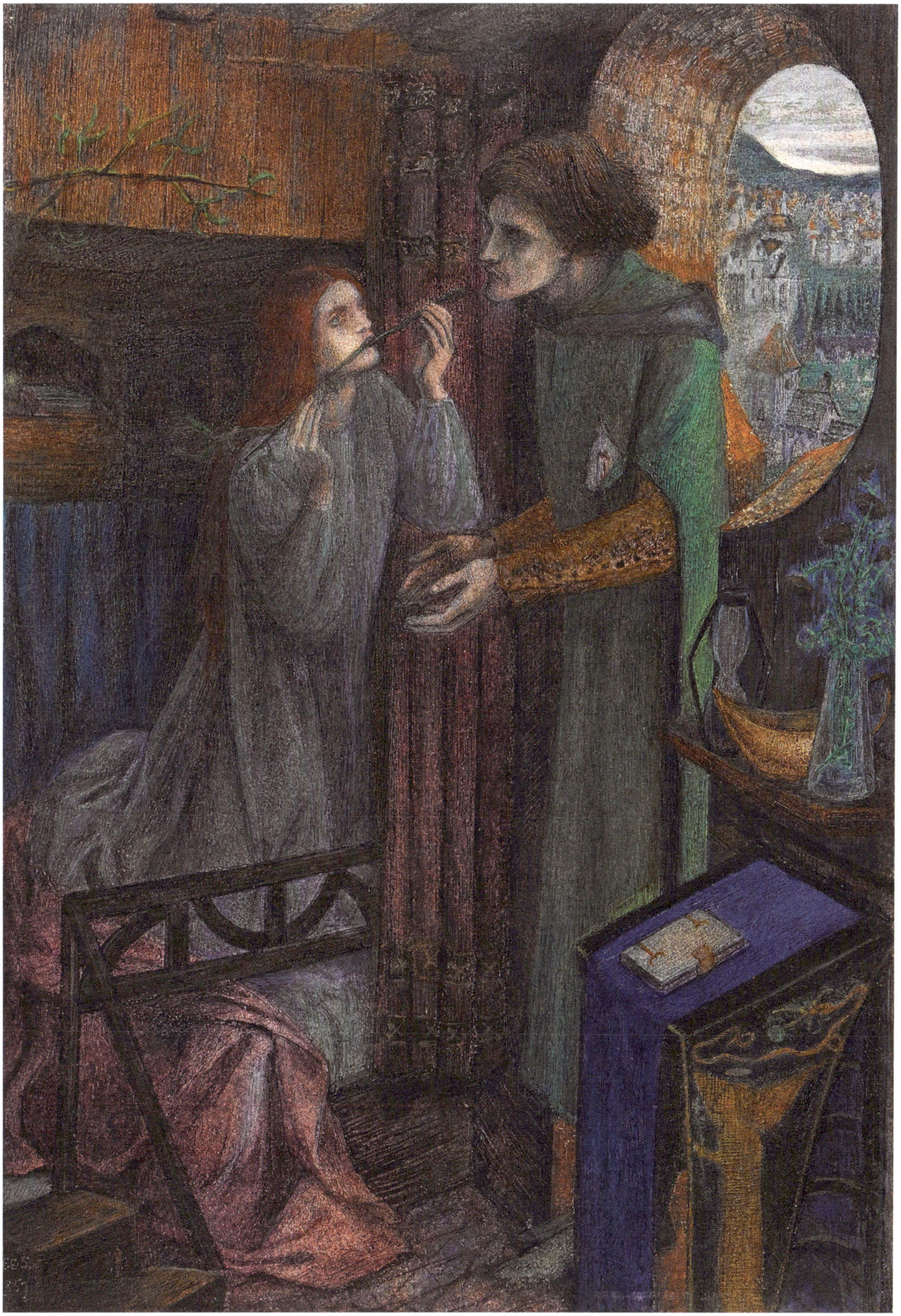

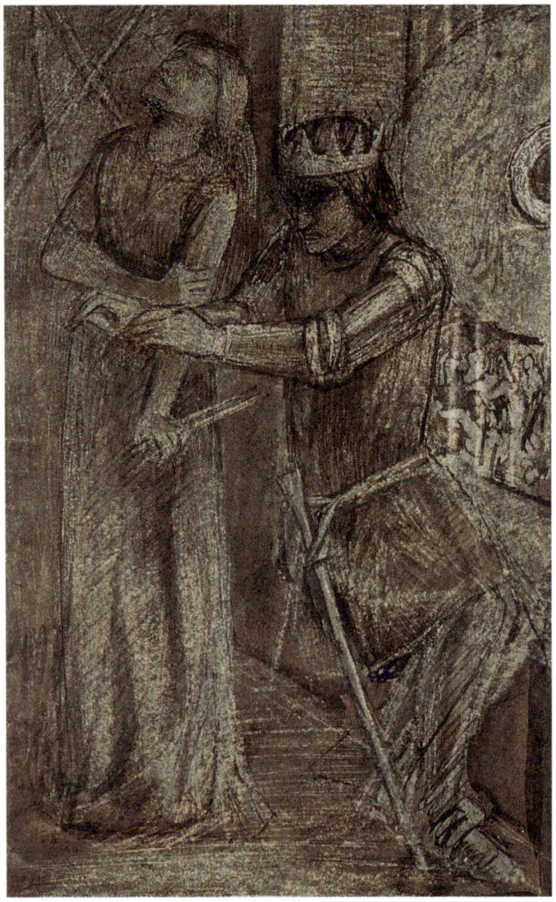

Elizabeth was not a melancholy passive dove, but a spirited independent woman, defying decorum by modelling for and with artists, aiming to exhibit, and more often than not living on her own. In contemporary terms, rather than meekly obedient to her elders and betters, she was wilful, headstrong and 'difficult'.[13] William Michael Rossetti judiciously described her as stand-offish: 'She maintained an attitude of reserve, self-controlling and alien from approach ... along with a decided inclination to order her mode of life according to her own liking, whether conformable or not to the views of the British matron, she was certainly distant.' Moreover, on social occasions her conversation was 'scanty; slight and scattered',[14] punctuated by remarks mocking polite custom. Her few surviving letters are either practical or relate events for comical effect.

So it is wise to be sceptical about descriptions of Elizabeth's character and emotions. One can, however, consider her actions - her travels, her friendships, and above all her artworks, as assessed in Glenda Youde's essay here (see p.114). The chief threads running through Elizabeth's career are the response to literary sources and the sense of shared endeavour.

Her earliest surviving works, after Tennyson and Browning, employ the linear quality, stiff figures and naïve aspect seen in certain Pre-Raphaelite works, including the engravings in *The Germ* drawn by Hunt and Deverell (see NO.71). Her best work is probably the much-lamented (because unlocated) *Self-Portrait*, the only known attempt in oils (NO.79). Many of the numerous sketches, including those depicting Sister Helen, Jephthah, La Belle Dame Sans Merci, the Nativity and the Macbeths (see NOS.135, 130, 86, 92), possess urgent intensity, with figural positions conveying dramatic emotion. Scenes such as *Lady Clare*, *Clerk Saunders*, the *Annunciation* and *Woeful Victory* (see NOS.124, 91, 137, 93) are theatrical in concept, as moments of dynamic tension, inviting viewers to imagine the back story and subsequent actions. While the devotional subjects are more reposeful, supernatural elements like revenants and angels often add to the drama. And it is no surprise that when Elizabeth planned an illustrated volume with Georgiana Burne-Jones, the themes were to be spooky and macabre, ghost stories and tales of terror.

After his poetic notebook was retrieved from Elizabeth's coffin, Gabriel wrote: 'no one so much as herself would have approved of my doing this... Had it been possible to her, I should have found the book on my pillow the night she was buried; and could she have opened the grave, no other hand would have been needed'.[15] The gothic image of a corpse in action is entirely appropriate to Elizabeth's own imagination. One can easily conceive of a composition, in picture or poem, which describes her own posthumous restitution of the precious manuscript.

Perhaps the most egregious of myths surrounding Elizabeth's art is the long-standing assertion that, in concept and practice, it was essentially created by Gabriel. Typically, its strengths are credited to him and its weaknesses to her. As his brother wrote: 'Her designs resembled those of Dante Rossetti at the same date: he had his defects, and she had the deficiencies of those defects.'[16] Subsequently collectors and dealers emphasised Gabriel's role,

ABOVE
NO.92 Elizabeth Siddal, *The Macbeths* 1850–62, ink with scratching out on paper, 21.4 × 13.5

OPPOSITE
NO.93 Elizabeth Siddal, *The Woeful Victory* c.1860, ink and graphite on paper, 16 × 12

claiming that he had worked on Elizabeth's watercolours, thereby enhancing their value and diminishing her achievement. A close analysis shows that in many cases the collaboration was in reverse order, with Gabriel adopting and responding to Elizabeth's ideas and execution. While she evidently kept to the medieval Pre-Raphaelite mode when Gabriel moved towards the 'Venetian' phase, the reciprocal nature of their earlier productions is clearly visible. As her brother-in-law noted, more generously, 'She had much facility of invention and composition, with eminent purity of feeling, dignified simplicity, and grace'.[17] The unique qualities of her art are only now being recognised and revalued

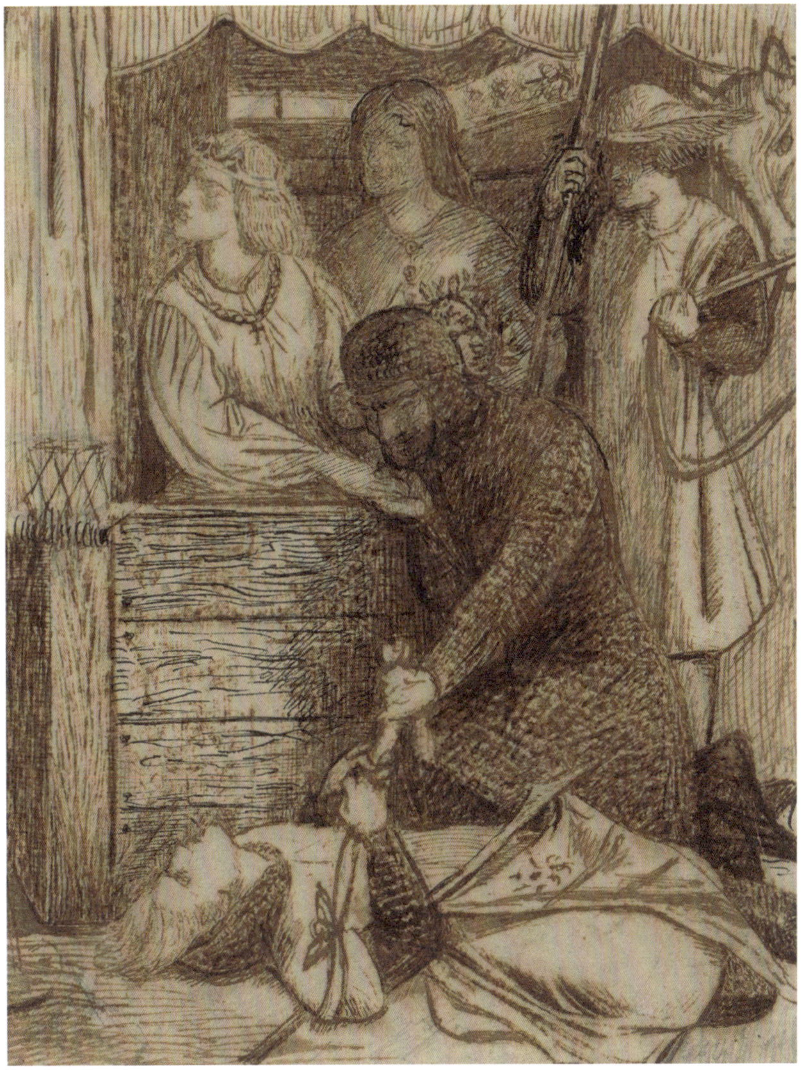

1 A quotation from *In Memoriam* by Alfred Tennyson, invoked by Dante Gabriel Rossetti in a letter to his sister Christina Rossetti, 4 August 1852.

2 William Ibbitt, 'The Death of Mrs D.G. Rossetta [*sic*]', *Sheffield Telegraph*, 28 Feb. 1862.

3 Information from Charles Collins to John Everett Millais, reported by Millais to William Holman Hunt, 4 November 1852; quoted in Diana Holman-Hunt, *My Grandfather, His Wives and Loves*, London 1969, p.92.

4 Sir Walter Scott (ed.), *Minstrelsy of the Scottish Border*, Edinburgh 1802 (1st edn); copy of 1830 edition in Fitzwilliam Museum, Cambridge.

5 Dante Gabriel Rossetti, Valentine verses, written in 1856.

6 At the inquest, Dante Gabriel Rossetti stated that his wife had 'expressed no wish to die ... and had ordered a new mantle which she intended to wear': 'Death of a lady', *Daily News*, 14 Feb. 1862, p.6.

7 Dante Gabriel Rossetti to William Michael Rossetti, 20 June 1853, in W.M. Rossetti, *Dante Gabriel Rossetti: His Family-Letters with a Memoir*, 2 vols., London 1895, vol.2, p.104.

8 Rossetti, Valentine verses, 1856.

9 'Rossetti unhappily called away through Miss Siddal's illness at Matlock', entry for 14 November 1857, in Cormell [Crom] Price's diary; cited in *Memorials of Edward Burne-Jones*, ed. Georgiana Burne-Jones, London 1904, vol.1, p.168.

10 J.G. Millais, *The Life and Letters of Sir John Everett Millais*, London 1899, vol.1, chap.ii.

11 Cited in *Letters of Dante Gabriel Rossetti to William Allingham, 1854–1870*, ed. George Birkbeck Hill, London 1897, pp.52–3.

12 G.E. Battersby, 'Rossetti and Siddal: Reconsidering the Rift 1858–1860', *The Journal of Pre-Raphaelite Studies*, vol.31, Fall 2022, pp.9–17, citing the discoveries by Norma Hampson in the archives of Lord Leycester Hospital and Shakespeare Birthplace.

13 John Ruskin told Mrs Henry Acland that Elizabeth was 'not ungrateful' but 'sickly headstrong'; *The Works of John Ruskin*, London 1901, vol.36, p.217.

14 William Michael Rossetti, 'Dante Rossetti and Elizabeth Siddal', *Burlington Magazine*, vol.1, no.3, May 1903, p.278.

15 Dante Gabriel Rossetti to Algernon Charles Swinburne, 26 October 1869, in *The Correspondence of Dante Gabriel Rossetti*, ed. William E. Fredeman, 10 vols., Cambridge, Woodbridge and Rochester, NY 2002–15, vol.4, p.312.

16 William Michael Rossetti 1903, p.278.

17 Ibid.

Carol Jacobi

Found: Love in a Capitalist Climate

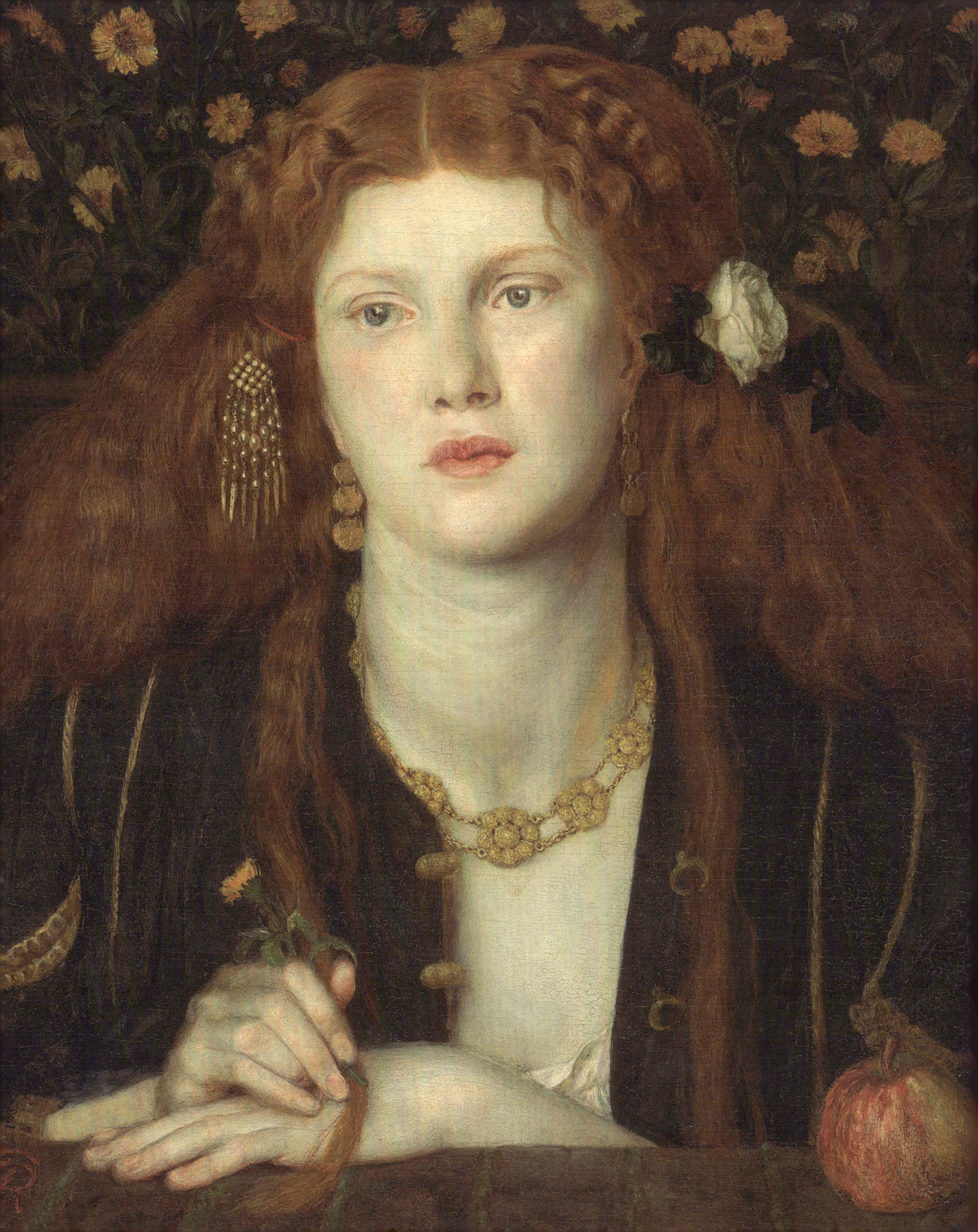

'He lured me to his palace home—
Woe's me for joy thereof—
To lead a shameless shameful life,
His plaything and his love.
He wore me like a silken knot,
He changed me like a glove; ...'

Christina Rossetti, 'Cousin Kate', 1860

From her late twenties to her late thirties, Christina Rossetti worked with women who had sold sex to men, as an Associate Sister at the St Mary Magdalene Penitentiary in Highgate, run by the Anglican Sisters of Mercy. In the 1850s, the new High Anglican Sisterhoods offered an alternative to conventional middle-class female roles. They departed from enclosed Catholic orders to promote social work in the world. Maria Rossetti had led the way in becoming an Associate Sister of All Saints Sisterhood, at Margaret Street, based just off Oxford Street, combining social work, lay ministry and fund-raising, and Christina volunteered at the Highgate Home for ten years.

Sex buying and selling was an aspect of the expansion of labour in Victorian cites, in a context of dramatic economic and social inequality between the classes and between women and men. A growing urban population supported themselves and others in domestic work, factory labour and other low-paid professions. In an age before a welfare state or labour rights, selling sex could supplement starvation wages and sometimes provide a better standard of living. Conducted across class divides, in theatres, dance halls, parks and streets, it was an urban spectacle visible to all.

The dominant discourse reflected middle-class perspectives and interests. Commentators characterised the sale of sex as a 'social evil' threatening norms of class and gender, although some saw it as a symptom of inequality and the need for social reform. The work of female actors, performers, models, even sales assistants on view in shops, was aligned with 'prostitution', and while working-class women laboured publically in all kinds of work, commercial activity could be considered flaunting and unsuitable for women of the middle class. The main career and position of status open to them was marriage and motherhood, alongside unpaid charitable activities. Women who had reached thirty or so without marrying were often described as 'redundant women'. A woman of any class who had sexual experience, lived or had children with a man outside wedlock, could be characterised as a 'prostitute' and typed as 'fallen'. They were sensationally represented in the media. Journalistic and fictional portrayals of 'fallen women' often ended with them taking or losing their life. Men who were seducers were mainstay villains of Victorian art and literature, but received less censure in real life. Men who bought sex were accorded scant attention, largely invisible in imagery and language focused on 'prostitution'. An exception

PAGE 93
NO.94 Dante Gabriel Rossetti, *Bocca Baciata* 1859, oil paint on panel, 32.1 × 27

OPPOSITE
NO.95 Elizabeth Siddal, *Pippa Passes* 1854, ink on paper, 23.3 × 29.6

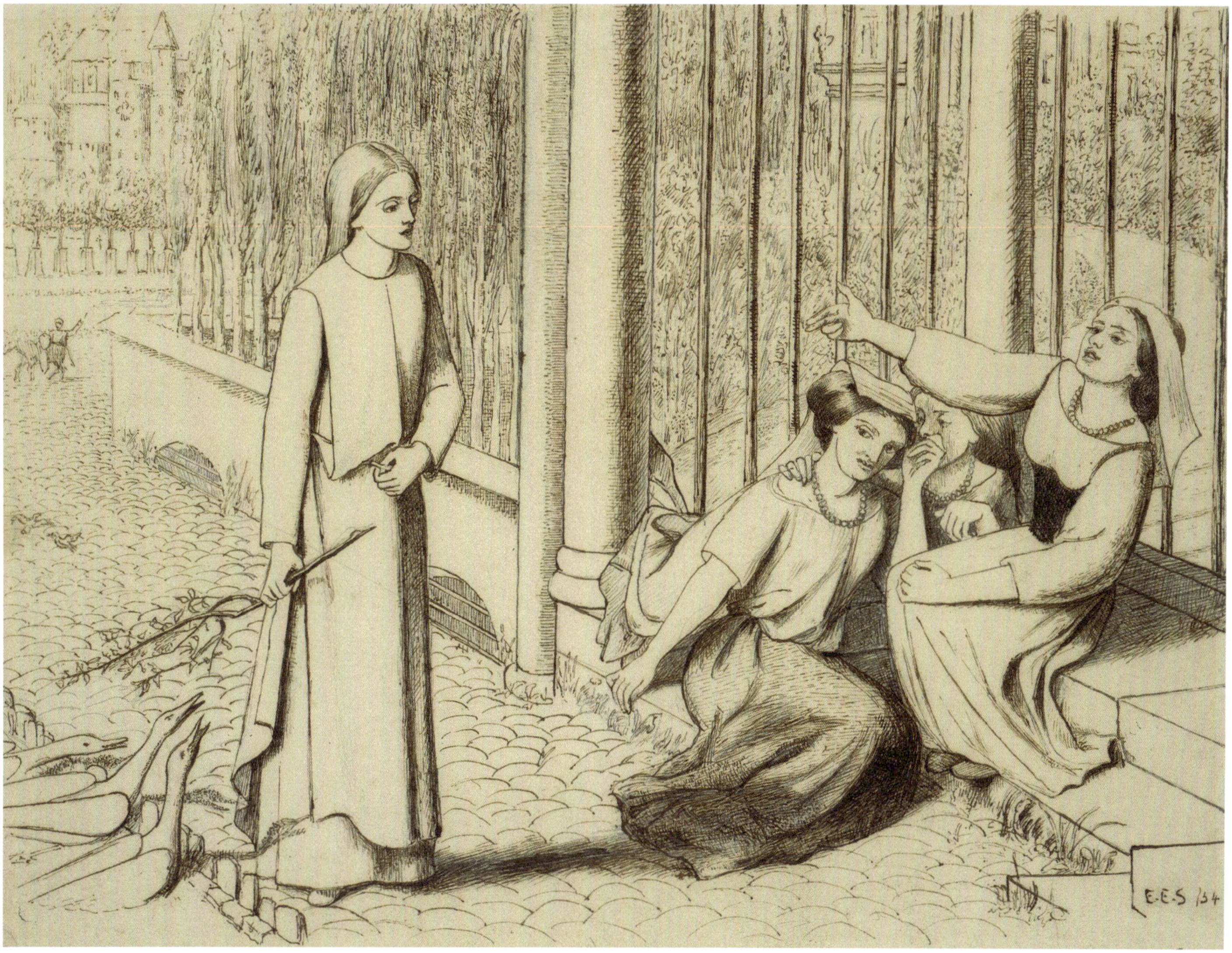

'I care not for my Lady's soul
Though I worship before her smile;
I care not where be my Lady's goal
When her beauty shall lose its wile. ...'

Elizabeth Siddal, 'The Lust of the Eyes', c.1855

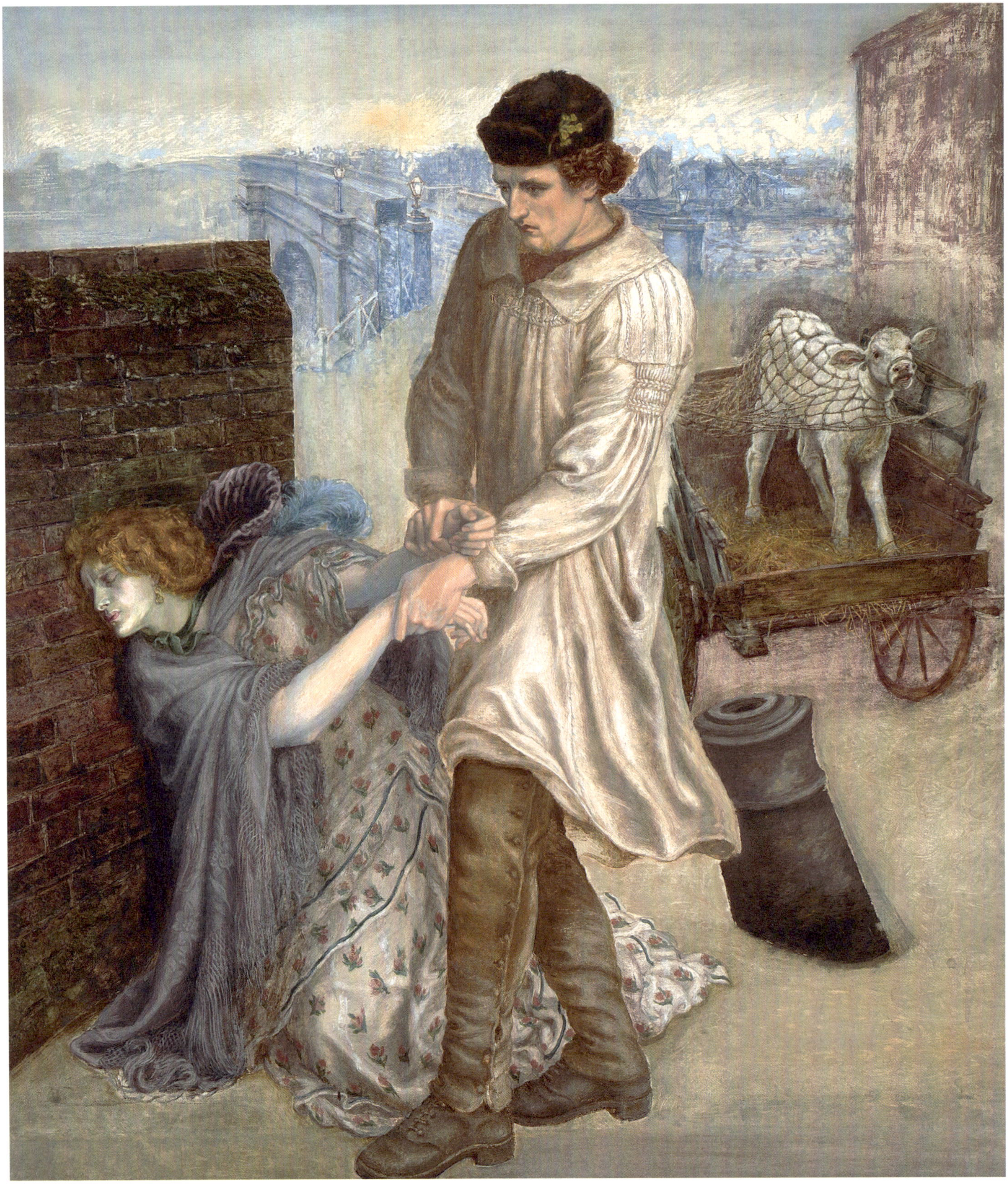

to this was Henry Mayhew's four-volume survey, *London Labour and the London Poor*, a collection of interviews with hundreds of working, poor and marginalised Londoners. The last volume, published in 1861, surveyed women who sold sex. Although it neglected buyers and framed sellers as a 'social evil', in the conventional way, the interviews themselves are a rare opportunity to hear their individual voices and glimpse their varied lived experience (see also p.107).

Public fascination with 'problem women', 'fallen women' and the 'social evil' of the market in sex gathered pace in the 1850s, focused by William Acton's book *Prostitution, Considered in Its Moral, Social, and Sanitary Aspects* (1857). The Rossettis engaged with the debates over this period, informed by their own lived relations with working women. They complicated the dominant narratives.

The Rossettis were middle-class, but their experience did not follow the typical pattern. Their insecure finances, ambitions and interests meant that both men and women worked. The brothers married late, and the sisters never took husbands at all. Furthermore, the siblings were lifelong Londoners where the streets were crowded with factory workers, vendors, the well-to-do, men and women in all kinds of professional and leisure occupations. William Michael and Gabriel were educated partly outside the home and freer to explore from an early age. The teenage Gabriel made pen sketches of characters in the insouciant style and spirit of French lithographs by Paul Gavarni, which he admired (see NO.27). At the age of eighteen, he drew *The Ladies of Marlboro' Street* (NO.97) and *The Bivouac after the Ball* (see NO.28). The latter shows an amorous couple on a doorstep, while revelry goes on beyond. Mayhew's interviews described similar transactions in which people might meet at a venue for drinking and dancing and then withdraw to the street or nearby rooms.[1]

One sketch, *Quartier Latin: The Modern Raphael and La Fornarina*, imagined a painter in his Paris studio embraced by an informally clad model (see NO.19). Within a couple of years, Gabriel and his fellow artists were browsing public spaces to appraise working-class women and seek to purchase their time as sitters. William Michael and other later biographers of the group characterised models with working-class origin stories: Annie Miller, Elizabeth Siddal and Fanny Cornforth were described as 'found' in these spaces – a pub, a shop and a park, respectively. Their real histories show that class and categories were permeable, however.[2] They became part of Gabriel's life, circle and household, although, with the exception of William Michael, they had little to do with the wider family. They all married. Elizabeth and Fanny pursued careers, and Annie was a mother and ran a prosperous household. Mayhew's interviews reveal that they were not untypical in moving between professions and social settings.

Elizabeth was a milliner who joined the circle as a professional model, which gave her more opportunities to paint and write. She worked and all but lived with Gabriel before marrying him in 1860. This, and her part in the commercial world, in her shop near Leicester Square and later selling her time as a model and an artist, put her in a socially ambiguous position. She addressed her exposed place in this world in an early drawing, *Pippa Passes* (NO.95), based on a poem by Robert Browning of the same name (1841). She could have

OPPOSITE
NO.96 Dante Gabriel Rossetti, *Found* 1854–5/1859–81, oil paint on canvas, 88.9 × 76.2

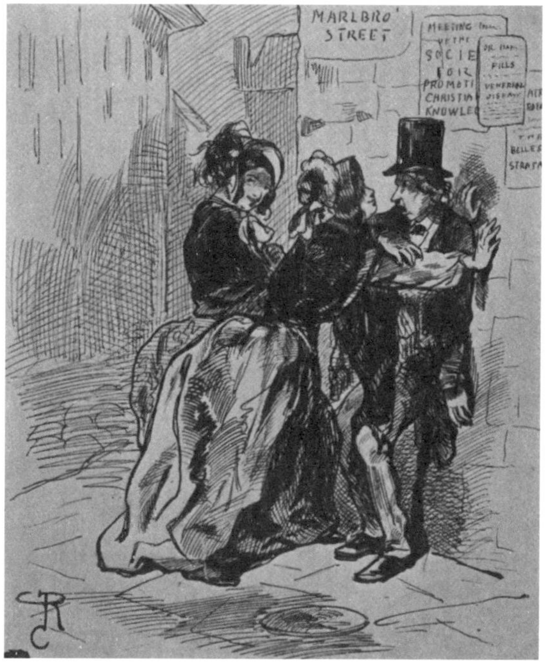

BELOW
NO.97 Dante Gabriel Rossetti, *The Ladies of Marlboro' Street* c.1846, ink on paper

'Poor beauty, so well worth a kiss!
But while my thought runs on like this
With wasteful whims more than enough,
I wonder what you're thinking of.'

Dante Gabriel Rossetti, 'Jenny', 1847

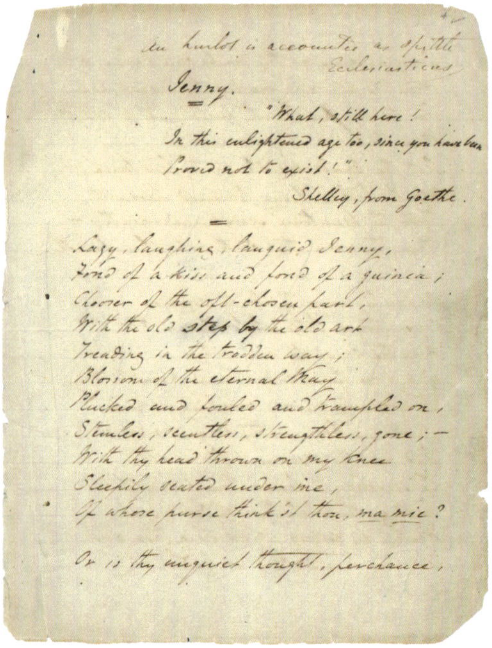

an harlot is accounted as spittle
Ecclesiasticus

Jenny.

"What, still here!
In this enlightened age too, since you have been
Proved not to exist!"
Shelley, from Goethe.

Lazy, laughing, languid Jenny,
Fond of a kiss and fond of a guinea;
Chooser of the oft-chosen part,
With the old step by the old art
Treading in the trodden way;
Blossom of the eternal May
Plucked and fouled and trampled on,
Stemless, scentless, strengthless, gone; —
With thy head thrown on my knee
Sleepily seated under me,
Of whose purse think'st thou, ma mie?

Or is thy unquiet thought, perchance,

NO.98 Dante Gabriel Rossetti, manuscript of first revised version of 'Jenny' 1860, ink on paper, 20.7 × 16.3

bought this in a cheap volume or come across it through Gabriel, with whom the Brownings were friends. The poem arose from Browning's determination not to write 'to flatter the pretensions of the great, but to speak for the masses ... cuffed and huffed from morn to midnight', and its heroine is a 'sad disheveled' silk worker.[3] Pippa walks through the medieval Italian town of Asolo, singing and passing unscathed; in fact, her song spreads a little good. A silk worker seems a sympathetic personification of Elizabeth the seamstress navigating modern London. The point is underlined by the episode she chose to illustrate: Pippa's gracious encounter with 'women of loose life'.

'Fallen' women were a cipher for the dangers of the modern, commercial world in general. Gabriel imaged modern political events in Europe in the sonnet 'After the French Liberation of Italy' (1859), in a startling metaphor of a man lying with 'a loveless whore', exhausted by the 'paid joys of love', and unaware that he has engendered 'a birth within, / The harlot's child, to scourge her for her sin!' (ll.11, 1, 13–14). For the Rossettis, stories of seduction, assault and rape, which left women pregnant and without status or future, foregrounded power structures of wealth, class and gender. A young Gabriel illustrated the seventeenth-century ballad 'Lady Anne Bothwell's Lament', in which the heroine addressed her baby born of a serial seducer (see NO.39).[4] Christina Rossetti and Elizabeth Siddal wrote poems in the voice of modern 'fallen' women, exposing a social hierarchy in which youth and beauty were a transient currency. The eponymous 'Cousin Kate' is confronted by a woman whom her husband has ruined: 'He wore me like a silken knot, / He changed me like a glove'. Kate knows her husband's past; indeed, she has exploited her own freshness and beauty to secure his hand, land and gold.

At nineteen, Gabriel penned a poem called 'Jenny' (1847/1870), inspired by William Bell Scott's 'Rosabell' (1838). Scott's long poem traced the standard popular story of a country girl, as – from 'eight years old' to 'age unknown' – she is groomed and tempted from life as a seamstress into forced sex, a fake marriage, selling sex, addiction, destitution and death.[5] Gabriel took a different approach to Scott. 'Jenny' contemplated past and future from only one episode focusing on both the seller and the buyer, and left the moral unresolved. He told it from the 'inner standing-point' of a casual lover who has met a woman at a dance and gone to her room.[6] Echoing, perhaps, the format of Lady Anne Bothwell's interior monologue to her child, we hear his thoughts as she sleeps on his lap (ll.1–4):

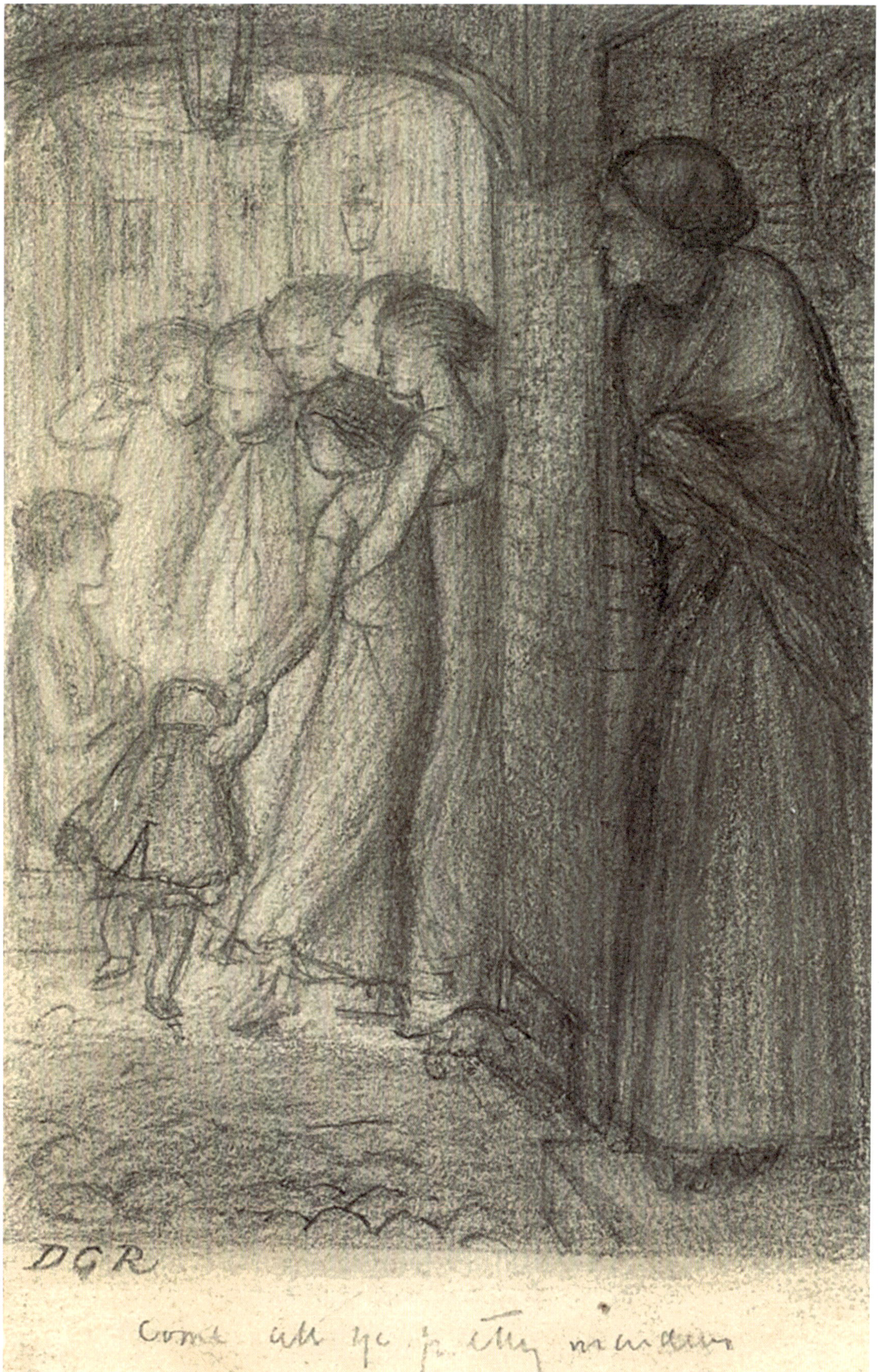

NO.99 Dante Gabriel Rossetti, *The Gate of Memory* 1853–4, graphite on paper, 14 × 8.6

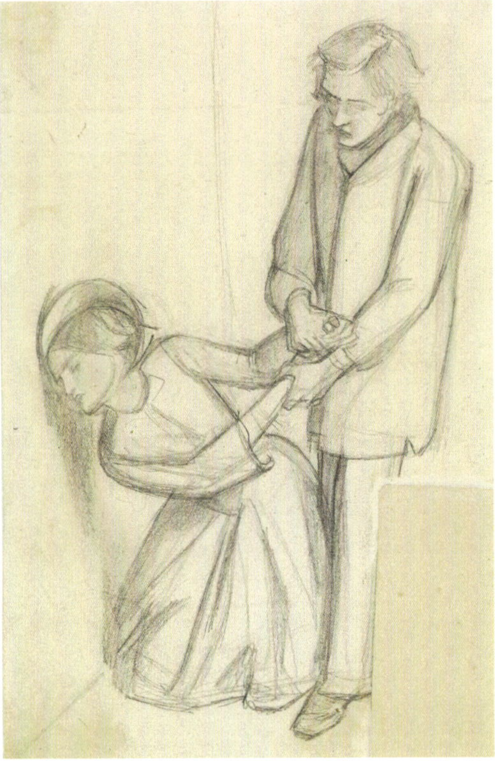

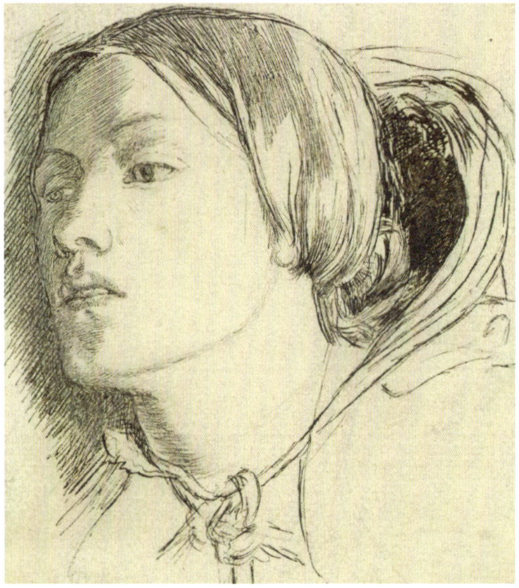

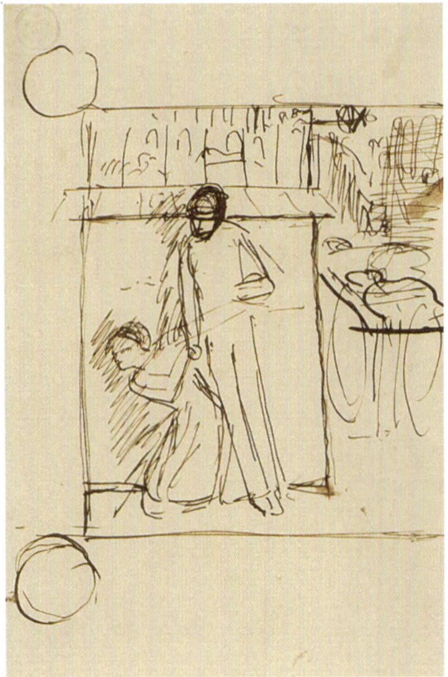

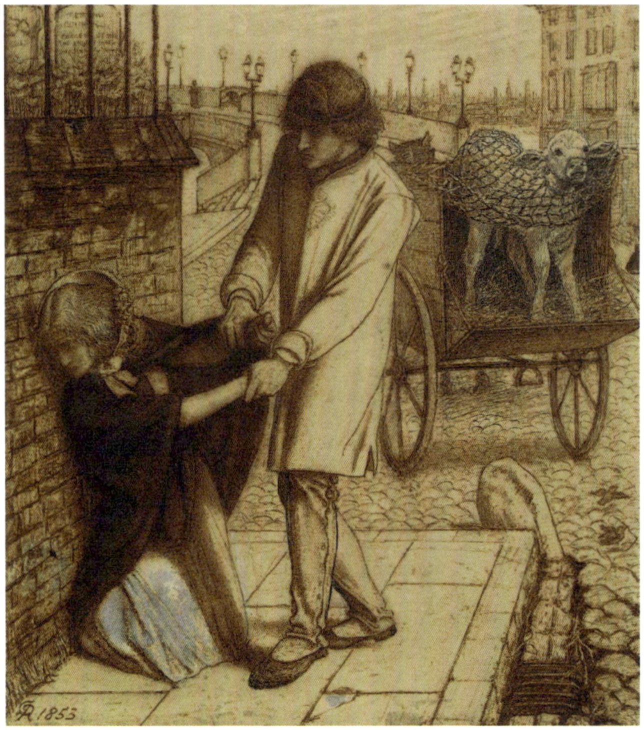

CLOCKWISE
FROM TOP LEFT

NO.100 Dante Gabriel Rossetti, *Found (Study for the Man and Woman Together)* 1853–4, graphite on paper, 24.3 × 16

NO.101 Dante Gabriel Rossetti, *Found (Study for the Woman's Head)* 1853–7, pen and ink over graphite on paper, 10.5 × 9.5

NO.102 Dante Gabriel Rossetti, *Found* 1853, ink and wash on paper, 20.5 × 18.1

NO.103 Dante Gabriel Rossetti, *A Sketch for 'Found'* c.1860, ink on paper, 18.1 × 11.1

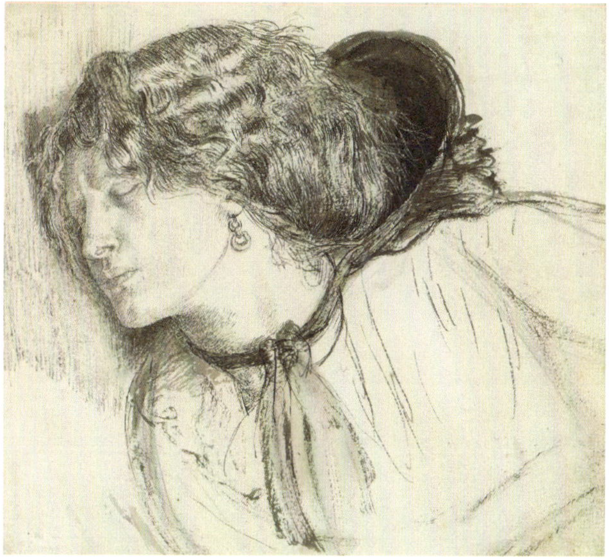

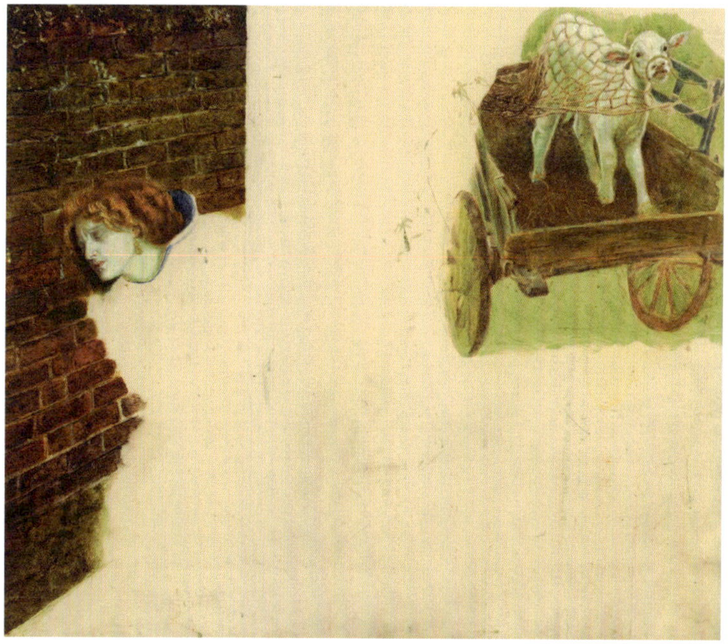

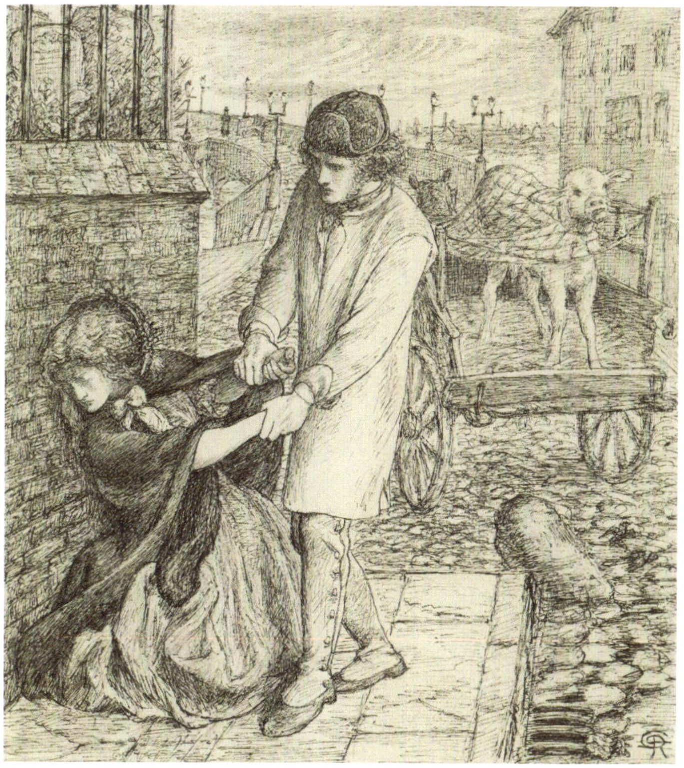

CLOCKWISE
FROM TOP LEFT

NO.104 Dante Gabriel Rossetti, *Found (Study for the Head of the Girl)* 1859–61, pen and ink with scratching out and wash on paper, 17.5 × 19.4

NO.105 Dante Gabriel Rossetti, *Found* 1849, oil paint on panel, 30.3 × 35.8

NO.106 Dante Gabriel Rossetti, *Found – Compositional Study* 1854–5, ink on paper, 39.3 × 38.1

BELOW
NO.107 Henry Treffry Dunn, *Study for the background of 'Found' by Dante Gabriel Rossetti* c.1869, graphite, crayon and watercolour on paper, 31.8 × 58.7

OPPOSITE
NO.108 Henry Treffry Dunn and Dante Gabriel Rossetti, *Found* 1870s, oil paint on canvas, 99.1 × 81.3

Lazy laughing languid Jenny,
Fond of a kiss and fond of a guinea,
Whose head upon my knee to-night
Rests for a while, as if grown light

Where Rosabell's seducers show no remorse, Gabriel's narrator reflects on his motivations as well as hers (ll.46–58):

Why, Jenny, as I watch you there,–
For all your wealth of loosened hair,
Your silk ungirdled and unlac'd
And warm sweets open to the waist,
...
Poor beauty, so well worth a kiss!
But while my thought runs on like this
With wasteful whims more than enough,
I wonder what you're thinking of.

Five years later, in 1853, Scott's poem inspired the radical modern-life Pre-Raphaelite paintings which concluded the group's association: William Holman Hunt's *The Awakening Conscience* and Gabriel's *Found* (see NO.102), modelled by Annie Miller. Like 'Jenny', they departed from popular 'fallen woman' narratives by interrogating the motivations of both a male and a female subject. Hunt's *The Awakening Conscience* translated Rosabell's interlude of faux marriage, kept in luxury by a wealthy aristocrat. Around the same time, Gabriel's first drawing for *Found* combined an earlier and a later episode from Scott's poem: the eighteen-year-old Rosabell's alienated encounter with her first lover and betrothed, the countryman Andrew, and her vagrancy by the time she is twenty-five. Its setting was, like Elizabeth's *Pippa Passes*, a cobbled city street, but it evoked Scott's chillier lines (XIII, ll.1–10):

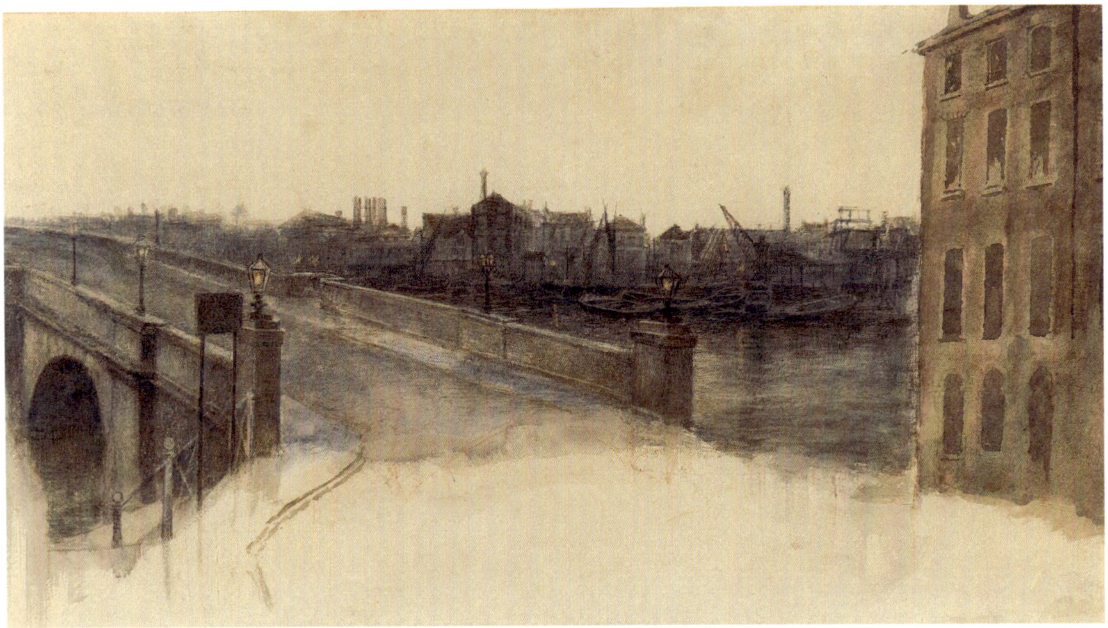

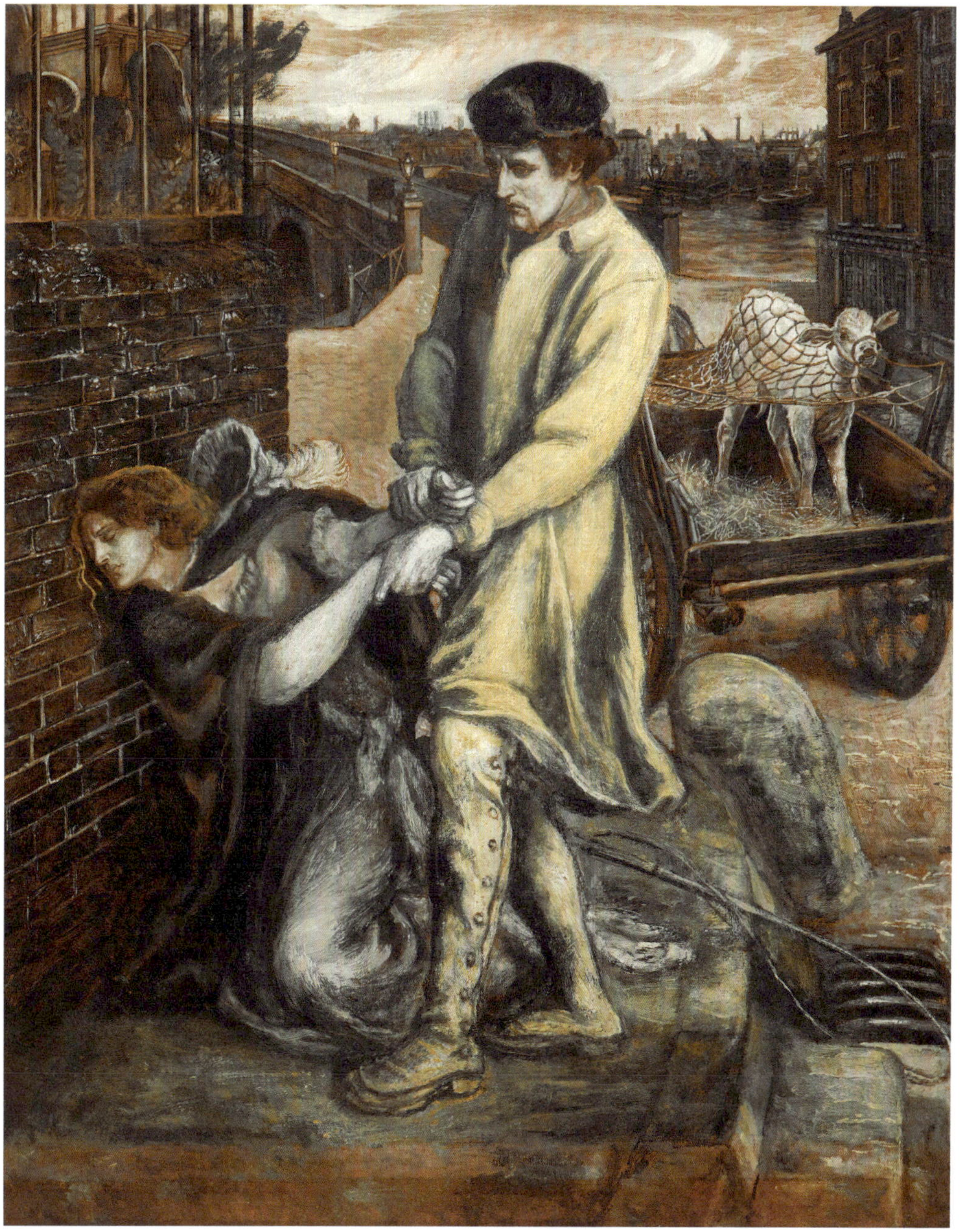

'Bocca baciata non perde ventura,
anzi rinnova come fa la luna'
(the kissed mouth loses not its favour,
but renews itself like the moon)

Giovanni Boccaccio, *The Decameron*, c.1350

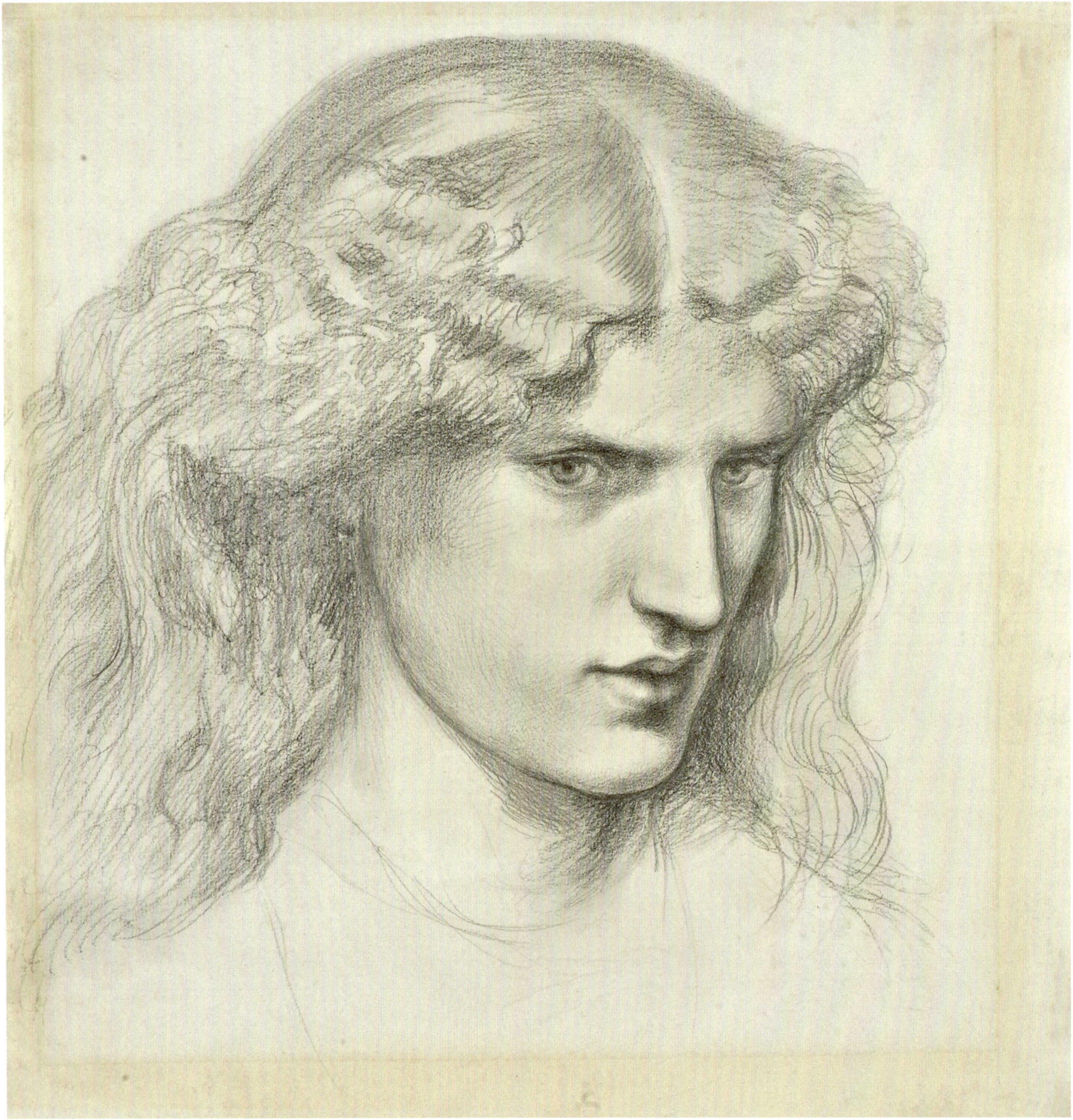

Down the wet pavement gleam the lamps,
While the wind whistles past them shrill;
A distant heel rings hurrying home,
It lessens into stillness now,
And she is left alone.
The rain-drops from the eaves are blown
Against her face; she turns;
The wind lifts up her dripping scarf,
(Faded now with its tinselling)
And flings it o'er her head.

The cemetery wall is modern brick. Weeds thread the gutter and paving on which the Rosabell figure kneels. The location is recognisably the north side of Blackfriars Bridge, near Gabriel and Elizabeth's studio. The area was described by Mayhew as a site where occasional or poorer women sold sex: 'there might be 600 of those wretched women and of all ages, from 15 to upwards of 40'.[7] Again, there is an attempt to penetrate some kind of 'inner standing-point'. Both Hunt's *The Awakening Conscience* and Gabriel's *Found* were distinguished by extreme expressions of anguish on each woman's face, uncomfortably different from conventional iconography. *Found* was never finished, and *The Awakening Conscience* was repainted with a more conventional countenance, at its owner's request, three years after its completion.

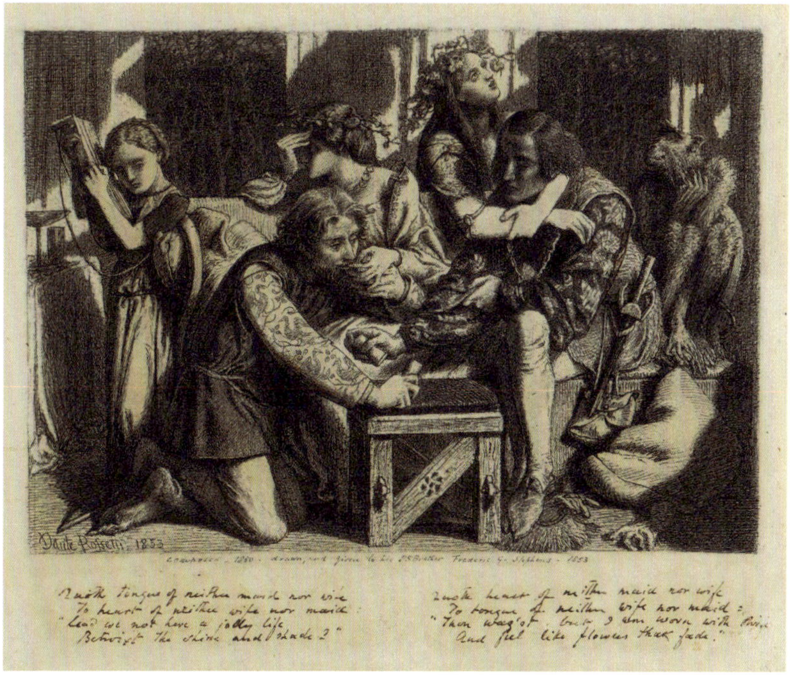

OPPOSITE
NO.109 Dante Gabriel Rossetti, *Annie Miller* c.1860, graphite on paper, 31.8 × 31.8

RIGHT
NO.110 Dante Gabriel Rossetti, *Hesterna Rosa* 1853, ink on paper, 21.9 × 26.3

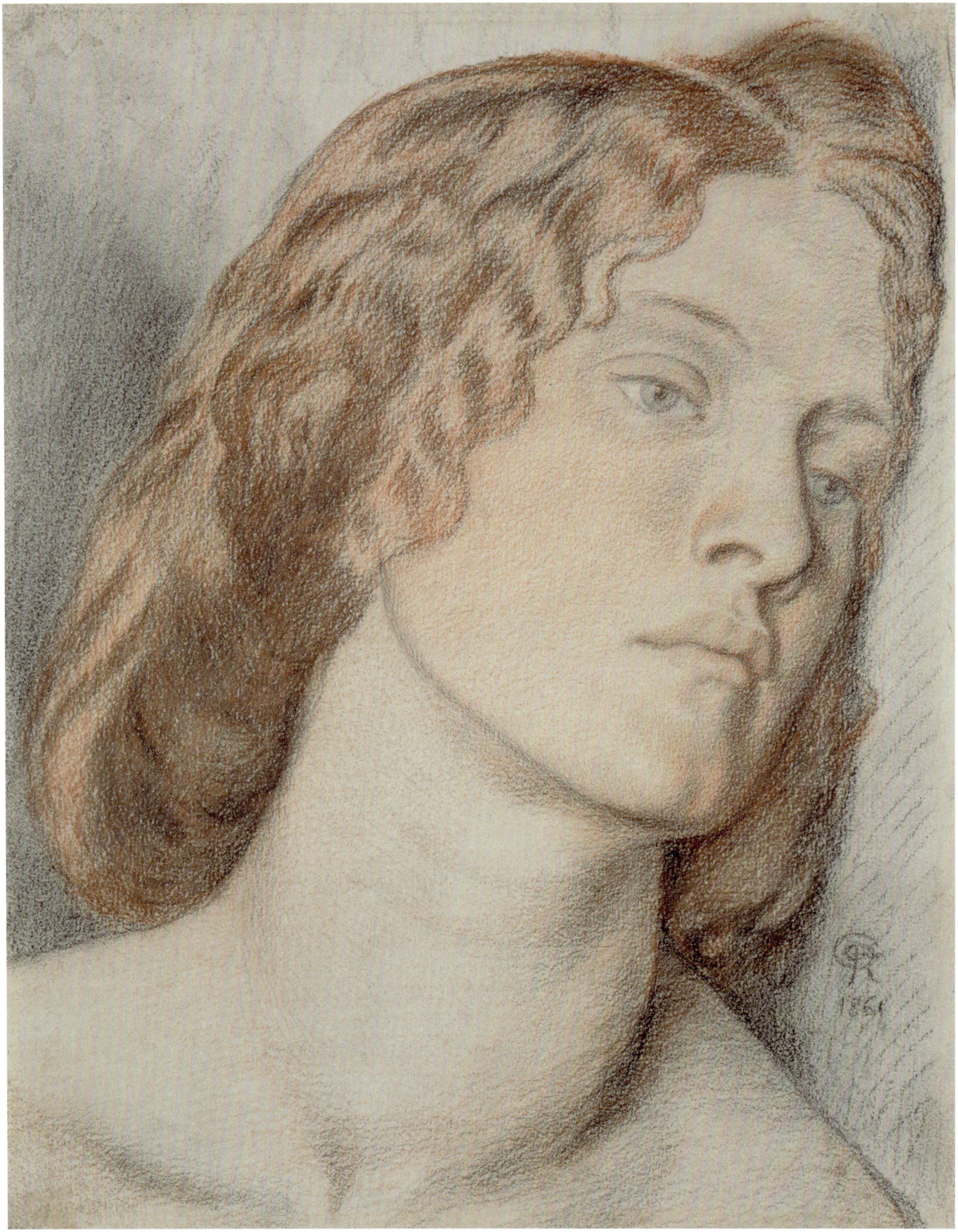

The following year, Gabriel revisited the subject in a different street scene based on Rosabell's end, called *The Gate of Memory* (NO.99). It showed a woman in the shadow of an arch, watching children dance and sing in the lamplight beyond. Women who sold sex, who spoke to Henry Mayhew, often described alienation and loss of feeling, especially those exposed to poverty, brutality and addiction: 'I don't want to live, and yet I don't care enough about dying to make away with myself. I arn't got that amount af feeling that some has, and that's where it is I'm kinder 'fraid of it.'[8] Scott's poem chimes with this piteously (XIV, ll.64–7):

> ... she stood
> As she were dead while still they sang;
> Then in her utter abandonment
> She loathed their loveliness.

However, Gabriel's title and the children's rhyme quoted below the drawing, infer an alternative ending – that the song has awakened memory and feeling. It parallels *The Awakening Conscience*, in which the woman rises from her lover's lap as a childhood song reminds her of a happier youth. A similar message is constructed by the title and textual glosses on the drawing of *Found*: a Biblical quote referring to Andrew, the childhood sweetheart, 'I remember thee: the kindness of thy youth, the love of thy betrothal' (Jeremiah 2:2); and another on the gravestone, referring to 'joy among the angels of God over one sinner that repenteth' (Luke 15:7). The streetlamps either side of Andrew's head allude to hope in a similar way to the single lamp in *The Gate of Memory*. However, in *Found*, such signs of redemption sit uncomfortably with the grittier realism, the grimness of the foreground setting, and the distress of the woman and the netted calf. Andrew's grip grapples, rather than gathering up, and she stays fallen.

The Gate of Memory was realised as a watercolour in 1857. Its generic style and redemptive message chimed with the narratives promoted by middle-class organisations like the Sisters of Mercy. The realism of *Found*, by contrast, refused to resolve. Annie Miller, for a while affianced to Hunt, was forbidden to come to Gabriel when Hunt went abroad in 1854, so the progress with a full-sized canvas in oil was limited to the netted calf and the cemetery wall. This changed in 1856, when Gabriel met Fanny Cornforth. Born Sarah Cox, into poverty, and one of the only surviving members of her family, she had been put out for domestic work at fourteen and came to London a little older than the fictional Rosabell, at twenty-one. Gabriel saw her in the crowds gathered in the Royal Surrey Gardens at Walworth on the occasion of a 'Dinner to the Medal Men of the Crimea Guard'. Their relative status is evident in her alias, Fanny, a name associated with sex selling, and in the familiar way Gabriel approached her, loosening her hair and inviting her to his studio to sit. Fanny recalled how, on her arrival there, 'he put my head against the wall' to finally paint the figure for *Found*.[9]

Where Annie Miller had left behind her hand-to-mouth survival living in the Cross Keys pub and was living as a professional model, by 1858 Fanny was staying in cheap lodgings at 24 Dean Street, Soho,

OPPOSITE
NO.111 Dante Gabriel Rossetti, *Fanny Cornforth (study for 'Fair Rosamund')* 1861, chalk on paper, 32.2 × 25.9

BELOW
NO.112 William Downey, *Fanny Cornforth* 1904–11, copy by Sanborn Studio, gelatin silver print of original (1863) albumen print, 13.7 × 10.8

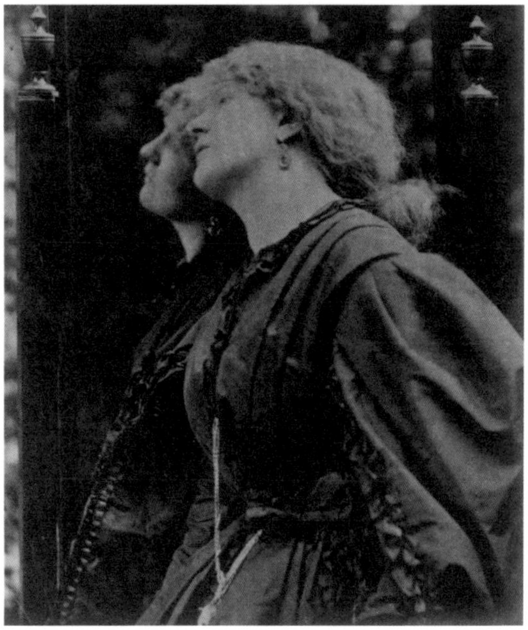

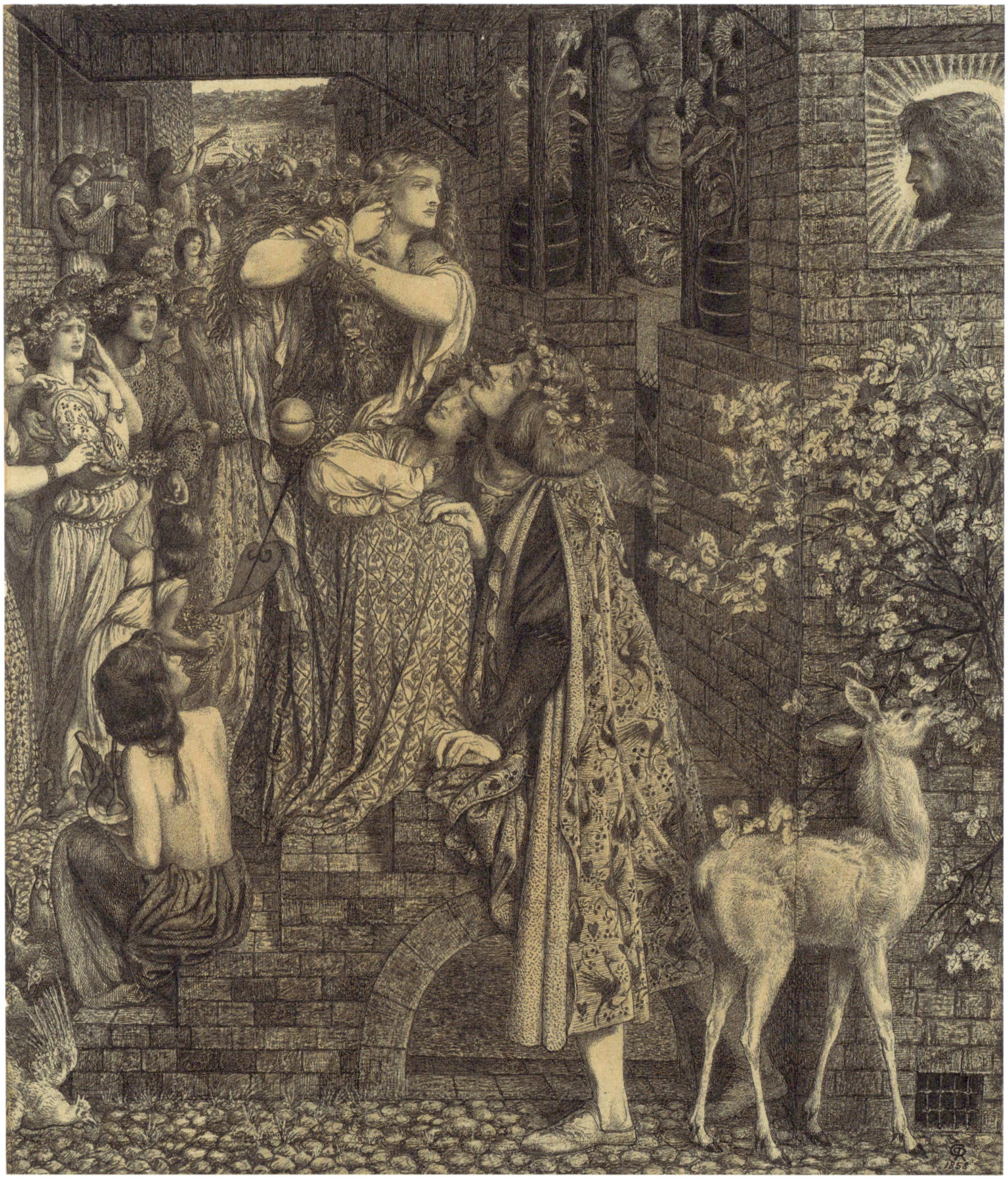

NO.113 Dante Gabriel Rossetti, *Mary Magdalene at the Door of Simon the Pharisee* 1858, pen and Indian ink on paper mounted on fine linen on a stretcher, 50.8 × 45.7

and frequenting nearby venues of fun and sexual commerce, such as the Argyll Rooms. Gabriel painted her more dishevelled and showily dressed in a decorated bonnet, golden earrings, ostrich feather, frilled dress and fringed shawl (see NO.108). However, like Annie, Fanny's real story challenged Scott's and Gabriel's fictional narratives of death or redemption. She was astute in accumulating her dues and valued independence. Her role as model and, probably, lover developed into friendships with Gabriel's circle, and especially with Gabriel himself. Her affectionate informality is evident in an unusual portrait he made of her in the studio with his friend and fellow artist, George Boyce (NO.114).

Gabriel's relationship with Fanny has been linked to a new sexuality which comes into view in the languorous description of 'paid joys of love' in 'After the French Liberation of Italy' in 1859 (ll.3–7):

> At length, and with one laugh of satiate bliss,
> The wearied man a minute rests above
> The wearied woman, no more urged to move
> In those long throes of longing, till they glide,
> Now lightlier clasped, each to the other's side

This intimate vignette of commercial sex sits oddly with its role as metaphor for national corruption in the final couplet ('the bought body holds a birth within'). Gabriel removed this poem from his first published collection in 1870 and it was not made public until after his death, but the sensuality heralded a new sexual narrative in his painting and his poetry. *Pippa Passes*, *The Awakening Conscience* and

BELOW
NO.114 Dante Gabriel Rossetti, *George Price Boyce with Fanny Cornforth in Rossetti's Studio, Chatham Place* c.1858, ink on paper, 22.2 × 31.8

PAGE 110
NO.115 Christina Rossetti, *Goblin Market and Other Poems* 1865 (second edition), frontispiece of book, 22.9 × 15.2

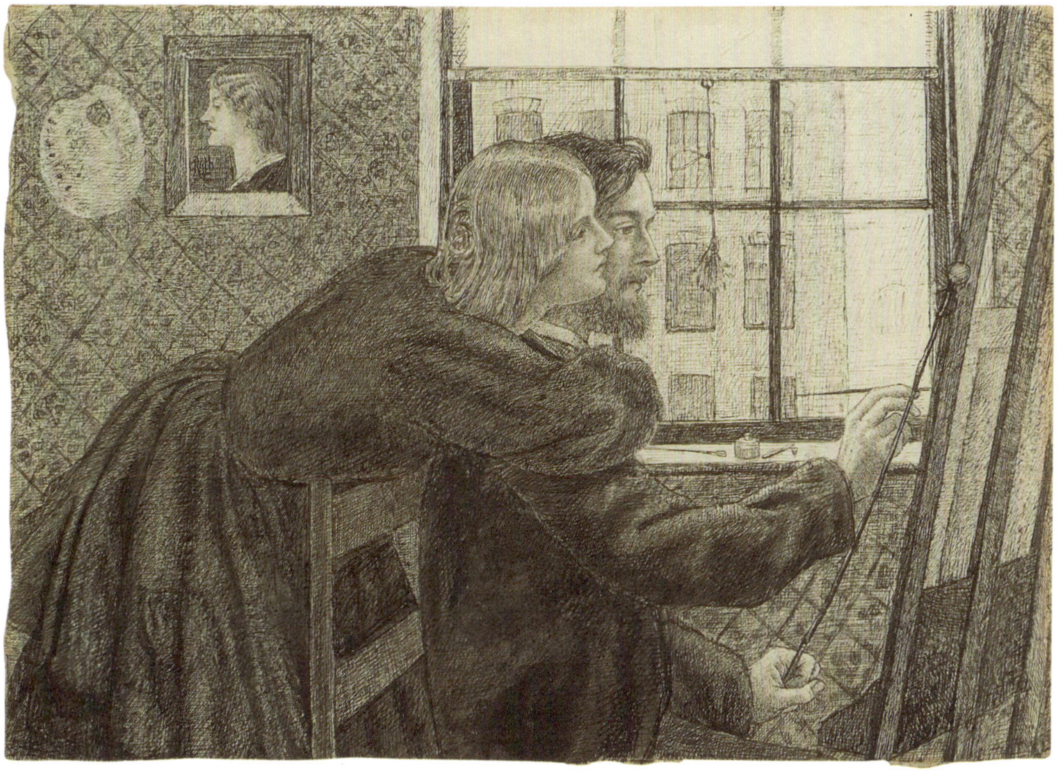

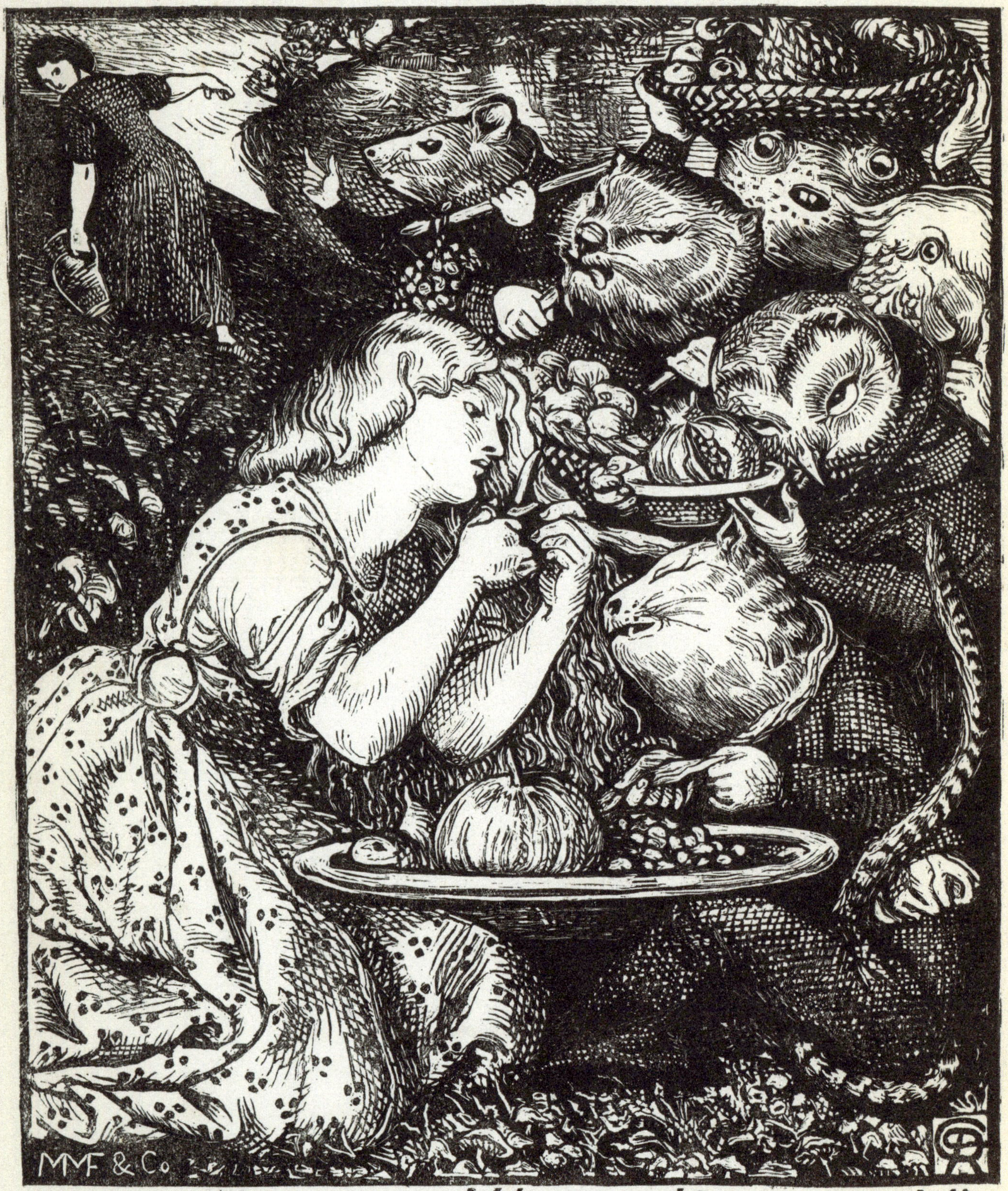

"Buy from us with a golden curl"

Goblin Market

by Christina Rossetti

Morning and evening
Maids heard the goblins cry:
"Come buy our orchard fruits,
Come buy, come buy:
Apples and quinces,
Lemons and oranges,
Plump unpecked cherries,
Melons and raspberries,
Bloom-down-cheeked peaches,
Swart-headed mulberries,
Wild free-born cranberries,
Crab-apples, dewberries,
Pine-apples, blackberries,
Apricots, strawberries;–
All ripe together
In summer weather,–
Morns that pass by,
Fair eves that fly;
Come buy, come buy:
Our grapes fresh from the vine,
Pomegranates full and fine,
Dates and sharp bullaces,
Rare pears and greengages,
Damsons and bilberries,
Taste them and try:
Currants and gooseberries,
Bright-fire-like barberries,
Figs to fill your mouth,
Citrons from the South,
Sweet to tongue and sound to eye;
Come buy, come buy." ...

'"You have much gold upon your head," They answer'd all together: "Buy from us with a golden curl."'

Christina Rossetti, 'Goblin Market', 1859

The Gate of Memory confronted the 'fallen' figure with the redeeming power of beauty and art, in the form of song. In the year Gabriel wrote 'After the French Liberation of Italy', he set aside *Found* and painted Fanny in a dramatically different way, in *Bocca Baciata* (NO.94). Here, corruption is transcended by the beauty of the woman herself. Fanny is cast as Alatiel, Babylonian princess and heroine of Boccaccio's medieval poem, *The Decameron*, whose sexual experiences with men from all corners of the world left her not 'ruined' but renewed, and she finally marries her betrothed. The title refers to an Italian quotation on the back of the painting: 'Bocca baciata non perde ventura, anzi rinnova come fa la luna' (the kissed mouth loses not its favour, but renews itself like the moon). It is in every way unlike *Found*. We are removed from the cold city to a private bower. Alatiel's head turns towards us rather than away, and she is intimately dressed in jewellery and a robe of Middle Eastern style, with neck bare and hair loose. Her worldly trials are metaphorised by marigolds, standing for suffering, while she proffers a pink carnation, symbol of allure.

Gabriel's image of a woman undimmed by her lived sexual experience of a commodified struggle in a commercial world develops Elizabeth Siddal's heroine, Pippa, who merely passes through it as a spectator. But it was Christina Rossetti who revised the 'fallen woman' narrative most radically that year, in her allegory of commercial sex, 'Goblin Market' (1859). She had little, if any, social contact with Annie or Fanny, but she wrote her poem at the beginning of her association with the St Mary Magdalene house. Henry Mayhew's interviews give us an insight into the voices and lives she would have encountered there. Many of the women described in earthy terms the temptations of a life of pleasure and comfort, sometimes sought out for their own sake, sometimes through the coercion of a lover. A few described appetite for and addiction to alcohol, a consolation for their increasingly hard life even as it shortened it. Christina would also have been aware of the part that Elizabeth's addiction to laudanum – an opiate dissolved in alcohol – played in her declining physical and mental health.

Like *Bocca Baciata*, 'Goblin Market' translated the world of commerce into an aestheticised allegory (ll.1–4):

> Morning and evening
> Maids heard the goblins cry:
> 'Come buy our orchard fruits,
> Come buy, come buy: ...'

In this case, redemption was brought about by the love of sisters, Laura and Lizzie. Gabriel's frontispiece depicted Fanny as Laura (NO.115), and again, doubled, in a second image of both sisters embracing in sleep (see NO.46). The sensuality of the poem went beyond *Bocca Baciata*, however. The repeated refrain 'Come buy' (with its double invitation) counterpoints the ravishing imagery and flattering words of the 'merchant men'. The girls know that the goblins' 'evil gifts' will 'harm' them (l.66), but Laura is tempted and, with no money, pays with parts of her body, a tear and a golden curl, to gorge on the fruit until she knows neither whether it is night or day. Having spent herself, Laura is unable to revisit the goblins or feed her addiction, and her health and spirit severely decline. Driven to desperation, her sister goes to the men with a penny, but they fall upon her, beat her, and:

> Held her hands and squeez'd their fruits
> Against her mouth to make her eat

Lizzie returns to Laura 'syrupped' with juice but having consumed none. She invites her sister, 'Eat me, drink me, love me' (l.471), and Laura covers her with kisses until she falls unconscious, as shown in the frontispiece. When she wakes, she is well.

Christina's incredibly visual and tactile imagery blends sensual, carnal, sisterly and eucharistic love. Lizzie's ordeal is Christ-like, evoking the belief that the communion of bread and wine is the real body and blood of Christ, which distinguished High Anglicans from other Anglican groups. The sisterly theme echoes Christina's mission with the Sisters of Mercy and her own sister's restraining influence. 'Goblin Market' was dedicated to Maria.

The Rossettis' inventive, evolving and ambivalent representation of the 'paid joys of love' reflected their lived experiences of the city and relationships with women of working backgrounds. Sexual buying and selling distilled the tension between commerce and performance and beauty and truth that reflected wider predicaments in the personal and professional lives of the Rossettis. Their exploration of the theme coincided with artistic turning points in 1853 and 1859. It was a vehicle with which to interrogate the vulnerabilities and possibilities for love in a materialistic world ruled by wealth, gender and class.

Afterword

Henry Mayhew's interviews reveal that the lives of women who diverted from conventional sexual expectations diverged from the stereotypes of the time. Neither Fanny Cornforth nor Annie Morris enacted the popular 'fallen woman' narrative. Their lives were dangerous and tough, and their social and financial independence hard-won, but they maintained it and, against popular myths, married and lived into old age. Annie dismissed William Holman Hunt, built a reputation as a model, and made connections in high society, marrying into an aristocratic family in her late twenties. Fanny's uncharacteristic illness when Gabriel Rossetti was reunited with and later married Elizabeth Siddal suggests an emotional as well as a practical connection. She married a mechanic, Timothy Hughes, but went to Gabriel when Elizabeth died, living with him as his housekeeper for fifteen years, until his failing health prompted his family to take over his care. Gabriel paid for a house nearby for Fanny, writing, 'you are the only person whom it is my duty to provide for'.[10] She remarried a publican and ran the Rose tavern in Westminster, but continued as Gabriel's occasional nurse and companion for the five years until his death. He systematically selected and transferred pictures to her ownership, so that she held an important collection and understanding of his work. For a time, she and her second husband ran a Rossetti Gallery, and her correspondence with the American collector Samuel Bancroft brought major works to Delaware Art Museum. She sold and distributed her pictures to keep herself until her last years, when she was placed by her daughter-in-law in a workhouse for the remainder of her life

1 See Henry Mayhew, *London Labour and the London Poor: A Cyclopædia of the Condition and Earnings of Those that* will *Work, Those that* cannot *Work, and Those that* will not *Work*, London 1851–62; esp. vol.1 (*The London Street-Folk*) and vol.4 (*Those that* will not *Work, comprising Prostitutes, Thieves, Swindlers, Beggars*).

2 Evidence about the lives of Annie Miller, Elizabeth Siddal and Fanny Cornforth (Sarah Cox) is discussed in Jan Marsh, *The Pre-Raphaelite Sisterhood*, London 1985; Jan Marsh (ed.), *Pre-Raphaelite Sisters*, London 2019; and Kirsty Stonell Walker, *Stunner: The Fall and Rise of Fanny Cornforth*, London 2006.

3 Robert Browning, in *The Browning Correspondence*, ed. Philip Kelley and Ronald Hudson, Winfield, KS 1984, vol.4, p.269.

4 See Robert Chambers, *The Scottish Ballads, Collected and Illustrated by Robert Chambers*, Edinburgh 1829, pp.118–21.

5 See William Bell Scott, 'My Story of Rosabell', *Monthly Repository*, Feb. 1838, pp.112–17, and March 1838, pp.189–96.

6 Dante Gabriel Rossetti first expressed his idea that 'the emotional influence' of art demands an 'inner standing-point' in a prose note to his 1869 poem 'Ave'; in 1871, he used the phrase again in response to an attack on 'Jenny' by the critic Robert Buchanan.

7 Mayhew 1851–62, 1, p.462.

8 Mayhew 1851–62, 4, p.241.

9 Anne Drewery, Julian Moore and Christopher Whittick, 'Re-presenting Fanny Cornforth: The Makings of an Historical Identity', *The British Art Journal*, vol.2, no.3, Spring/Summer 2001, pp.3–15 (p.6).

10 Dante Gabriel Rossetti to Fanny Cornforth, 11 September 1872; see original letter reproduced online, Delaware Art Museum digital archives, DAM_SB_20A_06.04 1–3, accessed 29 November 2022.

Glenda Youde

Dante Gabriel and Elizabeth Eleanor Rossetti: The Artistic Partnership

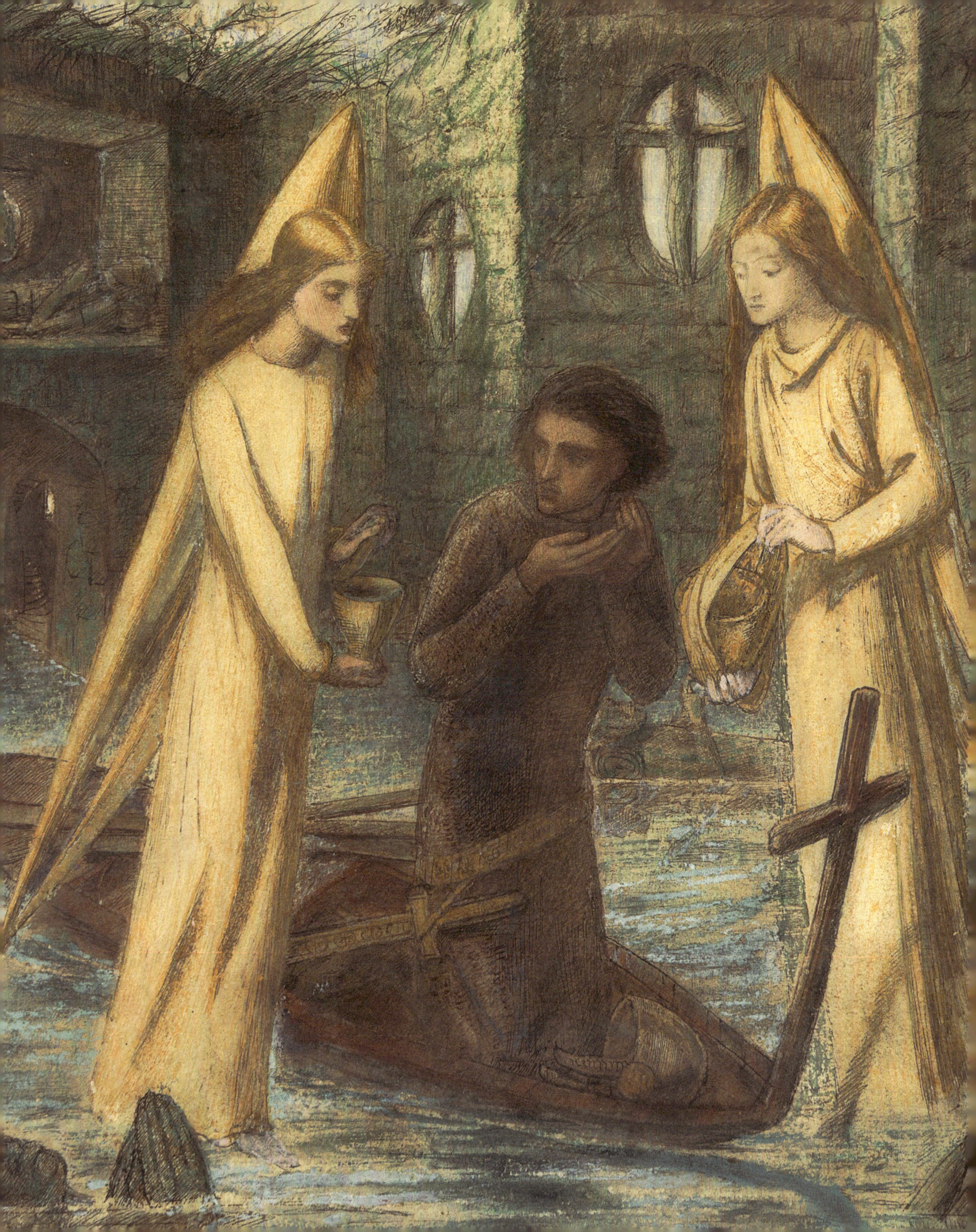

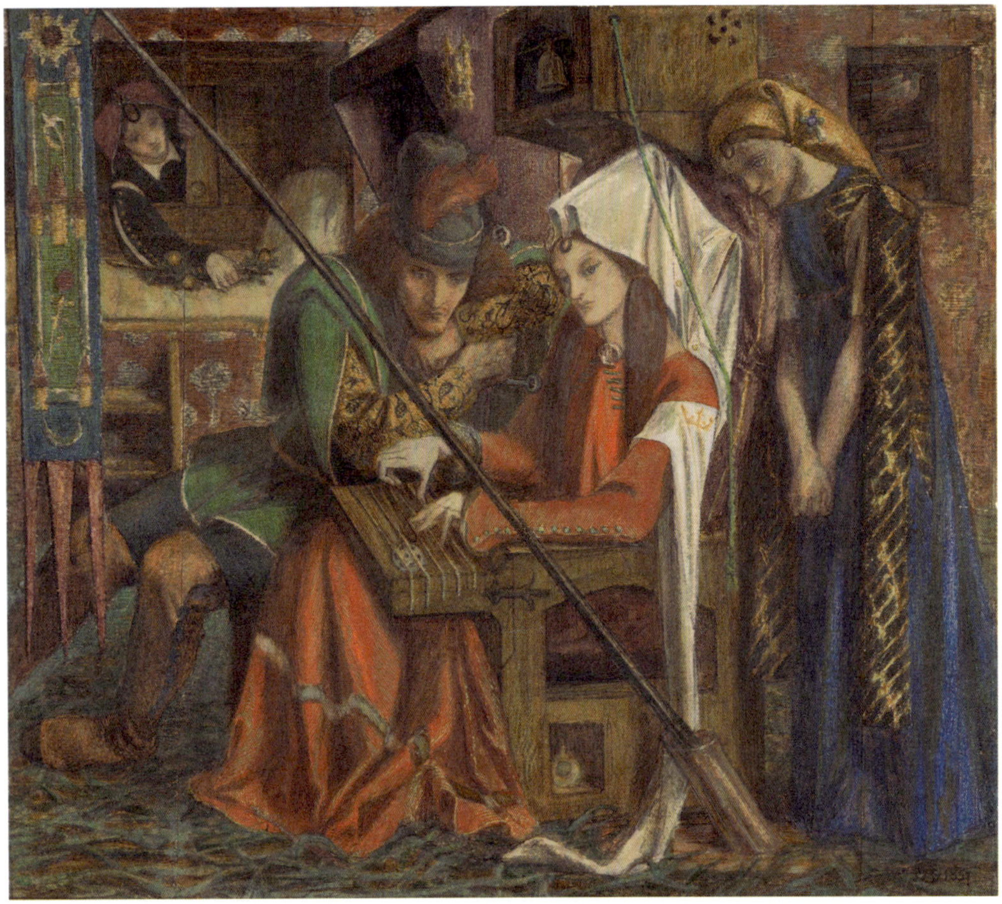

PAGE 115
NO.116 Dante Gabriel Rossetti and Elizabeth Siddal, *Sir Galahad and the Holy Grail* c.1855–7 (detail), watercolour on paper, 28 × 23.8

Despite the popular interest in their personal relationship, the artistic partnership between Elizabeth and Dante Gabriel Rossetti has received little attention.[1] Yet during the early years of the 1850s Elizabeth spent much of her time in Gabriel's studio, posing for him, learning her craft as his pupil, or working on individual and collaborative projects. Gabriel was gregarious and it is impossible to believe that the two artists worked together in silence. A typical day in the studio may have included discussion of colour, technique, composition, motifs and figure poses, as the artists' ideas were developed and worked on. Subconscious recollection or conscious adoption of an observed motif may then have infiltrated a later preparatory sketch. The resulting similarities between the work produced by the two artists would have led to the conventional art-historical viewpoint which dismisses Elizabeth's work as imitative or derivative, merely a poor copy of that of her tutor.[2] In this essay I will argue the opposite, showing how Elizabeth's original ideas so inspired Gabriel that he had all her drawings photographed and continued to 'borrow' from her designs long after her death.

ABOVE
NO.117 Dante Gabriel Rossetti, *The Tune of the Seven Towers* 1857, watercolour on paper, 31.4 × 36.5

OPPOSITE
NO.118 Elizabeth Siddal, *Lady Affixing Pennant to a Knight's Spear* c.1856, watercolour on paper, 13.7 × 13.7

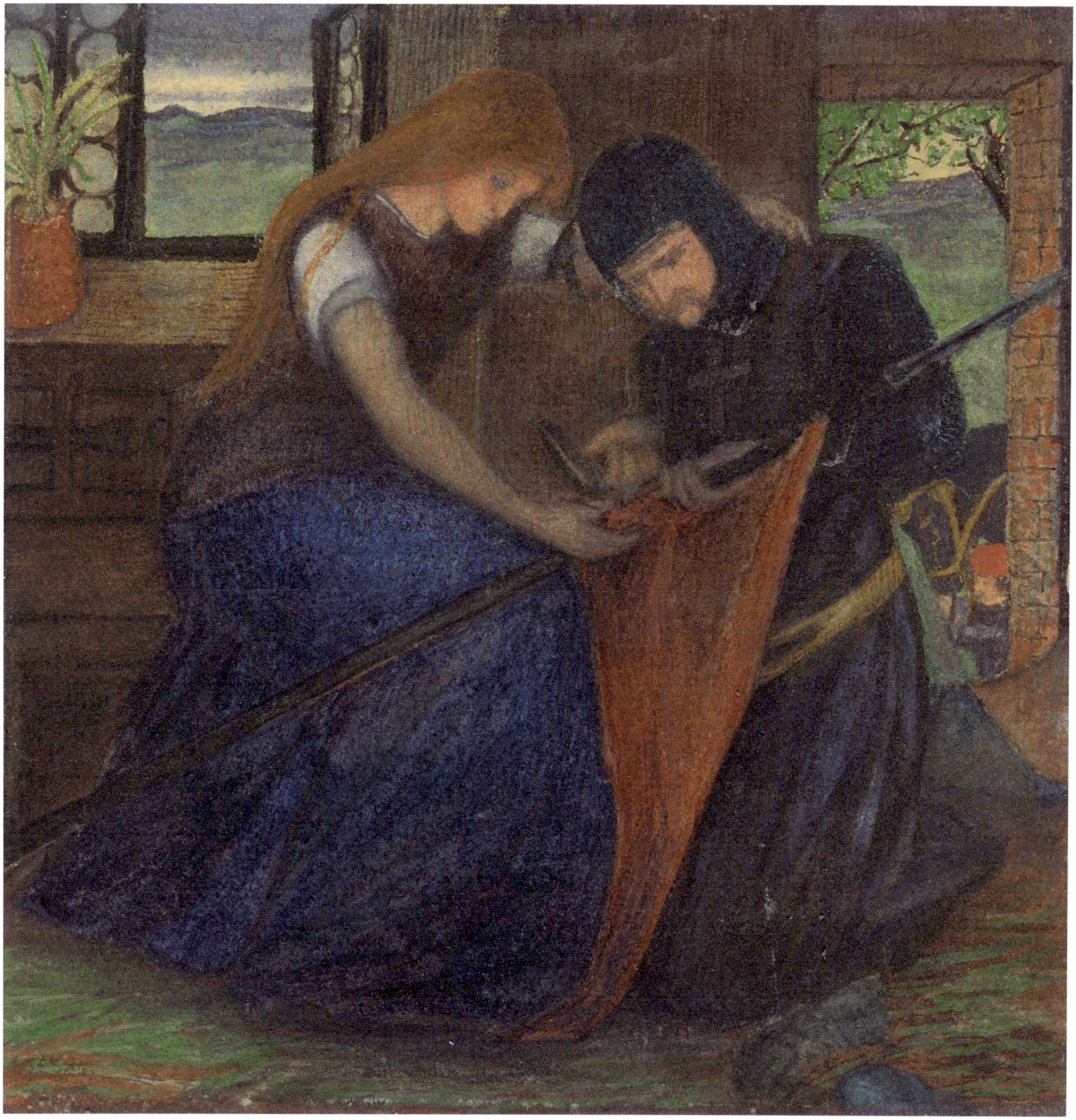

'I have no doubt it preceded Rossetti's design, and therefore this detail of invention properly belongs to Miss Siddal'

William Michael Rossetti

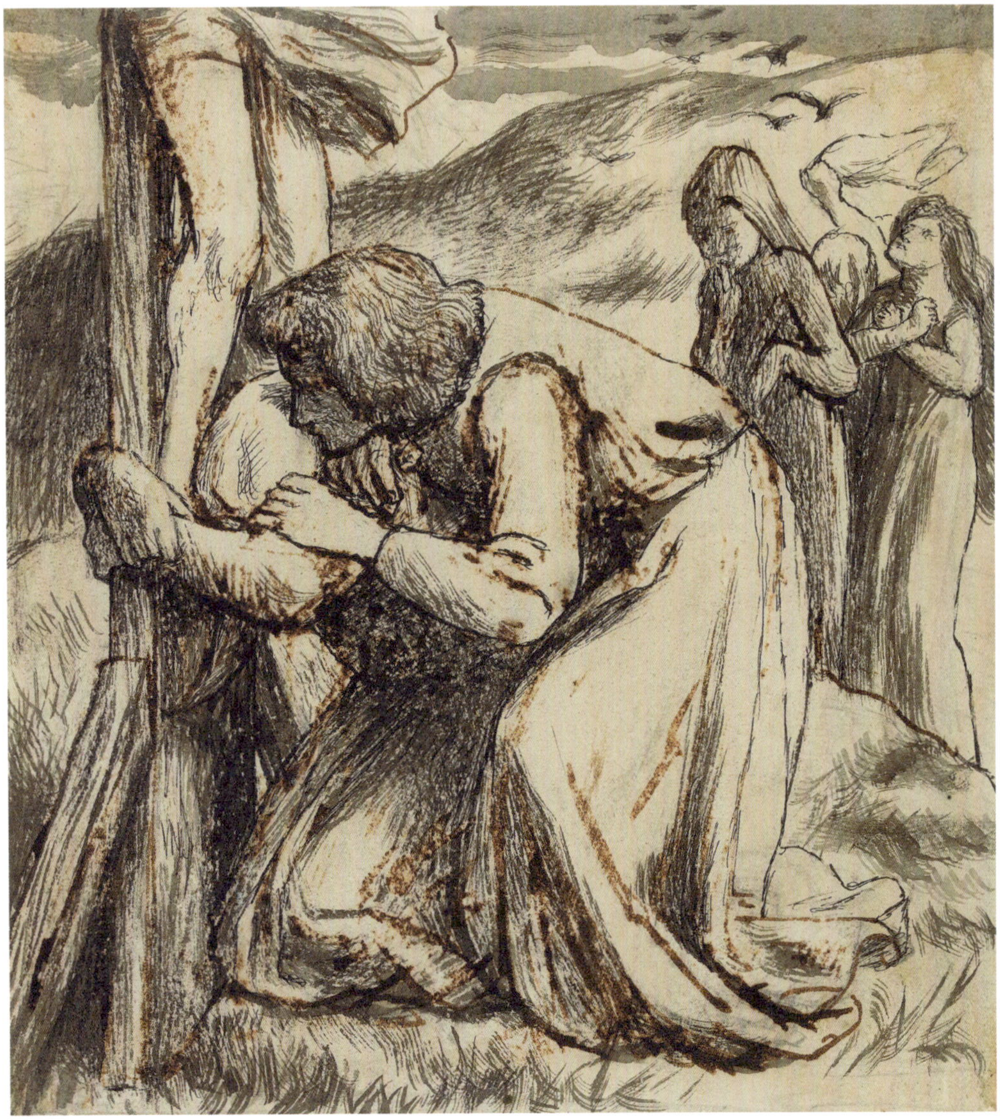

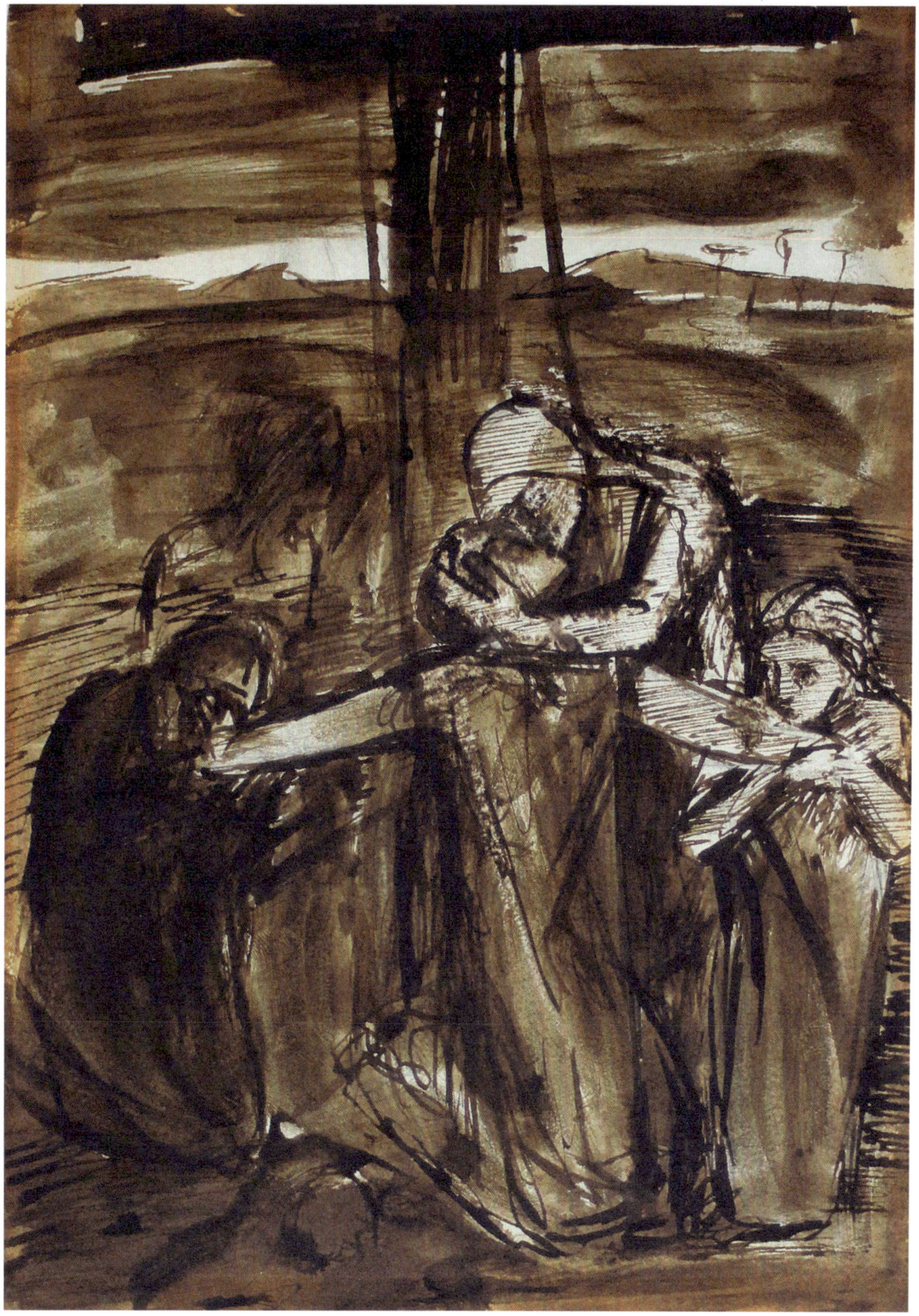

OPPOSITE
NO.119 Dante Gabriel Rossetti, *St John Comforting the Virgin at the Foot of the Cross* 1868, ink and wash on paper, 16.4 × 15.2

ABOVE
NO.120 Elizabeth Siddal, *Last Farewell Before Crucifixion* 1850–62, pen, black ink and brown wash on paper, 19.7 × 14

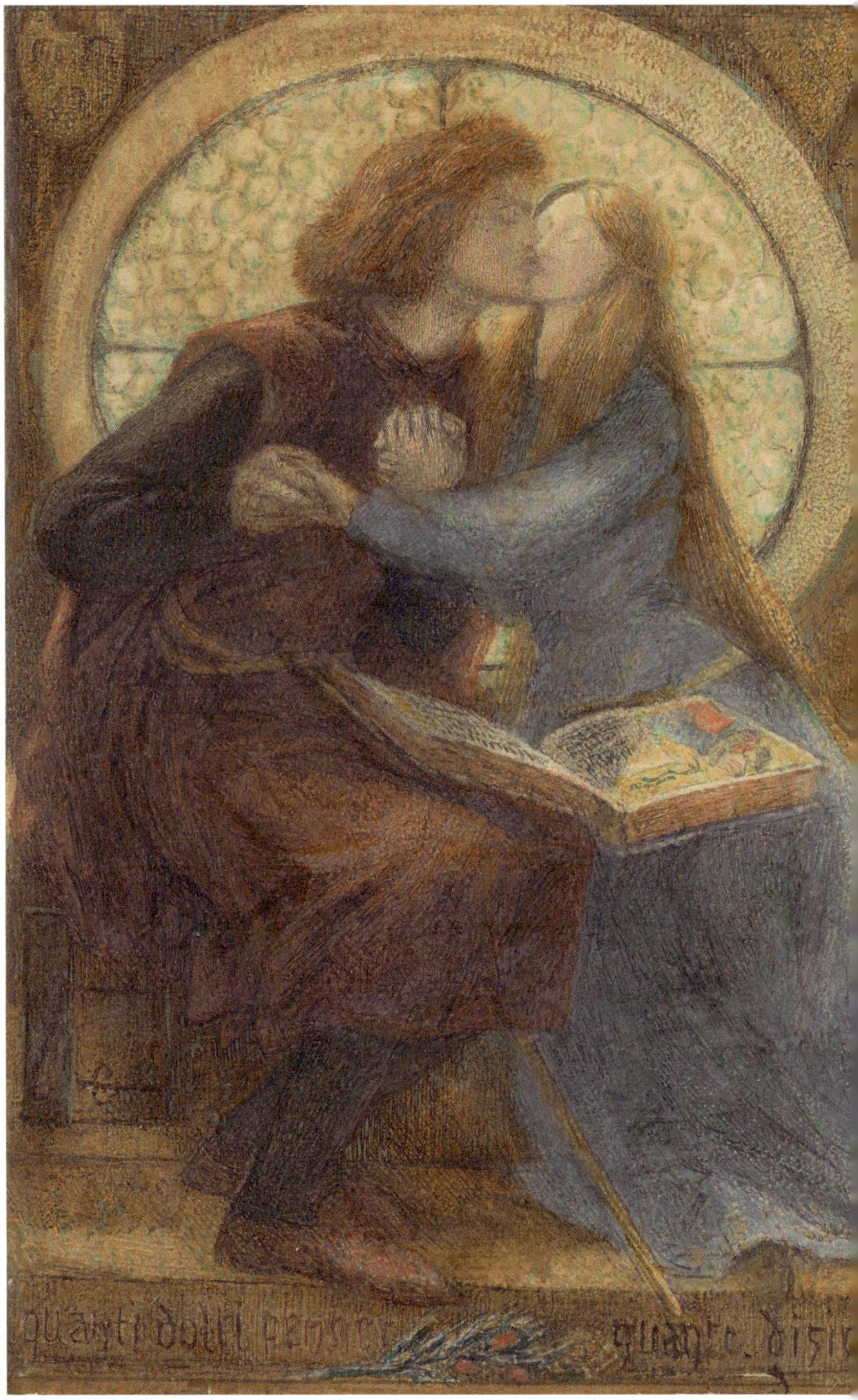

NO.121 Dante Gabriel Rossetti, *Paolo and Francesca da Rimini* 1855, watercolour on paper, 25.4 × 44.9

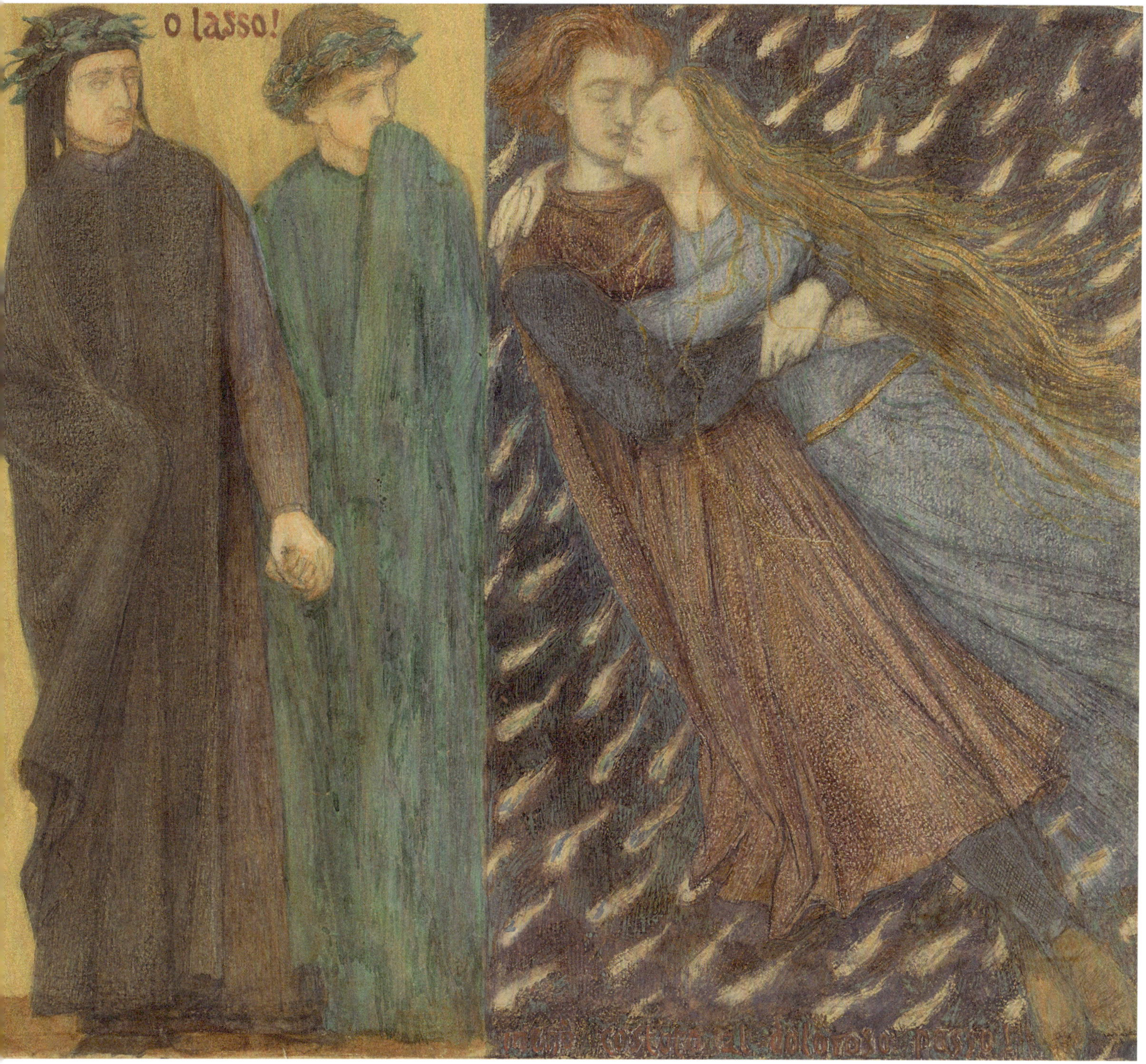
O lasso!
costoro al doloroso passo!

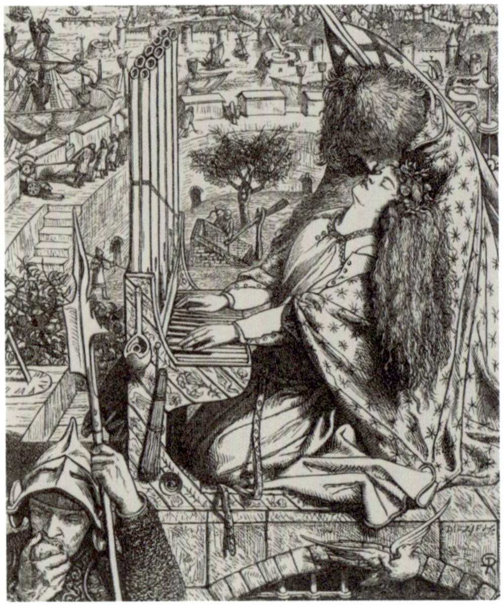

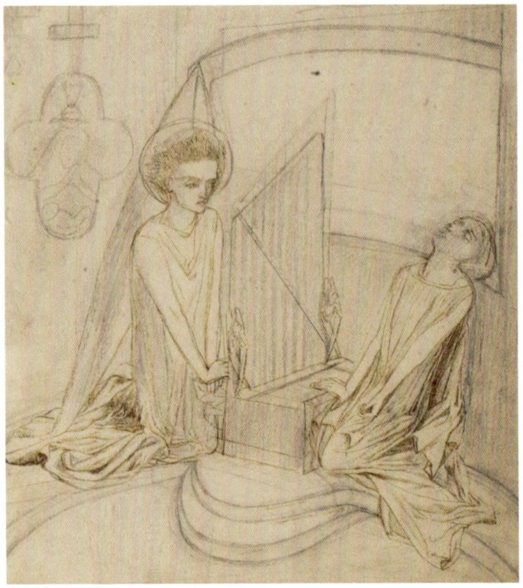

TOP
NO.122 Alfred Tennyson, *Poems* 1857, book, 22.9 × 16.8

ABOVE
NO.123 Elizabeth Siddal, *St Cecilia* c.1854–5, ink on paper, 21.5 × 20

Although she began as his model, as their relationship developed, Elizabeth's artistic output – her ideas, drawings and sketches – became increasingly significant to Gabriel, in effect taking over the role of 'muse' from her persona. Her drawings inspired him; he strove to achieve the same naïve effect in his own work. The pair often worked in parallel on similar themes: the medieval watercolours produced in the mid-1850s, Gabriel's *The Tune of the Seven Towers* (NO.117) and Elizabeth's *Lady Affixing Pennant to a Knight's Spear* (NO.118) show similarities in design, not least the diagonally placed spear which bisects each image. William Michael Rossetti recognised Elizabeth's contribution to his brother's work, stating of her drawing for *St Cecilia* (NO.123): 'I have no doubt it preceded Rossetti's design, and therefore this detail of invention properly belongs to Miss Siddal', confirming that ideas flowed both ways in the working relationship.[3]

Further evidence of the sharing of ideas is visible in Gabriel's sketches for his unfinished painting *Found* (see NO.129) and Elizabeth's *Pippa Passes* (NO.128). The many visual parallels between the motifs depicted in the sketches provide an insight into the working relationship in Gabriel's studio. Ideas appear to have bounced back and forth between the two artists as their drawings took shape. The most prominent parallel is the way in which strong verticals strengthen both compositions, with railings enclosing part of the picture space in each drawing. In *Found*, the railings surround a cemetery with an inscribed tombstone, whereas in *Pippa Passes* they appear to enclose a garden; the boundary between garden and street is echoed by the vertical trunks of sapling trees.

Both Gabriel and Elizabeth present the fallen women in their works as a juxtaposition of town and country. The figures representing the country, the drover and Pippa are depicted as innocent and pure, indicated by their simple and unadorned clothing and their erect stance. The theme of moral difference is highlighted in both cases by the dress code of the fallen women, whose attire is more elaborate and accessorised, reflecting their profession. In both images the innocence of the countryside seems to be depicted as confined or protected: Elizabeth's garden is enclosed, while Gabriel's calf is netted. However, to the right of Gabriel's drover a pair of birds gather nesting material, while Elizabeth has included two tiny birds flying to the left of Pippa as she drives her geese to market. Since the birds are positioned in the 'country' side of both drawings, this may be representative of the freedom of the countryside compared with the confinement of the city.

Additionally, both artists make extensive use of the drawn line to give a sense of place. The streets are cobbled, and the fallen women are positioned on a raised flagstone pavement or steps. A similar cross-hatching technique is used to form shadows, while distance and perspective are created with background buildings and figures. This perhaps offers evidence of the master/pupil relationship, whereby Elizabeth learned her craft through observation of Gabriel's hand at work.

It is notable that one of Elizabeth's fallen women presents a mirror image of the prostitute's pose in Gabriel's sketch for *Found*. Since his drawing was created first, this would appear to offer further evidence of the master's influence on his pupil's work.

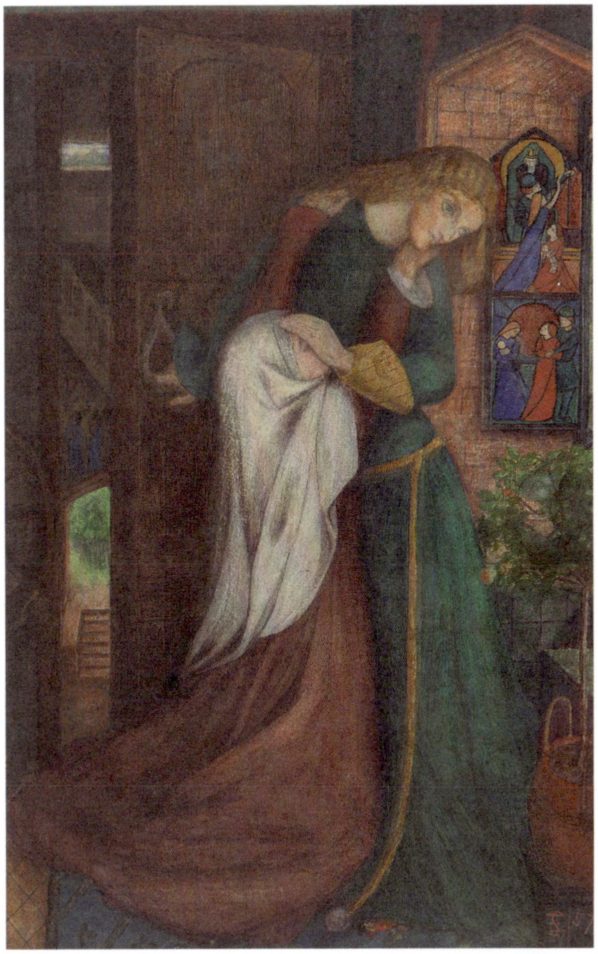

LEFT
NO.124 Elizabeth Siddal, *Lady Clare* 1854–7, watercolour on paper, 33.8 × 25.4

BELOW
NO.125 Dante Gabriel Rossetti, *Arthur's Tomb* 1860, watercolour on paper, 23.5 × 36.8

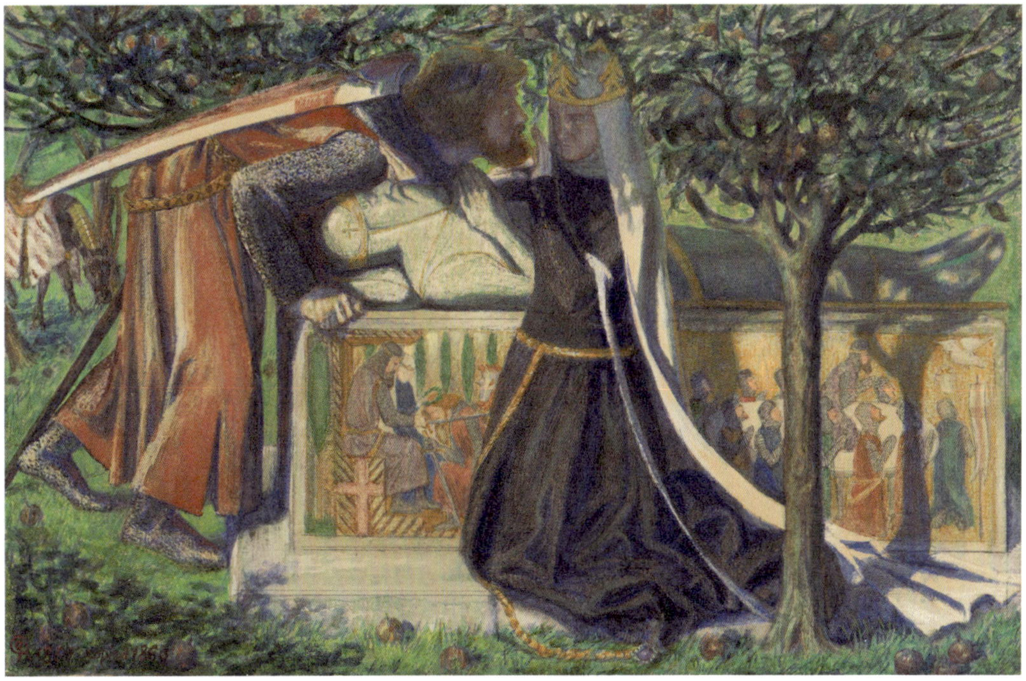

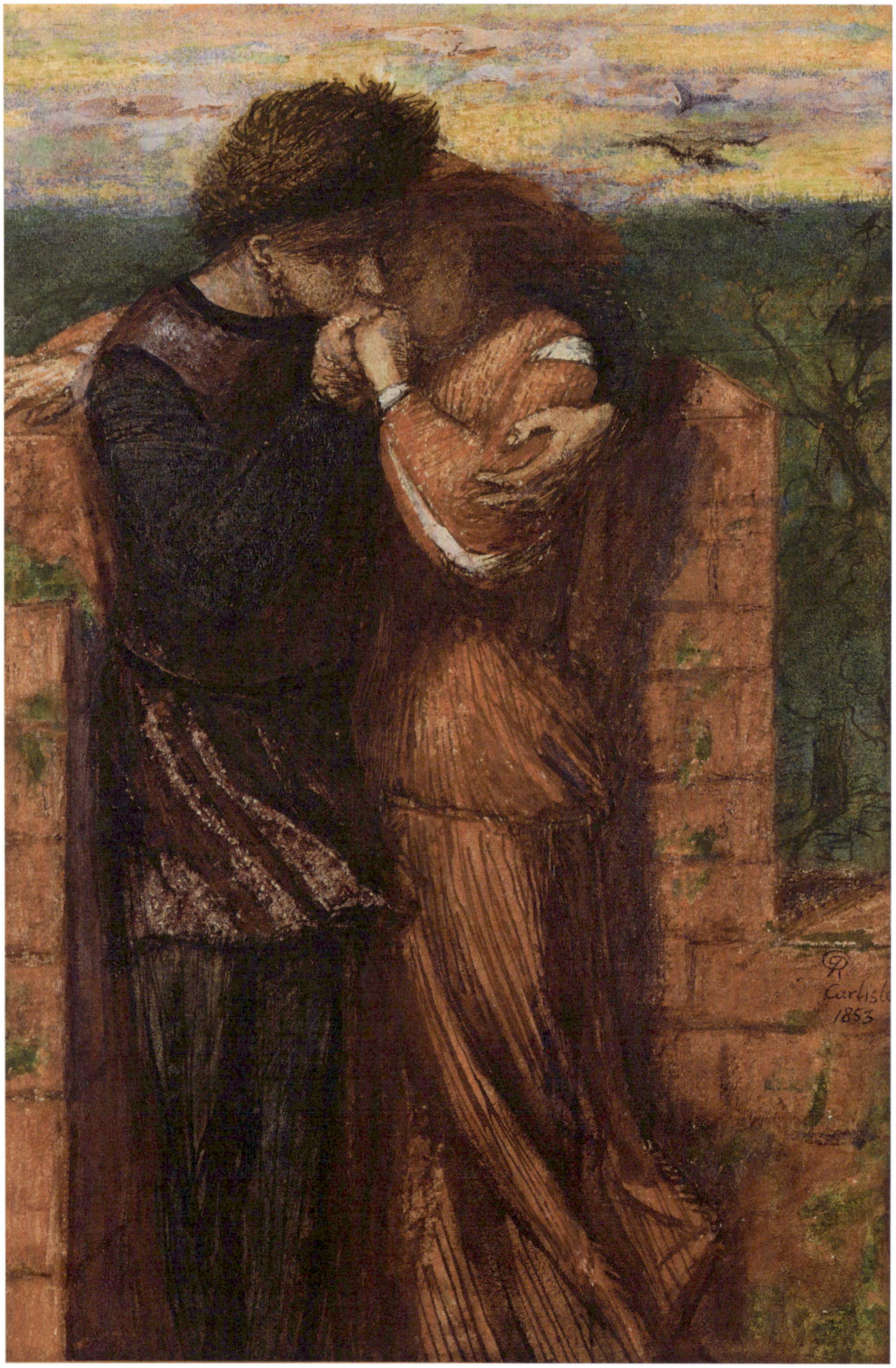

LEFT
NO.126 Dante Gabriel Rossetti, *Carlisle Wall (The Lovers)* 1853, watercolour on paper, 24.1 × 16.8

OPPOSITE
NO.127 Dante Gabriel Rossetti, *The Wedding of St George and Princess Sabra* 1857, watercolour on paper, 36.5 × 36.5

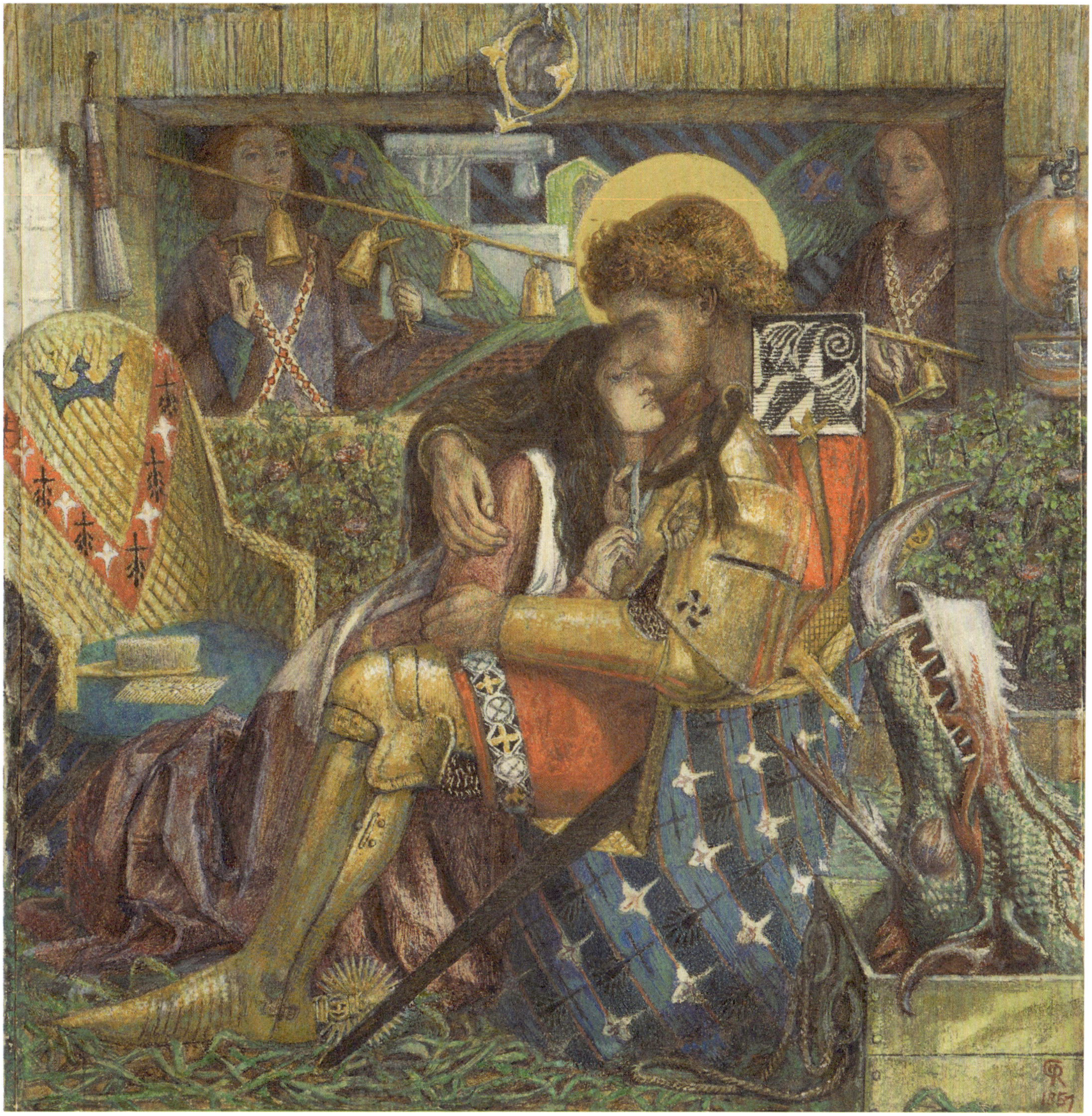

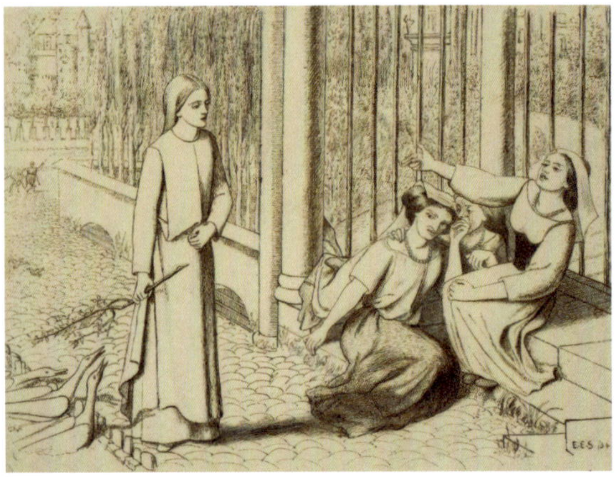

NO.128 Elizabeth Siddal, *Pippa Passes* 1854, ink on paper, 23.3 × 29.6

However, Elizabeth has not simply copied Gabriel's pre-existing drawing, but has absorbed its essence and created a new image which subtly references the former. This demonstrates not only her independence as an artist, but also her participation in the sharing of ideas which existed within the Pre-Raphaelite circle. Conversely, the clothing worn by the fallen woman in Gabriel's unfinished painting of his scene is much more elaborate than in his original sketch. Elizabeth's drawing with her elegant 'poor girls' may well have inspired his more ostentatious representation. The two-way transmission of ideas would have easily occurred subconsciously within the working environment of a shared studio.

When Elizabeth died on 11 February 1862, Gabriel lost his creative muse. He sought consolation completing his painting *Beata Beatrix* (see NO.10) from sketches made before her death. He then began the process of retrieving what he called the 'scraps and scrawls' that constituted her lifetime's work, with the intention of having them photographed.[4] The resulting images were collated into albums and presented to his friends. At least four copies, now referred to as photographic portfolios, have survived, allowing scholars an insight into the true extent of Elizabeth's oeuvre.[5]

Although it is not known who photographed Elizabeth's drawings, the most likely candidate is John Robert Parsons. Gabriel held Parsons's work in high esteem; he was elated with Parsons's photographs of Jane Morris in the gardens of Tudor House taken in July 1865 (see NOS.199, 201) and referred to them often. That same year, on 9 October, Gabriel wrote to one of his patrons, Liverpool merchant and passionate art collector John Miller:

> I am now having some drawings by my late wife photographed, and when I get copies shall beg your acceptance of some. I forget whether I ever drew your attention much to any of her designs, but am sure you will find them repay examination, as she had real inventive genius.[6]

NO.129 Dante Gabriel Rossetti, *Found – Compositional Study* 1854–5, black ink, framed in graphite, on paper, 39.3 × 38.1

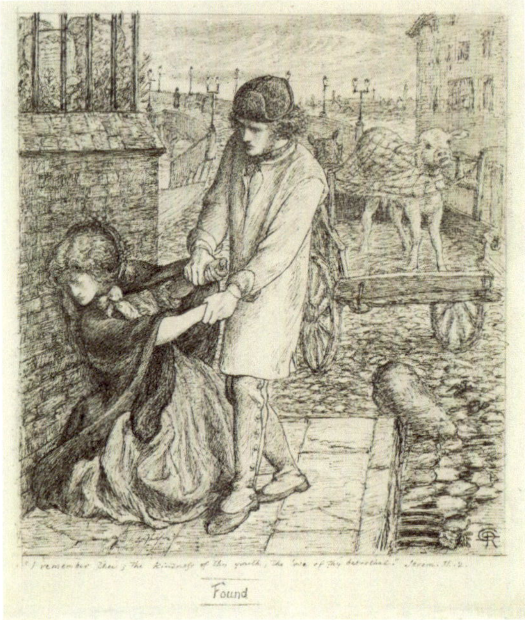

This letter provides a firm date as to when the photographs were taken. The images of Jane Morris were albumen prints, produced from glass negatives using the wet collodion process, cropped from the standard full plate negative of 21.7 × 16.8 cm. Both process and plate size were identical with those used for the photographs of Elizabeth's drawings. Parsons's work would still have been fresh in Gabriel's mind in the autumn, which perhaps made him the photographer of choice for the portfolios of Elizabeth's precious drawings.

Critically, these photographs are fundamental to understanding Elizabeth's artistic legacy as they contain images of sixty-seven authenticated drawings by her hand, providing a firm basis on which to begin building a true picture of her oeuvre. A complete photographic portfolio consists of sixty-nine images. Sixty-seven are photographs of drawings by Elizabeth, and the remaining two depict sketches of Elizabeth by Gabriel. Most significantly, twenty-seven of Elizabeth's drawings are known only from these photographs. They include all her designs for *The Lass of Lochroyan*; several studies for *La Belle Dame Sans*

Merci, *Jephthah's Daughter* and *Lady Clare*; her only drawings for *The Gay Goshawk* and *Landscape with Castle, Tree and Landing Stage*; and a selection of other sketches. Some, such as *The Lass of Lochroyan*, are mentioned in Gabriel's correspondence, but he remained silent on many others. Without the portfolios these drawings would have been lost completely. Conversely, it cannot be assumed that the portfolios contain *all* Elizabeth's 'scraps and scrawls'. In recent years, several drawings which were not included in the portfolios have been sold at auction from secure Rossetti family provenance. This implies that Gabriel had been unsuccessful in retrieving all her drawings from their owners before the photographic session. It also suggests there may be more drawings yet to be discovered.

It is believed Gabriel kept one copy of the photographic portfolio for himself, as the Ashmolean collection includes a portion of the original board cover. On the reverse is an explanatory note: 'Cut from the cover of the deteriorating portfolio included in the Bryson Bequest. September 1987. NBP'.[7] The fact that the original printed text on the label has been crossed through and annotated by hand adds further credence to that possibility. Unfortunately, this fragment is all that remains as physical evidence of ownership, since the card sheets containing the photographs are now loose and preserved in a random order in a museum storage box. Such damage to a bound volume is most likely to occur when the item in question is a well-used favourite, subject to continued opening, closing and page-turning, potentially caused by Gabriel's repeated use of his copy as a source book.

This possibility is further evidenced by Gabriel's own illustration for his poem 'Sister Helen' (NO.131), included in a volume of poetry published in 1870. The poem narrates a conversation between the protagonist, Helen, who uses witchcraft to avenge her deceitful lover, and her little brother. Gabriel's image depicts a central female figure seated with arms outstretched in front and head inclined towards her left shoulder. Behind her and to the viewer's right a child appears to be climbing up onto a ledge. To the left is a shadowy figure apparently carrying, or tied to, a long stick. The architectural detail suggests the interior of a room. At first glance the image appears very 'Rossettian'; the wavy hair and position of the figure's head are echoed in many of his oil paintings. Yet a detailed knowledge of Elizabeth's oeuvre suggests this is not an original illustration, but a compilation of several of her earlier ideas, all of which were included in the photographic portfolios of her work.

Some fifteen years before Gabriel began his drawing of Sister Helen, Elizabeth had made three known illustrations for this poem (NO.135), two of which are known only from the photographic portfolios. Gabriel wrote to the poet William Allingham on 23 July 1854 that 'Miss S[iddal] has made a splendid design from that *Sister Helen* of mine'.[8] It is not known which of the drawings he is referring to, but since he describes it as 'splendid' it may well be the most finished drawing, suggesting the rougher sketches may have been completed earlier. Gabriel's design shows a marked similarity to Elizabeth's drawings.

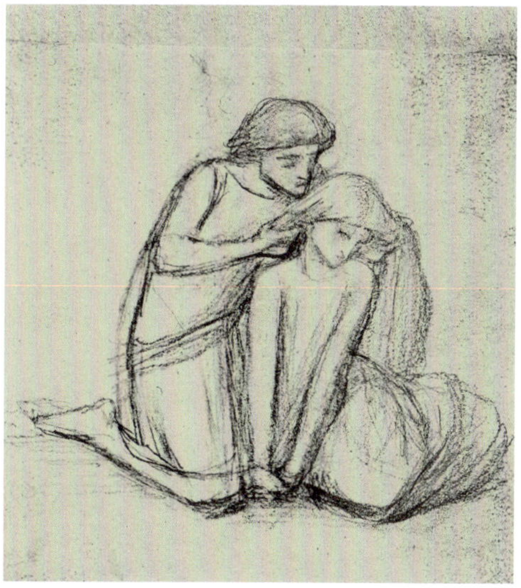

NO.130 Detail of photograph after Elizabeth Siddal, *La Belle Dame Sans Merci*, original drawing c.1855, graphite on paper, c.13 × 14

NO.131 Dante Gabriel Rossetti, *Sister Helen* c.1870, graphite and ink on paper mounted on board, 21.1 × 16.7

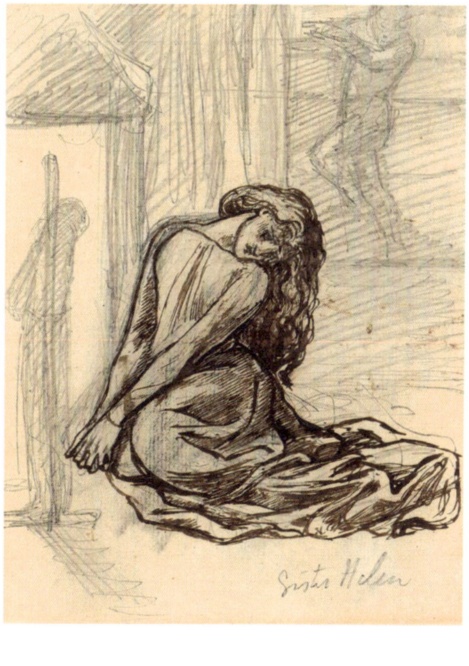

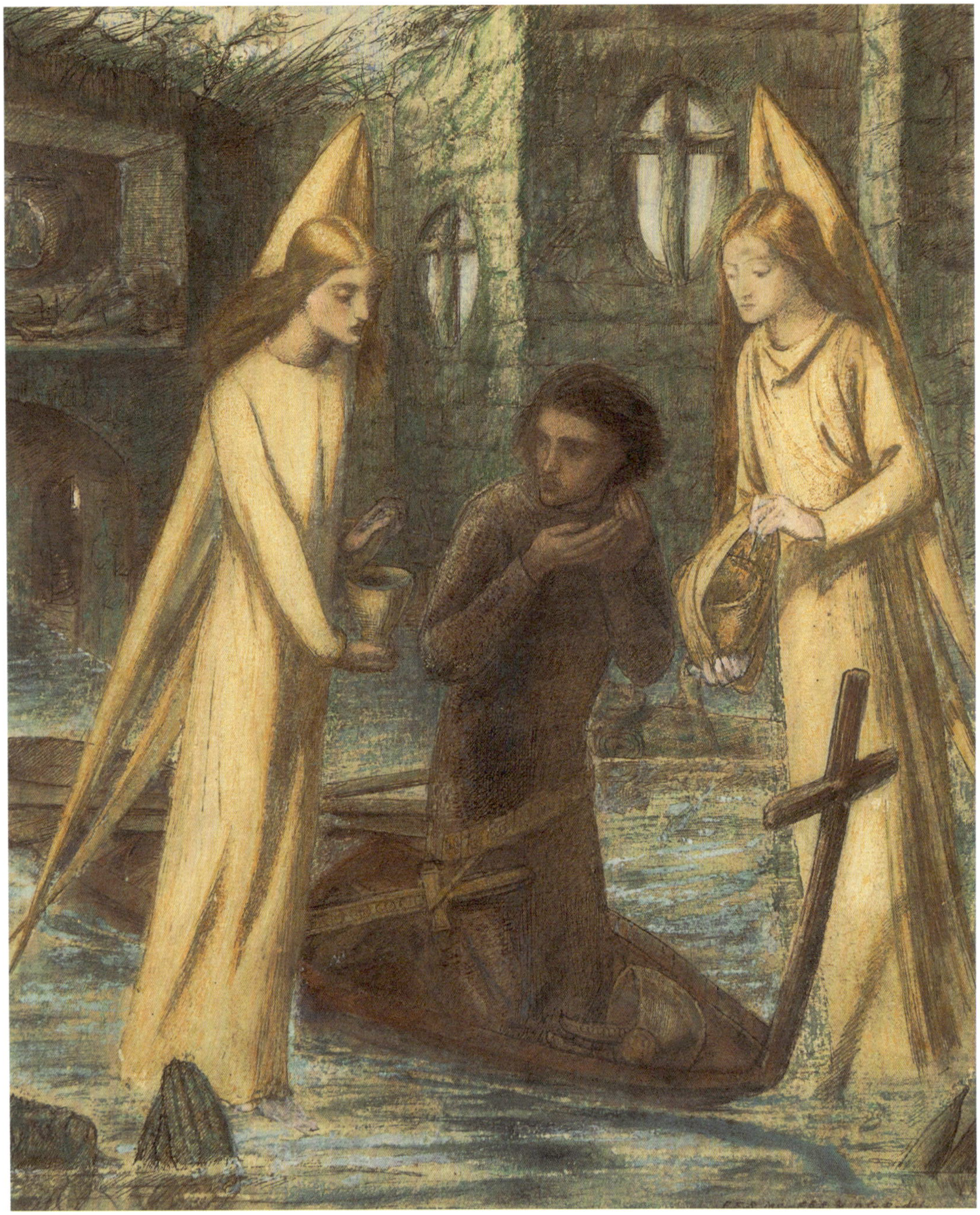

LEFT
NO.132 Dante Gabriel Rossetti and Elizabeth Siddal, *Sir Galahad and the Holy Grail* c.1855–7, watercolour on paper, 28 × 23.8

OPPOSITE ABOVE
NO.133 Dante Gabriel Rossetti, *Sir Galahad, Sir Bors and Sir Percival receiving the Sanc Grael, but Sir Percival's Sister died by the Way* 1857, ink, chalk, graphite and wash on paper, 25.1 × 35.2

OPPOSITE BELOW
NO.134 Dante Gabriel Rossetti, *How Sir Galahad, Sir Bors and Sir Percival Were Fed with the Sanct Grael; but Sir Percival's Sister Died by the Way* 1864, watercolour and gouache on paper, 29.2 × 41.9

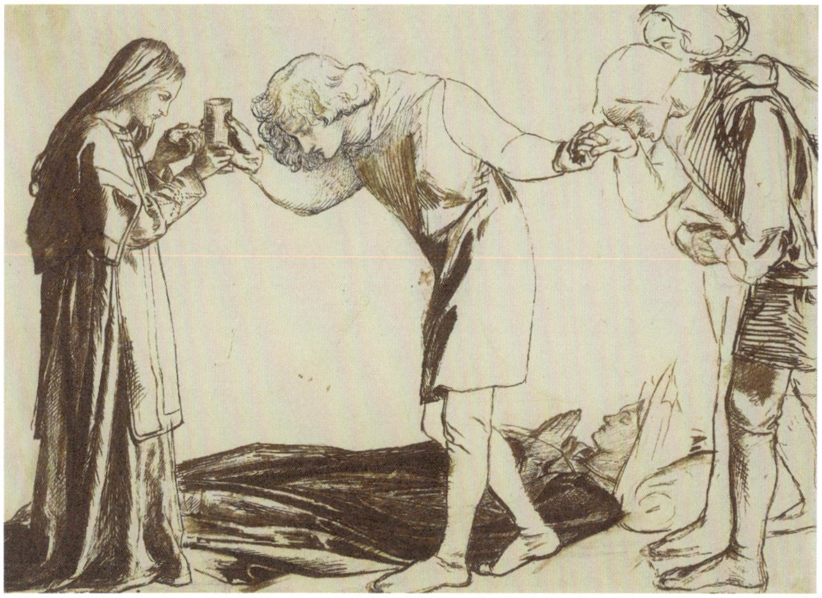

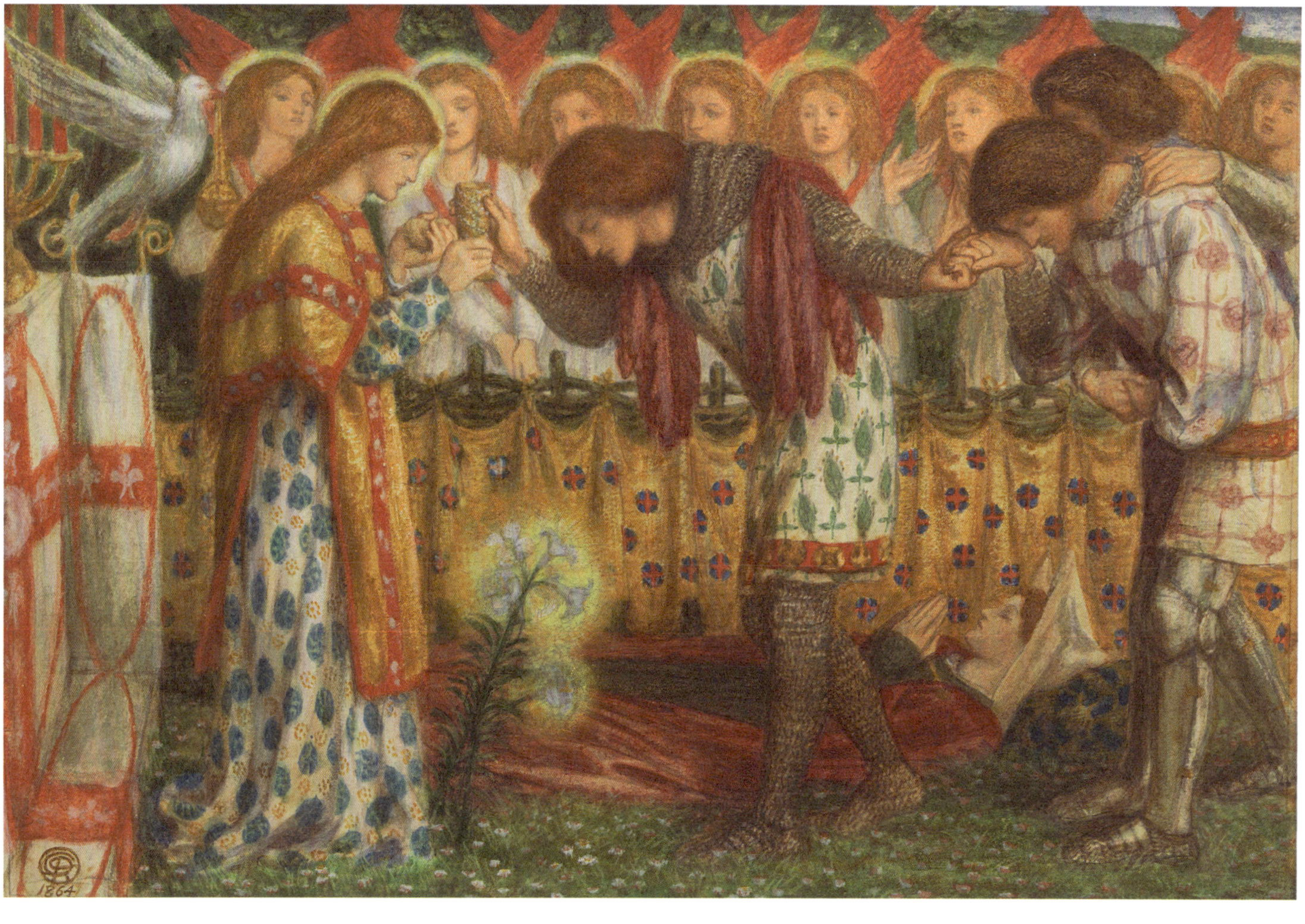

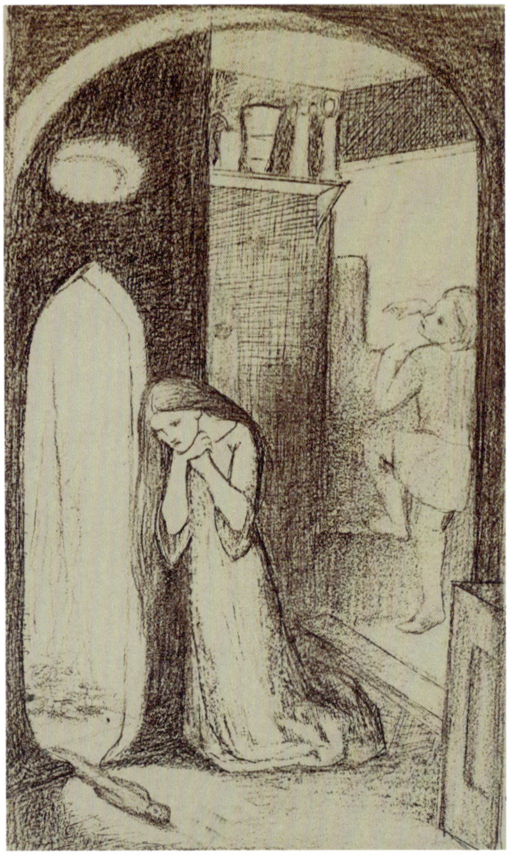

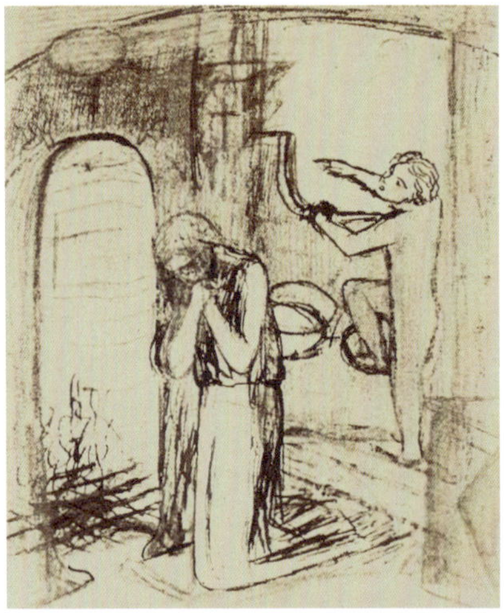

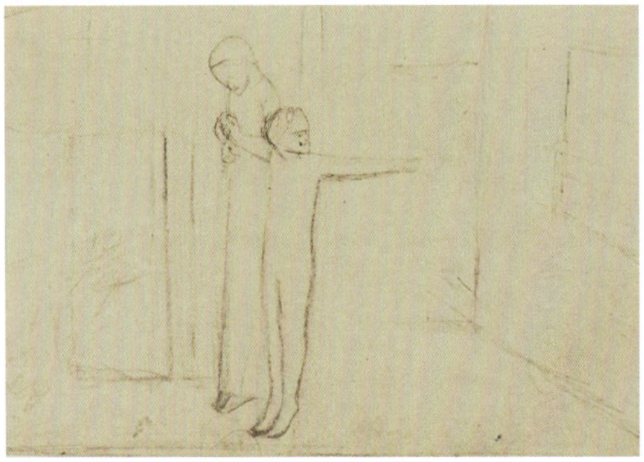

'I am now having some drawings by my late wife photographed, and when I get copies shall beg your acceptance of some.'

Dante Gabriel Rossetti

OPPOSITE
NO.135 Photographic album of works by Elizabeth Siddal, c.1866, open to three studies for *Sister Helen*, 57 × 45.5

Both Elizabeth's and Gabriel's images illustrate the seventh stanza, in which Helen melts a waxen doll in front of the fire. Her brother tirelessly questions her actions and reports what he sees from 'without the gallery door'. The seventh stanza reads:

> 'Here high up in the balcony,
> Sister Helen,
> The moon flies face to face with me.'
> 'Aye, look and say whatever you see,
> Little brother.'

Elizabeth's inspiration appears to derive from these lines. Her drawings depict an aperture representing the gallery door with Helen's sibling climbing 'high up' to reach the balcony and report what he can see. It is difficult to accept it was pure coincidence that Elizabeth and Gabriel chose to illustrate the identical scene, since the published poem of 1870 contains thirty-four stanzas (238 lines). Gabriel could have selected any other stanza to illustrate, yet he clearly followed Elizabeth's choice, as can be seen from the photographic portfolio (NO.135).

Gabriel depicts Helen's brother climbing onto a ledge in a similar position and pose to those previously chosen by Elizabeth. Close analysis of the figure of the child shows that although Gabriel has positioned his figure's head differently, the pose is similar. The child stands on one leg, with the other raised as if climbing. In Gabriel's drawing and Elizabeth's more finished sketch, it is the left knee that is raised, but in her rough sketch, it is the right knee. All three sketches show the child pointing, with his index finger extended. Despite the limitations of working with photographs rather than original drawings, the similarities between the figure poses are undeniable, suggesting that Gabriel copied Elizabeth's ideas.

It is easy to view the main figure as simply another 'Rossetti' female, resembling many, such as the siren in *A Sea Spell*. However, there are also striking similarities to two drawings Elizabeth produced to illustrate Keats's poem 'La Belle Dame Sans Merci', known only from the photographic portfolio. It is immediately obvious that the figure pose is visually similar in both drawings (see NO.130). The female figure is seated on the ground, with her body facing the viewer and her knees drawn up to the side. The folds of her skirt disguise the placement of her legs, but a rough indication of her knee position is visible in each drawing. The most striking feature is the placement of the figure's arms, extended straight forward with hands clasped. This motif is unique to Elizabeth, seen only in the two drawings mentioned. Gabriel undoubtedly referred to the photographs of Elizabeth's *La Belle Dame Sans Merci* in his copy of the photographic portfolio for his inspiration.

It is also evident from the photographs that Elizabeth made various changes to the positioning of some elements between her two sketches; these are critical to the analysis of Gabriel's figure. Most notably, the outstretched arms have been rotated slightly in Elizabeth's more refined drawing, making the figure's right arm almost perpendicular. Additionally, the head is inclined slightly further towards her left shoulder. It appears that Gabriel has noted

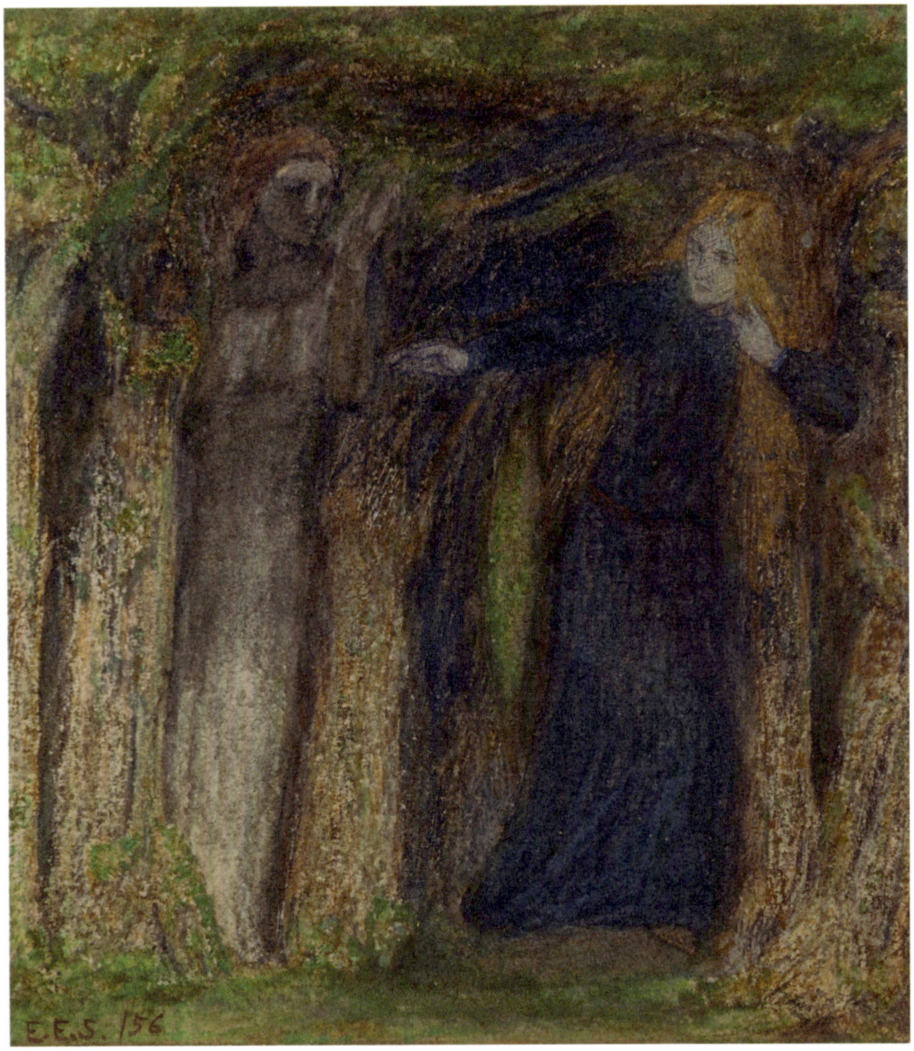

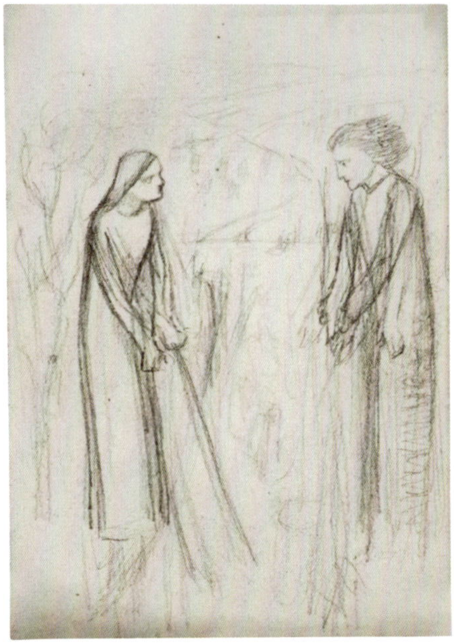

ABOVE
NO.136 Elizabeth Siddal, *The Haunted Wood* 1856, gouache on paper, 12 × 11

RIGHT
NO.137 Photograph after Elizabeth Siddal, *Annunciation* c.1850–60, black and white photograph printed on paper, 18.6 × 13.6

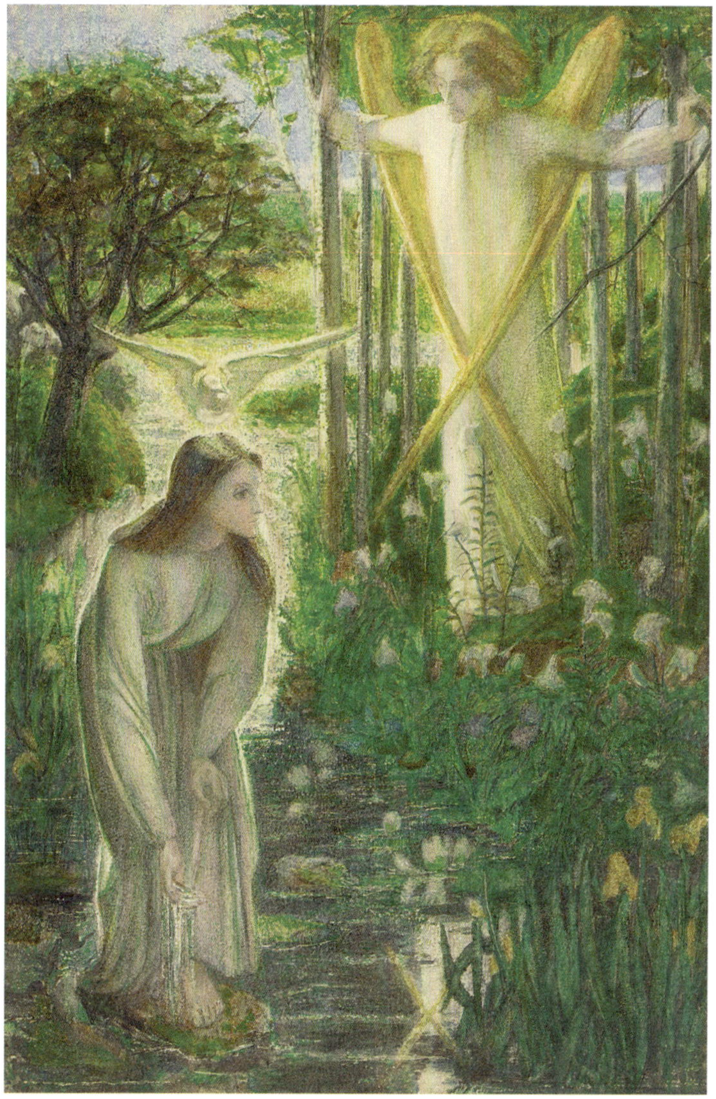

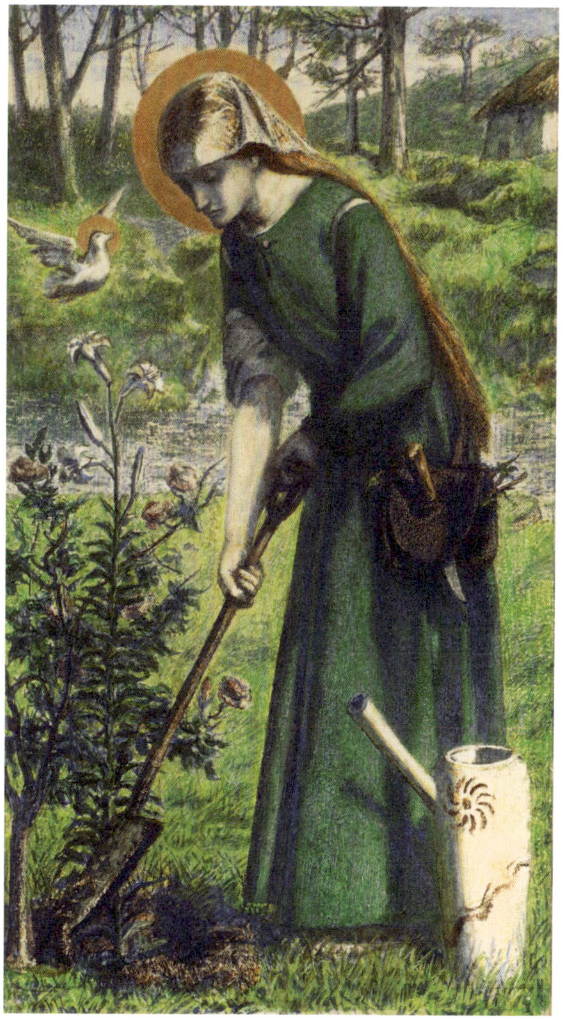

ABOVE
NO.138 Dante Gabriel Rossetti, *The Annunciation* 1855–8, watercolour on paper, 35.9 × 24.8

RIGHT
NO.139 Dante Gabriel Rossetti, *Mary Nazarene* 1857, watercolour on paper, 34.3 × 19.7

"'Here high up in the balcony, Sister Helen, / The moon flies face to face with me.' / 'Aye, look and say whatever you see, / Little brother.'"

Dante Gabriel Rossetti, 'Sister Helen', c.1852

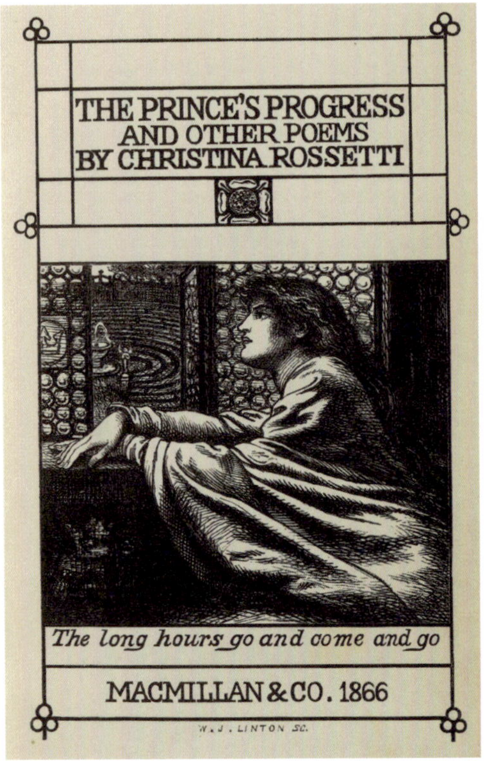

these two modifications and exaggerated them, since he has rotated the position of his figure's arms clockwise, so the right arm is at an even more acute angle. In addition, the incline of his figure's head and neck has been accentuated. The most significant similarity between all three drawings is the repetition of the straight extended arms and the acute angle created where they meet at the hands. Gabriel's duplication and modification of this unique motif suggest that he had a copy of the photographic portfolio open in front of him while he was working on his own illustration.

A further point of parallelism can be seen in the architectural setting and the shadowy figure Gabriel has positioned to the left of his drawing. This may represent the 'waxen man' mentioned in the first line of the poem, but the figure also exhibits a strong visual resemblance to one of Elizabeth's sketches illustrating Tennyson's poem 'St Agnes' Eve' (NO.141). The shadowy figures in both Elizabeth's and Gabriel's drawings are enclosed in a similar rectangular architectural space, and the angle of the incline of both bodies appears almost identical. Elizabeth's drawing of *St Agnes' Eve* was known only from the photographic portfolio until it was sold at Christie's Auction House, London, in June 2014 from Rossetti family provenance. This suggests that both the photographic portfolio and the original drawing were in Gabriel's possession when he worked on his design, providing ample opportunity for him to browse Elizabeth's work for inspiration.

Gabriel's heroic effort to preserve Elizabeth's work for the future should not go unnoticed. It clearly demonstrates his admiration for, and perhaps his dependence on, her untutored imagination. The methodical practice of cropping the photographs of her drawings and pasting them into the portfolios would have given him comfort in the years after Elizabeth's death; perhaps also the feeling that she was still there, working in the studio with him. The cathartic process would have enabled him to develop designs, subconsciously absorbing Elizabeth's ideas through constant exposure to her drawings. The existence of the damaged fragment of board cover along with the glass negatives shows there is a strong possibility that Gabriel retained a copy of the photographic portfolio for personal use as a source book, enabling him to continue the relationship with his muse beyond the grave. Far from being an imitator, Elizabeth was an innovator, evidence of which can be seen throughout Gabriel's oeuvre

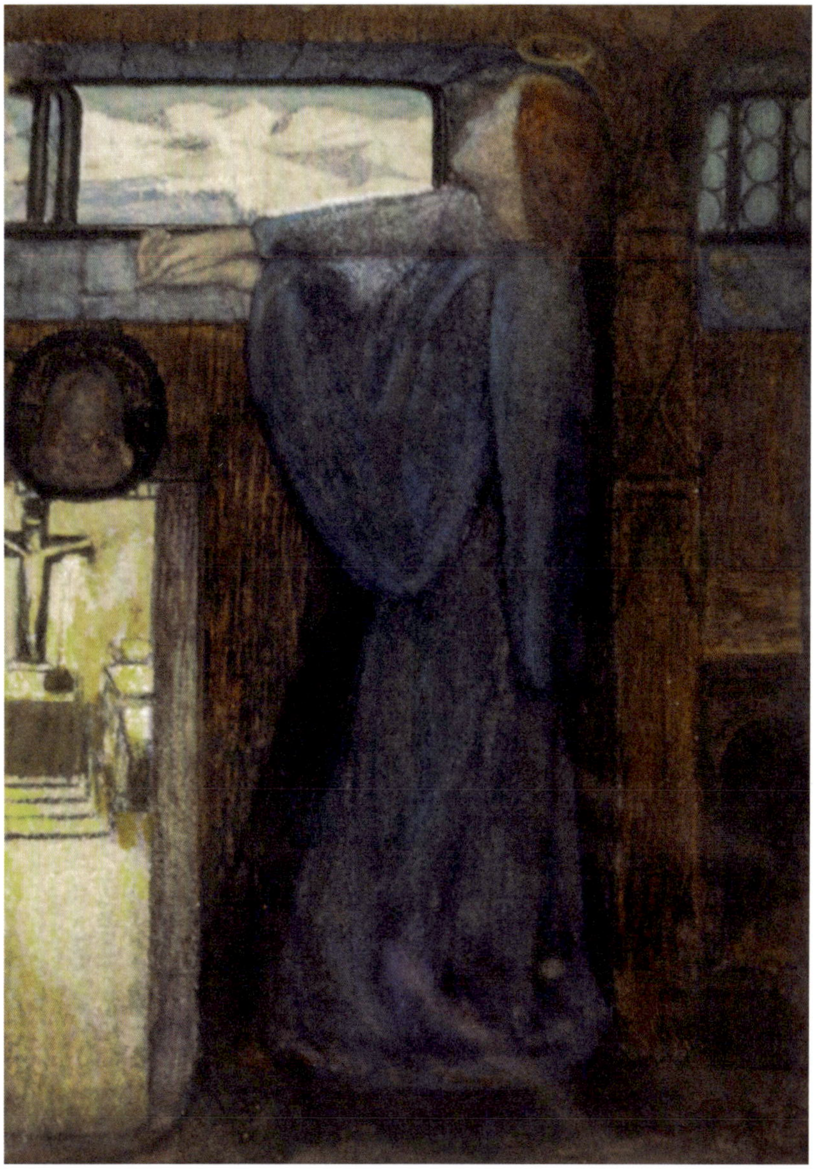

OPPOSITE
NO.140 Dante Gabriel Rossetti, frontispece to Christina Rossetti's *The Prince's Progress and Other Poems* 1866, book, 17.8 × 11.4

ABOVE
NO.141 Elizabeth Siddal, *St Agnes' Eve* 1853–60, gouache on paper, 16.5 × 12

1 To differentiate Elizabeth, the Pre-Raphaelite artist and poet, from 'Lizzie Siddal', the red-haired 'stunner', I have chosen to use her married name: Elizabeth Eleanor Rossetti. This essay is derived from research undertaken for my 'Beyond *Ophelia*: The Artistic Legacy of Elizabeth Eleanor Rossetti (née Siddall)' thesis, University of York, 2022.

2 See, for example, John Gere, 'Introduction', in *Dante Gabriel Rossetti*, ed. Julian Treuherz, Elizabeth Prettejohn and Edwin Becker, London 2003, p.14.

3 William Michael Rossetti, 'Dante Rossetti and Elizabeth Siddal', *Burlington Magazine*, vol.1, no.3, May 1903, p.295.

4 William E. Fredeman (ed.), *The Correspondence of Dante Gabriel Rossetti*, 10 vols., Cambridge, Woodbridge and Rochester, NY 2002–15, vol.4, pp.175–6.

5 Two incomplete copies of the photographic portfolio are held at the Ashmolean Museum, Oxford; a complete bound copy is in the Fitzwilliam Museum, Cambridge; and a complete unbound copy resides in the Princeton University Library, New Jersey, USA. A fifth copy was bequeathed to the Victoria and Albert Museum, London, in 1911 but is currently unlocated in the stores.

6 Fredeman 2002–15, 3, p.337.

7 'NBP' is believed to refer to Sir Nicholas Beaver Penny, Keeper of Western Art at the Ashmolean Museum from 1984 to 1989 (Caroline Palmer, Western Art Print Room).

8 Fredeman 2002–15, 1, p.363.

Gursimran Oberoi

The Collective Self-Portrait: Drawing Elizabeth Siddal in the New Woman Sisterhood

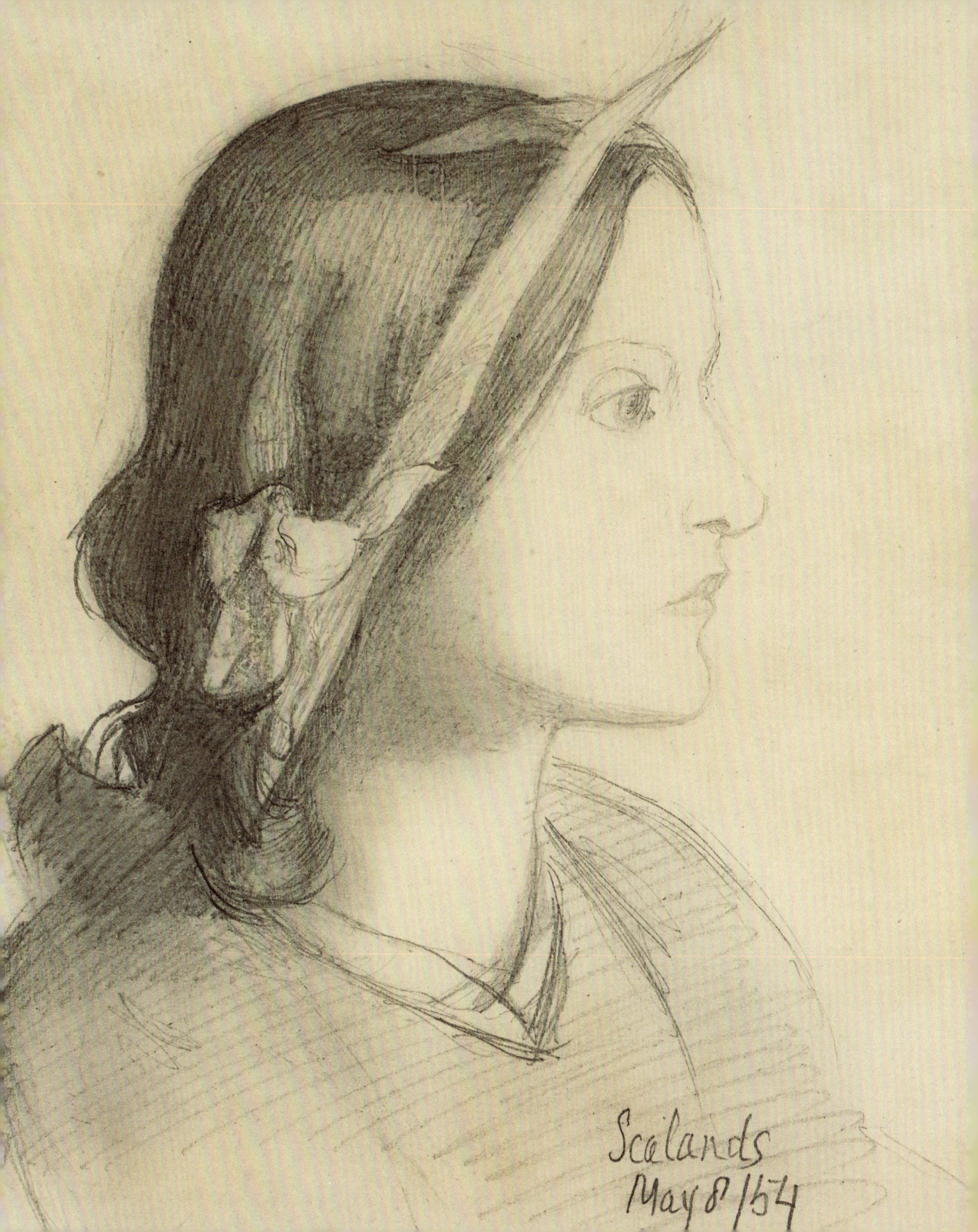
Scalands
May 8/54

PAGE 137
NO.142 Dante Gabriel Rossetti, *Profile Portrait of Elizabeth Siddal with Irises in her Hair* 1854, graphite on wove paper, 18.7 × 12.3

BELOW
NO.143 Dante Gabriel Rossetti, *Elizabeth Siddal* 1860, graphite on paper, 26 × 25.4

Artist, poet, 'model and muse'. Elizabeth Siddal has captivated Pre-Raphaelite enthusiasts with her skilful hand, maidenly beauty and untimely death at the age of thirty-two. Elizabeth is perhaps best remembered as the mystical figure in countless paintings by her husband, Dante Gabriel Rossetti, who exhumed her coffin one night at Highgate Cemetery in 1868 to retrieve a collection of his unpublished poems. This shocking legend – with its repeated emphasis on how Elizabeth's auburn hair had grown in the six years since they had parted – has permeated Pre-Raphaelite discussions. It has intersected with considerations of John Everett Millais's masterful portrayal of Elizabeth as the lifeless, floating Shakespearian Ophelia in the Tate collection. As Ophelia limply clasps poppies and other flowers in death, Elizabeth tragically died from a laudanum overdose (an opioid derived from poppies). Elizabeth's ethereal countenance, as painted by the founding members of the Pre-Raphaelite Brotherhood, has dominated public perceptions for more than a century.

Today, there is a new wave of feminist scholarship investigating the art, education and politics of Pre-Raphaelite women. This momentum was originally launched by the historian Jan Marsh in the 1980s and has been supported in recent years by emerging scholars Catia Rodrigues, Alex Round and Serena Trowbridge.[1] Together they uncover how female artists often recognised in the 'second and third phases' of Pre-Raphaelitism were in fact a sisterhood of independent, forward-thinking individuals who challenged gendered stereotypes in their lives and a patriarchal Victorian art world in their careers. These developments help us decentre the popularised myth that is 'Lizzie Siddal: model and muse', and instead rediscover her as the eponymous hero of her own journey and the effervescent self-portrait of nineteenth-century New Womanhood.

Drawing Elizabeth into this progressive and dynamic circle of women is more complicated than one might expect. In contrast to her non-familial sisters in art, there is very little biographical information about Elizabeth. Indeed, the array of primary material relating to the lives and works of Georgiana Burne-Jones, Anna Mary Howitt, Barbara Leigh Smith Bodichon and Mary Watts, for example, far outweighs the passing notes made about Elizabeth in correspondence and biographical histories of Gabriel and other Victorians. Judith Flanders's compelling account of the Macdonald sisters, who included the Pre-Raphaelite Georgiana (married to Edward Burne-Jones), has shown how four lower-middle-class women navigated Victorian class structures to great advantage.[2] Anna Mary Howitt's feminist activity in art, literature and social reform embodied the 'sisterhood in Art' she conceived with her friends. This collective deconstructed 'the romantic model of artistic manhood' championed by the Brotherhood.[3] The 'feminist, artist and rebel' Barbara Bodichon was among Howitt's sisters.[4] In a society that favoured matrimony, Bodichon had an unconventional upbringing in that her parents never married. She was raised to be an independent woman and founded both Girton College, Cambridge, and the Married Woman's Property Committee. The latter, established in 1855, contributed to the passing of the Married Women's Property Act of 1870 which enabled thousands of women in Britain to legally control any money they earned and inherited (including property). Given Elizabeth's

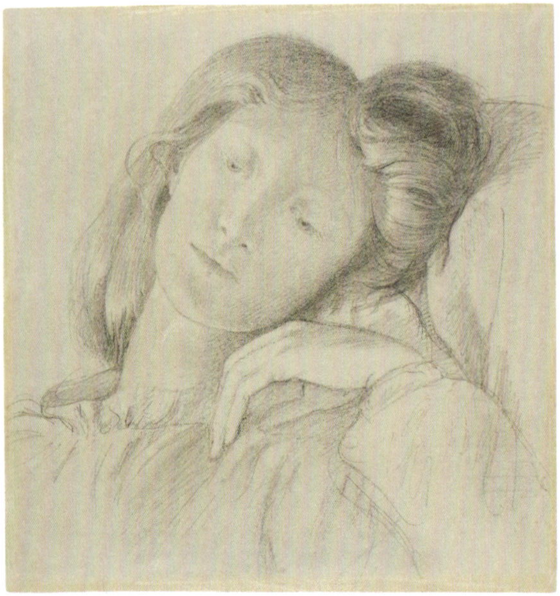

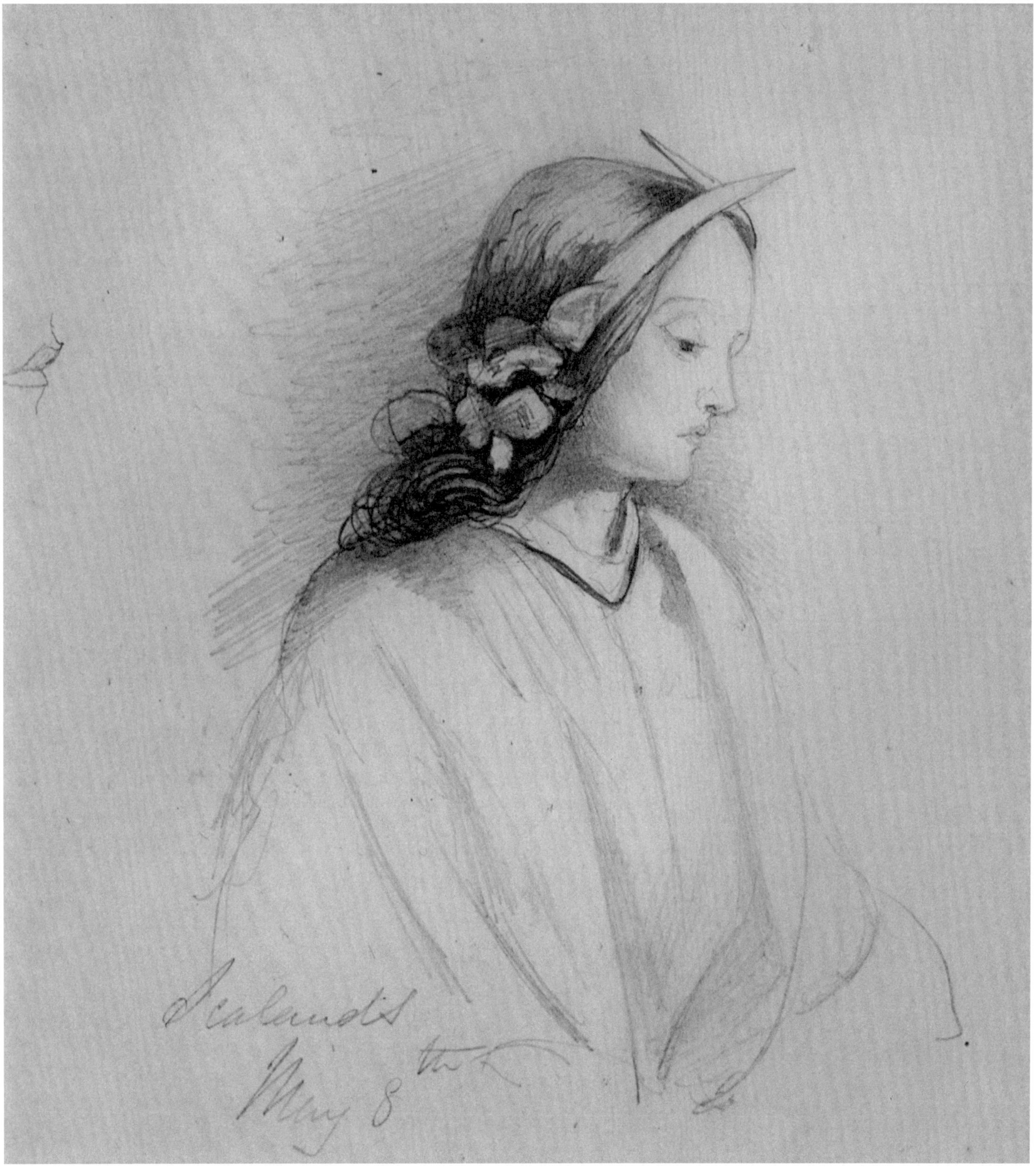

NO.144 Anna Mary Howitt, *Elizabeth Siddal* 1854, graphite on paper, 12.8 × 11.1

'Everyone adores and reveres Lizzy. Barbara Smith, Miss Howitt, and I, made sketches of her dear head with iris stuck in her dear hair the other day'

Dante Gabriel Rossetti

radiant career and her ties to such a vast creative and politically minded network, why has she been reduced to the rudimentary ideal of 'model and muse'? Surely there is more to her character than meets the eye.

As an upcoming professional artist and Pre-Raphaelite role model, Elizabeth exemplified the makings of a modern woman, or a 'New Woman', as they became known in the late nineteenth century. The term was coined in 1894 to characterise the many working, politically conscious and/or sexually liberated cultural luminaries whom we champion in contemporary society (for example, George Eliot, Cornelia Sorabji and Virginia Woolf). Simply put, the New Woman was a social and cultural phenomenon, who was perceived as destabilising the status quo. Yet, rather than existing in isolation, she found belonging in the respect and communal labour of her sisterhood. In emerging from a working-class background to sharing a studio and home with Gabriel outside of marriage, Elizabeth embodied the very characteristics of a New Woman.

Of the many myths surrounding her 'discovery' by the Pre-Raphaelite Brotherhood, it is believed that she was either approached while working in a hat shop by Walter Deverell to model as Viola in his *Twelfth Night* of 1850 or introduced by a mutual friend, the poet William Allingham, who had been courting a fellow milliner. Marsh challenges these assumptions, showing how Elizabeth utilised her contact with Deverell's father, then Secretary of the Government School of Design in London, to begin an artistic career among fellow craft persons. By 1853, she was modelling exclusively for Gabriel while developing her own medieval-inspired artistic expression, as we see in *Lady Clare* 1854–7 and *Lady Affixing Pennant to a Knight's Spear* c.1856 (see NOS.124, 118). Elizabeth and Gabriel developed a deep romantic attachment and later married, on 23 May 1860, in Hastings (an evidently important location for the couple). Elizabeth earned recognition as a Pre-Raphaelite of her own accord as the only woman to be exhibited beside the Brotherhood at the inaugural 'Pre-Raphaelite Exhibition' in 1857, and she was sponsored by the writer and artist John Ruskin for £150 per year. Ruskin dictated Victorian artistic tastes in many ways, so in dubbing Elizabeth an outright 'genius' he shone a light on her that other women were not easily afforded.[5] Despite these references, there is still little understood about Elizabeth's connection with other women artists or her political allegiances.

Indeed, the tension between the biographical omissions of Elizabeth's *political* opinions versus her deep *romantic* attachment to Gabriel need not continue framing our perceptions. If we are to truly understand Elizabeth, we must see past the historical accounts that have positioned her as the subservient muse of the Pre-Raphaelite Brotherhood. Turning our attention to three drawings of Elizabeth, we see how deconstructing this outdated classification ultimately enriches our understanding of Pre-Raphaelitism. These works were drawn by Bodichon, Howitt and Gabriel in the spring of 1854 while on holiday with Elizabeth at Scalands Farm. Scalands was Bodichon's ancestral home near the seaside town of Hastings. It became a place of refuge for many nineteenth-century New Women, including Jane Morris, George Eliot, Gertrude Jekyll and Elizabeth Blackwell (the first woman physician of the United States).[6] In the

NO.145 Dante Gabriel Rossetti, *Elizabeth Siddal in a Chair* c.1853, graphite on paper, 26 × 18.4

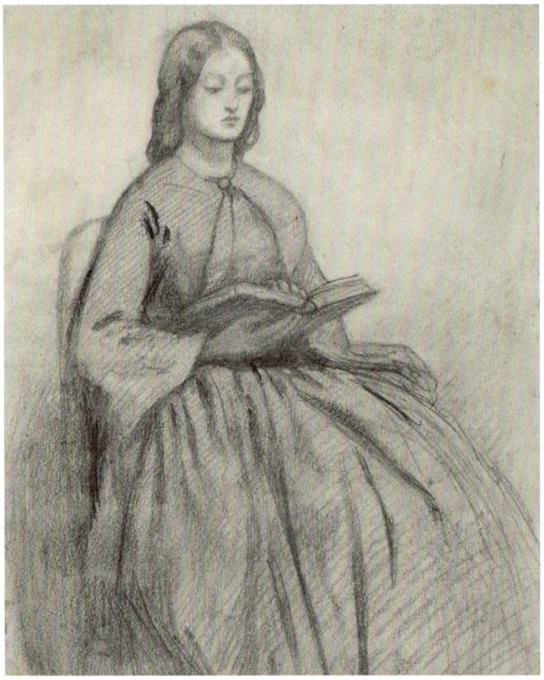

same year as the holiday, Bodichon importantly published *A Brief Summary, in Plain Language, of the Most Important Laws Concerning Women* (1854) - a treatise concerning the legal restrictions imposed upon her sex. Turning our attention to the drawings, the first by Bodichon shows Elizabeth's side profile (NO.149). Her soft wavy hair is pulled back from her face and adorned by a crown made of irises. These flowers, even in monochromatic graphite, draw our attention to her pearly skin. Bodichon signed this work and wrote the inscription 'Scalands. May 8th 1854'. Howitt's drawing developed Bodichon's design by presenting Elizabeth in three-quarter-length form (NO.144). Extending our eye from Elizabeth's downcast gaze to her dress and shawl, we are immediately granted more insight into Elizabeth's personality and self-expression. The V-shaped neckline of her dress meets the crown to frame Elizabeth's face as if she were a three-dimensional diamond. At first glance, Elizabeth appears silent and submissive like the stereotypical 'Angel in the House' championed by men of her century. Yet, the angularity of the head-dress and her unmistakable contemplation suggest something more is at work than meets the eye. The third and final sketch produced on this holiday, by Gabriel, shows a determined Elizabeth (NO.142). Less dejected than the previous sketches, her direct gaze and gently pursed lips emphasise a gravity of character and inner strength often omitted from previous biographical accounts. It is unsigned, but we know from Gabriel's correspondence that the trio sketched Elizabeth on this holiday. As he confided to his brother:

> Everyone adores and reveres Lizzy. Barbara Smith, Miss Howitt, and I, made sketches of her dear head with iris stuck in her dear hair the other day, and we all wrote up our monograms on the panel of the window, in memorial of the very pleasant day we had spent at the farm.[7]

Each of these portraits shows different aspects of Elizabeth's character, as perceived and interpreted by a group of artists in a single sitting. They invite us to see beyond clichéd categorisations, and instead reposition Elizabeth as a multifaceted New Woman artist and writer who operated within a wider artistic and feminist network that was forging a communal identity much like the Brotherhood.

In sketching Elizabeth from three different perspectives, Bodichon, Howitt and Gabriel shone a light on her multidimensional New Womanhood. However, in the Victorian period, the radicalism of a New Woman was reduced to the binary of either a feminist and champion of other social reform agendas or a prostitute. In art and literature, she was seen as either a conduit for the female mind or the apparent 'threat' it posed to convention. For example, in Woolf's essay, *A Room of One's Own* (1929), she embodied the intellectual independence of an educated woman; whereas, in John William Waterhouse's painting *Hylas and the Nymphs* 1896, she personified the deadly alluring qualities of the femme fatale which threatened masculinity. By way of contrast, the portraits of Elizabeth moved beyond reductive impressions of the female subject to instead harness her full potential. The intention behind these designs was far more in keeping with works by the Women's Suffrage Campaign, which represented New Womanhood using the spiritual and physical

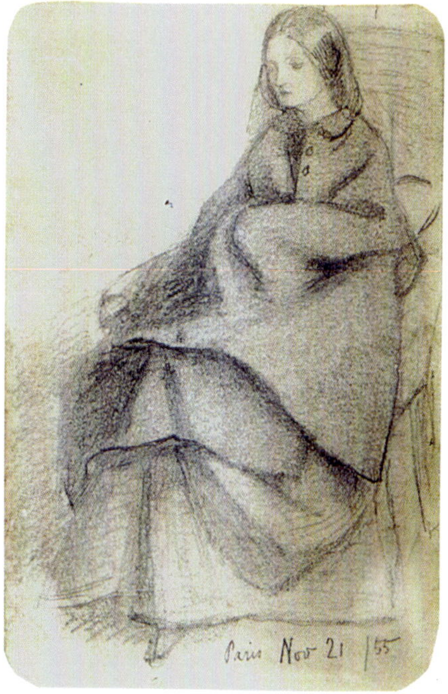

NO.146 Dante Gabriel Rossetti, *Elizabeth Siddal* 1855, graphite on paper, 12 × 9

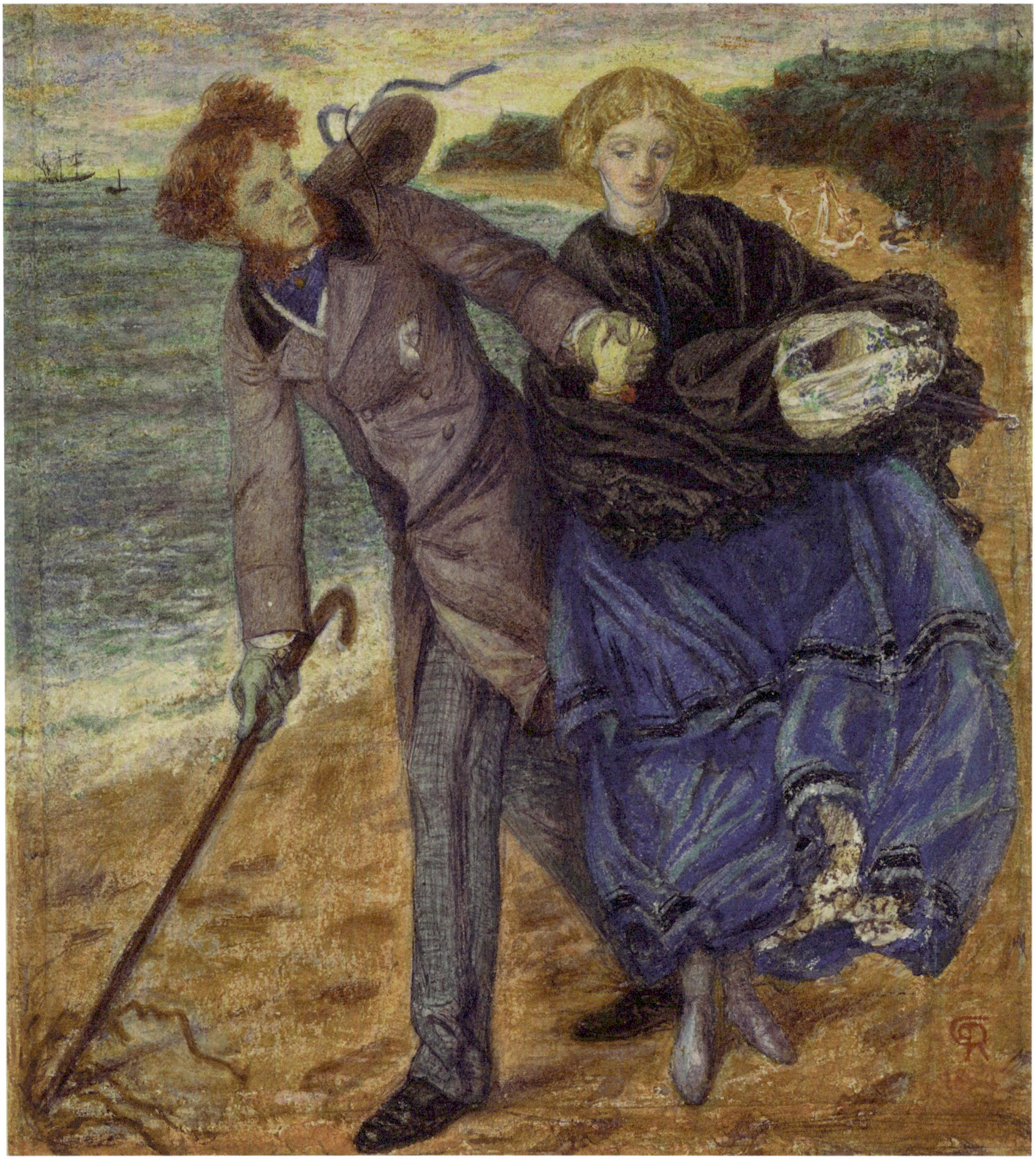

prowess of Joan of Arc (see works by Annie Swynnerton and Walter Crane for reference). The symbolism of the armoured saint recalled Gabriel's painting of the same subject produced in 1882 (see NO.218).

Given the political activities of Elizabeth's group, is it too big a leap to suggest that she shared the same values as Bodichon and Howitt? Although her sister-in-law, Christina Rossetti, was fiercely against women's suffrage, Elizabeth surrounded herself with many pro-women's rights supporters. Howitt first conceived the idea for an 'artistic sisterhood' with Bodichon and Bessie Rainer Parks (an equally committed feminist poet and founder of the *English Woman's Journal*) in the early 1850s. As Alexandra Wettlaufer, a historian in gender studies, describes: 'these women painted and wrote together, travelled through Europe, and strove to establish a new model of the female artist'.[8] By the mid-1850s, their extended network included Elizabeth, the artist Jane Benham, and many other women in the field of culture production. This sisterhood was inspired by, firstly, the collective efforts of the female spiritual community and, secondly, the contemporaneous fraternity of the Pre-Raphaelite Brotherhood. As a good-humoured sketch by Bodichon titled *Ye Newe Generation* illustrates (NO.148), these women intended to use palette, paint brushes and maulsticks to challenge not only the bullish art world but also the immobility, political disenfranchisement and tight-laced fashions of their sex. Elizabeth similarly utilised her artistic practice, networks, employment as painter and model, self-presentation, and unconventional and at times volatile relationship with Gabriel to forge her place in society.

The holiday to Hastings proved to be a key moment of sisterly compassion exhibited by the group to support Elizabeth in her physical and mental health. Gabriel had previously sought the counsel of these women with the hope that they might be able to sympathise with and help Elizabeth. He had trained with Howitt at Sass's Art School in the 1840s, and they remained good friends who contributed to the first instalment of the 'Folio' sketch club together with Bodichon in 1854.[9] The trip was organised by Bodichon who secured lodgings for Elizabeth at 5 High Street, Hastings, near to her own family home. Bodichon and Howitt were deeply concerned about Elizabeth's spirits and so urged Gabriel to travel up. He joined them shortly after his father's funeral, and it is said that the group spent a happy time together filled with lively conversation, good food and sympathetic understanding. Even so, the motivations behind this trip have prompted much discussion. Why did Elizabeth travel to Hastings? Was it to breathe the fresh sea air and relieve her consumption, which Bodichon believed explained many of her ailments? Or was the holiday taken for the change of scenery and the hope that it would lighten her spirits? Alternatively, was it to spend time with like-minded individuals? According to Diana Holman-Hunt, the granddaughter to the Pre-Raphaelite painter William Holman Hunt, Elizabeth journeyed to Hastings to convalesce from an illegal abortion. While we should never rely on speculation, one could read deep sorrow etched onto her countenance in two of the drawings (NOS.144, 149). Who is to say that her journey was not prompted by a combination of any or all of the above? Whatever the reaso\n, this trip and the culminative drawings reveal Elizabeth's character in greater depth.

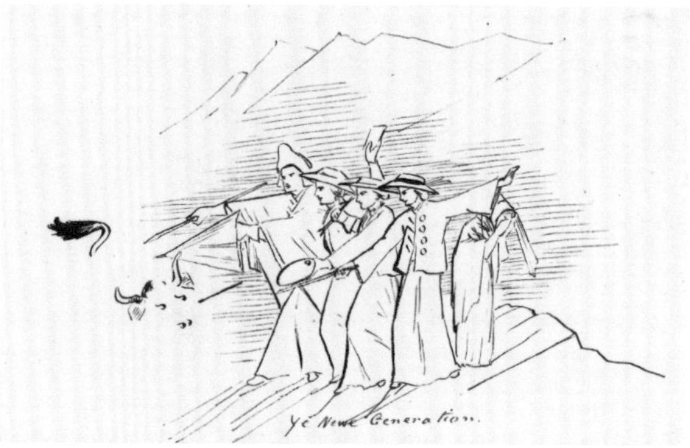

OPPOSITE
NO.147 Dante Gabriel Rossetti, *Writing on the Sand* 1858–9, watercolour on paper, 26.3 × 24.1

ABOVE
NO.148 Barbara Leigh Smith Bodichon, *Ye Newe Generation* c.1850, ink on paper, 11.2 × 17.5

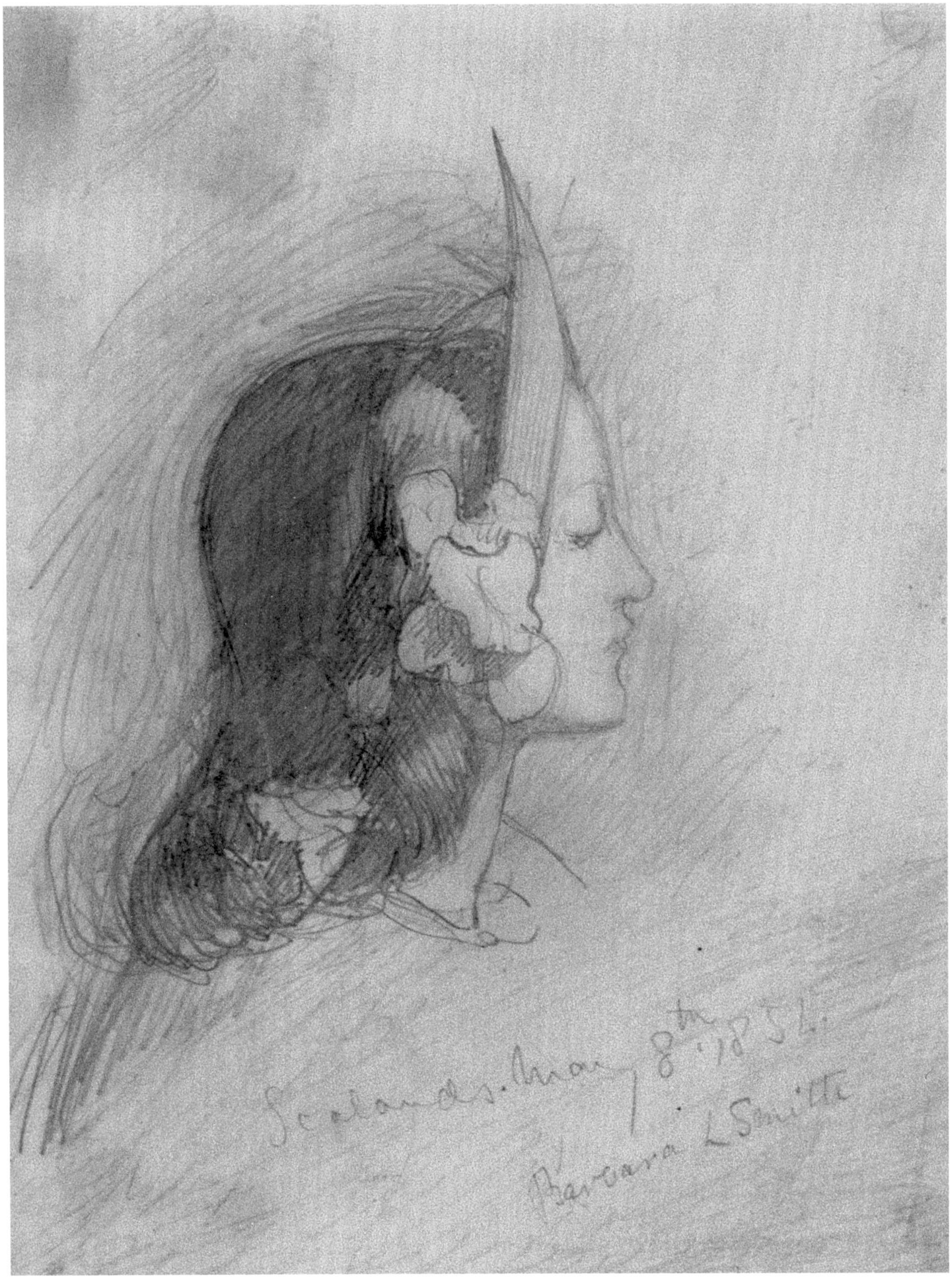

NO.149 Barbara Leigh Smith Bodichon, *Elizabeth Siddal* 1854, graphite on paper, 11 × 9

Recognising the three-dimensional New Elizabeth before us means we can better understand the hardships of New Women at a time when they were reduced to binaries. When society dictated that a woman should be caged, submissive and refrained, Bodichon and Howitt reinterpreted each of these gendered stereotypes to reflect the many radical ideals championed in *Ye Newe Generation*. Firstly, in selecting an unmarried, working woman as their chosen subject, Bodichon and Howitt immediately challenged conventional standards. Secondly, Elizabeth's downcast gaze in Howitt's drawing would traditionally be synonymous with female subjugation. Yet, Howitt externalises the inner torment of Elizabeth's life – an undoubtedly relatable emotional context for many women. Thirdly, Bodichon's interpretation and the final illustration further capture the grace exhibited by countless women to master their own thoughts and feelings – the same strength of character we see reflected in the political activities of Bodichon and other women's rights campaigners. Elizabeth's headdress of irises and leaves, therefore, becomes a coat of armour, a crown against the tide of patriarchal biases. It gives new meaning to a flower commonly associated with leadership, wisdom, purity and passion. Elizabeth's apparent 'refrain' is in fact based on the understanding of her own power and potential. Hence, these drawings can be viewed as a collective self-portrait for a new age of nineteenth-century womanhood.

'But where is Gabriel in this history?', one may ask. While the sisterhood embraced the collegial origins of the female spiritual community and effectively countered the fraternal spirit of the Pre-Raphaelite Brotherhood, their everyday activities worked in dialogue with their male counterparts. As this holiday shows, Gabriel was a key member of this collective. He, Howitt and Bodichon were long-standing friends who together recognised Elizabeth's strength of character, creativity and new womanhood. The third illustration by Gabriel (NO.142) moves beyond his customary portrayal of Elizabeth as the virgin mother (*The Girlhood of Mary Virgin* 1848–9; *Ecce Ancilla Domini! (The Annunciation)* 1849–50; see NOS.53, 73) or the doomed lover from various medieval tales (*Paolo and Francesca da Rimini* 1855; *Dante's Dream at the Time of the Death of Beatrice* 1856; see NOS.121, 76). Its emphasis on her psychology is far more in keeping with *Beata Beatrix* c.1864–70 (see NO.10), which he painted while mourning Elizabeth's death.

Elizabeth has been described as a secondary artist compared to her husband. She has been viewed as a 'model and muse' through the lens of male Pre-Raphaelitism rather than its sisterhood of New Women. These classifications run the risk of understating her significant contribution to art history, social history and the fight for women's rights. The trio of drawings analysed in this chapter represent the clear challenge made by both women and men artists against rudimentary social standards. Like the original works that Elizabeth modelled in and painted, she habitually saw herself as a modern-day Guinevere. Intelligent, beautiful, and without subscribing to social and economic norms, she embodied the virtue, potential and reality of women throughout history. In speaking to all these moments, these drawings mark the self-portraits of a sisterhood at work in the past, present and future. They importantly reveal a New Elizabeth to Pre-Raphaelite audiences

1 Jan Marsh, *The Legend of Elizabeth Siddal*, London 1989; Catia Rodrigues, '(De)Constructing Aesthetics: The Employment of Professional Models by the Pre-Raphaelite Group, 1848–1865', British Association for Victorian Studies Annual Conference, University of Birmingham, 1 June 2022; Alex Round, 'Transcending Boundaries: Race and Ethnicity in Rebecca Solomon's "The Young Teacher"', British Association for Victorian Studies Annual Conference, University of Birmingham, 1 June 2022; Serena Trowbridge, 'The Drama of Womanhood: Literary Portraits by Emma Sandys', British Association for Victorian Studies Annual Conference, University of Birmingham, 1 June 2022. See also Glenda Youde and Robert Wilkes (eds.), *Pre-Raphaelite Sisters: Art, Poetry and Female Agency in Victorian Britain*, Oxford 2022.

2 Alongside Georgiana's artistic career and life with Edward Burne-Jones, her sisters Alice, Agnes and Louisa made notable contributions to nineteenth-century art and literature. In addition, Alice married Lockwood Kipling and raised their son, the laureate Rudyard Kipling. Agnes married the Royal Academician Edward Poynter, who became both the director of the National Gallery and president of the Royal Society. Louisa married Alfred Baldwin and their son, Stanley Baldwin, served as Prime Minister three times. Judith Flanders, *A Circle of Sisters: Alice Kipling, Georgiana Burne-Jones, Agnes Poynter and Louisa Baldwin*, London 2002.

3 Alexandra Wettlaufer quoting Herbert Sussman, in Wettlaufer, 'The Politics and Poetics of Sisterhood: Anna Mary Howitt's "The Sisters in Art"', *Victorian Review*, vol.36, no.1, Spring 2010, p.130.

4 Pamela Hirsch, *Barbara Leigh Smith Bodichon: Feminist, Artist and Rebel*, London 1998.

5 William Michael Rossetti (ed.), *Ruskin, Rossetti, Preraphaelitism: Papers 1854 to 1862*, New York 1899, p.63.

6 Scalands was also visited by male luminaries such as John Ruskin and Henry Fawcett (a women's rights campaigner, married to the suffragist Millicent Fawcett, who campaigned peacefully for political change).

7 William Michael Rossetti 1899, pp.7–8.

8 Wettlaufer 2010, p.132.

9 This club was founded by John Everett Millais. Members (who were predominantly male and female Pre-Raphaelites) contributed sketches of artworks in progress to a Russian leather portfolio on a monthly basis and received feedback. While we cannot know if the three sketches of Elizabeth were intended for the Folio Club, it is interesting to note that Gabriel may have taken the portfolio with him to Scalands in May. See Roger W. Peattie (ed.), *Selected Letters of William Michael Rossetti*, London 1990, p.50.

Carol Jacobi

The House of Life: Designs for Living

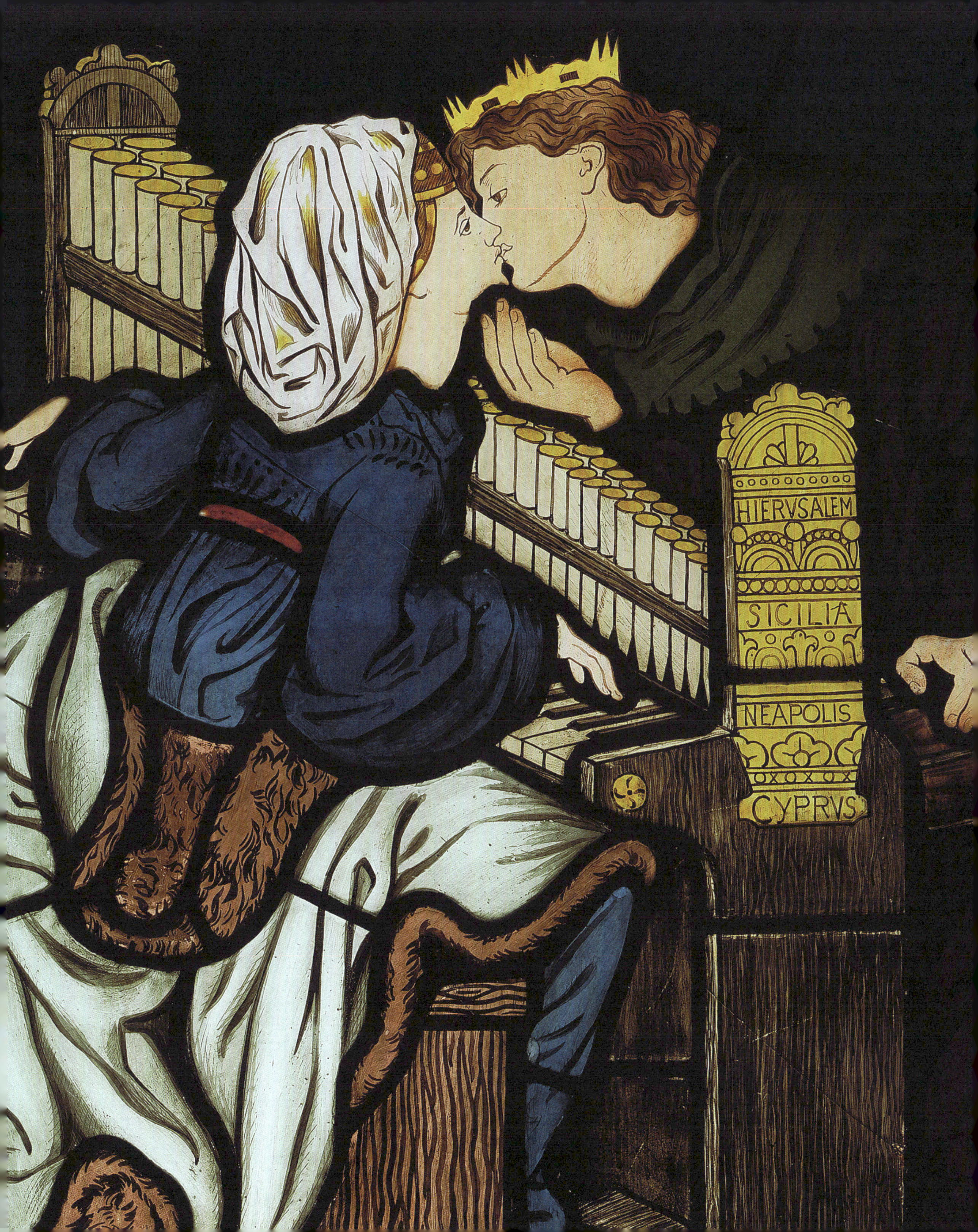

HIERVSALEM
SICILIA
NEAPOLIS
CYPRVS

'I was a child beneath her touch,—a man
When breast to breast we clung, even I and she,—
A spirit when her spirit looked through me,—
A god when all our life-breath met to fan
Our life-blood, till love's emulous ardours ran,
Fire within fire, desire in deity.'

Dante Gabriel Rossetti, 'The Kiss',
The House of Life, c.1860

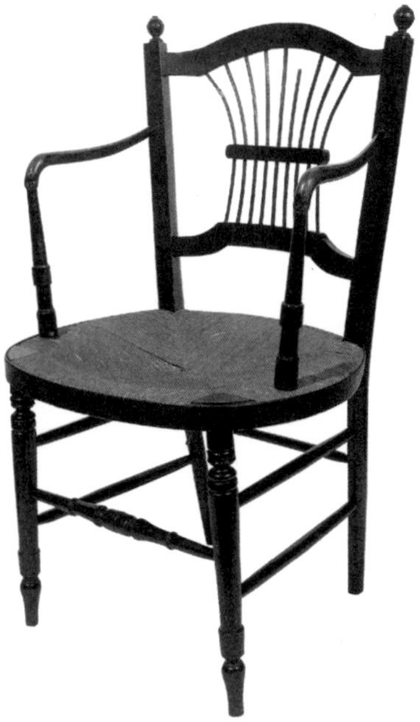

The Rossettis reinvented the way they loved and lived, and reflected this in their domestic environments. Their passions were pursued and performed in a range of domestic models outside the conventional framework of marriage. Maria and Christina Rossetti stayed with their mother in Bloomsbury until their deaths, devoted to writing, teaching and community work through the Anglican church. Cross-class relationships had scope for greater flexibility, adapting more informal working-class lifestyles and master-student, servant-employer models. Gabriel and Elizabeth dwelt in close association at 14 Chatham Place, Blackfriars, for six years, without marrying. His later, long relationship with Fanny Cornforth was accommodated in a bachelor household at 16 Cheyne Walk, Chelsea, which he shared with male associates (and an animal menagerie), and where she was described as 'housekeeper'. William Michael would remain single until his forties, moving between the female and mainly male households of his sisters and his brother.

The Rossettis' correspondence suggests that they carefully considered the emotional and existential implications of love and marriage; its complexities were a central theme of their art. Poems and paintings explored asymmetrical power relationships between men and women and people of different socio-economic status, and the group associated with campaigners for improved marriage rights for women. When marriage was not rejected, as in the case of Christina and Maria, it was reimagined. Gabriel and Elizabeth defied class conventions to wed, in May 1860, after a period of estrangement. Elizabeth died 21 months later, in February 1862. William Michael and the artist and writer Lucy Madox Brown married in 1874. They were the only members of the generation to raise children, after which they separated and remained in touch. Elizabeth and Lucy maintained their careers, but with a reduced scope.

Gabriel and Elizabeth's short marriage was part of a rethinking of domestic love in their wider circle that was to have enormous implications for art and artists. Another working and working-class woman, Jane Burden, had recently wed Gabriel's young associate William Morris, and Ford Madox Brown was discreetly married to Emma Hill. The artists Georgiana Macdonald and Edward Burne-Jones wed a few months later. All these couples were setting up new lives in new homes. Their unconventional households came together in a decisive moment of redefinition to create new art and designs for living. These new homes helped lay the foundation for the Aesthetic movement, which unified the arts and realised the concept of the palace of art, or *Gesamtkunstwerk*.

These relationships accorded with the emerging spirit of socialism that the friends shared. In an echo of Maria and Christina's community work, Gabriel, Ford Madox Brown, John Ruskin and others in the circle taught at the Working Men's College from its establishment in Camden in 1854, in the aftermath of Chartism. It was the first liberal adult education of its kind in Europe. William Morris and Edward Burne-Jones joined them, and Morris would go on to be a political writer and one of the founding members of the first organised socialist political parties. The collaborative Rossetti model that catalysed their careers and the Pre-Raphaelite project was continued in William and Jane Morris's commission of Red House as home and commune.

The Rossettis were people of their times: their art and correspondence reveal prejudices of their day around gender, race and class, but their community were rethinking many of these questions. A degree of equality is reflected in the roles of women and people of working-class background, like Elizabeth and Jane, as writers, artists and craftspeople. The Rossettis associated with important campaigners for women's rights and education, such as Anna Mary Howitt, Barbara Leigh Smith Bodichon, and Elizabeth and Robert Browning. Christina famously did not sign up to women's suffrage, but argued for female representation in Parliament and against the exploitation of women in sexual commerce or arranged marriages. Regarding race, the group were generally against imperial oppression and slavery. Anti-slavery was a mainstream position by this time, however, and they retained racialised European fantasies of an imagined 'orient'.

The conspicuous consumption that characterised fashionable Victorian interior design did not suit the group's tastes and became associated with more conservative Victorian values. Classically inspired carving and gilding enhanced by cheap gesso and shiny veneers – like those in William Holman Hunt's modern life painting *The Awakening Conscience* – were seen as meretricious, and the circle aspired to express more authentic lives in authentic environments. They co-operated in searching out and adapting items of furniture that were beautiful and basic, true to their materials and methods of making. They found this beauty in handcraft, such as wood turning or embroidery, rather than elaborate ornament. They were inspired by vernacular folk crafts, Asian artefacts flooding into Britain via the Empire, and revivals of medieval styles. The open, gracefully turned and simply painted shapes of Regency and Regency revival furniture, for example, appealed. Gabriel painted little oval insets representing Love, the Loving or Lover, and the Beloved onto a Regency revival sofa for Chatham Place (NO.152).

PAGE 147
NO.150 Dante Gabriel Rossetti, *King René's Honeymoon – Music* c.1863 (detail), stained and painted glass, 64.2 × 54.7

OPPOSITE
NO.151 Morris & Co., 'Rossetti' chair c.1870, ebonised beech and rush, 82 × 52 × 45.5

BELOW
NO.152 Dante Gabriel Rossetti and Morris, Marshall, Faulkner & Co., sofa and cushion c.1862, open-back sofa of wood painted black and partially gilded, the back painted with three figures in oval medallions inscribed 'Amor', 'Amans' and 'Amata' (Love, the Loving or Lover, and the Beloved), upholstered with contemporary green cut velvet, 82.6 × 198.1 × 66

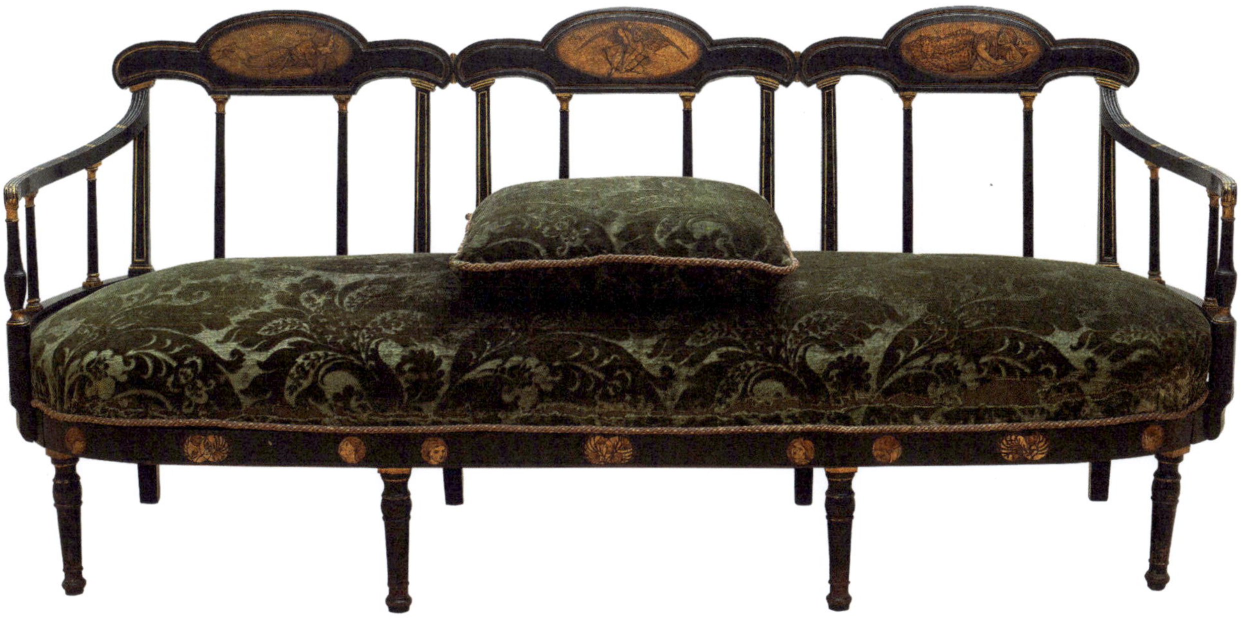

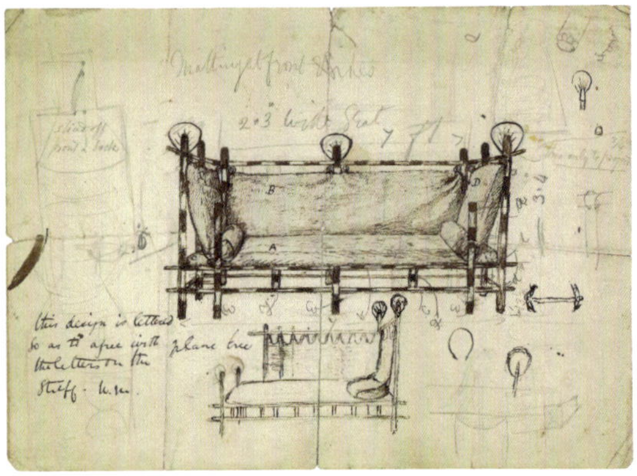

NO.153 Dante Gabriel Rossetti, *Two Designs for a Sofa* 1861–2, brown ink, over graphite, on paper, 24.3 × 33.9

He and Elizabeth liked nimble French Provincial chairs with unupholstered rush seating and simple, inexpensive furniture woven from rattan from East Asia (see NOS.160, 161). The couple searched out decorative objects and textiles which they associated with medieval and global cultures, most famously seen in Gabriel's collection of blue and white pottery and porcelain from China. They developed an aesthetic fed by an 'orientalist' European fantasy of Asian, African and South American cultures as exotic, mysterious and archaic.

Plain items were bought or commissioned for the purpose of painting, in the spirit of Ford Madox Brown's, Gabriel's and Elizabeth's medieval-modern watercolours and oils. These were more widely known since they had been exhibited in the *Pre-Raphaelites* exhibition in Russell Square in 1857. Edward Burne-Jones decorated a wardrobe as a wedding present for Jane and William Morris on which she featured as the Virgin Mary in Geoffrey Chaucer's medieval *Prioress's Tale*. Gabriel gave them three large panels for a settle depicting Dante Alighieri's *New Life*: *The Salutation of Beatrice in Florence*, *Dante's Love* (*Dantis Amor*, symbolising Beatrice's death) and *The Salutation in the Garden of Eden*, while Elizabeth joined Morris, Ford Madox Brown and others in painting a mural of life-sized Biblical figures in Jane and William's bedroom.

She and Gabriel decorated a jewel casket with medieval scenes after a manuscript by the medieval Italian Christine de Pizan which was eventually given to Jane (NOs.156, 157). Pizan's proto-feminist celebration of eminent women was little known in the nineteenth century but appears to have been an enthusiasm for the Rossettis' circle. At the same time, Jane Morris was beginning a series of embroideries of eminent women for the Red House dining room and Gabriel's last painting of her was in the role of one of these, Joan of Arc (see NO.218).

Elizabeth and Gabriel also planned new, modern wallpaper based on natural rather than classical forms and traditional rather than industrially produced colours. His design modernised the garden of love motif, giving the effect of life-size trees at dusk in which apples glow in the starlight. The wallpaper was never realised, only the drawing and colour notes are known, but a sense of its appearance can be gained today from the reconstruction by the artist Ilyanna Kerr (NO.154). In 1862, William Morris designed his first wallpaper on a similar garden theme, based on a trellis at Red House, in which roses rather than apples evoked love. On this occasion, he worked for two years to develop a viable method of production, printing with wood blocks, and went on to develop a range of wall-hangings.

Morris, the wealthiest of the friends, was the most indefatigable in his commissions and creations of furnishings and furniture that expressed the circle's emotional, aesthetic and social needs. In 1861, Gabriel was one of six collaborators in a commercial design cooperative, Morris, Marshall, Faulkner & Co., Fine Art Workmen in Painting, Carving, Furniture and the Metals, which made and marketed these for a wider clientele. The French provincial chair was adapted and reproduced as the 'Rossetti' chair, for example (NO.151). Gabriel contributed three of ten painted panels for the *King René's Honeymoon Cabinet* for the architectural office of John P. Seddon (NO.159). It celebrated the fifteenth-century patron of the arts, King René of Anjou, who created a castle for his new wife, Jeanne de Laval. It was reminiscent of the 'Palace of Art' in Tennyson's poem of

NO.154 Ilyanna Kerr after Dante Gabriel Rossetti, wallpaper design, 2023

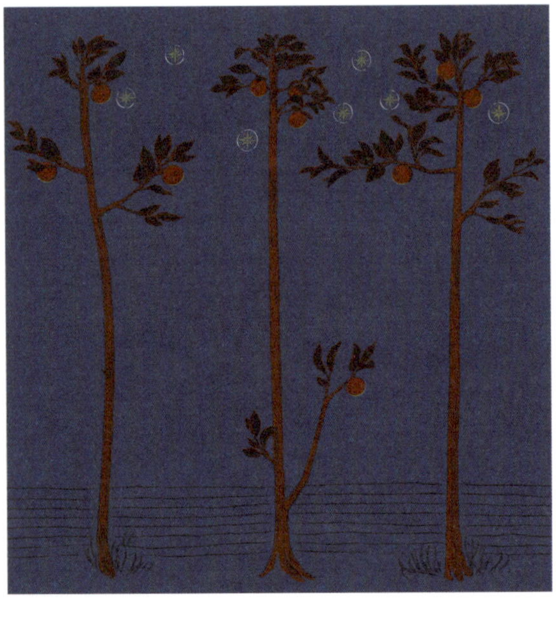

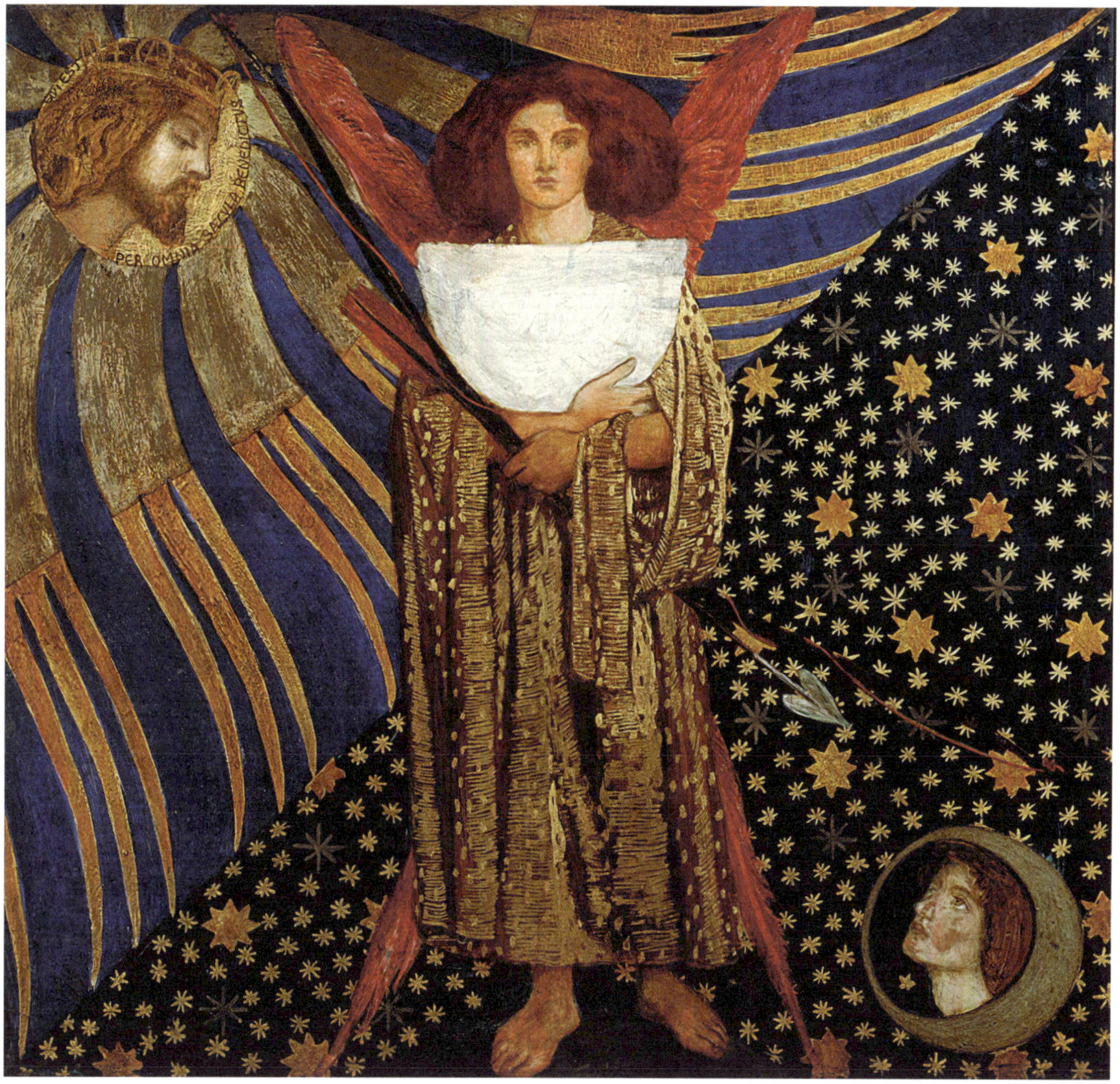

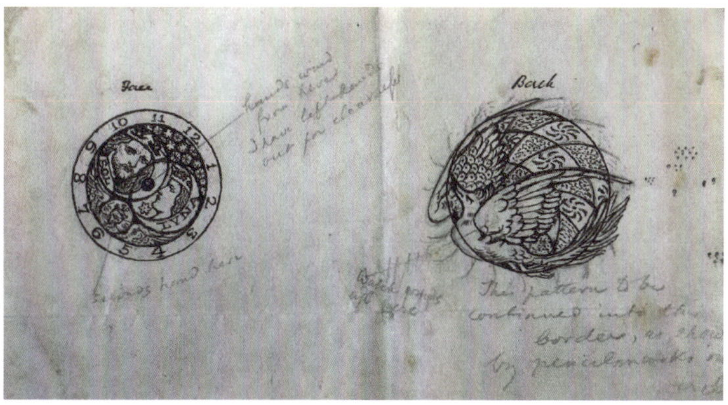

NO.155a Dante Gabriel Rossetti, *Dantis Amor* 1860, oil paint on mahogany, 74.9 × 81.3

NO.155b Dante Gabriel Rossetti, *Design for the front and back of a watch* 1862, ink and graphite on paper, 11 × 20.5

RIGHT
NO.156 French School, 'A hundred ballads of a lady and her lover' c.1410–15, from the works of Christine de Pizan, Queen's Manuscript (London, British Library, Harley 4431, folio 376 recto)

BELOW
NO.157 Dante Gabriel Rossetti and Elizabeth Siddal, medieval-style jewel casket, belonging to Jane Morris, c.1859, wood bound with studded iron bands, 17.7 × 29.2 × 17.7

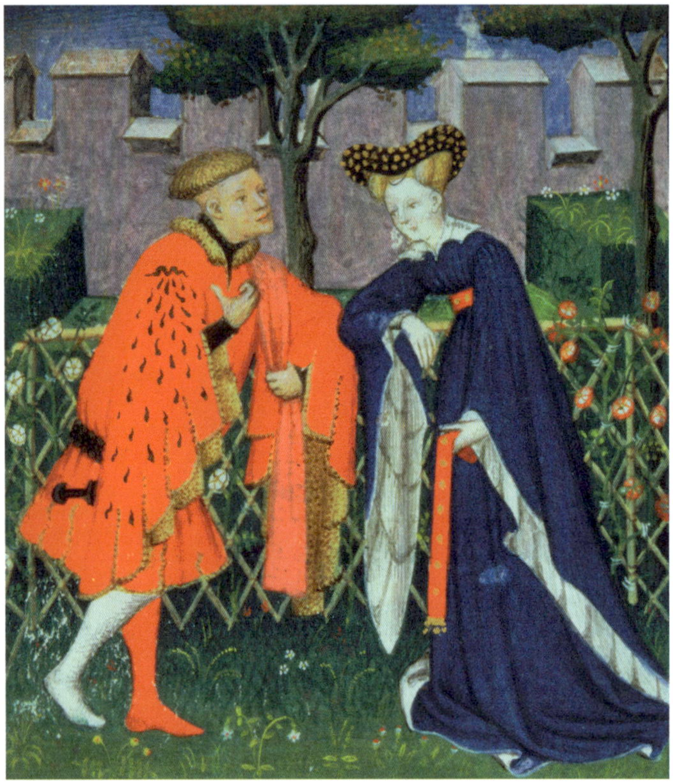

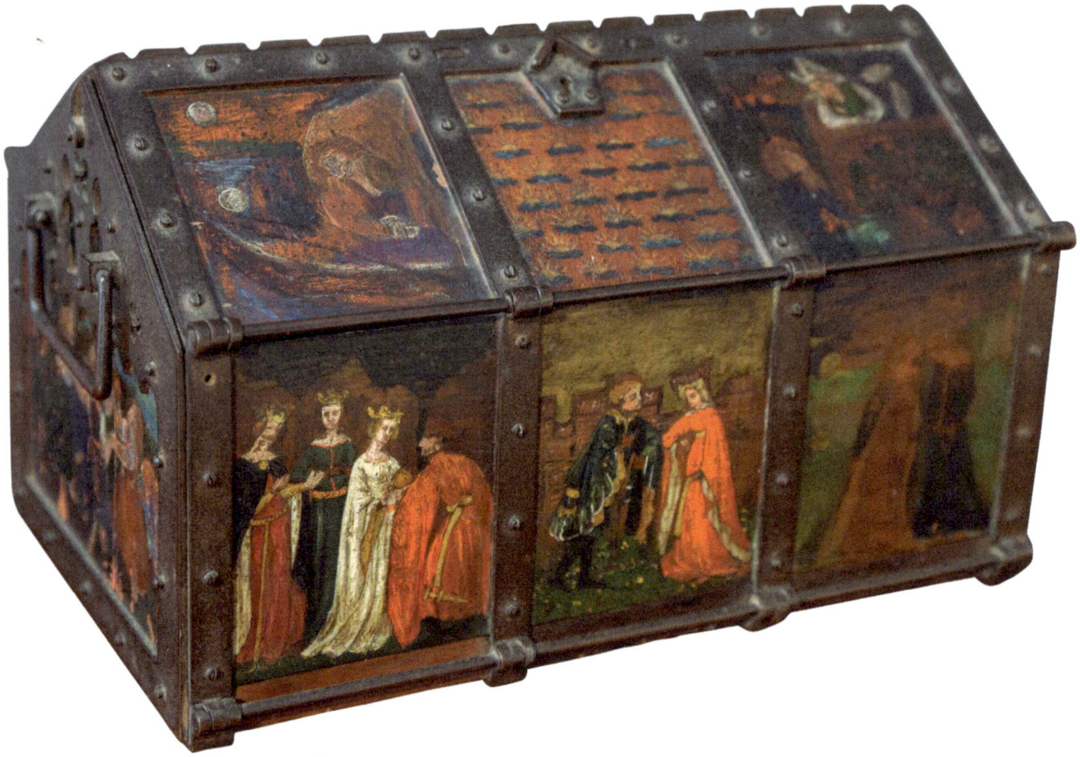

RIGHT
NO.158 Dante Gabriel Rossetti, *King René's Honeymoon – Music* c.1863, stained and painted glass, 64.2 × 54.7

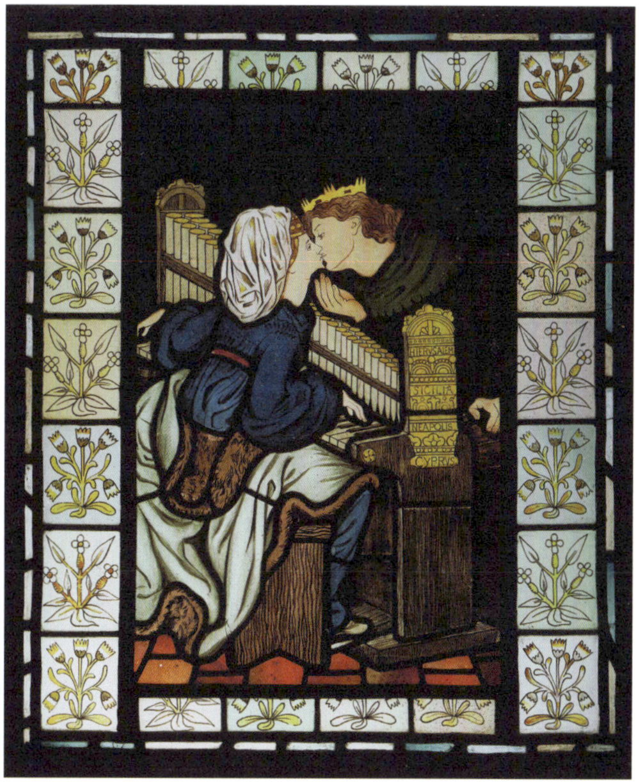

BELOW
NO.159 Ford Madox Brown, Edward Coley Burne-Jones, William Morris, Valentine Cameron Prinsep, Dante Gabriel Rossetti and John Pollard Seddon, *King René's Honeymoon Cabinet* 1861, oak, inlaid with various woods, with painted metalwork and painted panels, 133.4 × 252 × 87

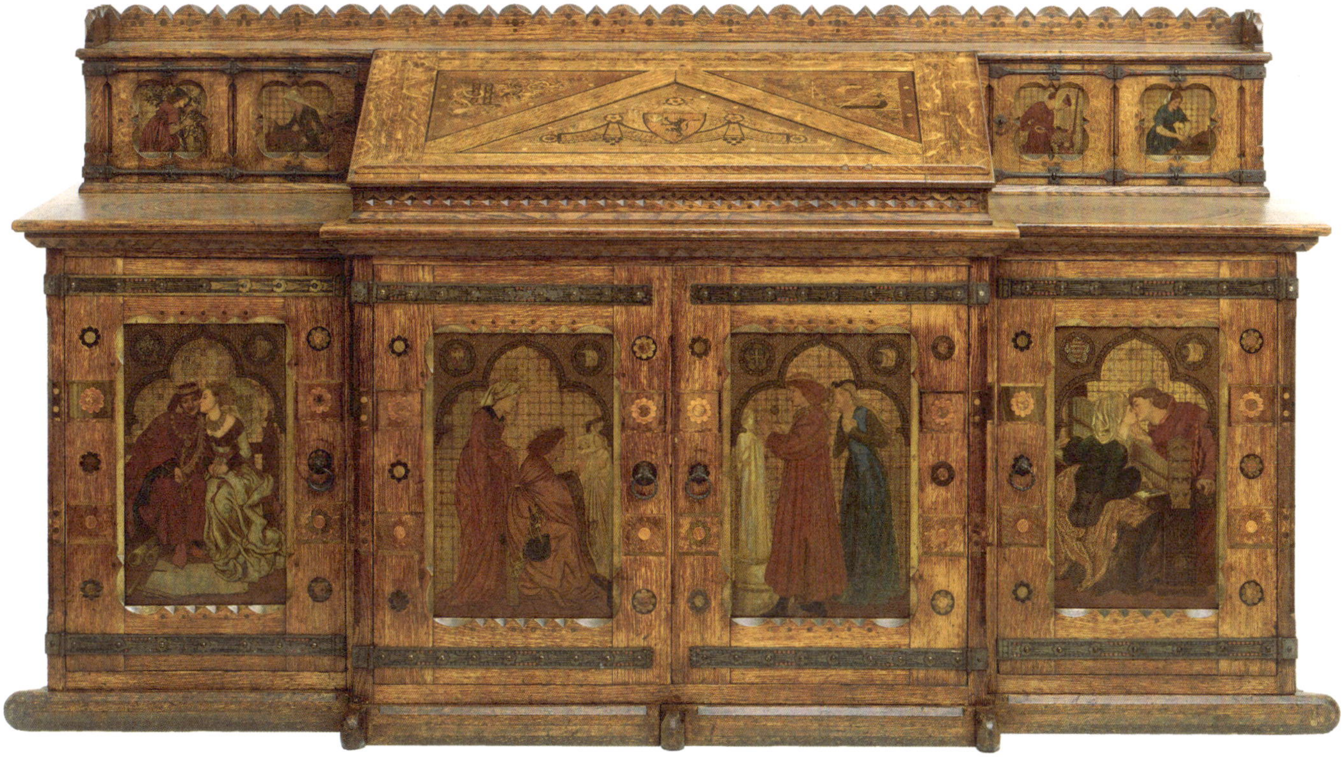

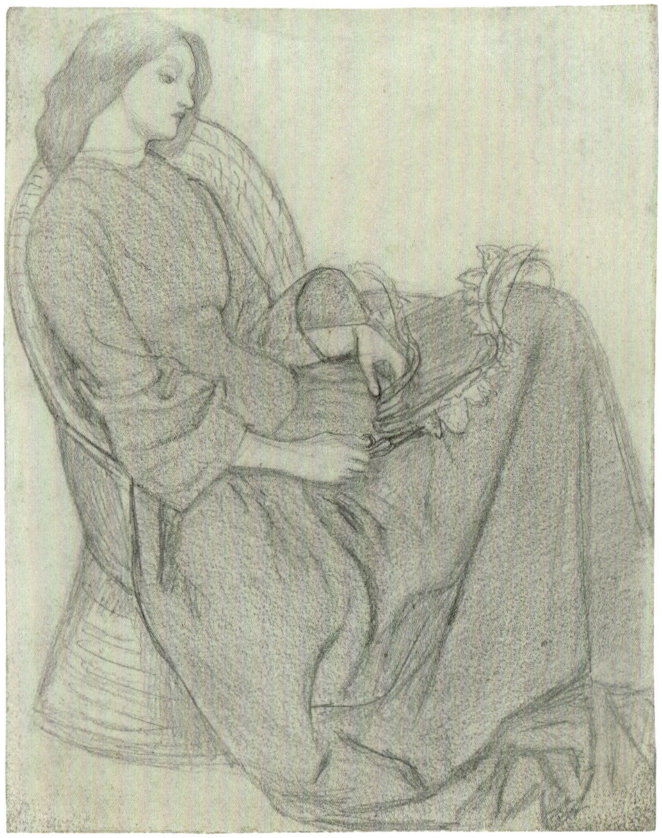

LEFT
NO.160 Dante Gabriel Rossetti, *Portrait of Elizabeth Siddal* c.1857, graphite on paper, 18.8 × 15.3

BELOW
NO.161 Dante Gabriel Rossetti, *Elizabeth Siddal in Basket Chair*, date not known, graphite on paper, 18.8 × 15.3

OPPOSITE
NO.162 Dante Gabriel Rossetti, *Elizabeth Siddal playing a stringed instrument* c.1852, graphite on paper, 18.4 × 12.1

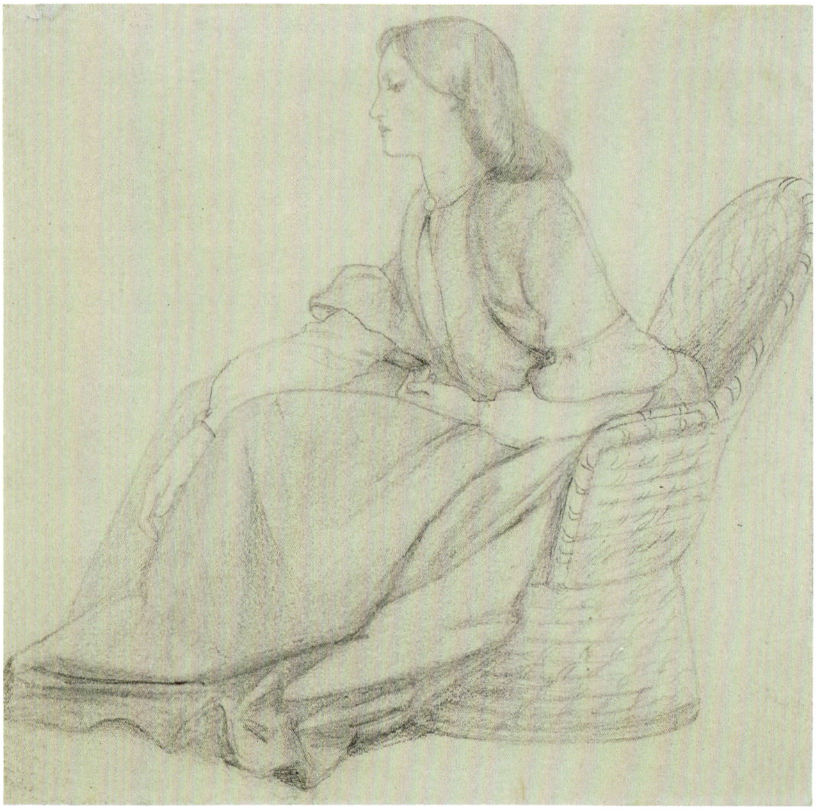

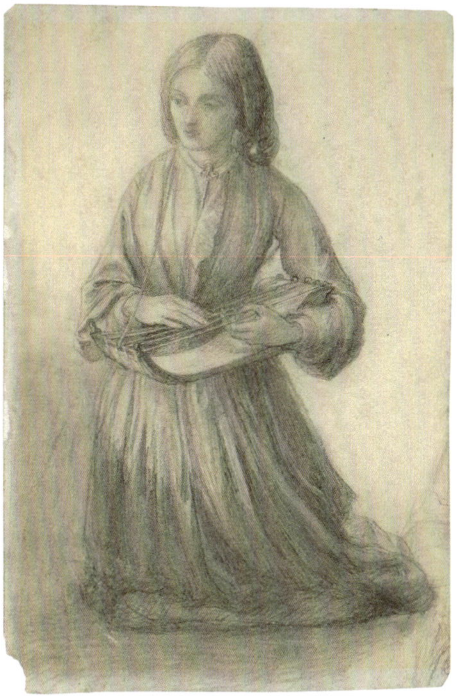

that name (1832) and a model for the Morris's Red House. The cabinet was imagined as an artefact commissioned for René and Jeanne's castle. Gabriel's panels celebrated gardening and music, adapting an earlier illustration of lovers meeting over a keyboard from 'Palace of Art', engraved by the Dalziel Brothers and published in 1857. The design was reused in a series of domestic stained-glass panels (see NO.158). Morris explored possibilities for growing the firm, combining modern and traditional methods which replaced exploitative and mass production with practices that respected individual creativity and labour. Women continued to play a major role, Jane becoming an internationally respected embroiderer and her daughter May taking a leading part. In 1875, William took over the firm as Morris & Co., which played a key role in the international Aesthetic and Arts and Crafts movements.

Men and women also evolved more authentic ways of dressing. Victorians aspired to the frills and crinolines of the rich, but Elizabeth devised a plainer look, with natural materials and an eye to colour. She was a trained seamstress and designed clothing without crinolines and corsets, based on looser gowns, conventionally worn for working or relaxing in private. They were less encumbered by cuffs and collars, and, at the same time, revealed the wrists and throat. Hair was also freed from buns and bonnets and worn in looser manners. Gabriel sketched Elizabeth like this, resting or painting, reading and plaiting her hair. An undated drawing shows Elizabeth seated in a rattan basket chair holding scissors as she snips a fabric, her plain dress falling loosely over her body and her hands free (NO.160). Elizabeth and Jane wore their graceful gowns outside the private realm, inspiring alternative fashions aligned with medieval styles and William Morris's Arts and Crafts firm, which became known as 'aesthetic' dress. Freedom of movement was associated with freedoms of other kinds. Gabriel went on to design jewellery, and even a watch framing the motif of time in the life and death imagery of 'Dantis Amor' (see NOS.155a, 155b).

Love was expressed in every creative form: art and poetry, design and music. Gabriel's wooded wallpaper recalled the wood of love guarded by a child, at once cupid and angel, in Elizabeth's drawing of *Lovers Listening to Music* c.1854 (NO.163). There is no story. Instead, Elizabeth creates a timeless and exotic atmosphere by including young women racialised to appear East Asian. Their instruments recall both medieval and East Asian designs, evoking an orientalist fantasy of archaic sound and song. Gabriel drew Elizabeth in a similarly fantasised role (NO.162). He was also moving away from story-telling in favour of atmosphere and aesthetic effect. Like *Lovers Listening to Music*, *The Blue Closet* 1857 combined two singers and two musicians, resembling Elizabeth (NO.164). A medieval and orientalist mood is created by archaic costume and instruments and the blue and white tiles. This interest in exchanges between the arts in the guise of colour, form, rhythm and musical sound was described by Pre-Raphaelite Brother and art critic Frederick Stephens: 'Colour is as much an art as music being in fact to the eye what music is to the ear – the expression of beauty.'[1] *The Blue Closet* is like a small *Gesamtkunstwerk*. It was an inspiration to William Morris, who owned it and wrote a poem of the same title.

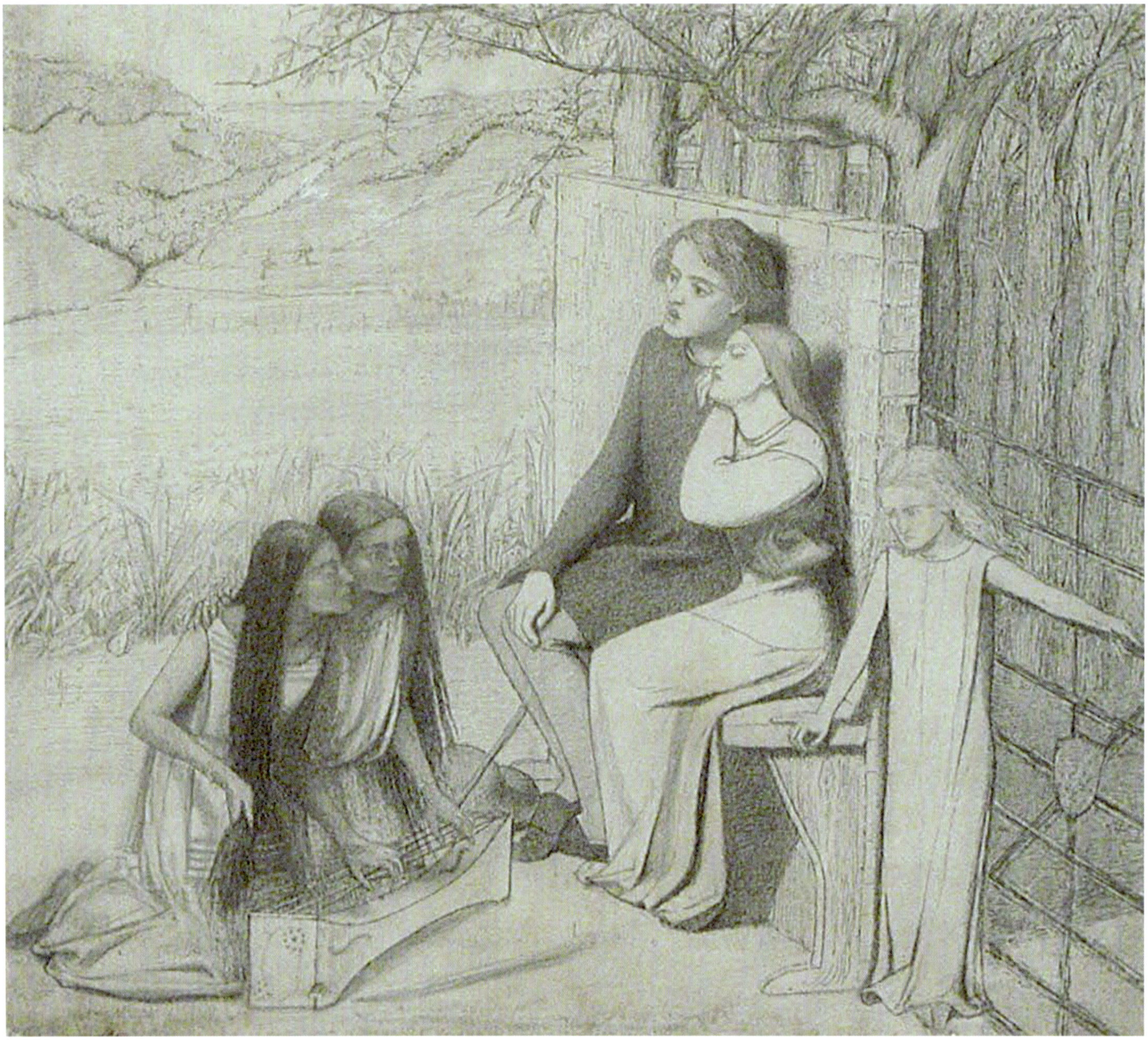

ABOVE
NO.163 Elizabeth Siddal, *Lovers Listening to Music* c.1854, graphite and ink on paper, 37.8 × 39.8

OPPOSITE
NO.164 Dante Gabriel Rossetti, *The Blue Closet* 1857, watercolour on paper, 35.4 × 26

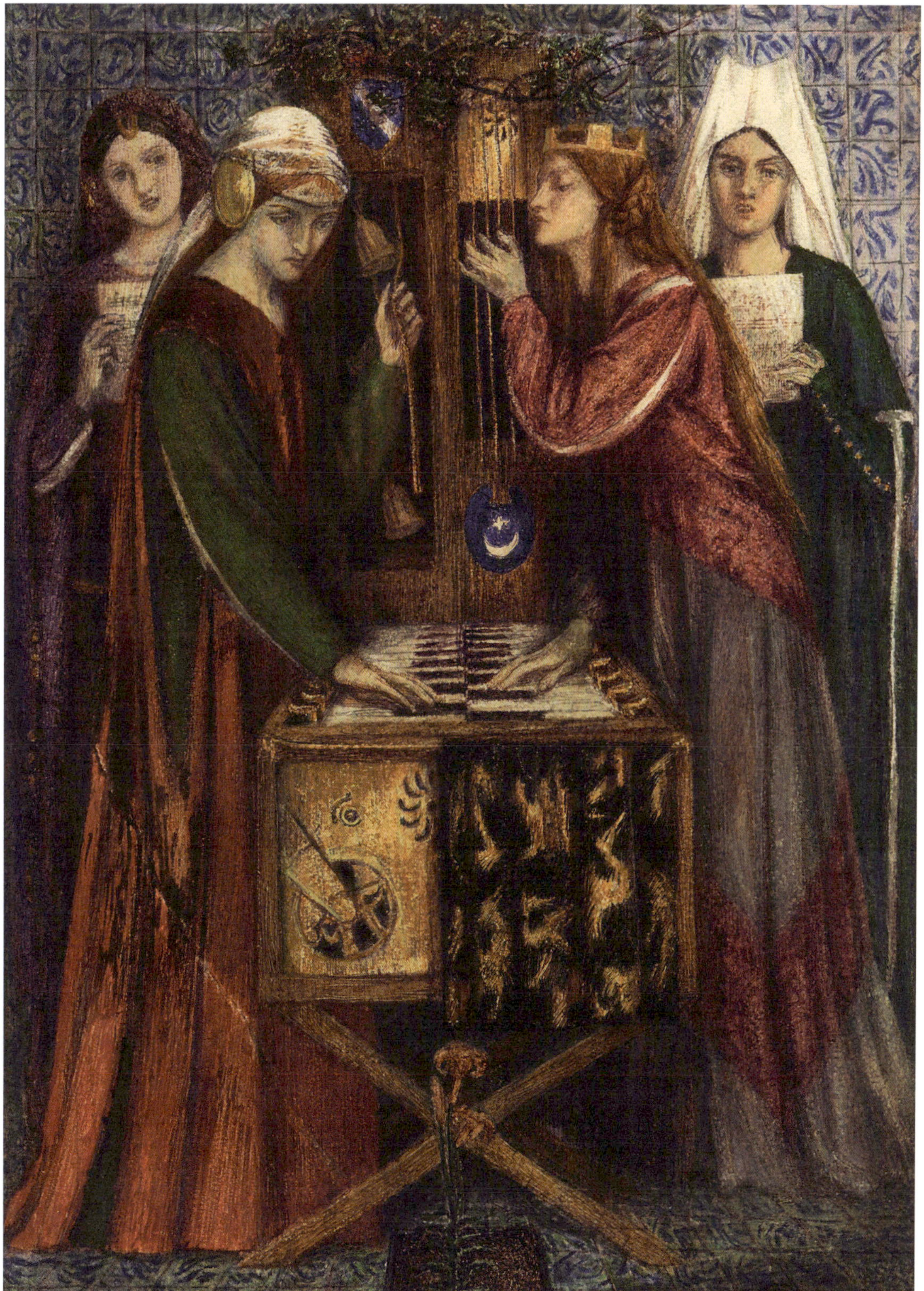

Nuptial Sleep

Dante Gabriel Rossetti

At length their long kiss severed, with sweet smart:
And as the last slow sudden drops are shed
From sparkling eaves when all the storm has fled,
So singly flagged the pulses of each heart.
Their bosoms sundered, with the opening start
Of married flowers to either side outspread
From the knit stem; yet still their mouths, burnt red,
Fawned on each other where they lay apart.

Sleep sank them lower than the tide of dreams,
And their dreams watched them sink, and slid away.
Slowly their souls swam up again, through gleams
Of watered light and dull drowned waifs of day;
Till from some wonder of new woods and streams
He woke, and wondered more: for there she lay. [c.1861]

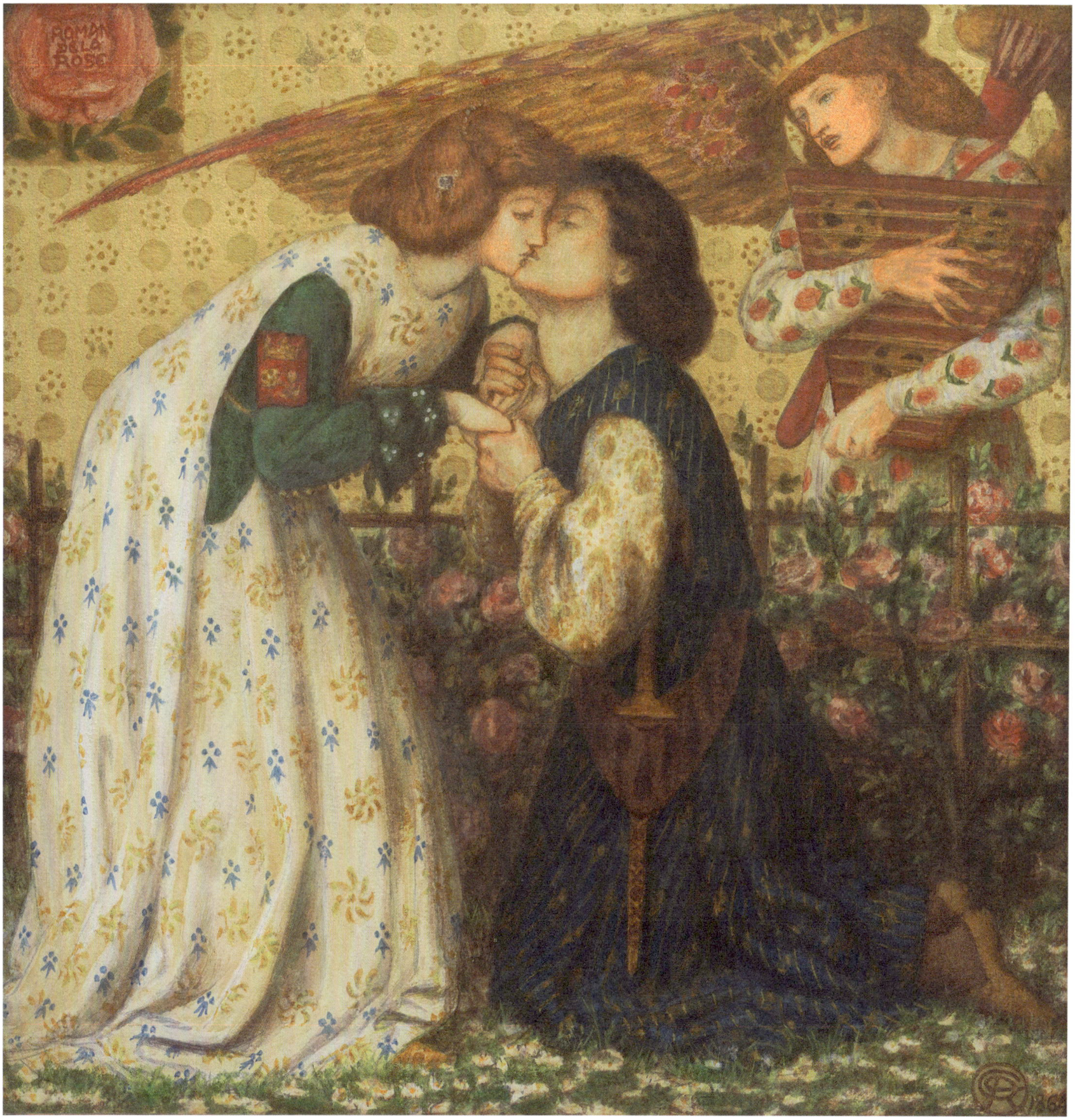
ROMAN
DE LA
ROSE
1864

PAGE 159
NO.165 Dante Gabriel Rossetti, *Roman de la Rose* 1864, watercolour on paper, 34.3 × 34.3

BELOW
NO.166 Dante Gabriel Rossetti, *The Early Italian Poets from Ciullo d'Alcamo to Dante Alighieri* 1861, book, open at frontispiece, 18 × 12

The spiritual and sensual convergence of love and art is distilled in Gabriel's paintings and poems around the theme of the kiss, a motif explored in *Carlisle Wall* and *The Wedding of St George and Princess Sabra* (see NOS.126, 127). In the first panel of *Paolo and Francesca da Rimini* (see NO.121), art in the form of a vivid medieval manuscript encourages the illicit embrace that will condemn the lovers to execution and Hell. Music inspires the kiss in *The Palace of Art, Music* and *Love's Greeting* (1861, Isabella Stewart Gardner Museum, Boston), in which an angel serenades lovers in another garden of love, inscribed in Italian, like the sofa, 'Love, the Lover and the Beloved'. *Love's Greeting* derived from a French thirteenth-century poem of courtly love, Guillaume de Lorris's *Romance of the Rose*, which Gabriel had translated ten years before. It was also realised as a design for his first book, *The Early Italian Poets* (1861; NO.166) and a later watercolour, *Roman de la Rose* (1864; NO.165).

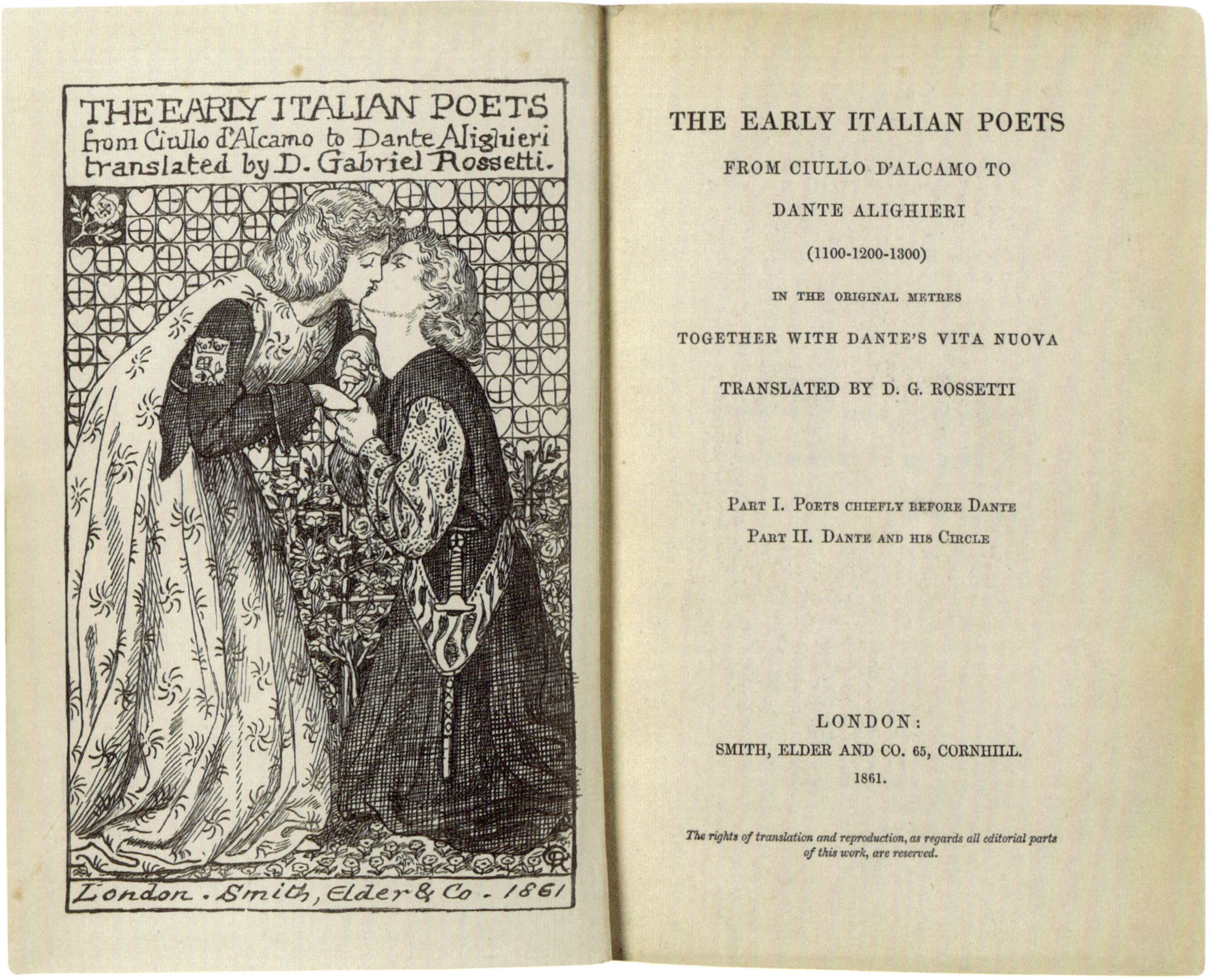

'Colour is as much an art as music being in fact to the eye what music is to the ear – the expression of beauty'

F.G. Stephens

The Early Italian Poets assembled translations of texts from the time of Dante Alighieri, culminating in *Vita Nuova*, Dante's reflection on his love of Beatrice, written in alternating sonnets and commentary. William Michael translated the prose and Gabriel the poems, prioritising their aesthetic aspects of rhythm and language over literal meaning. This project was entwined with Gabriel's ambition to create his own *Vita Nuova*. He traced his own and Elizabeth's emotional and artistic journey in a series of poems, called *The House of Life*, which modernised Dante's text. In the work, Gabriel reflected on love in his own terms and personal voice, dwelling on the sensual and aesthetic, most powerfully evoked in the sonnets 'The Kiss' (see p.148) and 'Placatâ Venere' (the peace of Venus, referring to sleep after sexual consummation).

Gabriel's work on his translations and on his own love poems throughout 1861 was suddenly interrupted by Elizabeth's death on 11 February 1862. Perhaps *The House of Life* project seemed over in all its aspects. For whatever reason, he made the drastic decision to place his poetry in Elizabeth's coffin. Although he continued to write, his first poetry volume, *Poems*, was not published until 1870, when he was 42, after the manuscript had been retrieved from Elizabeth's tomb. He had left out the most earthy poem from *Early Italian Poets* ten years before, but when he finally published the unfinished *The House of Life*, in *Poems*, he included 'Placatâ Venere', under the more direct English title, 'Nuptial Sleep' (see p.158). It is tempting to wonder whether he was partially encouraged by William Michael's edition of Walt Whitman's poems in 1868. *Poems* was well-received and influential within the Aesthetic circle, but was generally condemned as obscenely 'fleshly' with a focus on 'Nuptial Sleep'.[2] Gabriel's poetic reputation did not reach that of his sister Christina during his lifetime, but the wider Aesthetic achievements developed during the short-lived experiment in living laid the foundation for the success of the embowered portraits in his mature style

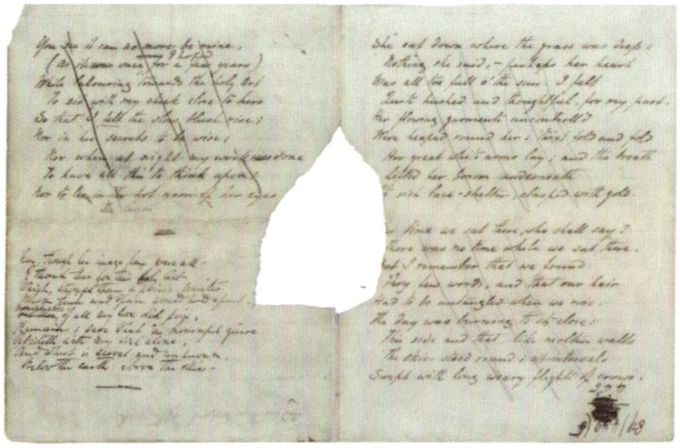

NO.167 Dante Gabriel Rossetti, manuscript of 'The Portrait in the Library' c.1847–50, ink on paper, 20.2 × 32.2

1 Frederick Stephens, 'The Royal Academy', *Macmillan's Magazine*, June 1860, p.160.

2 Robert Buchanan, 'The Fleshly School of Poetry', *The Contemporary Review*, August–November 1871, vol.18, pp.334–50.

Chiedza Mhondoro

Sensitivity and Possibility: Reading Dante Gabriel Rossetti's *The Beloved* Through Fiction

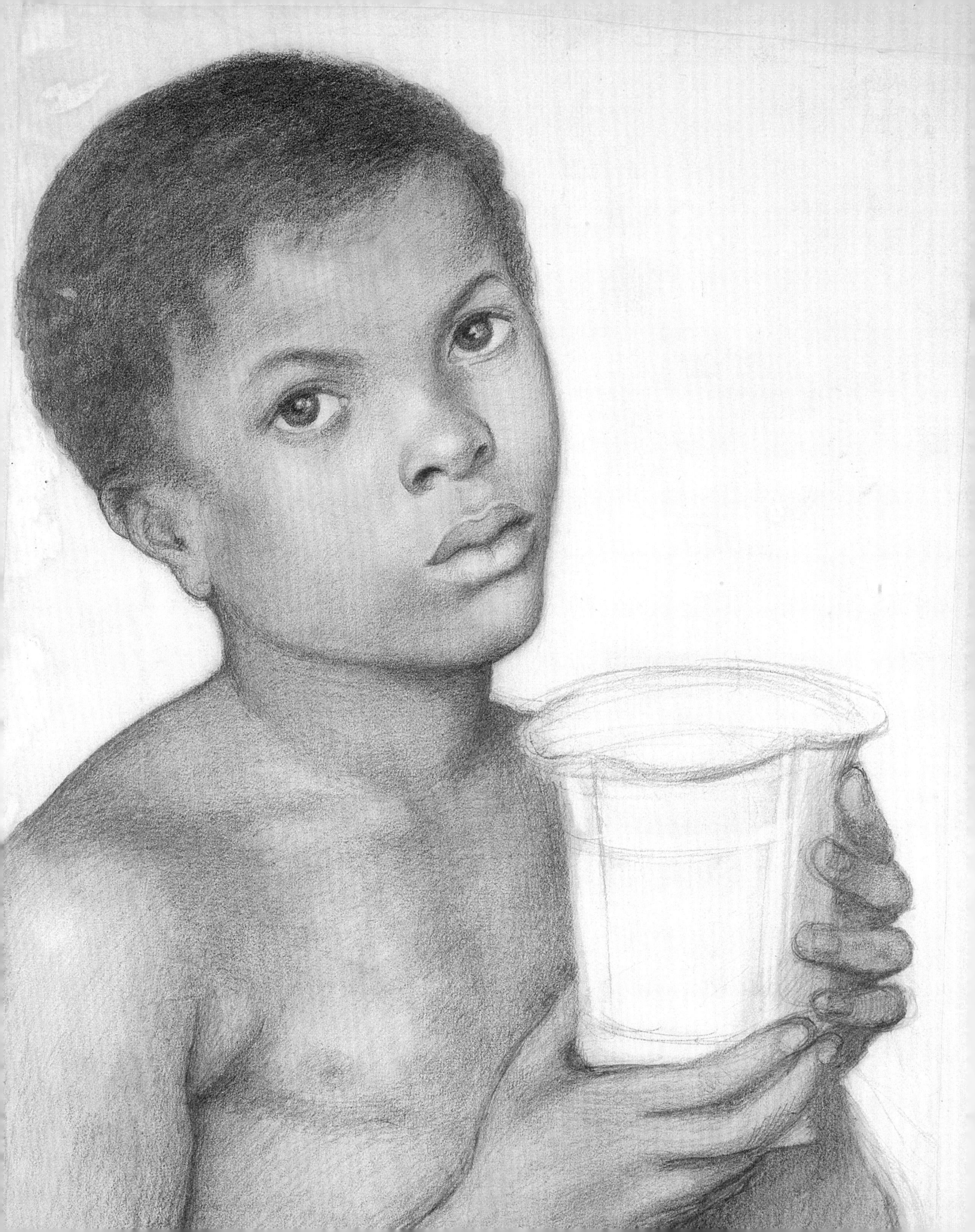

'Sit still!' He wants to continue drawing me now. Why's he happy I'm crying? Won't that ruin his picture? I only wanted to play in the garden and see all the beasts he said he had. I didn't mean for him to get angry. Will he tell Sir? I was told to be good. He's really looking at me, sit still. Am I replacing the girl in the picture because she was bad? My stomach's hurting again. Will he paint it hurting, or just my head and shoulders like the girl's? Mr Ro-sse-tti. Dan-te Gabriel Ro-sse-tti. Funny name, but he sounds just like the other men Sir's come to meet in London. He's strange though...

'Ar-ma-di-llo.' He's telling me about the animals again. Ar-ma-di-llo. Arma-dillo. Do all houses in Chelsea (is that where the cab driver said we were going?) have so many beasts in the garden? Wombats, dormice, owls, peacocks, a white bull ... oh to see a white bull in here with all this china. He'd smash it all, and the clocks and frames and cabinets and looking glasses. He'd smash the other beasts in the garden too! Sir would never allow his gardens to be this wild. He'd surely tell Winston and Charlie to keep them tidy. I feel better now ... but mustn't smile or talk or move my neck. Did the girl cry too when she sat like this?

'Song of Solomon!' He's seen me looking at his picture of the women. 'Pure black boy.' I'm the pure black boy. But boys don't wear jewels. Who's Solomon? 'Mulatto', he called the girl I'm replacing. One, two, three, four, five; me and five ladies. Their robes and jewels... I've never seen anything like it. Looks like they're coming out of the picture to me. Is the white lady in the middle sad or happy? She must be the special one and the others her friends. And I'm the most different. That's why he came to me outside the hotel. They don't have eyes or hair like me, and their lips are so pink. Do they have children? Have they left them somewhere?

'Eyes here!' He's really looking at me. His pencil moves so fast. Does the girl have a master like me, or her mammy still? I've never met a painter before. Not when travelling with Sir, or running errands, or at the house. Where's Mr Rossetti's helper? Will he draw me too? I want the cab back. Ar-ma-di-llo. Arma-dillo. Armadillo. I like when Mr Rossetti tells me about the beasts.

'Turn to the side!' He's come so close again, look away. His eyes are so grey. And sad. Warm fingers, look away. I don't want him to get angry at me again. Chin down, turn to the side, sit still. A 'canvas' he called those. Can-vas. I'm cold and want my shirt back. '*Venus Verticordia*.' I don't understand. He's looking at the canvas too. Is that the lady's name? Was she cold when she worked for Mr Rossetti like me? Naked skin and flowers too. But I'm different. There are no Black boys in any other pictures here. Or Black men and women. I'm the only one here. And in the house. My stomach hurts again... Sit still.

'A few more minutes...' My neck hurts and I want my shirt back. The windows are tall and it's bright but there's no warmth coming through. I don't want to be looked at anymore. But Sir said I must be good. Don't cry, he's looking. The Solomon women are looking too, and Venus, and the others in all the pictures. They're all looking. Don't cry. I'm crying. He's stopped drawing. 'Do you miss your mammy?' There's no air. Is the cab back? Don't cry be good Sir said be good. I do want my mammy. He's so close again. Why won't he stop looking at me?

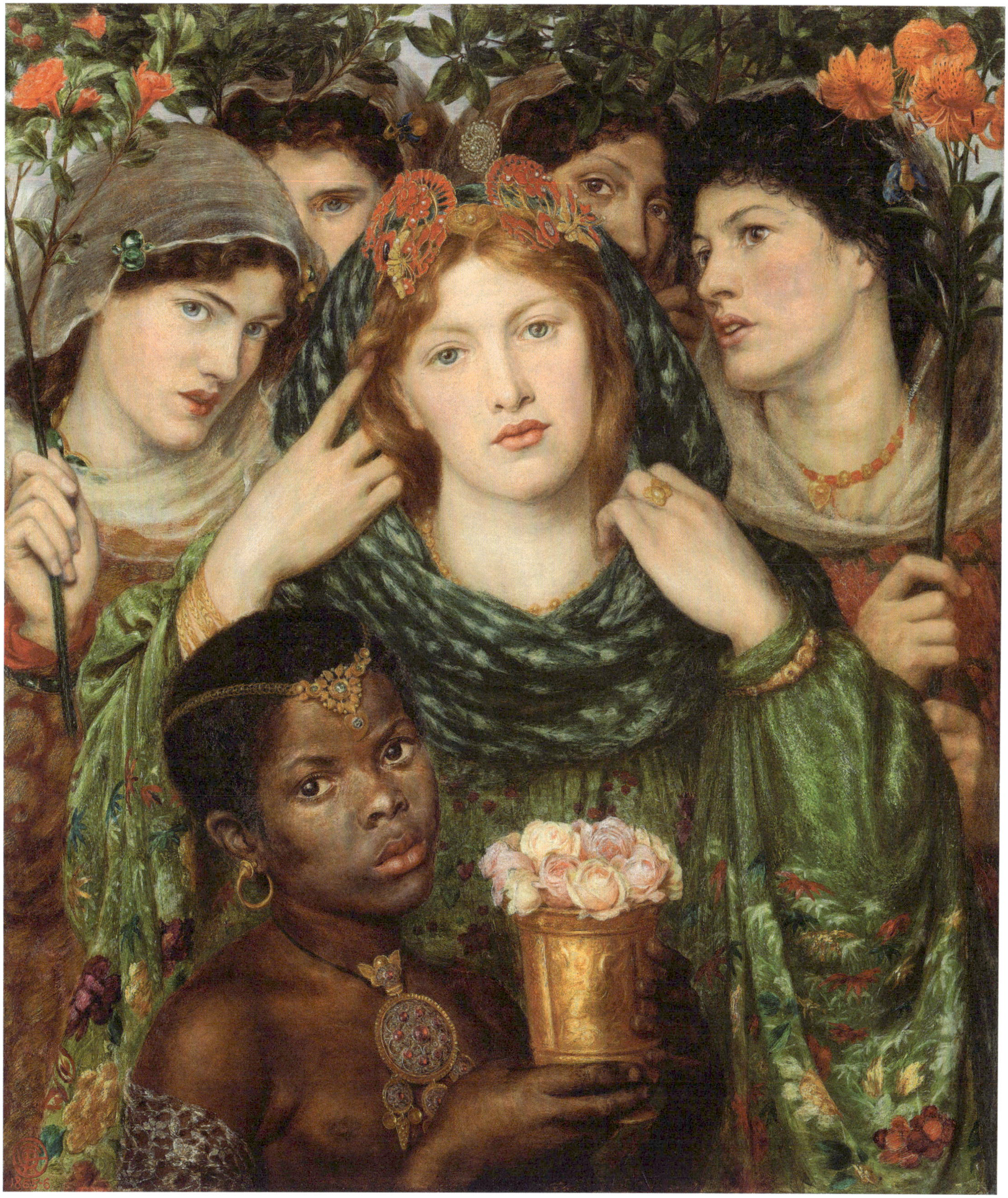

PAGE 163
NO.168 Dante Gabriel Rossetti, *The Beloved – Study for a Boy* 1865–6, black chalk over graphite on cream wove paper, 49.5 × 37.4

PAGE 165
NO.169 Dante Gabriel Rossetti, *The Beloved ('The Bride')* 1865–6, oil paint on canvas, 82.5 × 76.2

In the spring of 1865, a young boy visited the studio of Dante Gabriel Rossetti to sit for his painting, *The Beloved* (NO.169). His identity is not recorded, beyond the fact that he was in the charge of an adult staying at a London hotel. The picture was nearly complete, but Gabriel wished to replace the girl child attendant he had previously painted. He made two preliminary drawings (NOS.168, 170), so the boy may have sat on more than one occasion. Gabriel immortalised the child's face in *The Beloved*, yet little is known about him, and he remains restricted within the social and racial hierarchies visualised in the artist's fantasy.

There are no archival records of the boy's life experiences, no biography, not even a name. Black presence in Victorian England is visualised in painting, drawing, photography, sculpture, illustration and ephemera, but the narratives were largely constructed by those whose racialisation did not match that of whom they depicted. It is difficult to determine how the visual record of Black sitters correlates with their experiences, as there are few first-hand accounts, or, as stated by Saidiya Hartman, 'there is no access to the subaltern consciousness outside dominant representations or elite documents'.[1] This essay began with an imagination of the boy's stream of consciousness as he sat for Gabriel. Where the experiences and presentation of the subaltern are dictated by the elite, can fiction provide a multi-dimensional perspective more sensitive to the lives of those who are deemed inferior?

Writing on the specific context of the archive of enslaved people in the United States, Hartman uses the term 'critical fabulation' to describe her strategy for portraying the lives of the enslaved as fully as possible. By rearranging fragments of the archive through literature, she attempts to 'displace the received or authorized account, and to imagine what might have happened or might have been said or might have been done'.[2] To the context of oppression and racism engendered by the promotion of Western or imperial scientific knowledge, post-colonial scholar Aimé Césaire argued for the ability of poetry and literature to fill the void created by the privileging of such knowledge.[3] The fictional narrative presented at the beginning of this essay is a creative exploration that borrows strategies from the disciplines of history and literature and combines the fragmented references to the child with scholarship on the Rossettis to sketch details of what might have been when the boy sat for Gabriel.

OPPOSITE, CLOCKWISE FROM TOP LEFT

NO.170 Dante Gabriel Rossetti, *The Beloved (Study of a Boy)*, reverse, likely 1865, 49.5 × 37.4

NO.171 Dante Gabriel Rossetti, *The Beloved (Study)* c.1865, chalk and graphite on paper, 41.2 × 30.1

NO.172 Dante Gabriel Rossetti, *The Beloved (Study of a Girl)* 1864–5, black chalk and graphite on paper, 43.1 × 35.5

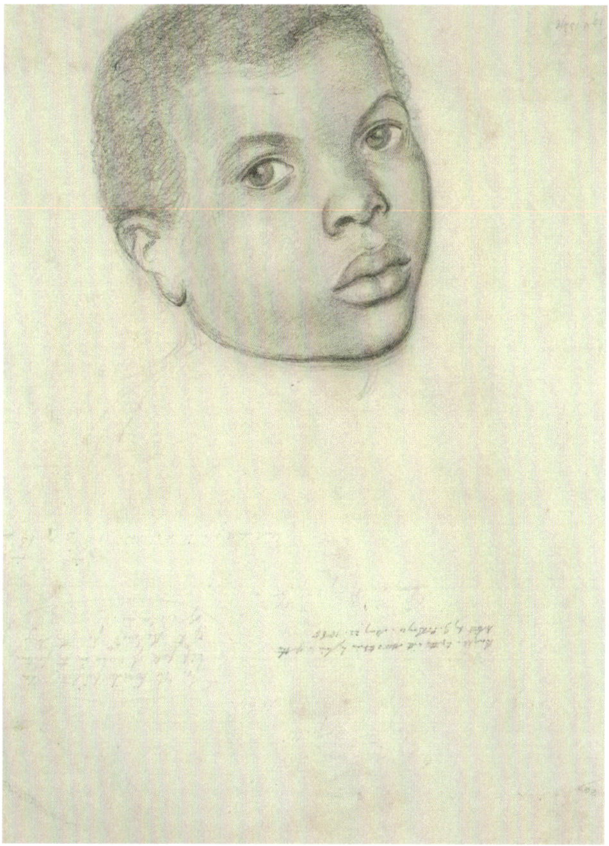

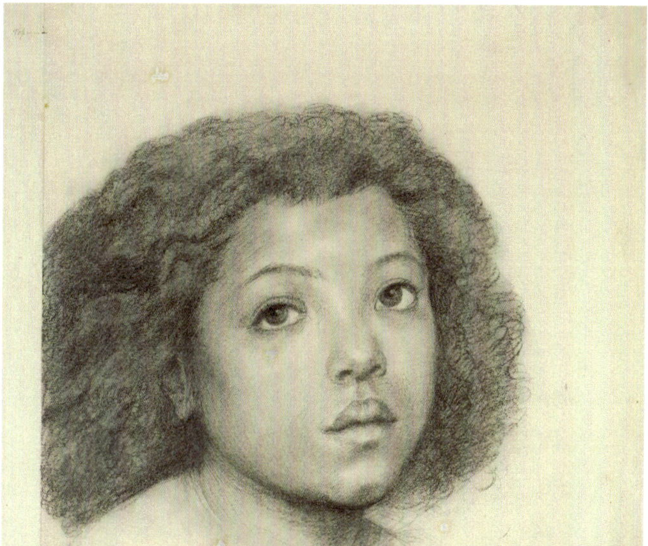

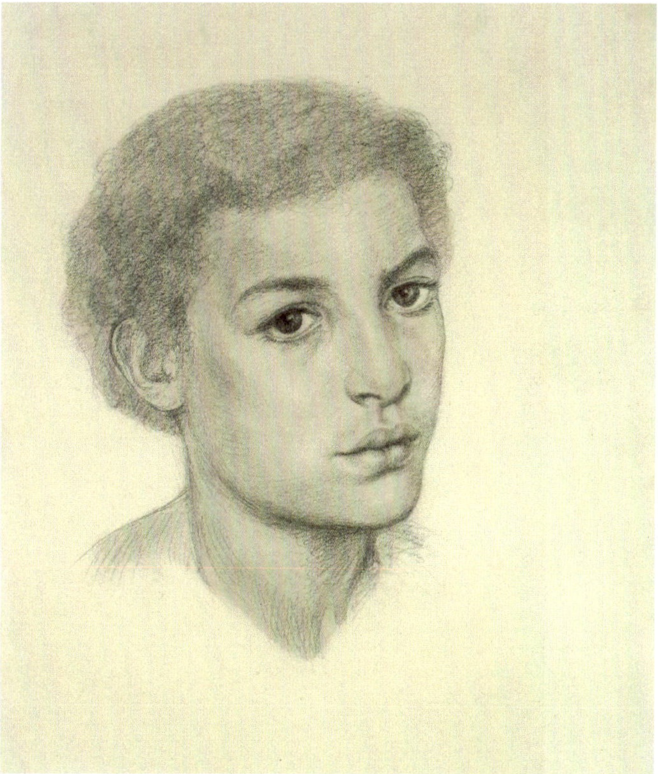

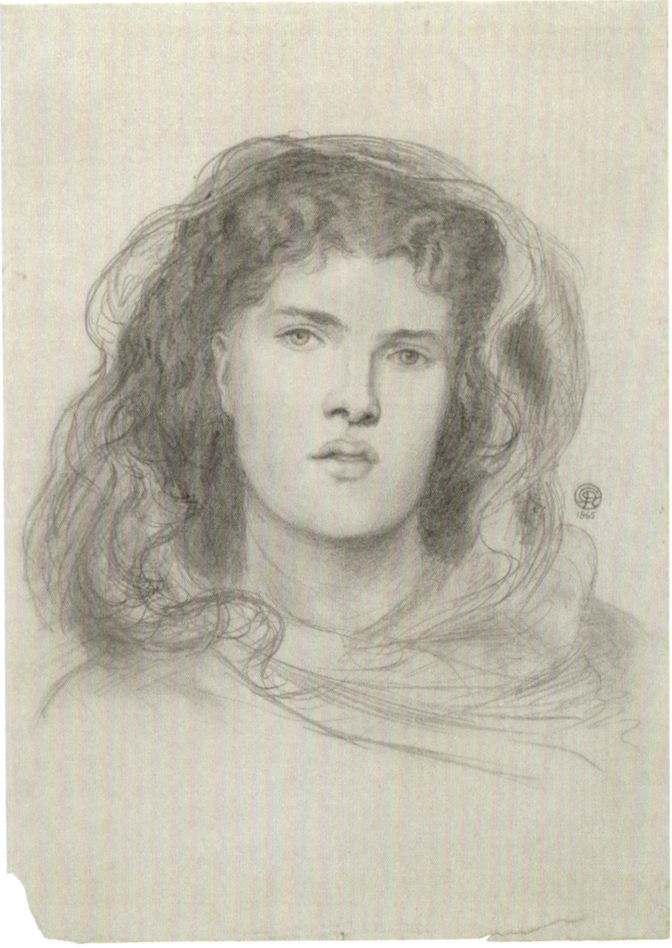
1865

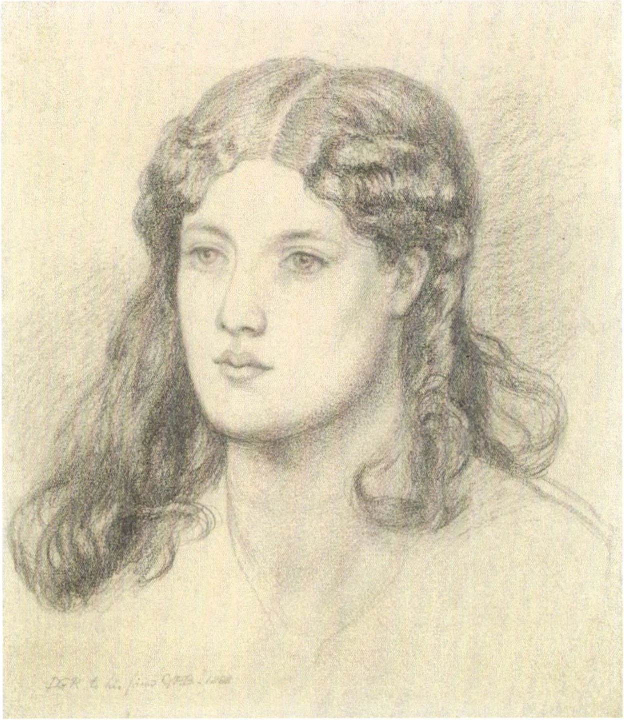

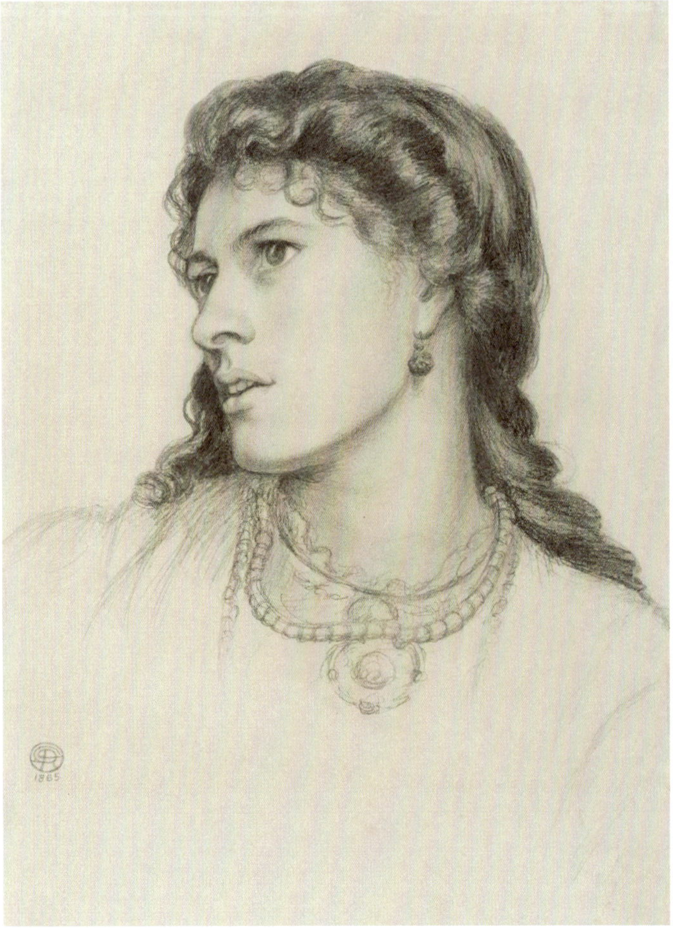
1865

Setting Racial and Social Hierarchies

Gabriel was preparing the painting that was to become *The Beloved* for the collector (and his patron) Ellen Heaton in the spring of 1863. He began a painting of the figure Beatrice, the twelfth-century noblewoman who is said to have inspired a significant proportion of Italian poet Dante Alighieri's work. Upon finding the complexion of his model Marie Ford 'bright' and 'irresistible',[4] he copied her face for a new painting inspired by the Old Testament 'Song of Solomon', which Dante had quoted in his *Divine Comedy*. This Gabriel presented to Liverpool-based banker George Rae who would eventually buy it for £300, and he completed another painting for Heaton.

The Beloved 1865–6 references two Old Testament passages: Song of Solomon and Psalm 45.[5] The former is an eight-chapter tale of romance, love, passion and pursuit. It narrates the story of two lovers, a bride who is a 'keeper of vineyards' and her groom, a shepherd. She describes herself as dark-skinned, so is perhaps a woman of African descent. Gabriel depicts the moment this bride, now of European descent, is presented to her beloved. The artist places her in the centre of the composition, luxuriously dressed and exuding a gentle sensuality that marks her as worthy of her groom's affection, and of ours as the viewers at whom she is also staring directly. Four women, 'the virgins that be her fellows' described in Psalm 45, accompany her in a procession. The foreground figure in the painting is an androgynous-looking boy of African descent.[6] He holds a burnished cup of pale roses, an allusion to the bride's skin and a contrast to his own.[7] The boy's difference in status is evident: he is unclothed, without a veil, the sole occupant of the bottom half of the composition, and pre-pubescent, perhaps nine or ten years old. He is the only Black figure ever painted in oils by the artist throughout his career.

Gabriel's visual narrative in *The Beloved* blends East with West and painting with poetry, for which he was well known.[8] In lowering her veil for her beloved, the bride exposes her auburn hair and a gold and ruby Chinese headdress. The bracelet on her left wrist takes the form of the East Asian motif of the *makara*, a legendary sea-creature. Her voluminously sleeved and embroidered robe is a kimono lent by an acquaintance of Gabriel's. The pendant worn by the boy is North African.[9] These references to Africa and Asia became generalised for the Western gaze to signify a foreign other.

OPPOSITE, CLOCKWISE FROM LEFT

NO.173 Dante Gabriel Rossetti, *Study for 'The Bride'* 1865, graphite on paper, 41.9 × 30.5

NO.174 Dante Gabriel Rossetti, *Portrait of Ellen Smith* 1863, graphite on paper, 24.3 × 21.7

NO.175 Dante Gabriel Rossetti, *The Beloved (study for bridesmaid)* 1865, graphite on paper, 41.9 × 30.5

Gabriel's melange continues with the appointment of a European protagonist in a story that takes place in the Middle East. The bride in the King James version of the Bible states, 'I am black, because the sun hath looked upon me.'[10] Ford's fairness, emphasised by her hair, the soft blush of her cheeks and the pink of her lips, deviates entirely from the Biblical narrative. A field worker who has elicited a strong love and desire from her groom, though explicitly described as dark-skinned, was in Gabriel's fantasy to be visualised as a white European. There is a form of racial and class erasure in this change to the narrative, the latter evident in the bride's ascension in status over her five attendants. Despite the erasure of the Biblical bride's dark skin, Gabriel reinserts his attention to race through a composition unique to the artist's work at the time, and through the inclusion of a Black attendant.[11]

Instead of the lone woman in a richly coloured and sumptuous setting, there are multiple figures in *The Beloved*, their alluring gazes drawing us into the intimacy of the scene. Typical of Gabriel's work, they each have a full cupid's bow lip and luxuriant hair. The women's sheer headscarves are drawn back by intricate jewels and ornaments to reveal hair darker than the bride's. Each is racialised, her difference highlighted by the skin tone of her companions. Working-class professional women modelled for the painting, echoing the narrative in the Song of Solomon of a working woman as the focus of a man's passion and desire, and serving as one of the many iterations of Gabriel's devotion to capturing the beauty he found in this social demographic.

The figure on the right is drawn from the Roma model Keomi Gray Bonnet. The model behind her is Fanny Eaton, a mixed-heritage Jamaican-born former laundress, who often sat for roles of varied origins in Gabriel's circle. Ellen Smith, an English former housemaid, poses for the attendant at left, and perhaps also for the olive-skinned figure whose face is largely obscured behind her. Marie Ford, whose biography is now lost but who was likely from a working-class background, poses for the bride, her wavy auburn hair and the green headscarf that frames her face emphasising the fairness of her skin and her whiteness. The bride's ability to arouse desire and love from her groom is coded in this atemporal and exotic setting - which is implied through the African, Asian and Middle Eastern referents - and relies upon the whiteness that empowers and differentiates her from the others.

It has been suggested, in an analysis of Gabriel's engagement with Black subjects, that the artist was likely thinking about the bride in the Song of Solomon and the execution of this painting when he visited his friend Édouard Manet in Paris. There he saw *Olympia* 1863 prior to its scandalous exhibition at the Paris Salon of 1865.[12] Laure, the Black attendant in Manet's painting, commands almost as much space as the reclining figure, and the attention with which she is rendered alludes to her importance as a pictorial counterpoint to the nude. She is, however, more a reflection of Paris's changing population and a move towards modernity than a visualisation of 'exoticism', which Gabriel deploys through the child's servitude, lack of clothing, and jewellery.

OPPOSITE
NO.176 Dante Gabriel Rossetti, *Head of a Young Woman [Mrs. Eaton?]* 1863–5, chalk and charcoal, with stumping, 46.5 × 31.5

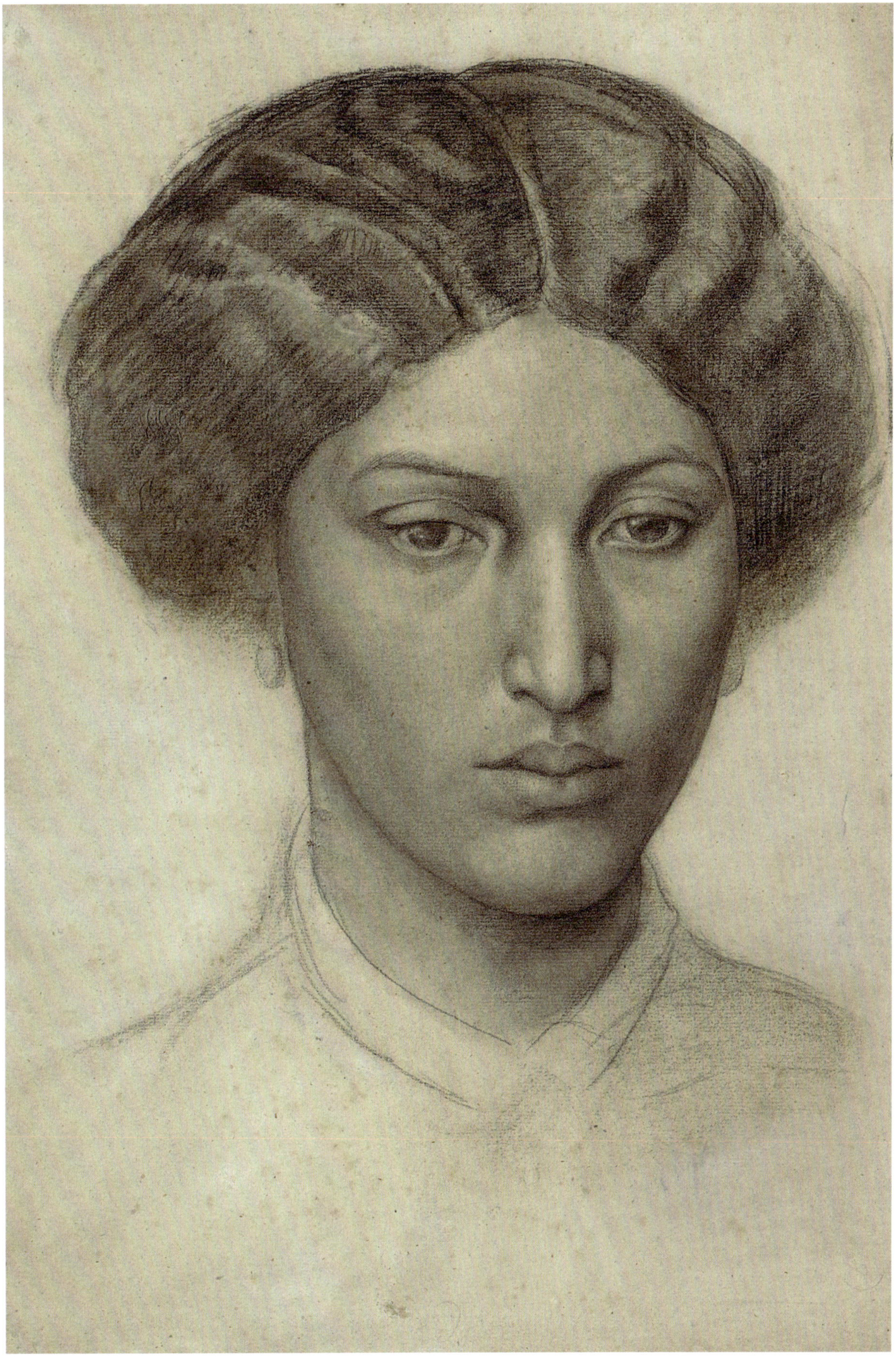

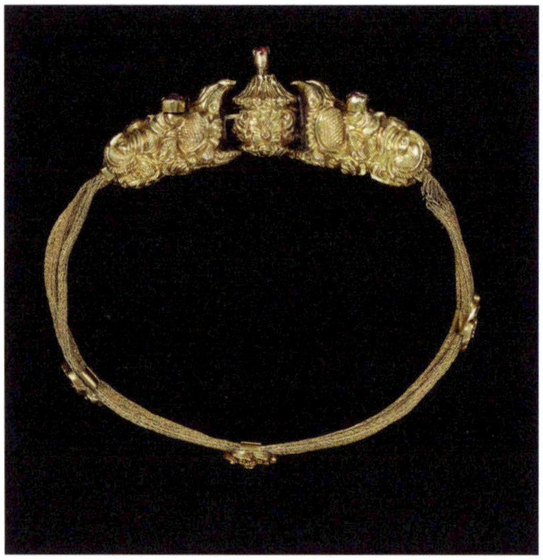

ABOVE
NO.177 Bracelet 1850, plaited gold and rubies, 6 × 6.2 × 1.1

OPPOSITE
NO.178 Unknown artist, *The Beloved* 1865, carbon print on paper, 26.5 × 24

More Than a Pure Black Boy

On his return to London from Paris in December 1864, Gabriel wrote to his friend the artist Ford Madox Brown about a search for 'a little nigger girl (real nigger) about 12 or so' or, alternatively, a child of mixed heritage to include in *The Beloved* as 'the foreground figure of all'.[13] Two young girls sat for Gabriel (NOS.171, 172). One was painted into the group in December 1864, and her likeness remained on the canvas until Gabriel resolved to find a darker-skinned Black child instead. In March 1865, Gabriel wrote about the substitution to George Rae: 'One change I propose is to take out the little mulatto girl and paint in a pure black girl or boy if I can get one. I mean the colour of my picture to be like jewels, and the jet would be invaluable.'[14] Gabriel then introduced the figure of the boy between March and December 1865, when he wrote to Rae of the painting's completion. The first pencil sketch appears to be a close likeness to the sitter (NO.168). The more finished drawing on the other side of the paper alters the angle and shape of his face to be closer to that of the child who appears in the painting (NO.170). It also alters the sitter's patient, slightly uncertain expression to accord with the final figure's more conventionally appealing gaze.

Gabriel's use of the word 'jet' in his March letter conflates jewel-like painting, notably the use of pigment, with the individuals he alludes to as being jewels. Jet, the black or dark-brown gemstone

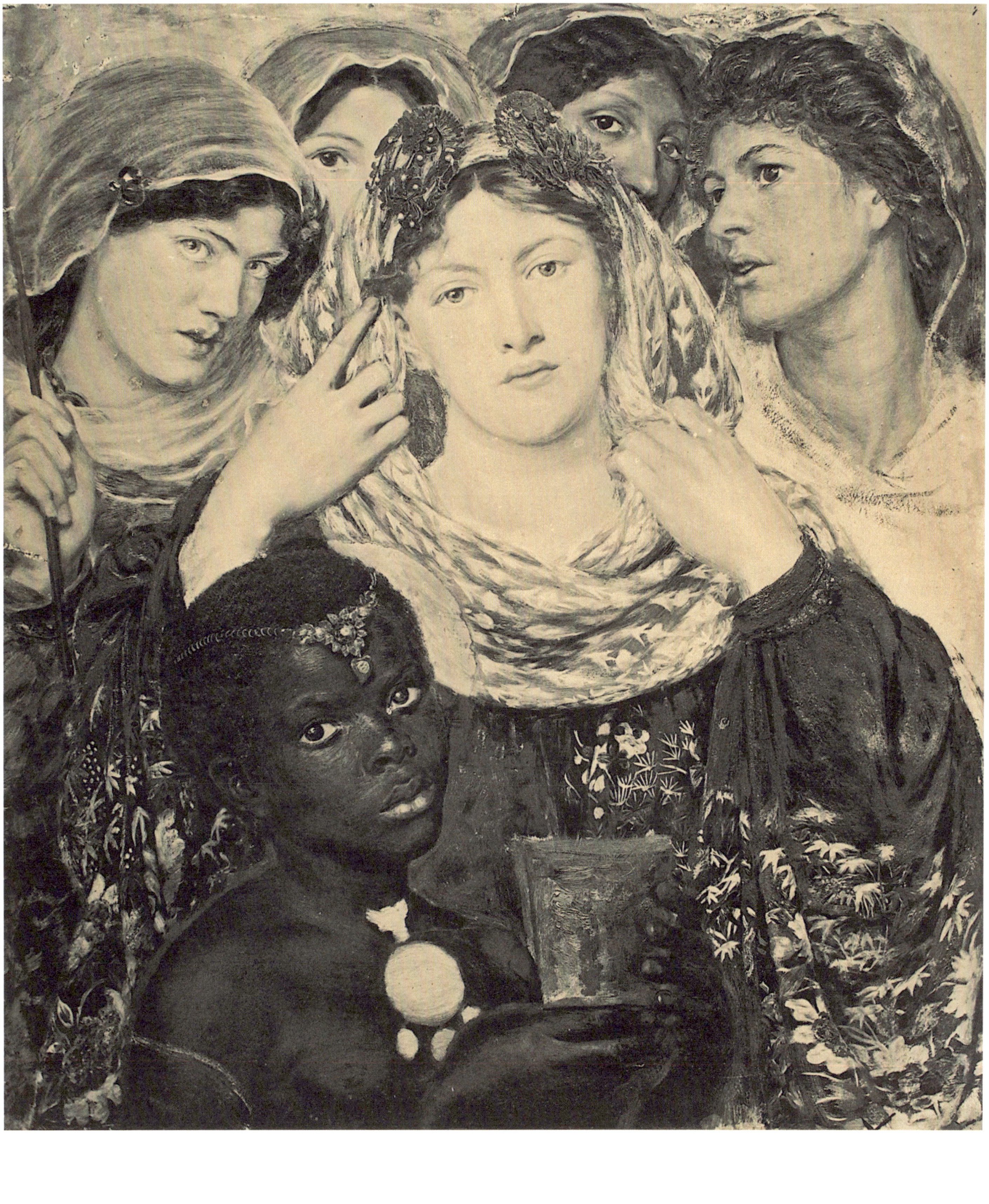

used to produce ornaments and jewellery, stands as a metaphor for the child. The word 'pure' in relation to his race has connotations of breeding and animal husbandry. Likewise, the archaic 'mulatto' as a derivative of the Latin for mule, a hybrid between a donkey and a horse, diminishes the humanity of the people it is intended to describe. A short excerpt from the letters of Gabriel's aunt Charlotte Polidori, which highlights the properties of the boy's skin, supports Gabriel's fascination with it. Either recalling a visit to Gabriel's studio or recounting a conversation with him, Polidori wrote in 1866:

> Whilst sitting the tears would run down his cheeks: the skin, as if it absorbed them as blotting-paper, would look darker. When not sitting he was accustomed to be most active, running and jumping etc. G[abriel] suggested that he might be thinking about his Mammy...[15]

The Beloved attempts to present us with this 'pure black boy', a pictorial tool employed to accentuate the colour values in the jewellery and robes of the women, and to highlight the beauty of the 'irresistible' white bride. Little of his humanity and childhood is reachable through the painting alone. His role remains one-dimensional. Moreover, the fantasy that pervades the visualisation of the elite with their Black attendants upholds the belief of the latter's willing acceptance of the subordinate role.

The child in the painting first encountered Gabriel at the entrance to a hotel when he was with his 'master', from whom Gabriel sought permission to paint him.[16] No archival evidence has been found to determine the legal status of the child, but the word 'master' at this time connotes servitude and an obligation to a presumably white man.[17] The child's decision to sit for Gabriel was not his to take but his *master's*. The experience would have been foreign to him. Perhaps he would have been delivered to Gabriel's house in Cheyne Walk, Chelsea, by cab. He would then have been told to partially undress by a man who was not known to him. What instructions had he been given beforehand? Perhaps he sat in Gabriel's studio surrounded by strange props, the artist's eclectic furniture and multiple paintings in progress, one of which was *Venus Verticordia* 1865.[18] Did Gabriel, a charming but brusque man who could be fascinated by a child's tears, make conversation with him? What stories did Gabriel tell to calm the boy down when perhaps he cried for his mother, as wondered by the artist? Possibly ones about the menagerie in his large garden.[19] Did the boy understand the narrative in which Gabriel wanted to include him? Could such a young child with a 'master' ever consent to his likeness existing perpetually in the context of Gabriel's racialised vision? Was he missing his mother?

None of these questions can ever be answered. The fictional writing at the beginning of this essay attempted to understand the experience of the child within the social and racial schemas of Gabriel's time. It foregrounded the boy's perspective, although it can never restore the voice that was not recorded in 1865. The writing cannot retrieve what has been lost to history, nor will it reveal a picture that can be deemed truer than Gabriel's painting. It is, however, an attempt at sensitivity and the exploration of what might have been

1 Saidiya Hartman, *Scenes of Subjection: Terror, Slavery, and Self-Making in Nineteenth-Century America*, New York and Oxford 1997, p.10.

2 Saidiya Hartman, 'Venus in Two Acts', *Small Axe*, vol.12, no.2, June 2008, pp.1–14 (p.11).

3 Aimé Césaire, 'Poetry and Knowledge', in *Lyric and Dramatic Poetry, 1946–82*, Charlottesville, VA 1990, p.xlii.

4 Dante Gabriel Rossetti to Ellen Heaton, 2 July 1863, in William E. Fredeman (ed.), *The Correspondence of Dante Gabriel Rossetti*, 10 vols., Cambridge, Woodbridge and Rochester, NY 2002–15, vol.3, p.61.

5 The two Biblical texts are engraved onto the original frame. The first comprises Song of Solomon 2:16 and 1:2. It reads: 'My Beloved is mine and I am his. / Let him kiss me with the kisses of his mouth: / for thy love is better than wine.' The second text, from Psalm 45:13–14, reads: 'She shall be brought unto the king in raiment of needle-work: the virgins that be her fellows shall bear her company, and shall be brought unto thee.'

6 For Victorian preoccupations with the androgyny, see Matthew Francis Rarey, '"And the Jet Would be Invaluable": Blackness, Bondage, and *The Beloved*', *Art Bulletin*, vol.102, no.3, Sept. 2020, pp.44–6.

7 For the meanings commonly attached to flowers in Victorian England and the principal translation of roses as love, see *The Language of Flowers, With Illustrative Poetry*, London 1841, pp.106–18.

8 Eleonora Sasso, *The Pre-Raphaelites and Orientalism: Language and Cognition in Remediations of the East*, Edinburgh 2018, pp.11–36.

9 See Charlotte Gere and Geoffrey C. Munn, *Artists' Jewellery: Pre-Raphaelite to Arts and Crafts*, Woodbridge 1989, p.109.

10 More recent Bible translations interpret 'black' as 'dark'. The verses inscribed on the original frame are from the King James version of the Bible.

11 *The Beloved* was painted against the backdrop of the American Civil war (1861–5) and anti-slavery campaigns on both sides of the Atlantic. Nonetheless, both contemporaneous accounts and recent scholarship demonstrate a reluctance to attach the inclusion of the boy to the socio-political concerns of the time. They, rather, underline Gabriel's ambivalence to race and the oppression of Black people, and his refusal to take an explicit stance. See Jan Marsh, *Dante Gabriel Rossetti: Painter and Poet*, London 1999, pp.292–4; Rarey 2020, p.30; and William Michael Rossetti (ed.), *The Works of Dante Gabriel Rossetti*, London 1911, pp.674–5.

12 Rarey 2020, p.41.

13 Fredeman 2002–15, 3, p.228: Dante Gabriel Rossetti to Ford Madox Brown, 19 December 1864 ('a little nigger girl'); Dante Gabriel Rossetti to George Rae, 20 December 1864 ('the foreground figure of all').

14 Ibid., p.272.

15 Charlotte Polidori, personal memorandum of 20 February 1866, reprinted in *Rossetti Papers, 1862 to 1870*, ed. William Michael Rossetti, London 1903, p.175.

16 Ibid.

17 The Slavery Abolition Act was passed in 1833, but Black servitude was deliberately ambiguous at this time both in Britain and in the United States. Jan Marsh has argued that this 'master' was American. See Marsh 1999, p.291.

18 See Marsh 1999, pp.247–88, and Fredeman 2002–15, 3, p.272.

19 John Simons, *Rossetti's Wombat: Pre-Raphaelites and Australian Animals in Victorian London*, London 2008, pp.63–87.

Margaretta Frederick

Troubling Women: Dante Gabriel Rossetti's Portrayals of Modern Beauty

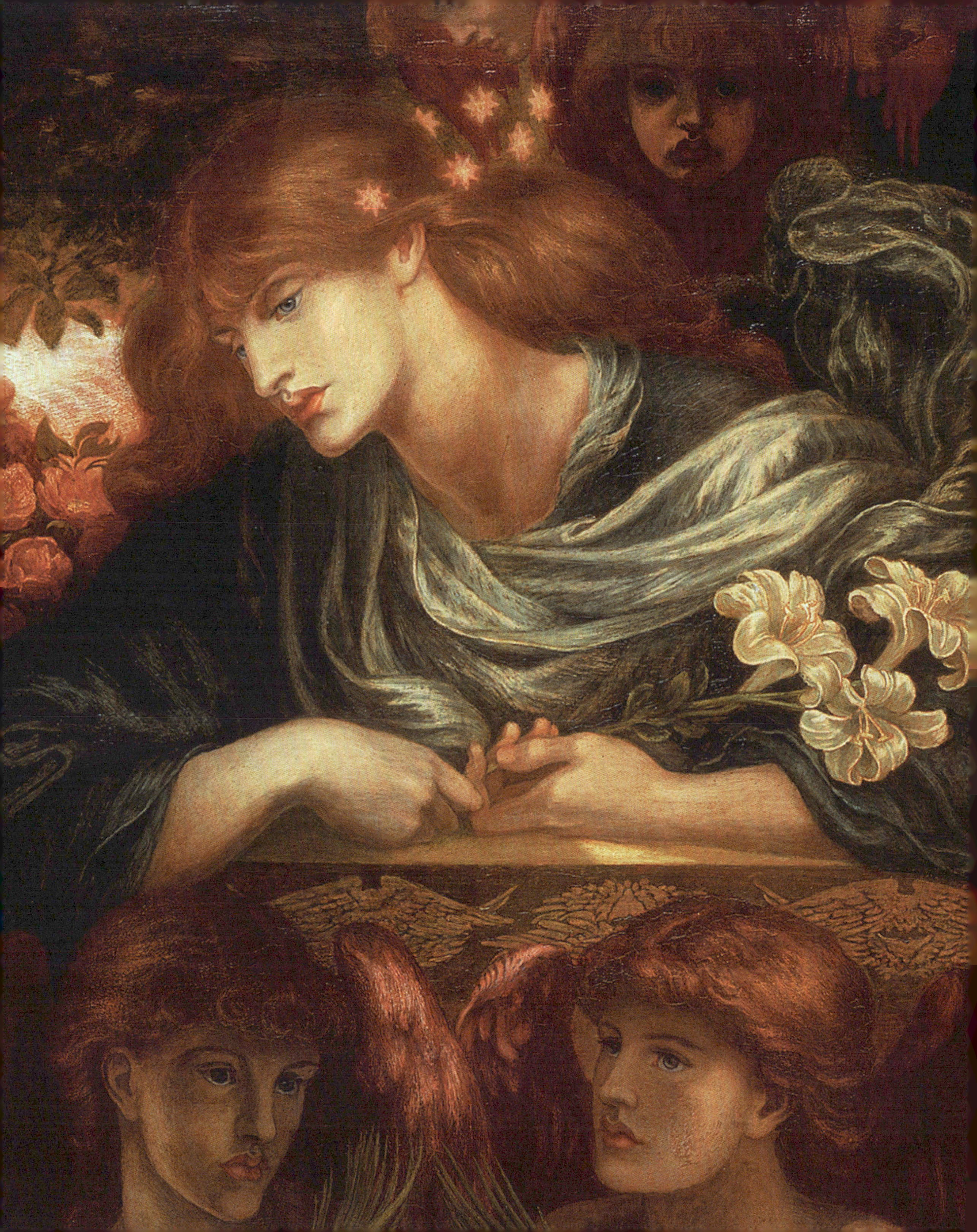

> [T]he artist ... has become the slave of his own predilections. He has found a particular cast of beauty, with lips at once full and pining, and eyes overshadowed by a great thunder-cloud of hair – he has found this, and the length of throat, the litheness of limb and sinuousness of pose that go with it, so consonant to his imaginative mood, that he repeats them again and again, sometimes with a mechanical insistence and exaggeration, especially in the drawing and colouring of the mouth, that almost degenerate into caricature. Technically he aims more and more at depth of tone, and at the same time his sense of colour becomes sicklied. In the flesh particularly, he in many pictures of this date gets a morbid tint into the shadows, and a dragging and stringy quality into the handling, that stand in the strongest contrast to the work of his healthier days.[1]

This essay investigates the images of women created by Dante Gabriel Rossetti from the early 1860s through the 1870s. They provoked discomfort, even disdain, in contemporaries such as Sidney Colvin (cited above), and continued to do so, raising the ire of feminists across decades and throughout cultural, social and societal negotiations of the definition of the gender. They are iconic renderings of beauty which overwhelm, their provocative bodies pushed to the limits of the pictorial foreground, defying perspectival placement and aggressively confronting the viewer. As such we are forced to reckon with their powerful and eminent presence. They are investigations of 'Womanhood' with a capital 'W'.

Gabriel's style, medium and pictorial imagery transformed in a frenzy of work at the beginning of the 1860s.[2] He effected 'a wholesale reconfiguration of the practice of painting, from the most basic level of materials and techniques up to the most abstract or conceptual level of the meanings and ideas that can be embodied in visual form'.[3] Discarding the carefully rendered, sincere presentations of medieval inspiration espoused by the early Pre-Raphaelite Brotherhood, Gabriel's oils from this period feature instead modern, iconic, half-length female figures.[4]

These images reside somewhere between portraits and ideal fantasies of the feminine, an 'entanglement of art and life, fiction and biography, character and model, subject paintings and portraiture'.[5] Here, I situate this record of male-female interaction within the broader context of the re-definition of womanhood which was unfolding during Gabriel's lifetime. I propose these paintings visualise a progressive internal dialogue in which the artist is negotiating the rapidly changing roles of women in society.

Beginning with the introduction of Elizabeth Eleanor Siddal – and followed by Fanny Cornforth, Jane Morris and Alexa Wilding, among others – Gabriel developed a habit of focusing on a single model and painting each in monomaniac repetition. In several cases, but not all, a romantic relationship was also initiated. Gabriel maintained the Pre-Raphaelite convention of using 'real people' as models for his work, choosing – particularly in the case of female figures – features that defied contemporary stereotypes and keepsake wholesomeness. In seeking these women quite literally on the streets, Gabriel stretched the definition of women who work/

PAGE 177
NO.179 Dante Gabriel Rossetti, *The Blessed Damozel* 1875–9, oil paint on canvas, 221.5 × 139 (frame)

BELOW
NO.180 Dante Gabriel Rossetti, *Lady having her hair combed out* 1855, ink and wash on paper, 15.3 × 11.5

OPPOSITE, CLOCKWISE FROM LEFT

NO.181 Dante Gabriel Rossetti, *Elizabeth Siddal Plaiting her Hair*, date not known, graphite on paper, 17.1 × 12.7

NO.182 Dante Gabriel Rossetti, *Fanny Cornforth* 1862, graphite on paper, 38.9 × 35.6

NO.183 Dante Gabriel Rossetti, *Study for Delia in 'The Return of Tibullus to Delia'* 1860–2, graphite on paper, mounted on card, 22.2 × 19.6

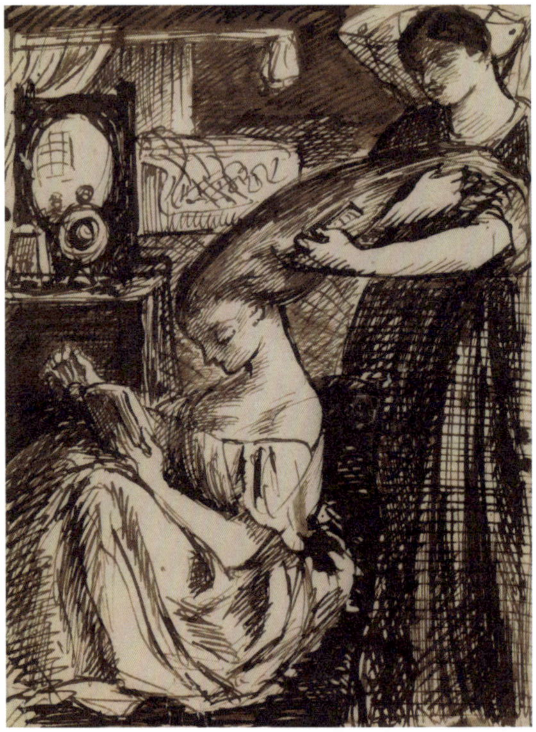

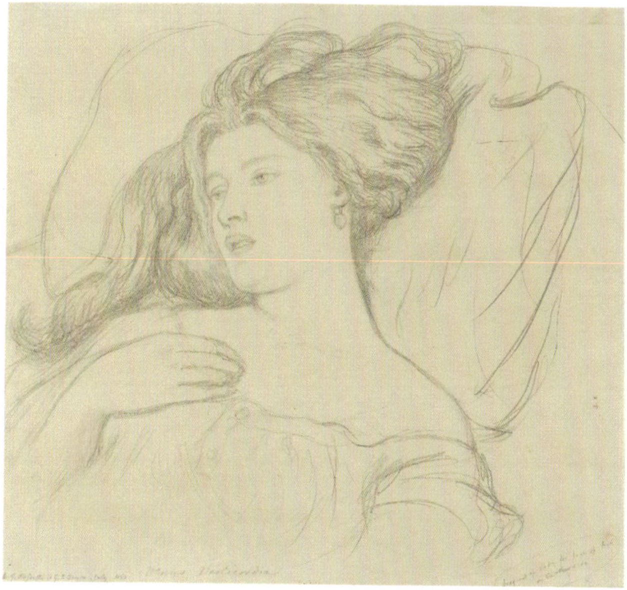

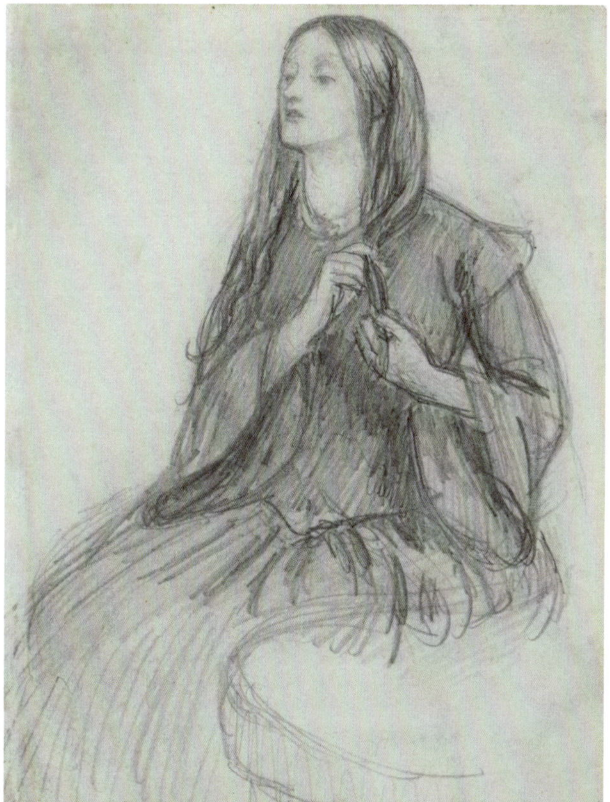

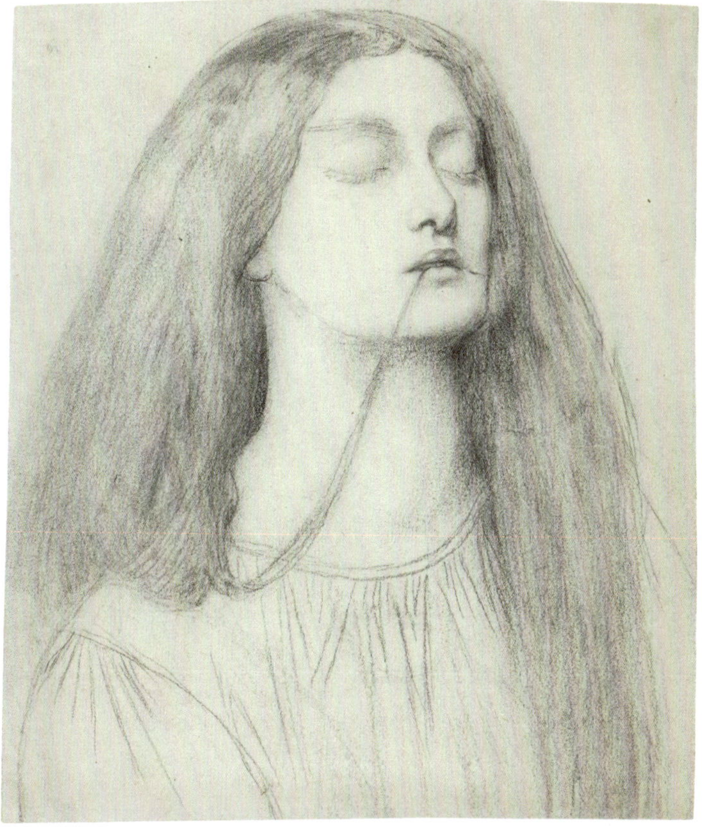

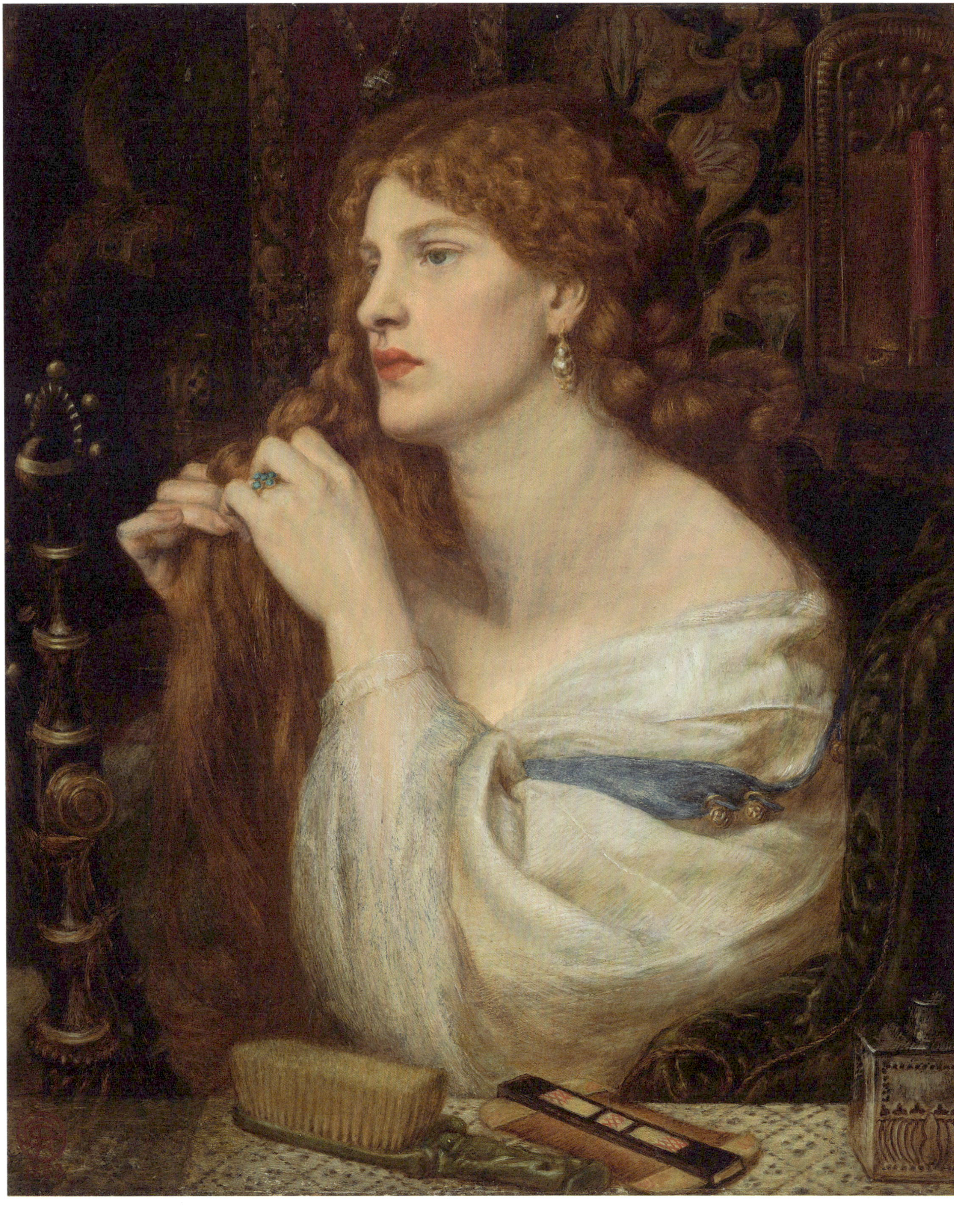

'He has found a particular cast of beauty, with lips at once full and pining, and eyes overshadowed by a great thunder-cloud of hair'

Sidney Colvin

working women. These depictions capture what were for Gabriel 'troubling women' who were exemplary of expanding female agency with the advent of the 'New Woman'. This phrase, which came into use in the 1880s (see also p.140), identified those who pushed the boundaries of tradition to participate in a more meaningful way in the cultural milieu.[6]

The paintings of this period reveal an obsession with the female subject, repeatedly refined and revised as the artist sought a way to depict this 'New Woman' and to re-conceptualise the look and definition of female beauty. His depictions vacillate between an embrace and a rejection of the feminine, an internal argument which is visible in some of his earliest works dating well before the 'stunner' portraits of Fanny Cornforth and Jane Morris. *Elizabeth Siddal Drawing Rossetti*, in which Gabriel has drawn his future wife as she in turn captures his likeness, bears witness to his simultaneous feelings of pride and unease in the talent he has mentored. He captures her in the act of creation, but in doing so essentially repossesses the seat at the easel, thereby overriding Elizabeth's artistic agency.

In May 1860, Gabriel and Elizabeth travelled to Paris on their honeymoon. Gabriel spent time at the Louvre where he was particularly drawn to sixteenth-century Italian painting, describing Veronese's *Marriage at Cana* as 'the greatest picture in the world beyond a doubt'.[7] Despite the anti-Raphael dogma of the Brotherhood, Gabriel was from his earliest years drawn to the seductive qualities of the art of this period and its sensual female imagery. This can be seen in the 1853 drawing *Giorgione Painting*, in which the Renaissance painter is seated in front of a female model (Elizabeth Siddal), oblivious to the onlookers crowding around him.

Bocca Baciata 1859 (see NO.94) exemplifies Gabriel's response to Venetian 'courtesan' portraits, a tradition of Renaissance painting in which single half-length females are portrayed in varying stages of undress. Gabriel updates and modernises the pictorial convention by foregoing three-dimensional perspective; the illusion of background is here replaced with a suffocating pattern of marigolds. The compressed picture plane and the confrontational gaze of the sitter create the illusion of her presence within the viewer's space. During the Renaissance period, a woman at a window signalled contradictory readings – a lack of decorum, discouraged as encouraging wanton behaviour, but contrarily often used in sacred depictions of the Madonna and Child.[8] Gabriel's use of this iconography initiates a sustained visual investigation of conflicting views of womanhood.

OPPOSITE
NO.184 Dante Gabriel Rossetti, *Aurelia (Fazio's Mistress)* 1863–73, oil paint on mahogany, 43.2 × 36.8

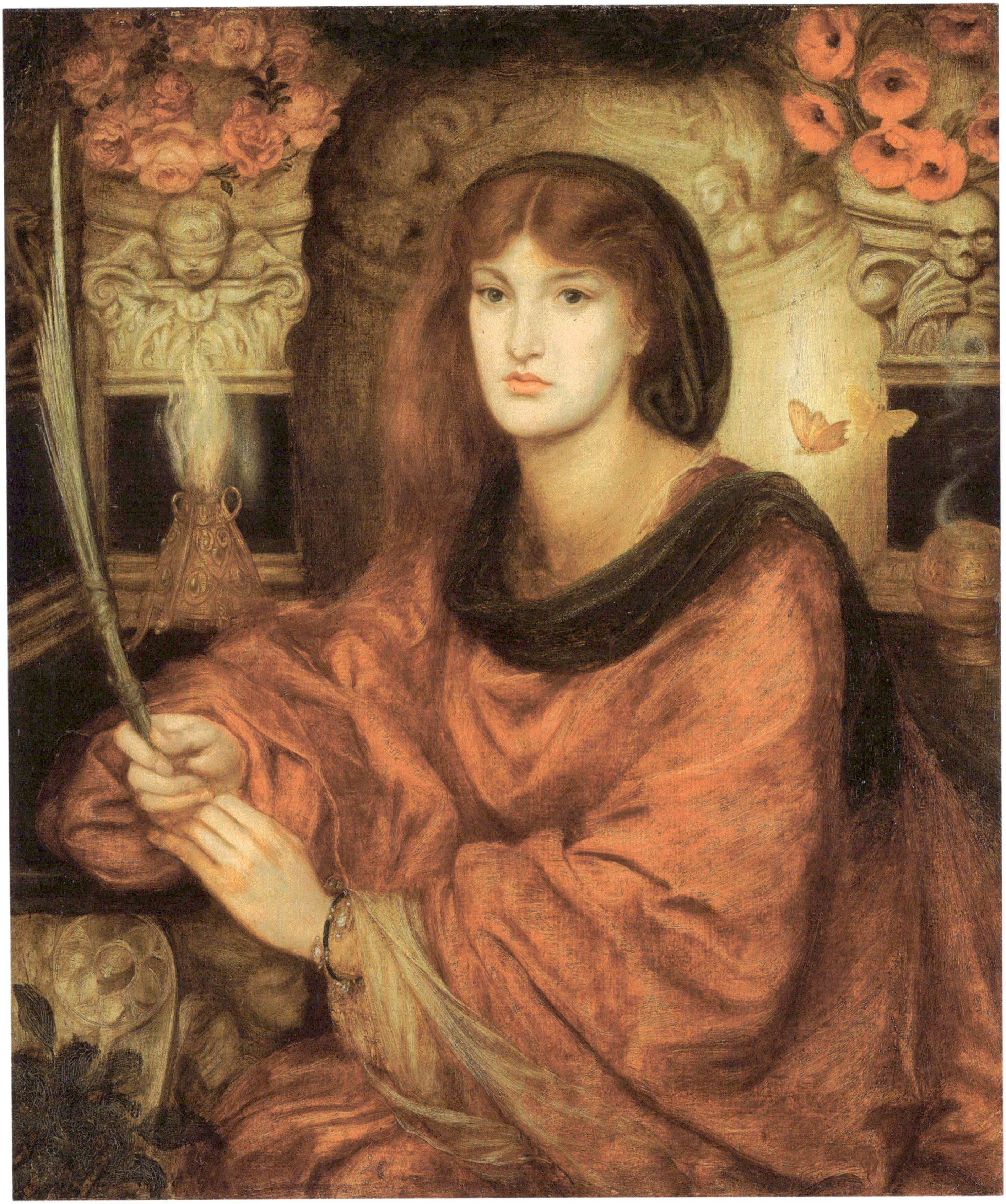

The painting is also exemplary of Gabriel's career-long synaesthetic impulses, combining the visual with the written word. In addition to the title referencing a line from Boccaccio's *Decameron*, the painting, in turn, inspired the artist's poem 'The Song of the Bower' (1860). This simultaneous working across genres was a pattern in Gabriel's creative process from the earliest days. A poem could refine a painting, or vice versa: a kind of 'double work of art'.[9]

When exhibited at the Hogarth Club in 1860, *Bocca Baciata* prompted a stern response from Pre-Raphaelite Brother William Holman Hunt, who described it as representative of 'gross sensuality ... advocating as a principle mere gratification of the eye and if any passion at all – the animal passion to be the aim of Art'.[10] The absence of narrative, the singular conceptualisation of feminine beauty, and the appeal to the senses mark *Bocca Baciata* as an early example of the 'art for art's sake' philosophy of the approaching Aesthetic movement.

In March 1863, James McNeill Whistler and his partner and model Joanna Heffernan moved to 7 Lindsey Row, Chelsea, near Gabriel's home at 16 Cheyne Walk, where Fanny Cornforth was now his housekeeper. The move initiated a friendship, socialising and, undoubtedly, the sharing of aesthetic ideology. Both Rossetti and Whistler were embarking on their mature careers, staking new ground in artistic expression. In moving the aesthetic needle forward, they were each indebted to live-in female partners who served as inspirational muses.

Fazio's Mistress, later renamed *Aurelia* (NO.184), dispenses with all semblance of decorum provided previously by the cloak of Renaissance compositional borrowings. The windowsill setting of *Bocca Baciata* has been replaced by a dressing table as the viewer is taken inside the private space of the female boudoir. The model is shown in the intimate act of 'plaiting her golden hair'.[11] She is seated facing left, gazing into a cheval glass, one pillar of which is depicted in the left foreground. A brush, a comb and a perfume vessel lie on the table before her. The title references a poem by the Renaissance poet Fazio degli Uberti, 'His Portrait of his Lady, Angiola of Verona', which Gabriel included in his work of translation *The Early Italian Poets* (1861). It is a paean to a beautiful woman, as the opening lines indicate:

> I look at the crisp golden-threaded hair
> Whereof, to thrall my heart, Love twists a net

These lines describe the devotion of the poet to his love, but also reveal an underlying foreboding of entrapment, reiterated at the poem's close:[12]

> That since the first fair woman ever made,
> Not one can have display'd
> More power upon all hearts than this one doth

Gabriel simultaneously celebrates this potency – in an image of compelling and seductive beauty – while indicating the underlying apprehension. The assumedly male viewer is here given access to a private female space, but is effectively ignored, by a figure who is indifferent to his presence, engaged in the contemplation of her own beauty. Gabriel was not unaware of the rising women's movement,

OPPOSITE
NO.185 Dante Gabriel Rossetti, *Sibylla Palmifera* 1865–70, oil paint on canvas, 98.4 × 85

Lilith

Dante Gabriel Rossetti

Of Adam's first wife, Lilith, it is told
(The witch he loved before the gift of Eve,)
That, ere the snake's, her sweet tongue could deceive,
And her enchanted hair was the first gold.
And still she sits, young while the earth is old,
And, subtly of herself contemplative,
Draws men to watch the bright net she can weave,
Till heart and body and life are in its hold.

The rose and poppy are her flowers; for where
Is he not found, O Lilith, whom shed scent
And soft-shed kisses and soft sleep shall snare?
Lo! as that youth's eyes burned at thine, so went
Thy spell through him, and left his straight neck bent,
And round his heart one strangling golden hair. [1866]

RIGHT
NO.186 Dante Gabriel Rossetti, *La Belle Dame Sans Merci* 1855–6, graphite and ink on paper, 33.2 × 43.2

BELOW
NO.187 Dante Gabriel Rossetti, *Lady Lilith* c.1869, ink and graphite on paper, 21.2 × 17.5

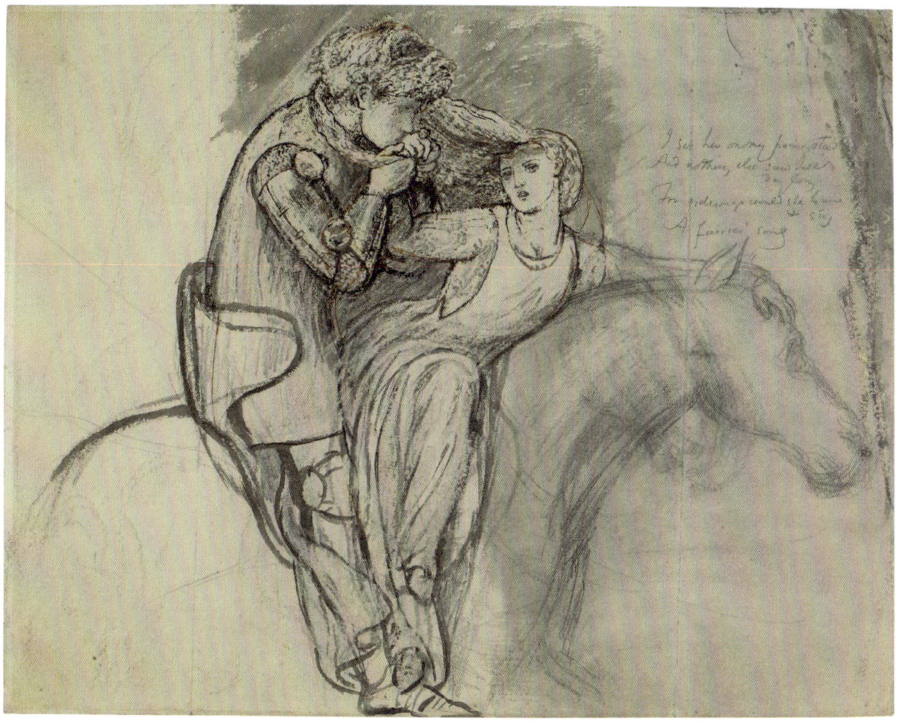

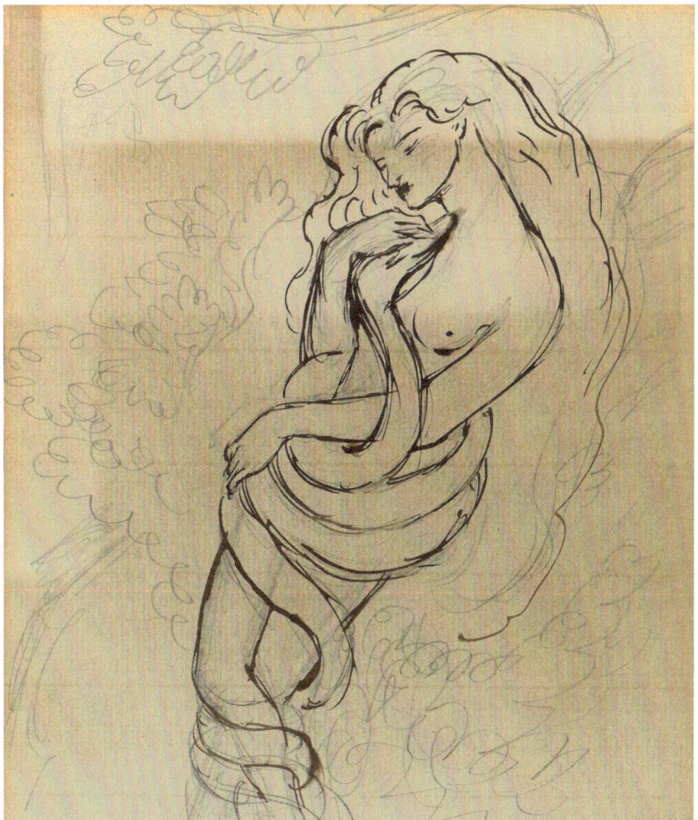

having developed a strong friendship with Barbara Leigh Smith Bodichon, an early advocate of women's education and suffrage.

In images such as this, Gabriel hit on a broadly shared patriarchal nerve, as there were buyers aplenty. While his fellow painter George Price Boyce purchased *Bocca Baciata*, *Fazio's Mistress* found a ready customer in lawyer and early patron William Blackmore, and later the banker George Rae. More patrons were to follow, often requesting replicas of original works.

An abundance of red or golden hair was a key component of all of these 'stunner' paintings, and is observed and refined in numerous drawings of the period. It was a particular attribute of Fanny Cornforth's, which Gabriel exploited, tapping into its cultural implications. During the Victorian period, hair was, as Sarah Heaton explains, 'a site of contested discourses' and 'patriarchal control'.[13] Young children wore their hair loose, but once adulthood – and marriage – was attained, hair was to be kept demurely under restraint. As women's public-facing roles expanded, including taking charge of personal presentation, these restrictions became more malleable. Gabriel's emphatic sexualisation of hair visualises this societal shift in female power and the tension it provoked. A drawing of Fanny reclined with her head on a pillow (NO.182), masses of hair swirling around her, implies the male presence – and ownership.

Lady Lilith (NO.188), 'My picture with the hair', as Gabriel described it,[14] is perhaps the culmination of these hair-centric compositions. The subject, continuing the internal dialogue on the definition of womanhood, was undoubtedly brought to Gabriel's attention through Goethe's *Faust*.[15] Said to be created at the same time and from the same earth as Adam, Lilith was his female equal. In the Talmudic story she refuses to take a secondary role to Adam, fleeing from Eden to escape the patriarchal tyranny. Lilith was, as described by medievalist historian Ponsonby Lyons, to whom Gabriel must have written for information after completion of the painting, 'the first strong-minded woman and the original advocate of women's rights'.[16] Gabriel explained to a friend:

> The picture is called *Lady Lilith* ... and represents a *modern Lilith* combing out her abundant golden hair and gazing on herself in the glass with that self-absorption by whose strange fascination such natures draw others within their own circle. The idea which you indicate (viz: of the perilous principle in the world being female from the first) is about the most essential notion of the sonnet.[17]

The painting in its present state depicts the model Alexa (born Alice) Wilding seated facing left, languorously passing a comb through definitive tresses of red hair as she gazes, abstractedly self-absorbed, into a hand-held mirror. An abundance of white fabric dominates the foreground – dressing gown, fringed wrap – falling in gentle folds and melding her body into the low-armed upholstered chair. The flattened picture plane thrusts her body alarmingly into the viewer's space. White roses surrounding her head and a poppy at lower right reference Lilith's sensory entrapment of men. At left, via a reflection in a mirror, we see a view of lush greenery outside a window. Lilith sits within an enchanted bower of her own making.

OPPOSITE
NO.188 Dante Gabriel Rossetti, *Lady Lilith* 1866–8, altered 1872–3, oil paint on canvas, 96.5 × 85.1

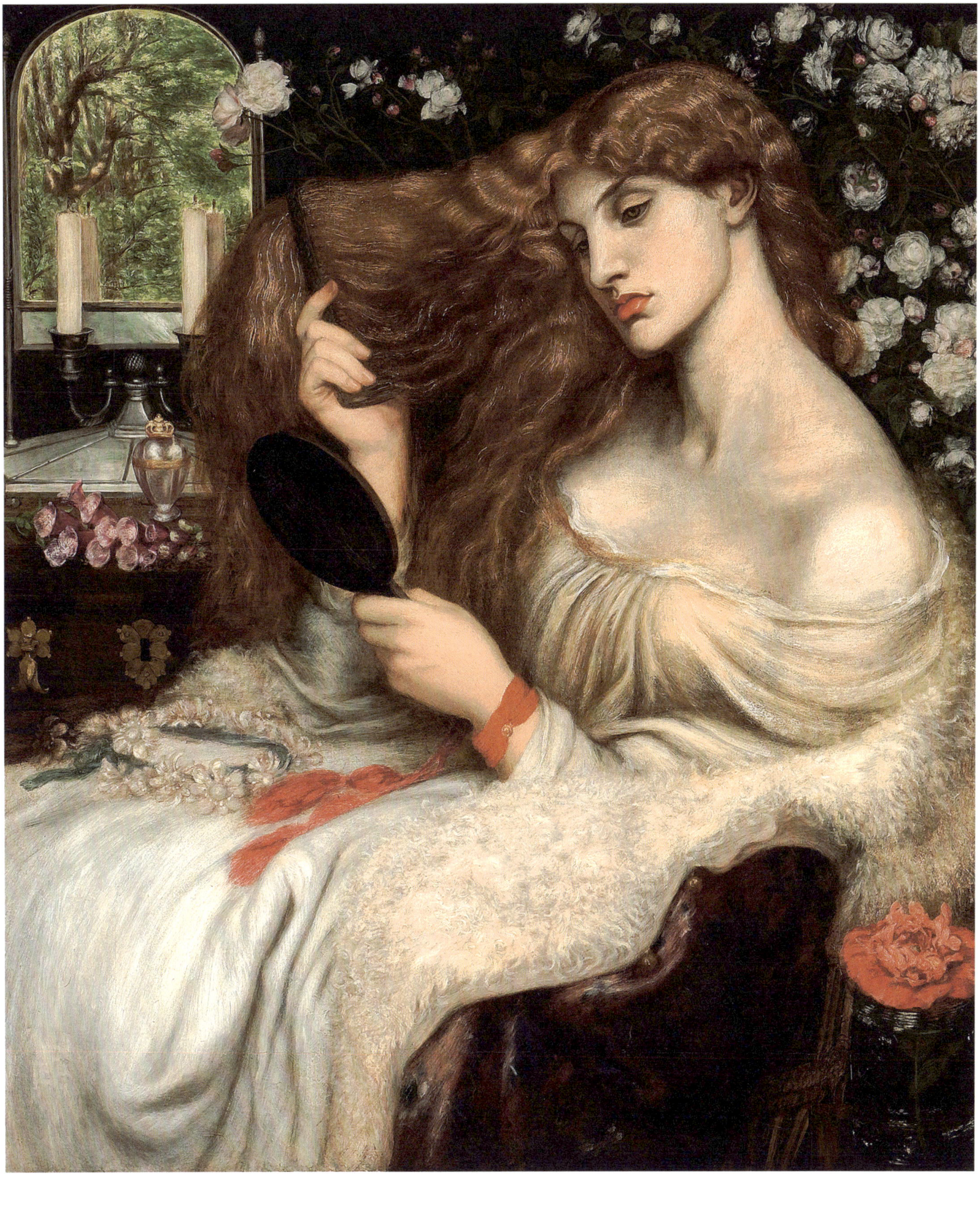

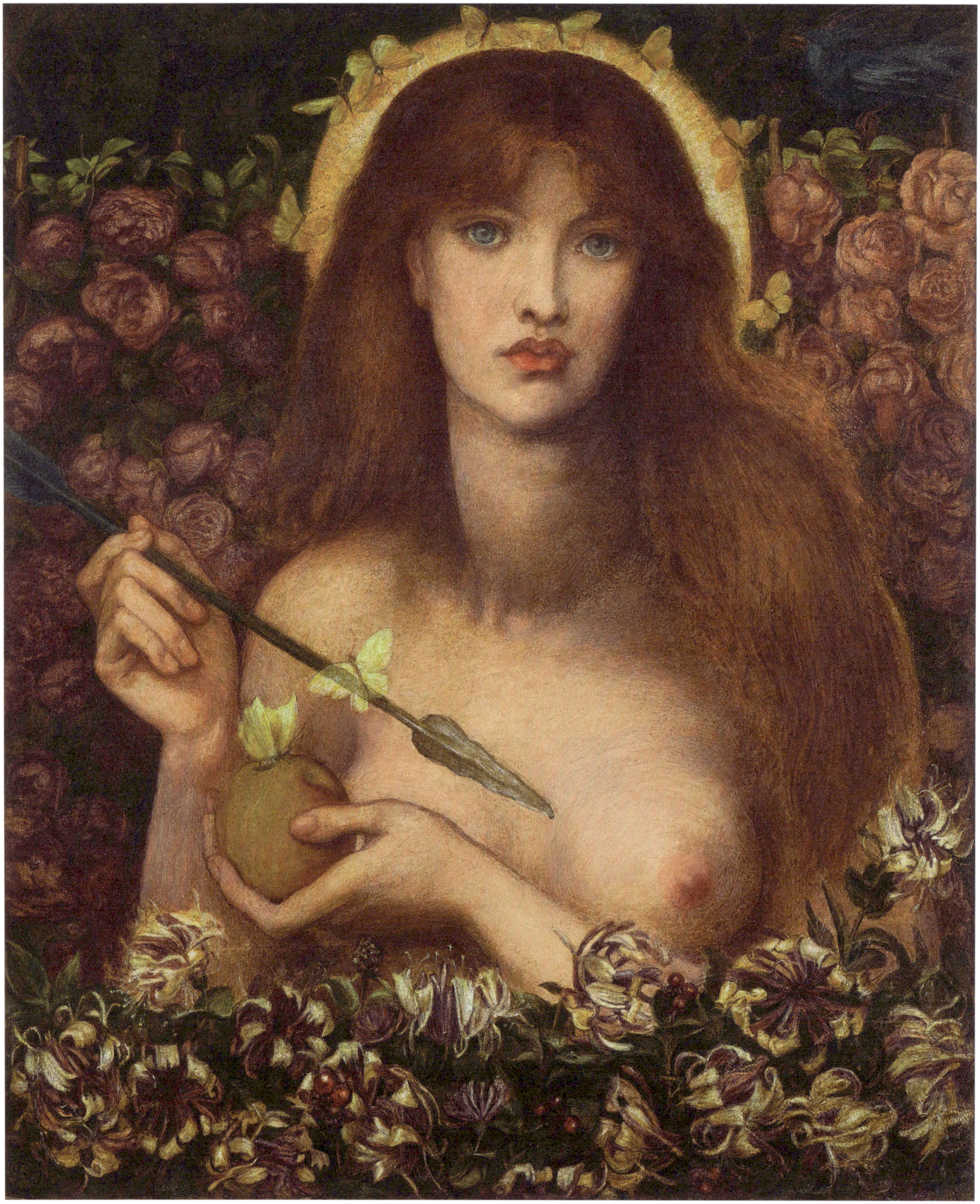

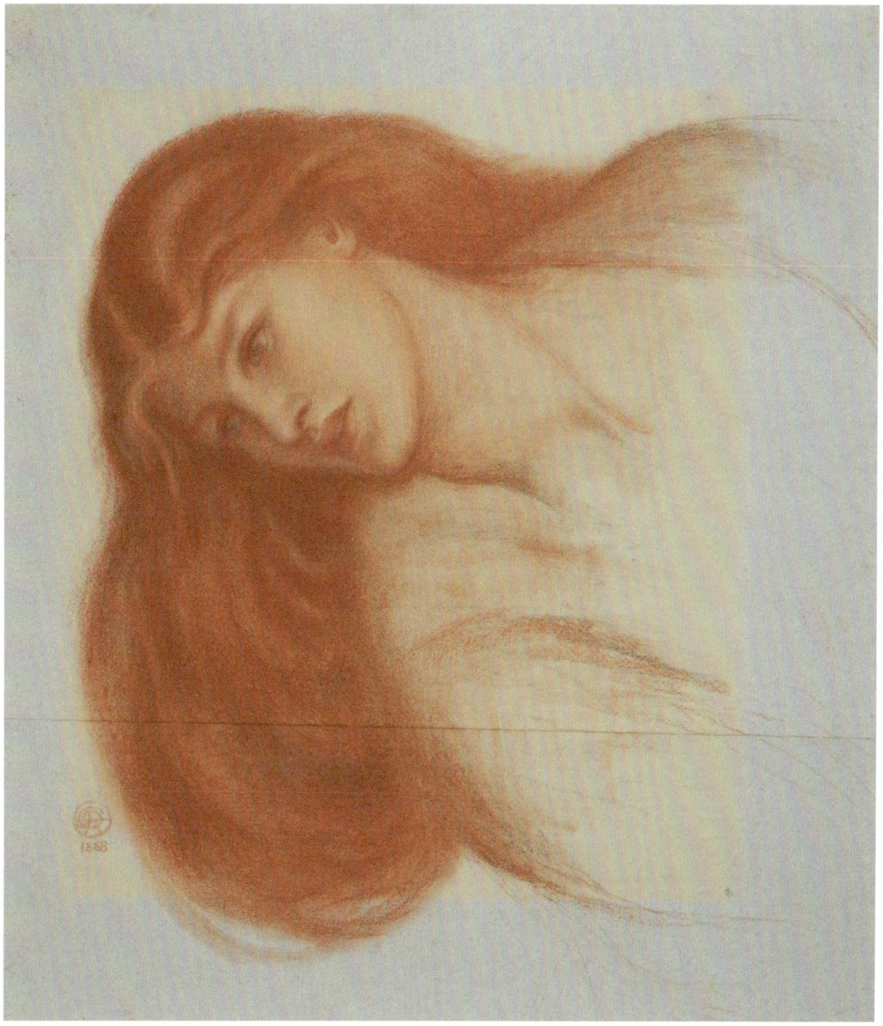

OPPOSITE
NO.189 Dante Gabriel Rossetti, *Venus Verticordia* 1868, watercolour and bodycolour on paper, 67 × 59

ABOVE
NO.190 Dante Gabriel Rossetti, *Head of Andromeda (Aspecta Medusa)* 1868, chalk on paper, 51.3 × 54.7

'I look at the crisp golden-threaded hair /
Whereof, to thrall my heart, Love twists a net'

Fazio degli Uberti, trans. Dante Gabriel Rossetti

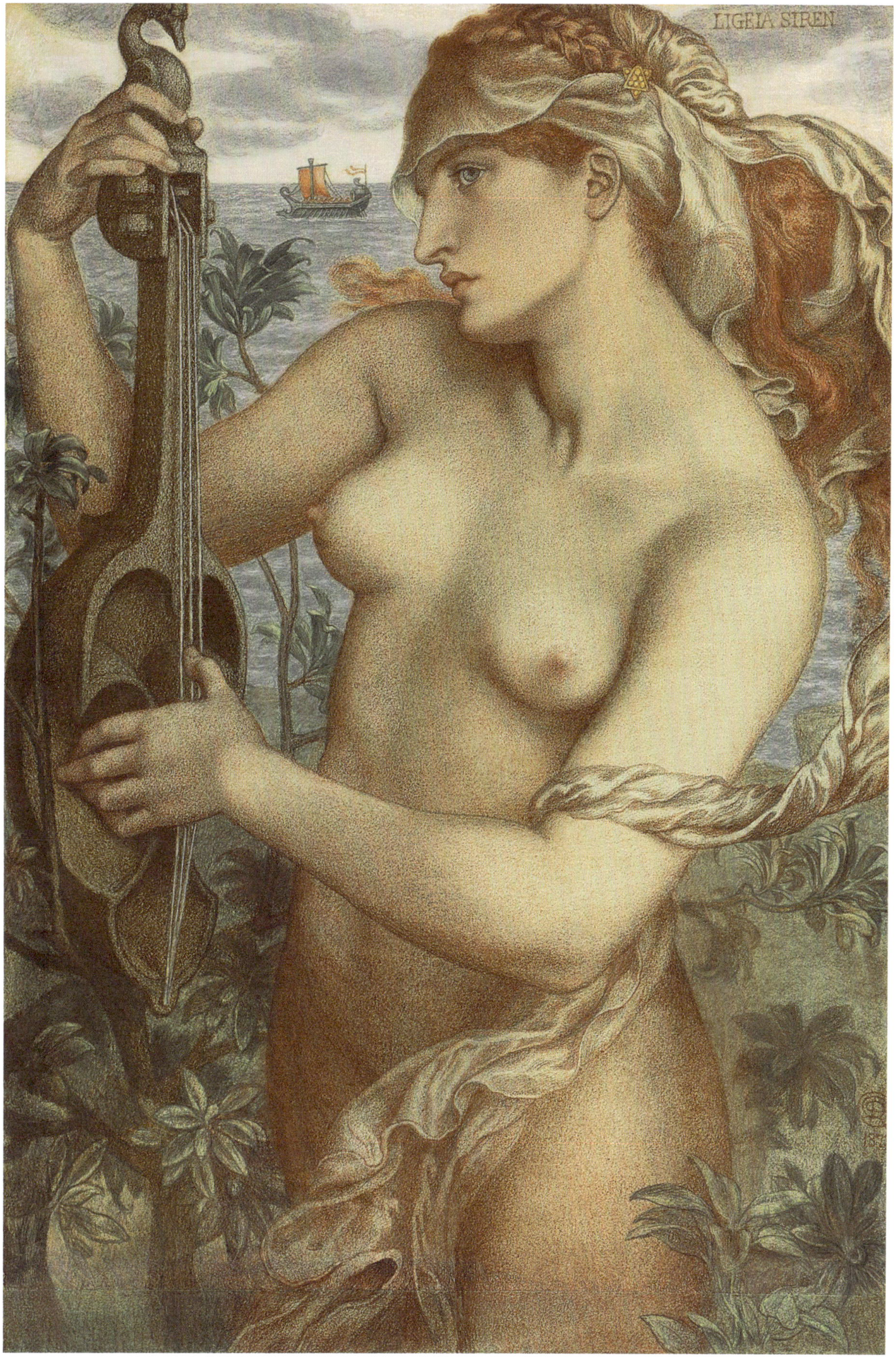
LIGEIA SIREN

'It was Lilith the wife of Adam: ... / Not a drop of her blood was human, / But she was made like a soft sweet woman'

Dante Gabriel Rossetti

The painting is associated with two poems, both of which address the subject of Adam's first wife. 'Body's Beauty' was composed in 1866 as Gabriel was still engaged in the creation of the painted composition. The two stanzas that make up the poem are included on the bottom section of the frame.[18] The second poem, 'Eden Bower', was begun in 1869 and tells a fuller - and darker - story of Lilith's life:

It was Lilith the wife of Adam:
  (Eden bower's in flower)
Not a drop of her blood was human,
But she was made like a soft sweet woman

Lilith stood on the skirts of Eden
  (And O the bower and the hour!)
She was the first that thence was driven;
With her was hell and with Eve was heaven

In the ear of the Snake said Lilith: –
  (Eden bower's in flower.)
'To thee I come when the rest is over;
A snake was I when thou wast my lover. ...'

Much of the ballad structure is taken up in a discourse between Lilith and the serpent as they bring about the fall of Adam and Lilith's replacement, Eve. A drawing of *Lady Lilith* from this later period (NO.187) depicts a nude female figure with a snake entwined around her body, suggesting the reciprocal working out of this prose-image relationship.

Virginia Allen has described Gabriel's engagement with the subject of Lilith as an expression of 'not only what men saw in the feminist movement in the broad sense, but what was understood to be the major hazard of that movement: the escape of women from male control of their sexuality'.[19] I would add to this a contiguous dialectic thread in which Gabriel positions women in a more positive role as strong and defiant in the face of patriarchal restrictions and confinement. As Jan Marsh has remarked, he was particularly supportive of his sister Christina's professional career, encouraging, promoting and editing as the need arose.[20] Gabriel's Lilith has no time to waste on the opposite sex, and in fact ignores the male gaze.

PAGE 191
NO.191 Dante Gabriel Rossetti, *Ligeia Siren* 1873, coloured chalks on paper, 80 × 55

OPPOSITE
NO.192 Dante Gabriel Rossetti, *Monna Vanna* 1866, oil paint on canvas, 88.9 × 86.4

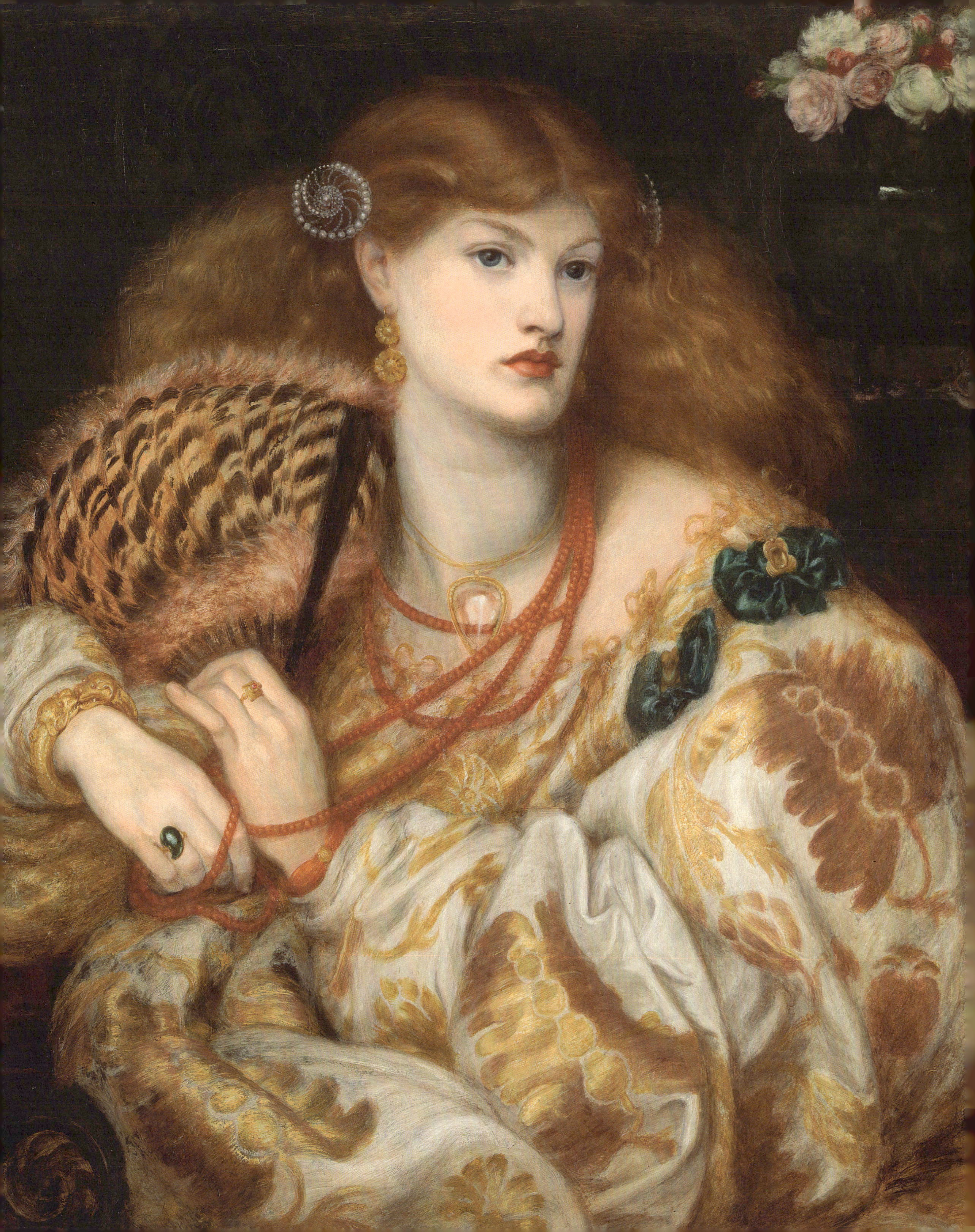

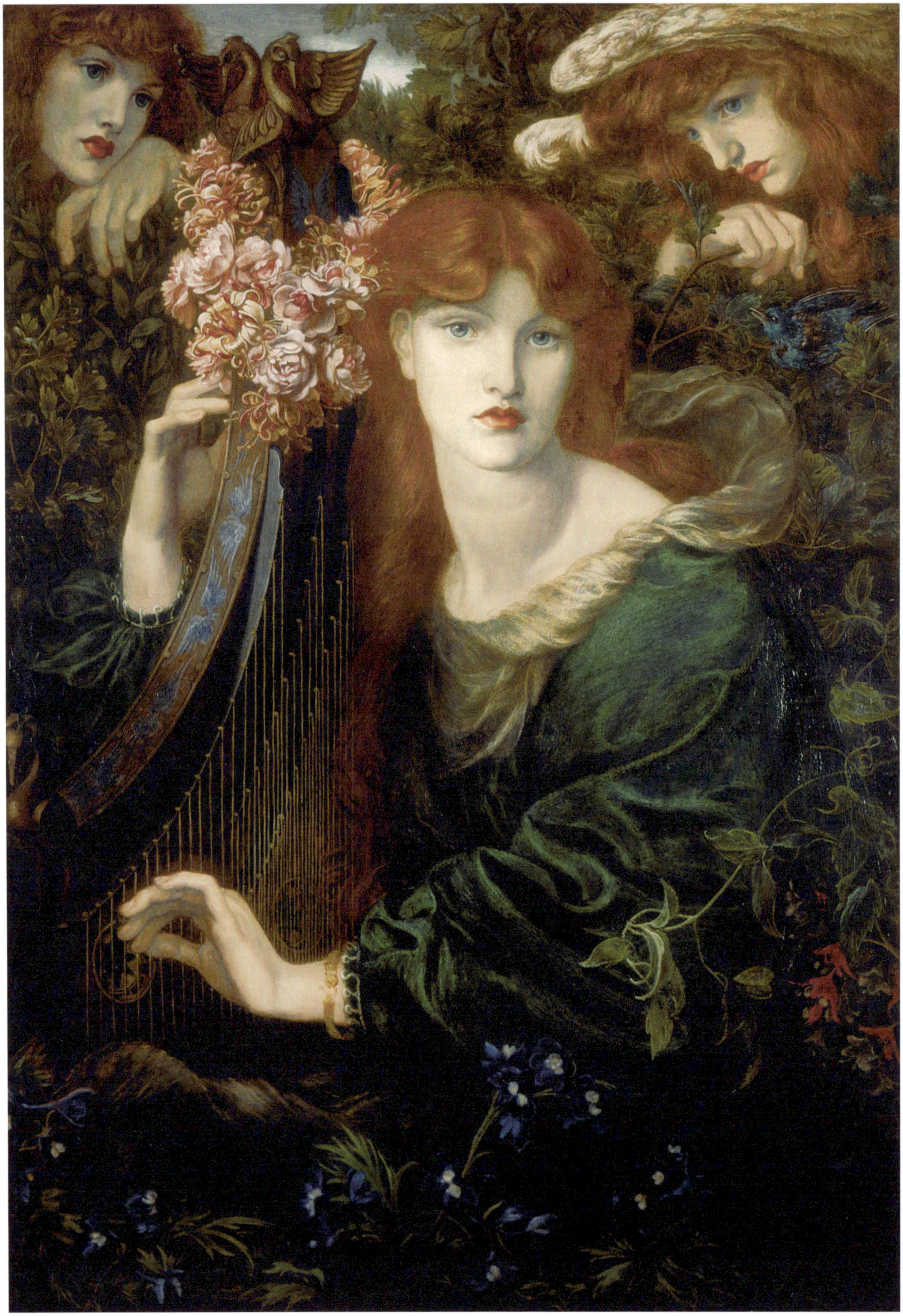

When the subject was first envisioned, the model was Fanny Cornforth, as shown in two surviving compositions, a chalk drawing and a watercolour. In 1872, Gabriel asked to have the painting back from the patron as he was reconsidering the arrangement. At this time Fanny's face was replaced with the cooler sensibility of the model Alexa Wilding. Wilding began sitting for Gabriel around 1865 and is featured in numerous works throughout the 1870s. She was literally encountered on a London street,[21] when Gabriel approached and asked her to pose for him. She came from a seemingly respectable working-class background, in comparison to Fanny. The substitution of Alexa as the figure of Lilith several years after its creation may well reflect the artist's continued personal revision and understanding of the current 'woman question'.[22]

The tastes of shipping magnate Frederick Leyland were particularly aligned with Gabriel's new concept of female beauty. Leyland was a self-made man who began amassing an art collection in the early 1860s. His commission for *Lady Lilith* included a companion piece entitled *Sibylla Palmifera* (NO.185), with an accompanying poem 'Soul's Beauty'. Both paintings were intended for the sumptuous display in the drawing room of his Prince's Gate home (NO.194). A shrine to Dante Gabriel Rossetti, the room included, in addition to this pair, *Monna Rosa*, *Proserpine*, *Mnemosyne* and *Veronica Veronese*, among others (see NOS.197, 195, 198). Leyland would later become infamous for his commission to Whistler for the Peacock Room – an undertaking which ended in the artist's dismissal and the vituperative severing of their relationship.

In considering *Lady Lilith* within the broader cultural sphere – and setting aside Gabriel's preoccupation with the woman question – the painting falls squarely in the thick of the Aesthetic movement. Marsh makes a strong argument for understanding *Lady Lilith* as Gabriel's direct response to Whistler's *Symphony in White, No. 1: The White Girl* (National Gallery, Washington), exhibited in London and Paris in 1862–3.[23] Whistler's painting incited critical derision for its sexual innuendo enhanced by the absence of any readable narrative. The painting depicts Joanna Heffernan, standing in virginal white, her red hair worn loose, her body turned just slightly to engage with the viewer. Gabriel's image of *Lilith* similarly employed his live-in muse, Fanny Cornforth (at least as originally intended), to convey an image of female detachment within the spotlight of patriarchal assessment, suggesting a new kind of woman for whom male esteem was no longer a marker of lifetime achievement.

For nearly a decade, Alexa Wilding would appear in almost as many of Gabriel's canvases as Jane Morris (see p.202).[24] Her beauty was demonstrably inspirational for the artist, but, like Fanny's, was not exemplary of current fashionable standards. Her red hair and lips, and particularly a palpable self-assured presence, served as the touchstone for Gabriel's continued conceptualisation of womanhood. He often had several compositions under-way simultaneously. While working on *Lilith*, with Fanny as the model, Gabriel was also considering a subject titled *Monna Vanna* (NO.192), for which Wilding sat. Devoid of narrative, *Monna Vanna* represents an adjustment of the definition of female beauty. Wilding dominates the now familiar shallow perspective, her body twisted to the right, as she gazes over her left shoulder, in cursory acknowledgement of the

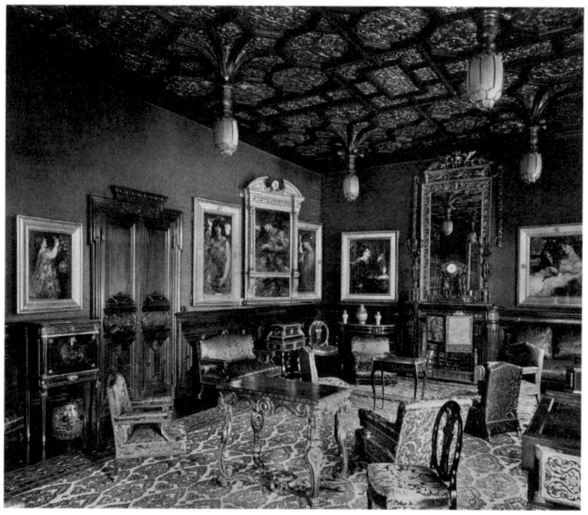

OPPOSITE
NO.193 Dante Gabriel Rossetti, *La Ghirlandata* 1873, oil paint on canvas, 124 × 85

ABOVE
NO.194 Bedford Lemere, photograph of home of Frederick Leyland, 49 Prince's Gate, May 1892, interior view in the drawing room, showing six paintings by Dante Gabriel Rossetti on the walls

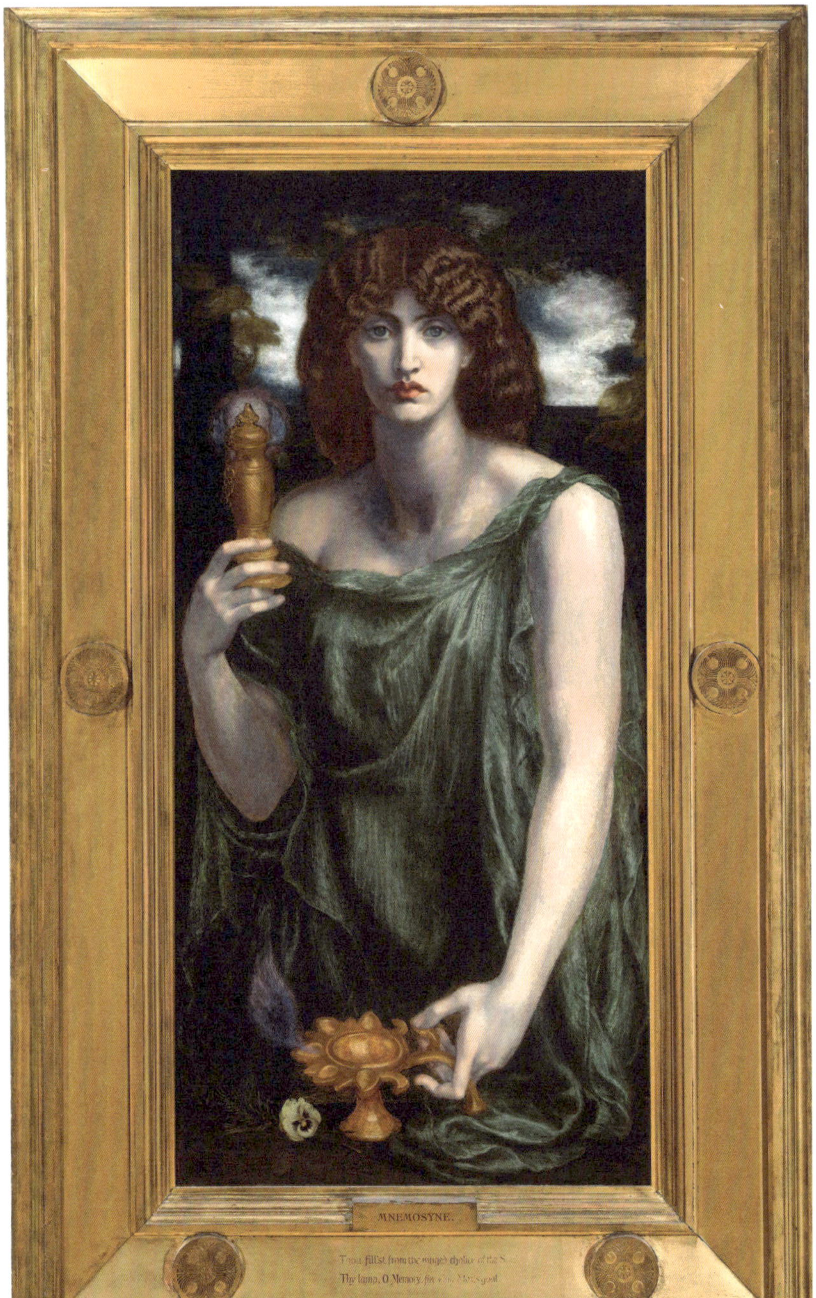
MNEMOSYNE.

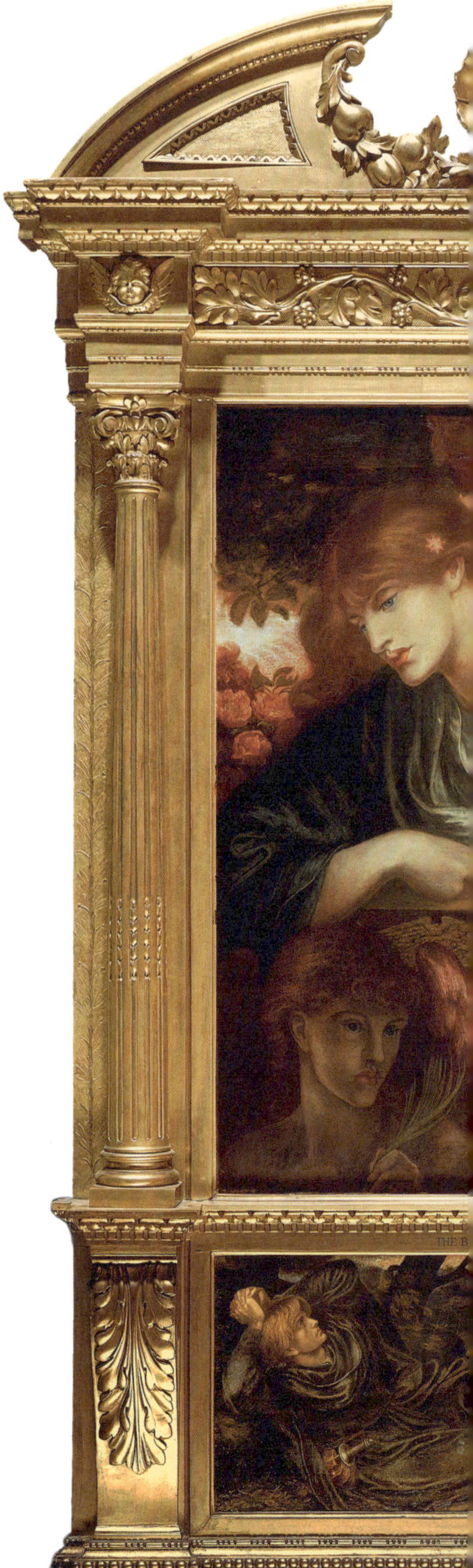

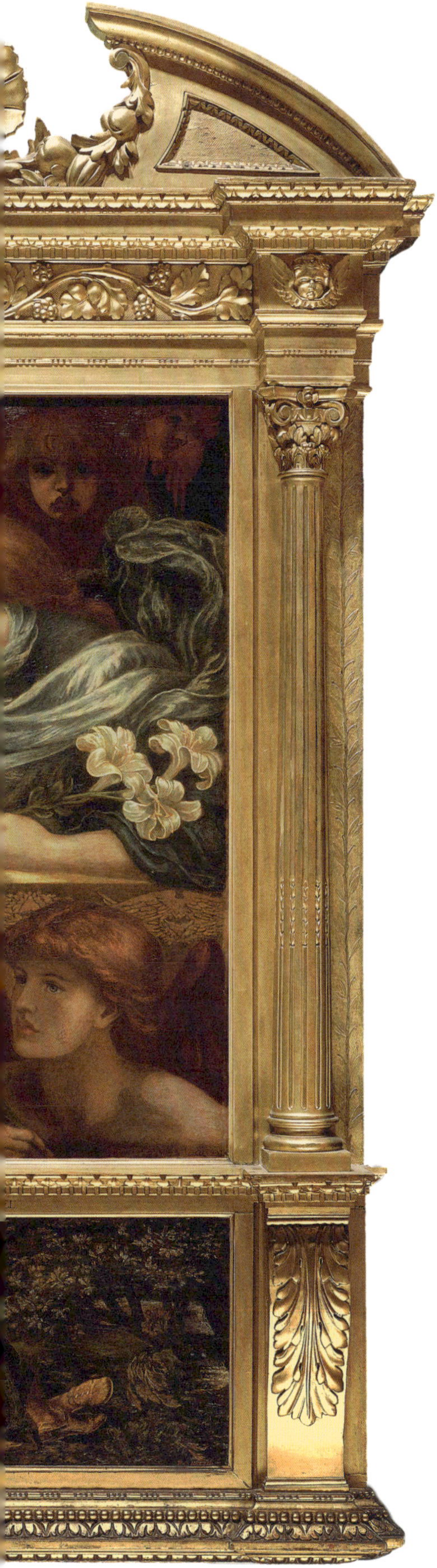

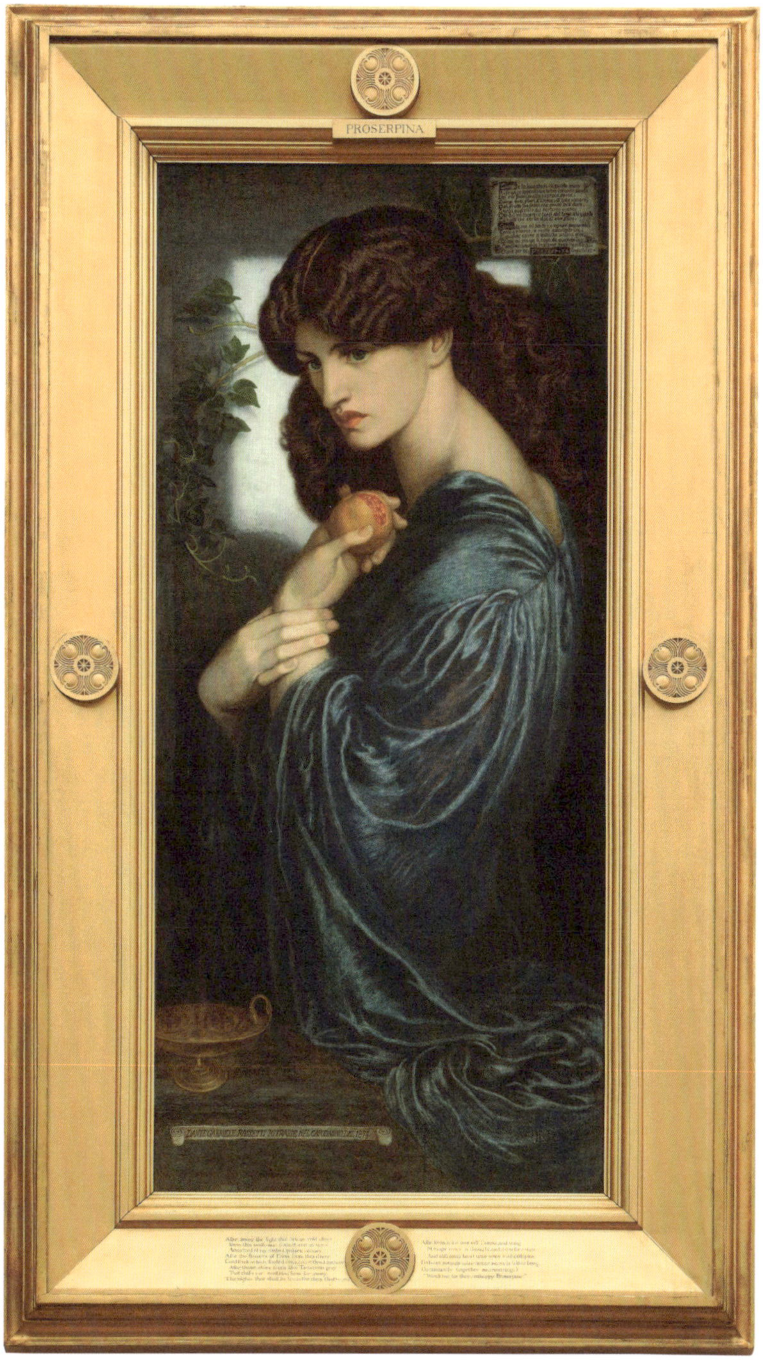
PROSERPINA

'The picture is called Lady Lilith ... *and represents* a modern Lilith *combing out her abundant golden hair and gazing on herself in the glass'*

Dante Gabriel Rossetti

PAGE 196
NO.195 Dante Gabriel Rossetti, *Mnemosyne* 1881, oil paint on canvas, 126.4 × 61

PAGES 196–7
NO.196 Dante Gabriel Rossetti, *The Blessed Damozel* 1875–9, oil on canvas, 221.5 × 139 (frame)

PAGE 197
NO.197 Dante Gabriel Rossetti, *Proserpine* 1874, oil paint on canvas, 125.1 × 61

OPPOSITE
NO.198 Dante Gabriel Rossetti, *Veronica Veronese* 1872, oil paint on canvas, 109.2 × 88.9

viewer. She is clothed, or rather engulfed, in a mass of gold brocade fabric, accessorised with jewellery – cockle-shaped clips in her hair, a crystal pendant and a red coral necklace, rings on both hands (standard appurtenances in Gabriel's compositions of the period) – and pressing an exotic feathered fan to her right shoulder.

The pose mimics traditional Venetian portraits, as does the flattening of the picture field (the painting was originally titled *Venus Veneta*). The great roll of the sleeve is also a sixteenth-century borrowing, as Alastair Grieve has suggested.[25] The title of the painting, *Monna* (or Lady), a contraction of Madonna, was drawn from Dante's *Vita Nuova*. The composition was retitled *Belcolore* when the artist reworked it in 1873.[26] In renaming the painting, Gabriel was further reducing any possibility for narrative interpretation, redirecting the viewer towards a purely formal analysis. Viewers were meant to hone in on the sensory elements – the smell of roses, the downy tactility of feathers, and the embodiment of female sensuality. William Sharp, writer and early Rossetti biographer, felt the painting to convey 'Beauty, as manifested in refined and exquisite feminine loveliness'.[27] Another contemporary, Frederick W.H. Myers, renowned promotor of psychical concepts, considered Gabriel's images of feminine beauty within the broader scope of their expanding agency. Describing them as 'the sacred pictures of a new religion', he saw in them evidence of 'the steady rise in the status of women; that constant deepening and complication of the commerce between the sexes which is one of the signs of progressive civilization'.[28]

Gabriel continued to amend and recast his conception of beauty throughout the 1870s, often using Alexa Wilding's features as inspiration. The images become subtler in their outright sexuality, as seen, for example, in *Veronica Veronese* (1872, Delaware Art Museum; NO.198) and *La Ghirlandata* (1873, Guildhall Art Gallery; NO.193). The focus is honed on defining the power inherent in feminine beauty, in these particular images, as allied to the arts of music and painting. Another source for this refined vision of womanhood was found in Jane Morris.

Potentially as early as 1871, Gabriel turned to the myth of Proserpine as subject, creating a chalk drawing of Morris facing left, holding a pomegranate (1871, Ashmolean Museum). As many as seven versions of the subject were conceived.[29] The majority of

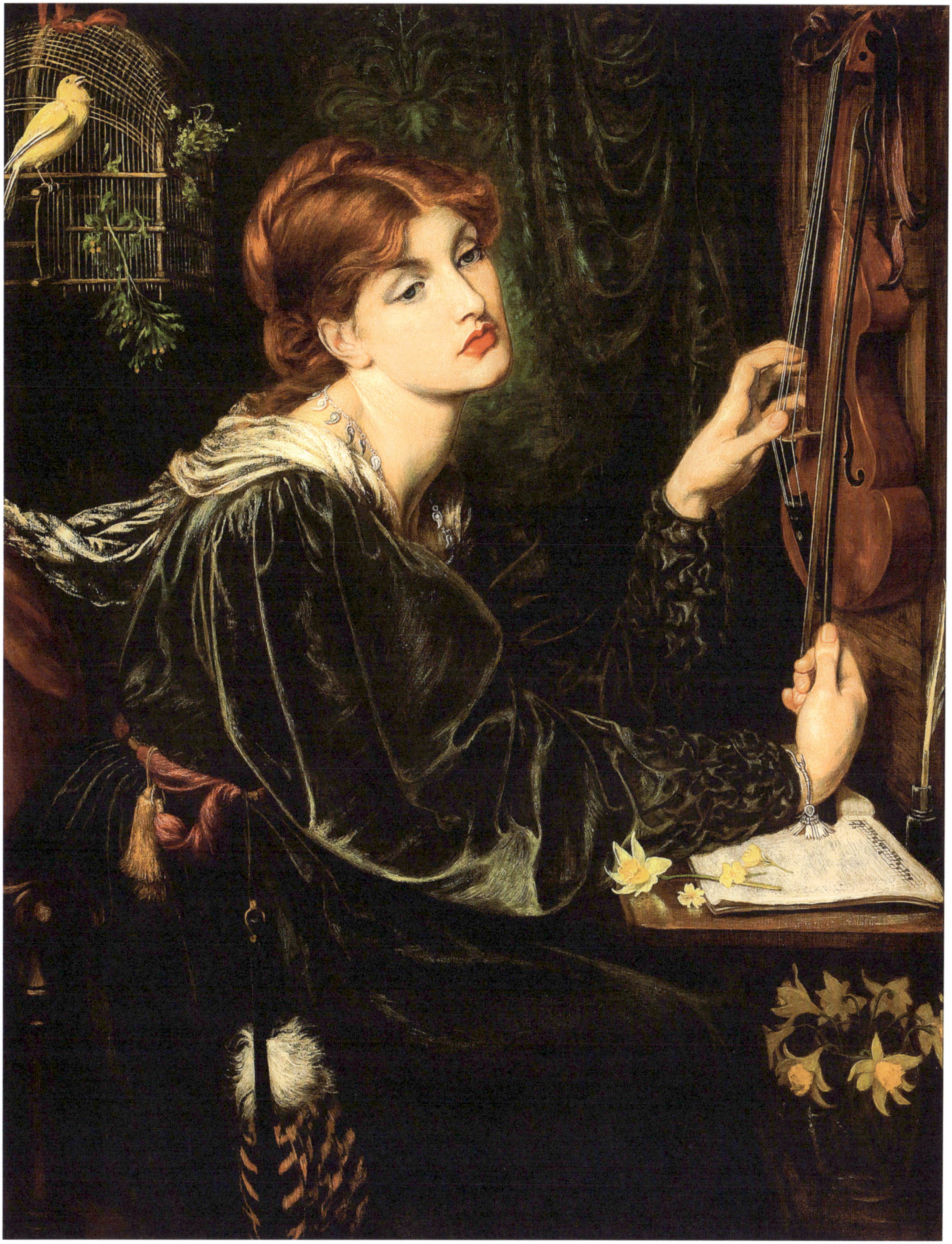

the attempts were created at Kelmscott (see p.220), all from the face of Jane Morris. What Allan Life designates the sixth version of Gabriel's *Proserpine* (NO.197) is by far the most comprehensive, including all appurtenances. In a tall, narrow format, Jane Morris stands, half-length, facing left and looking slightly downward. She holds a pomegranate in her left hand, her arm firmly pressed towards her shoulder. A sprig of ivy and an incense burner at upper and lower left, respectively, complete the goddess's accessories. In comparison to earlier works such as *Veronica Veronese* and *La Bella Mano* (1875, Delaware Art Museum), these ancillary trappings are significantly reduced - a paring down that continues into the last years of Gabriel's life.

At upper right, Gabriel has included a trompe l'œil rendering of a small piece of paper, or 'cartellino', inscribed with his own sonnet 'Proserpina (For a Picture)'. Here, the accompanying poem has moved off the surrounding frame to become embedded within the composition, fully uniting word and image. As Maryan Wynn Ainsworth explains, 'Rossetti saw the poem and painting of a particular theme as linked not only intellectually but also physically ... inextricably bound together'.[30]

Afar away the light that brings cold cheer
Unto this wall, - one instant and no more
Admitted at my distant palace-door

Recent unframing has revealed the letters 'JANE' written vertically along the lower left side of the canvas, previously hidden by the rabbet - a surprise and an anomaly still to be explained. When compared to the early portrait of Jane Morris, *The Blue Silk Dress* of 1868 (see NO.208), this version of *Proserpine* illustrates a gradual idealisation of her face, what William Michael Rossetti described as a necessary reduction in order for the artist to achieve his pictorial goal: 'For idealizing there was but one process - to realize.'[31] With the completion of *Proserpine* in 1874, Gabriel had moved from realising to the idealisation his brother explains. Jane Morris is depicted like a statue in an ancient temple, a figure worthy of veneration.

The gradual abstraction of Morris's features is taken to the extreme in the paintings created in the last years of Gabriel's life. In 1875, he began work on a composition for what would become both *Astarte Syriaca* and *Mnemosyne* or *Ricordanza* (NO.195). Both are three-quarter-length images of Jane Morris as a 'Syrian Venus' and a goddess of memory, respectively. In these two late paintings, Morris's appearance is virtually unrecognisable. The larger-than-life figure who fills the picture plane of *Mnemosyne* is an androgynous mythic creature, a symbol of time passing and the life hereafter. One of the last canvases completed prior to Gabriel's death, it is his final statement on womanhood. Depicting a figure in which male and female characteristics are now merged, it suggests a gender détente in which the sexes harmoniously co-exist in one body. It is both a summing up of the past and a view into the world to come, as indicated by the lines inscribed on the frame:

Thou fill'st from the winged chalice of the soul
Thy lamp, O Memory, fire-winged to its goal

1 Sidney Colvin, 'Rossetti as a Painter', *The Magazine of Art*, vol.6, Jan. 1883, p.183.

2 Jan Marsh, *Dante Gabriel Rossetti: Painter and Poet*, London 1999, p.273.

3 Elizabeth Prettejohn, '"Beautiful women with floral adjuncts": Rossetti's New Style', in *Dante Gabriel Rossetti*, ed. Julian Treuherz, Elizabeth Prettejohn and Edwin Becker, London 2003, p.54.

4 While the change in style was clearly initiated, the production of medieval watercolours continued with diminishing frequency to satisfy early patrons and to identify those amenable to the new work.

5 Sylvie Broussine and Christopher Newall, *Rossetti's Portraits*, London 2021, p.65.

6 For the introduction of the phrase, see Greg Buzwell, 'Daughters of Decadence: The New Woman in the Victorian Fin de Siècle', British Library (online), 15 May 2014, accessed 2 November 2022. For more on the definition of the New Woman, see for instance Marianne Berger Woods, *The New Woman in Print and Pictures*, Jefferson, NC 2009.

7 Dante Gabriel Rossetti to William Michael Rossetti, 6 June 1860, in *The Correspondence of Dante Gabriel Rossetti*, ed. William E. Fredeman, 10 vols., Cambridge, Woodbridge and Rochester, NY 2002–15, vol.2, p.298.

8 For a comprehensive account of the iconography of the woman at the window imagery, see Jennifer Sliwka, *Reframed: The Woman in the Window*, London 2022.

9 Maryan Wynn Ainsworth, *Dante Gabriel Rossetti and the Double Work of Art*, New Haven, CT 1976, p.1.

10 This letter is cited in Deborah Cherry, 'The Hogarth Club: 1858–1861', *Burlington Magazine*, vol.122, no.925, April 1980, p.241; Hunt to Thomas Combe, 12 Feb. 1860, Bodleian Library.

11 Dante Gabriel Rossetti to Ellen Heaton, 24 October 1863, in Fredeman 2002–15, 3, p.83.

12 Alastair Grieve first drew attention to the poem's suggestion of female entrapment in *The Pre-Raphaelites*, ed. Leslie Parris, London 1984, p.98.

13 See Sarah Heaton, 'Gender and Sexuality: Tresses Adorned and Adored, Locks Coiled and Cut', in *A Cultural History of Hair in the Age of Empire*, ed. S. Heaton, London 2019, vol.5, pp.101–16.

14 Dante Gabriel Rossetti to James Smetham, 1 August 1866, in Fredeman 2002–15, 3, p.456.

15 The importance of *Faust* as an inspirational source is visible from the very earliest of Dante Gabriel Rossetti's work. See, for instance, the adolescent drawings in the collection of the National Trust, Wightwick Manor.

16 Dante Gabriel Rossetti to Ponsonby Lyons, 18 November 1869, reprinted in William Michael Rossetti, *Rossetti Papers, 1862 to 1870*, London 1903, pp.484–6.

17 Dante Gabriel Rossetti to Thomas Gordon Hake, 21 April 1870, in Fredeman 2002–15, 4, p.449.

18 The first line of the second stanza inscribed on the frame is slightly altered from that of the poem as printed in 1881 in *House of Life*.

19 Virginia M. Allen, '"One strangling golden hair": Dante Gabriel Rossetti's *Lady Lilith*', *Art Bulletin*, vol.66, no.2, June 1984, p.294.

20 Marsh 1999, p.297.

21 See Allan and Page Life, 'Monna Innominata: Alexa Wilding', in Fredeman 2002–15, 6, p.608.

22 Charles Fairfax Murray understood the change in model for the figure of Lilith to be the desire of both the painter and the patron (see letter, Fairfax Murray to Bancroft, 6 September 1893, in *The Correspondence between Samuel Bancroft, Jr. and Charles Fairfax Murray, 1892–1916*, ed. Rowland Elzea, Wilmington, DE 1980, p.33). Outside of Fairfax Murray's missive, there is no surviving evidence that the patron, Frederick Leyland, was dissatisfied with the model's face, despite this being the historical consensus to date. Dante Gabriel Rossetti had a habit of re-working compositions over time. We do know that the painting was back in his studio by January of 1872, although of the specific changes we have only his enthusiastic summary: 'I have done a great deal' and 'it is now a complete success' (*Dante Gabriel Rossetti: An Annotated Bibliography*, ed. Francis L. Fennell, New York 1981, p.35). Fairfax Murray's retelling may well reflect his own bias towards Fanny.

23 Jan Marsh, 'Pre-Raphaelite Models: Elizabeth Siddal, Fanny Eaton, Fanny Cornforth' paper, for 'Reframing the Muse' course, Royal Academy, 21 May 2022.

24 A. and P. Life, 'Monna Innominata', in Fredeman 2002–15, 6, p.605.

25 Alastair Grieve, in Parris 1984, p.214.

26 There is evidence of the canvas having been expanded, although this may have been done during the original creation and not in 1873. My thanks to Joyce Townsend, Senior Conservation Scientist, Tate, for this information.

27 William Sharp, *Dante Gabriel Rossetti: A Record and a Study*, London 1882, p.200.

28 F.W.H. Myers, 'Rossetti and the Religion of Beauty', in Myers, *Essays – Modern*, London 1883, pp.325, 319.

29 According to Allan Life, in its original conception the female figure may have been holding an apple, the subject intended to have been Eve; see Fredeman 2002–15, 6, p.590.

30 Ainsworth 1976, p.6.

31 William Michael Rossetti, *Dante Gabriel Rossetti: His Family-Letters with a Memoir*, 2 vols., London 1895, vol.1, p.244.

Wendy Parkins

‘The works are there to tell their own tale’: Jane Morris in the Art of Dante Gabriel Rossetti

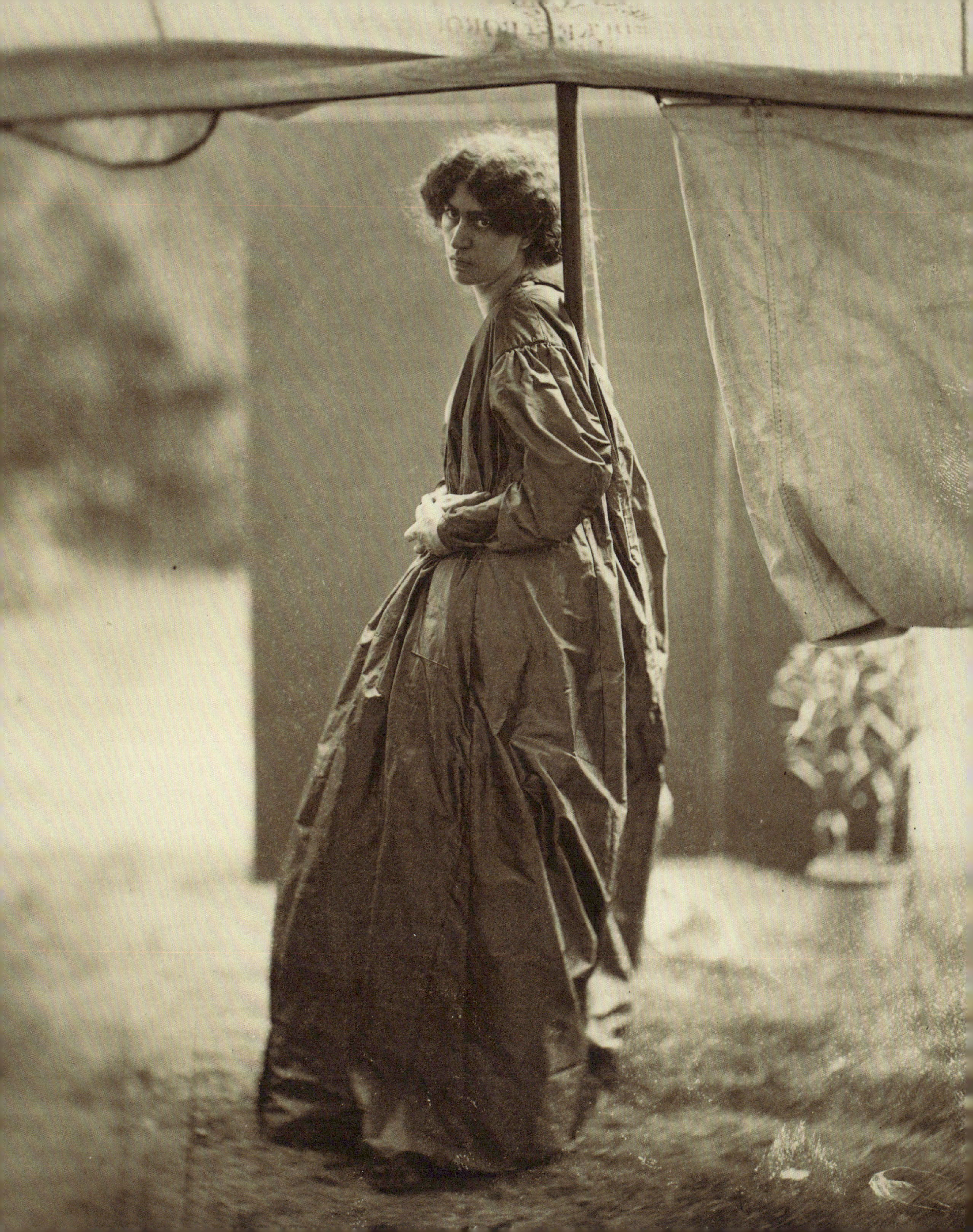

Truth and fiction have always proved difficult to distinguish in the life of Jane Burden, the daughter of a laundress and a stableman. Within two years of meeting Dante Gabriel Rossetti in Oxford in 1857, she would become Jane Morris, wife of designer and poet William Morris, and established as an admired artist's model. Gabriel's first sketches of Morris in Oxford (see NO.200) beautifully captured her distinctive features, such as her full lips, strong brow and nose, long neck, thick dark hair and tapered fingers.

Although traces of her humble origins are present in these early drawings – in the simple manner in which her hair is arranged, her plain dress, and absence of ornamentation, for instance – Gabriel's art more commonly endowed Morris with an exotic femininity that contemporaries often assumed to be foreign in origin. As William Michael Rossetti, the artist's brother, wrote: 'For a Pia, Pandora, Mariana, Proserpine, Venus Astarte, or Mnemosyne, there was hardly such another head to be found in England.'[1] Her face 'was at once tragic, mystic, passionate, calm, beautiful, and gracious ... a face ... not at all like that of an Englishwoman, but rather of an Ionian Greek'.[2]

Perhaps the best example of Gabriel's attempt to endow Morris with exotic, if not other-worldly, characteristics is his monumental *Astarte Syriaca* 1877, a work of confronting physicality with its voluptuous rendering of a bare-shouldered Morris. Here, she is simultaneously a Syrian goddess far removed from earthly origins and the embodiment of a bold carnality at odds with Victorian conventions of genteel femininity.

Given such Rossettian depictions, then, it might not seem surprising that in her own lifetime Morris came to be seen as something of a mythic figure herself. To those meeting her in real life, she could seem just as unearthly as her depictions on canvas. The novelist Henry James, for instance, found her 'an apparition of fearful and wonderful intensity', a portrait come to life:

> It's hard to say whether she's a grand synthesis of all the Pre-Raphaelite pictures ever made ... whether she's an original or a copy. In either case she is a wonder. Imagine a tall lean woman in a long dress of some dead purple stuff, guiltless of hoops (or of anything else I should say), with a maze of crisp black hair, heaped in a great wavy projections [*sic*] on each of her temples, a thin pale face, great thick black oblique brows, joined in the middle and tucking themselves away under her hair, a mouth like the "Oriana" in our illustrated Tennyson, a long neck, without any collar, and in lieu thereof some dozen strings of outlandish beads. In fine complete.[3]

If Henry James's admiration had more than a hint of ambivalence, others were even more pointed in their rendering of such encounters. The artist James McNeill Whistler drily recalled observing 'Rossetti and Mrs Morris, sitting side by side in state, being worshipped' at a social gathering, while the *Punch* cartoonist George du Maurier described a dinner at which he 'was depressed by Mrs Morris, Rossetti's famous model, sitting opposite in an old Florentine costume and her old Florentine face above it'.[4]

PAGE 203
NO.199 From John Robert Parsons, *Thirteen Photographs of Jane Morris Posing in the Garden of Rossetti's House* 1865. 'Jane Morris posed by Rossetti in his garden at 16 Cheyne Walk', photograph 10/13. Albumen print on paper from wet collodion glass negative, 21.8 × 15.7

OPPOSITE
NO.200 Dante Gabriel Rossetti, *Jane Burden* 1858, ink, graphite and wash with white highlights on paper, 48.3 × 35.3

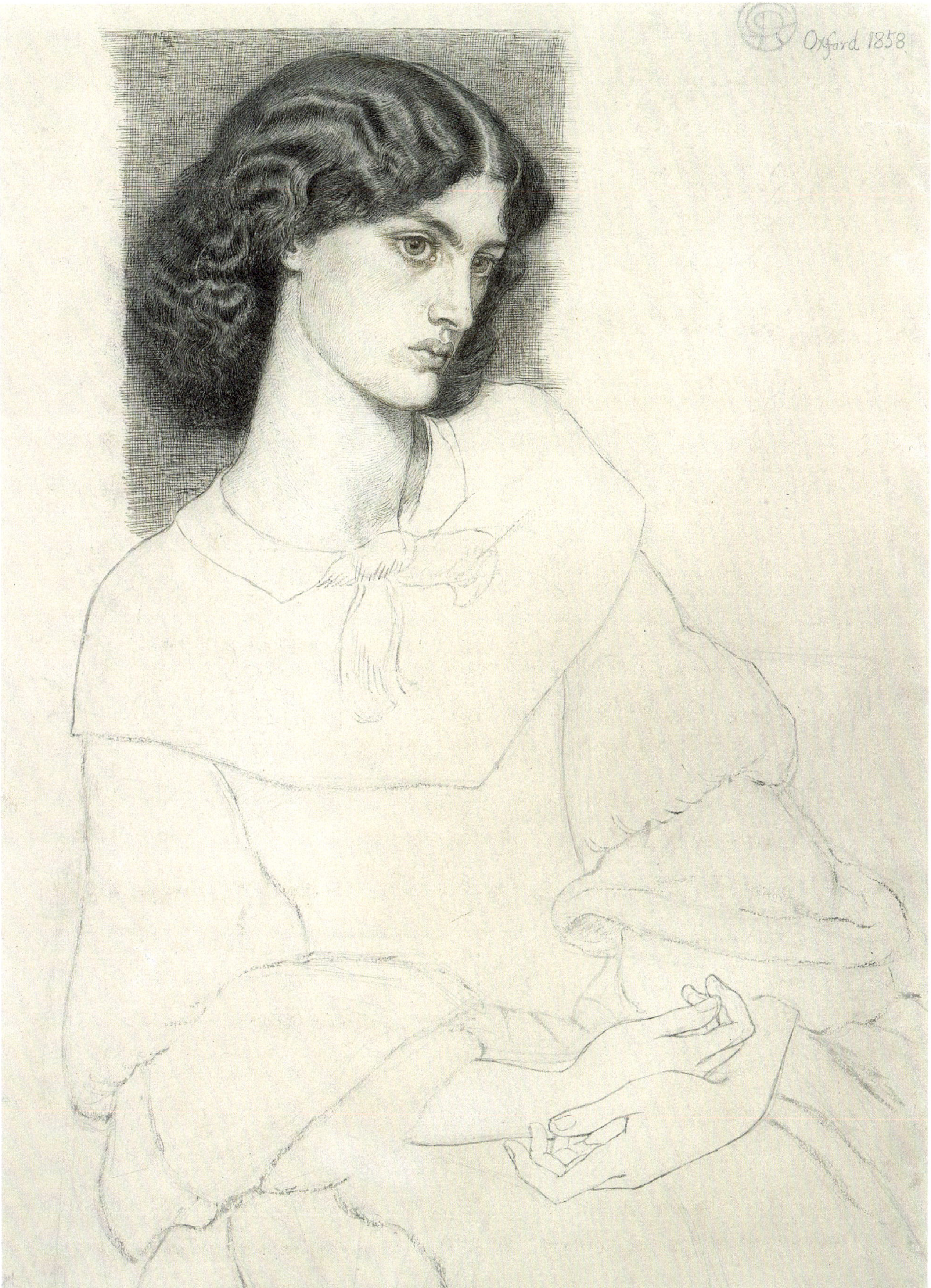
Oxford 1858

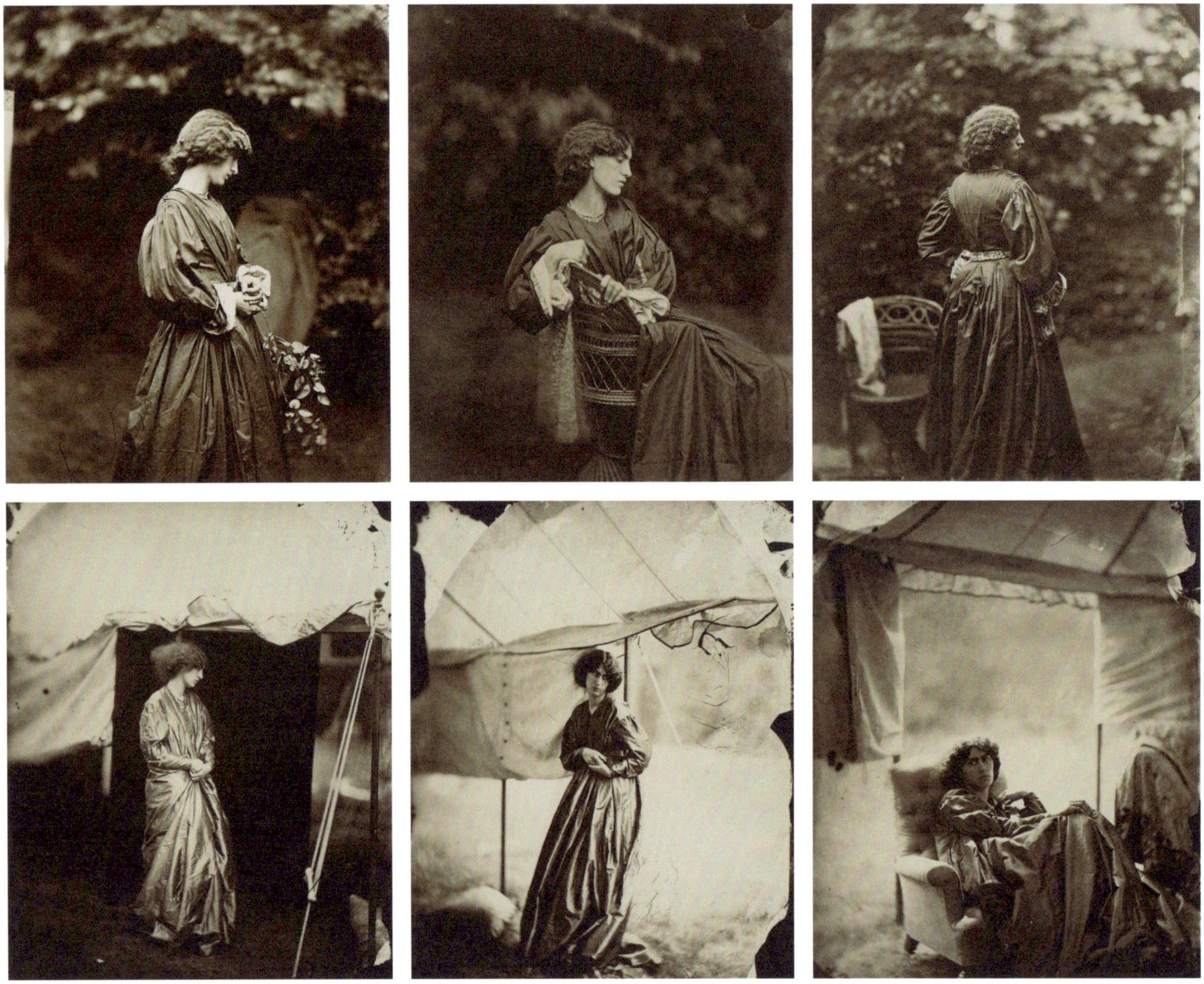

THIS PAGE, AND OPPOSITE, CLOCKWISE FROM TOP LEFT

NO.201 From John Robert Parsons, *Thirteen Photographs of Jane Morris Posing in the Garden of Rossetti's House* 1865. 'Jane Morris posed by Rossetti in his garden at 16 Cheyne Walk', photographs 3, 9, 1, 12, 11, 13 and 2, 5, 6, 8, 7, 4/13. Albumen prints on paper from wet collodion glass negatives, each 21.8 × 15.7

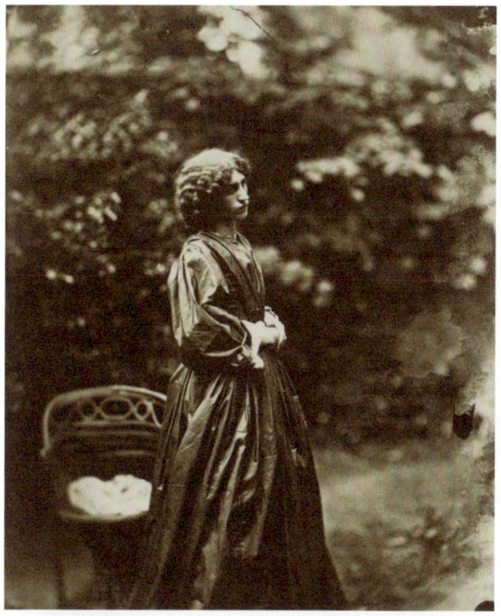
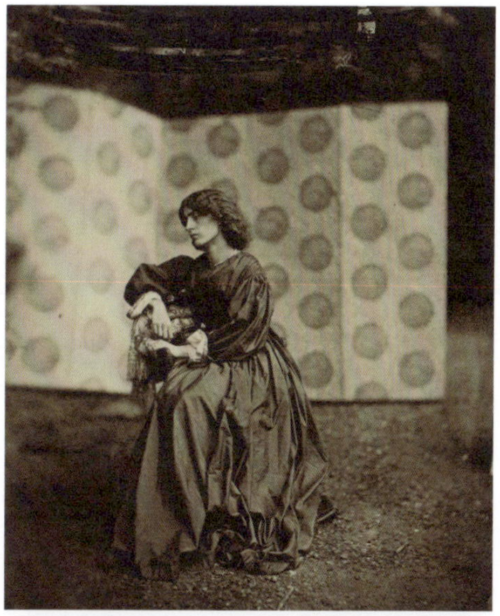
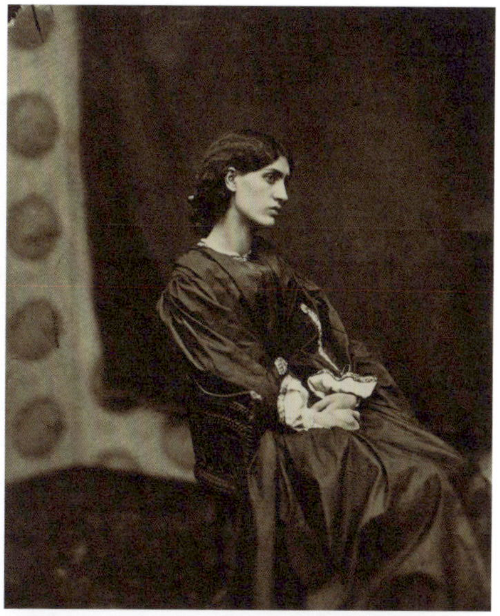
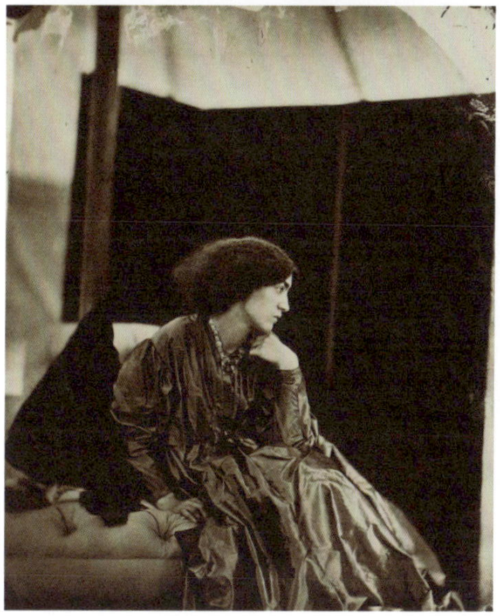
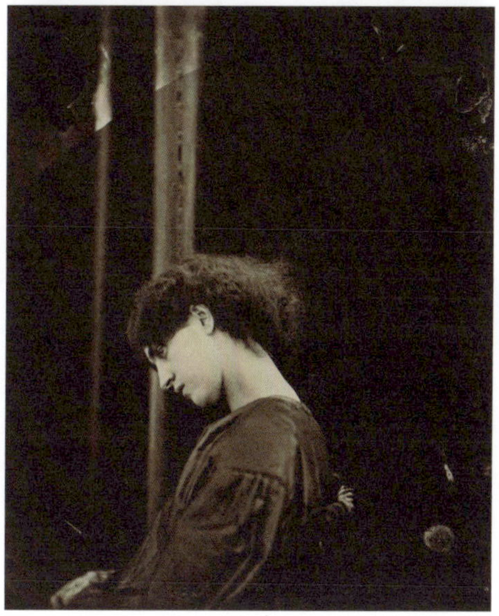
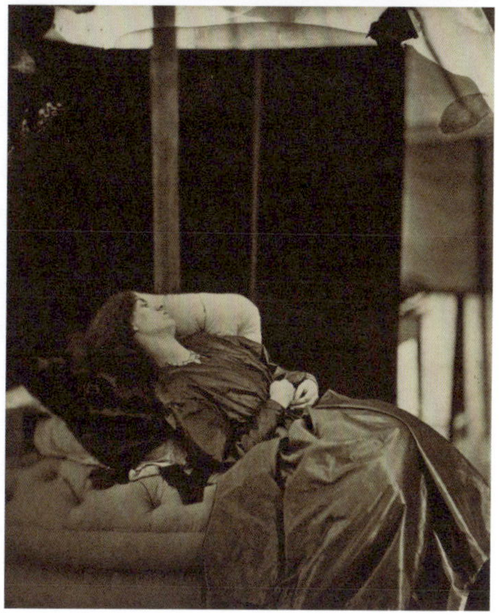

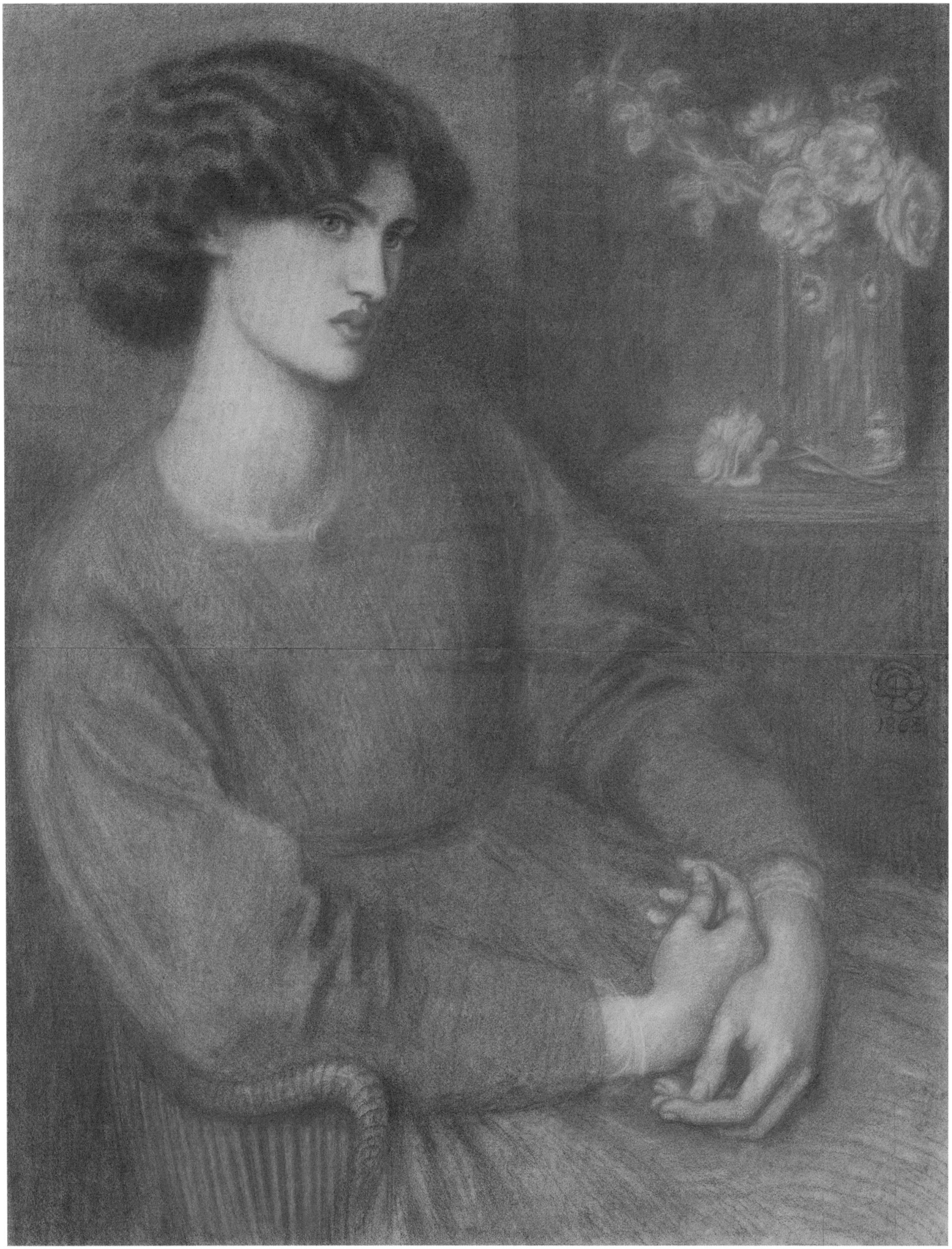

'For a Pia, Pandora, Mariana, Proserpine, Venus Astarte, or Mnemosyne, there was hardly such another head to be found in England'

William Michael Rossetti

Such somewhat gossipy recollections of Morris, however, should not be taken at face value (as it were), not least because they were the impressions of those who moved in social circles in which Gabriel and Morris were much talked about. Gabriel was notoriously reluctant to exhibit his work publicly, as well as increasingly reclusive in later life. Instead, he relied on patrons' commissions and 'an inner circle of worshipping and influential friends who could at odd moments whet the public appetite for some unforthcoming work of their caged genius', as one contemporary put it.[5] Gabriel's letters, in fact, show that he was at pains to keep Morris's name from public attention – or perhaps just from public association with his – writing to her in 1878: 'I have finished an old watercolour of the head of your portrait, and it comes well... I did not want it to be talked about among strangers by your name, so have christened it *Bruna Brunelleschi*, of course bearing on the dark complexion.'[6]

Many in Gabriel's 'inner circle', though, were well aware that his connection with Morris was not confined to art, a knowledge that no doubt also rippled out through networks associated with Pre-Raphaelitism and aestheticism. Although Gabriel had been sketching and painting Morris since 1857, an affair between artist and model is only believed to have begun in 1868. The romantic relationship continued well into the 1870s, with William Morris's knowledge but the disapproval of Gabriel's closest friends, who unfairly held Jane Morris responsible for Gabriel's addiction to chloral hydrate (a dangerously powerful sedative that depressed the central nervous system) and the breakdown of his health.[7]

Following Gabriel's death in 1882, however, when his artistic work began to be reviewed and evaluated more extensively, the significance and influence of Jane Morris on his art was more publicly discussed, often unfavourably. One critic, for instance, wrote of the 'monotony' and 'melancholy madness' of Gabriel's late work, complaining of 'the same face, the same stare, nearly the same attitude,

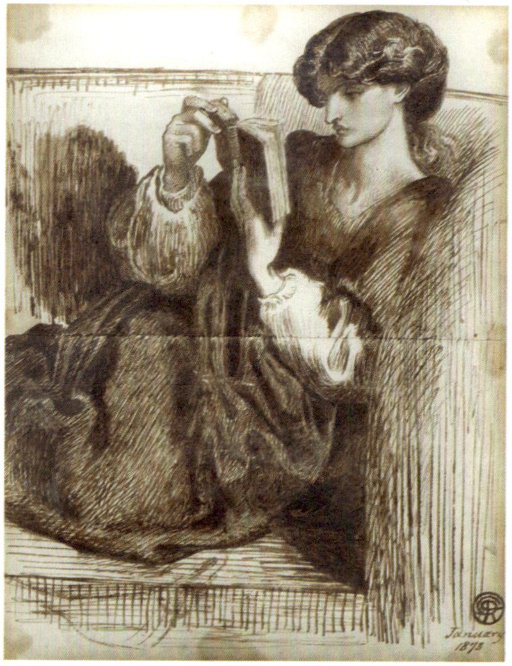

OPPOSITE
NO.202 Dante Gabriel Rossetti, *Jane Morris* 1868, coloured chalks on paper, 87.6 × 71.1

ABOVE
NO.203 Dante Gabriel Rossetti, *Portrait of Jane Morris* 1873, ink on paper, 22 × 17

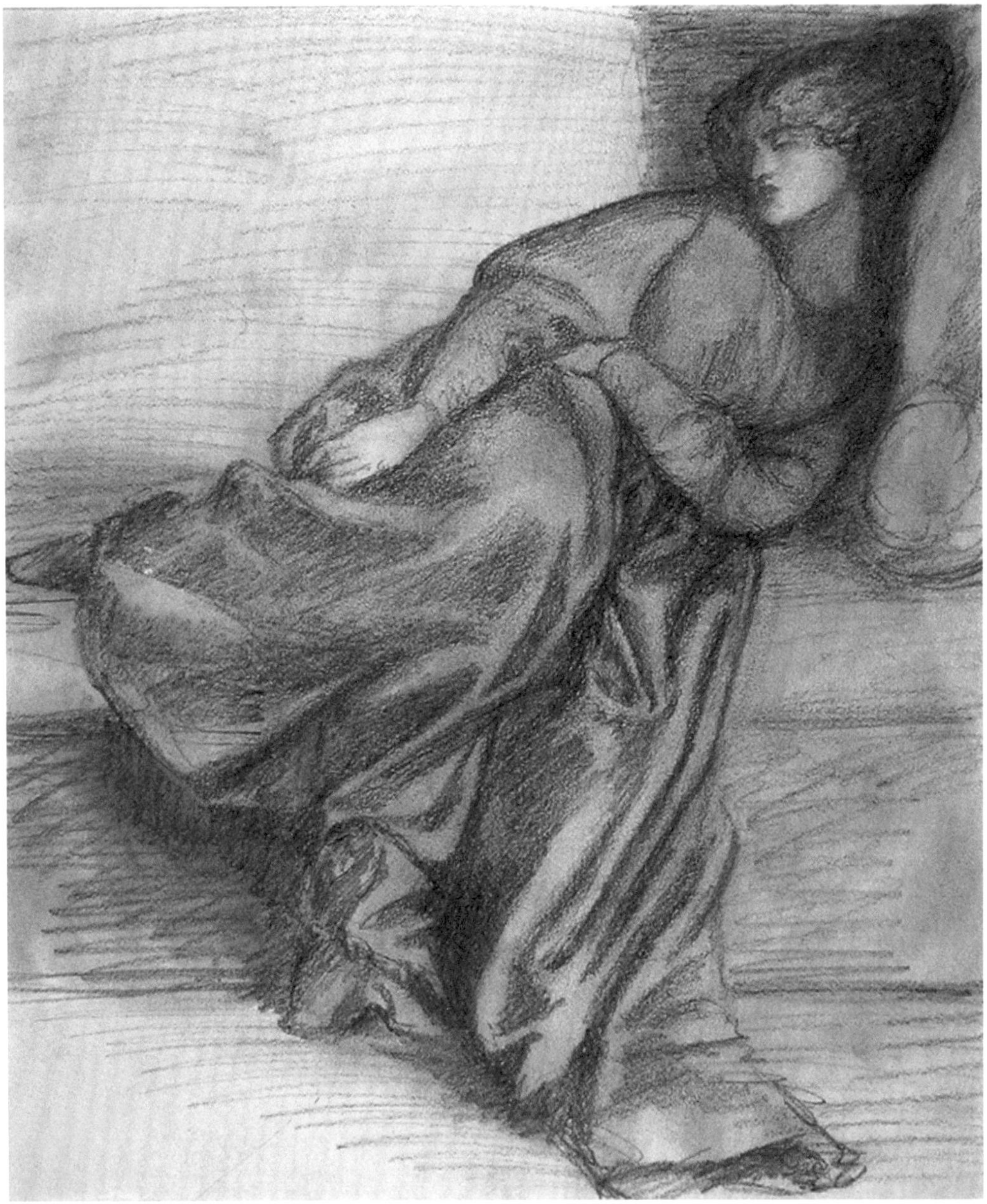

NO.204 Dante Gabriel Rossetti, *Jane Morris* 1870, graphite on paper, 35 × 30

'There were no lessons to be had, everything had to be laboured at for a time often unsuccessfully … but the failures were amusing too'

Jane Morris

on every wall', with the clear implication that the perceived deterioration in his artistic achievement was attributable to this model.[8] Even friends eager to defend Gabriel, such as the writer Theodore Watts-Dunton, concurred that 'The Truth About Rossetti' (the title of an essay by Watts-Dunton) was his obsession with one particular model – Jane Morris.[9]

As these posthumous evaluations suggest, then, Gabriel's artworks have left us a fixed image of Jane Morris, unable to speak for herself. It is only her body that speaks, or rather her body as mediated through the renderings and interpretations of others. Gabriel's pictures, for example, often borrowed literary tropes to depict Morris as a sad or tragic wife, as in *La Pia de' Tolomei* or *Proserpine* (see NOS.197, 210–12), where the artist sympathetically draws attention to the woman's suffering while implicitly absolving himself of any role in it.

Positioning Jane Morris in an imaginary past in this way not only endowed her with an air of timeless melancholy, it also occluded the active role that she played in Gabriel's artistic work. In the correspondence between Gabriel and Morris, a distinct picture of professional collaboration between artist and model emerges. For instance, regarding the portrait *Mrs William Morris (The Blue Silk Dress)* (NO.208), Gabriel wrote to his sitter in early 1868:

> About the blue silk dress it occurs to me to say that I think the sleeves should be as full at the top as is consistent with simplicity of outline, and perhaps would gain by being lined with some soft material, but of this you will be the best judge. The pieces of gold embroidery in front might (if you have time to make it) be something like this [*an outline in pen of a stitched pattern on a smocked bodice panel*], unless as is very possible a better idea strikes you. However it is a great pity that … the embroidery which you propose to put at the back will be hidden.[10]

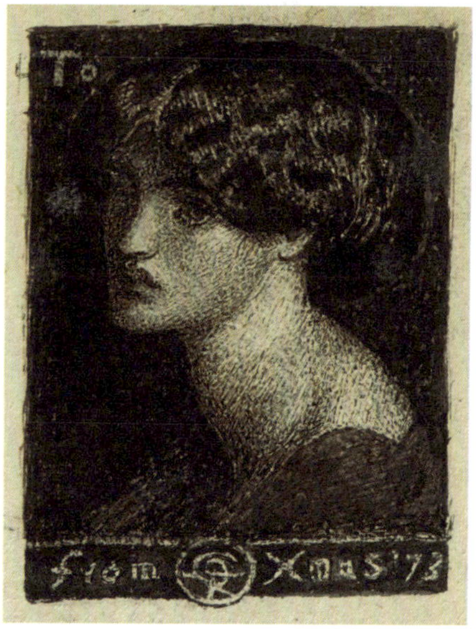

NO.205 Dante Gabriel Rossetti, portrait of Jane Morris on the flyleaf of Rossetti's and Morris's copy of Robert Burton's 1651 book *The Anatomy of Melancholy*, 19 × 14

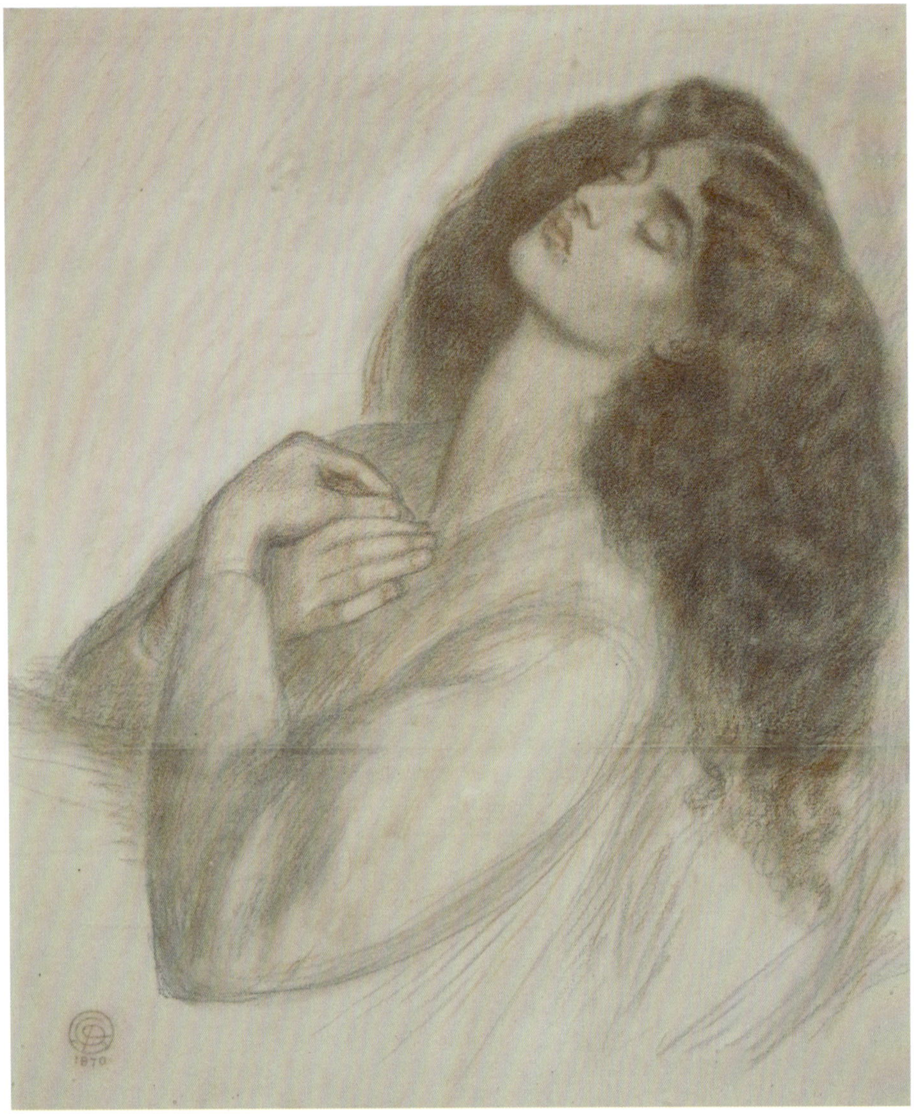

ABOVE
NO.206 Dante Gabriel Rossetti, *Jane Morris (Study for 'Dante's Dream')* 1870, chalk on paper, 60 × 51.1

OPPOSITE
NO.207 Dante Gabriel Rossetti, *The Salutation of Beatrice* 1869, oil paint on canvas, 57.1 × 47

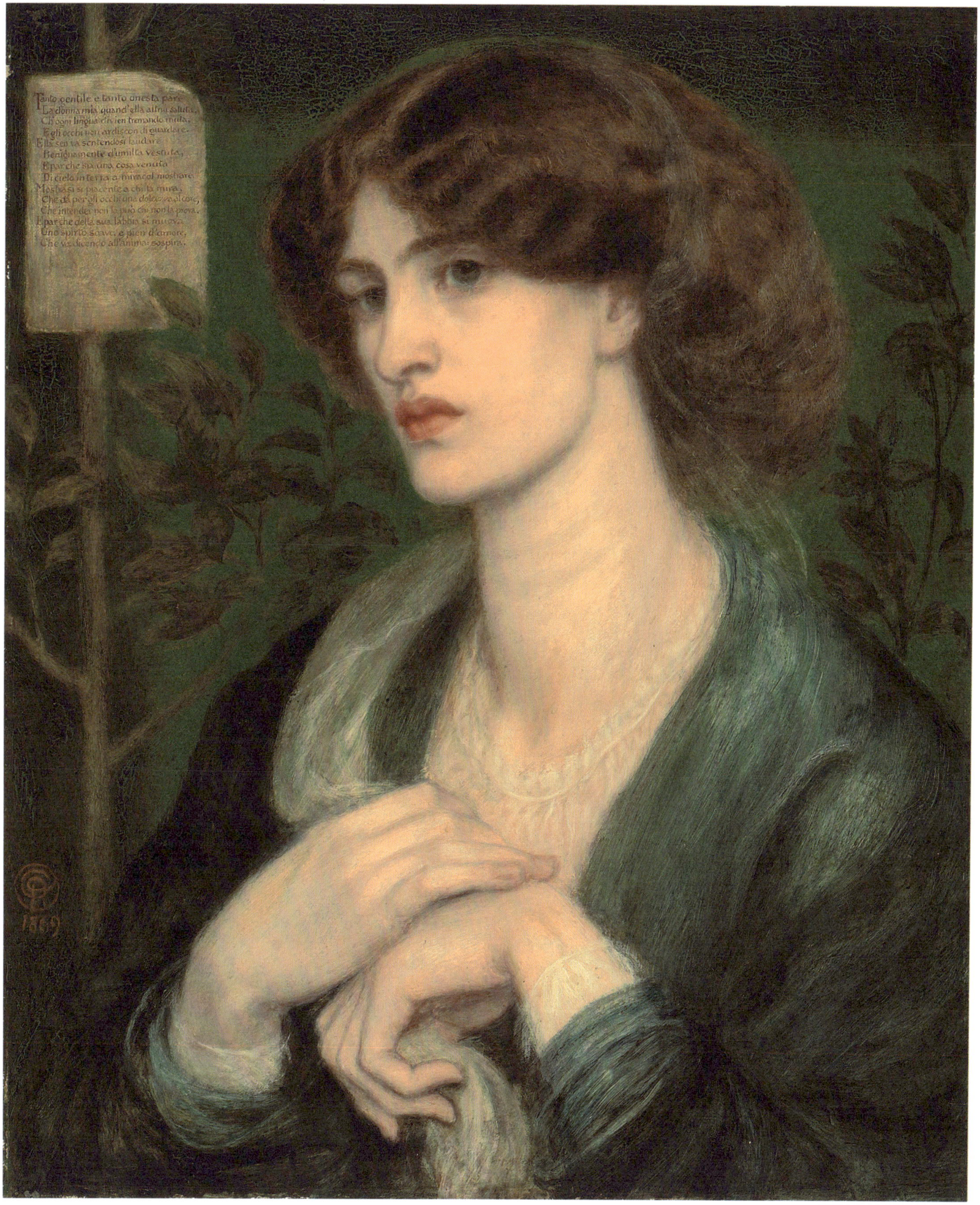
Tanto gentile e tanto onesta pare
La donna mia quand'ella altrui saluta,
Ch'ogni lingua divien tremando muta,
E gli occhi non ardiscon di guardare.
Ella sen va sentendosi laudare
Benignamente d'umilta vestuta,
E par che sia una cosa venuta
Di cielo in terra a miracol mostrare.
Mostrasi si piacente a chi la mira,
Che dà per gli occhi una dolcezza al core,
Che intender non la può chi non la prova.
E par che della sua labbia si muova
Uno spirto soave, e pien d'amore,
Che va dicendo all'anima: sospira.
1869

'I don't know why I am writing all this to you, but I feel that I want to talk to some one about him'

Jane Morris

This letter makes clear that the blue silk dress of the portrait was made and embroidered by Morris herself, and that Gabriel was happy to consult with her concerning its styling and design, even deferring to her creative decisions. Notable, too, is Gabriel's reference to 'the embroidery which you propose to put at the back', which would not appear in the finished painting, implying that Morris's vision for the dress was not simply as an artist's prop but as a more holistic design, an aesthetic creation in its own right.

This blue silk dress closely resembled the one which Morris wore in a striking series of photographs by John Robert Parsons, commissioned by Gabriel three years earlier, and staged in his Chelsea garden in 1865 (NOS.199, 201). Whether the dress in these photographs was made or simply modified by Morris is unknown, but the Parsons photographs have been identified as one of the earliest documented examples of aesthetic dress.[11] Looser, flowing dress styles associated with aestheticism marked an implicit rejection of the confining hoops and corsets of mainstream Victorian fashion in favour of a radical, if romantic, simplicity of costume.

Viewed as a sequence, these photographs also provide a sense of the diverse embodied skills that Jane Morris brought to modelling. The varied arrangements of dress imply the hand of a stylist – whether Gabriel, Morris herself, or a collaboration between the two. Sometimes the waist is accentuated with a contrasting belt; sometimes the dress is arranged in a billowing fullness. The use of accessories varies, too, with the inclusion of lace or beads at the neck in some shots, as does the arrangement of Morris's abundant hair and the poses she adopts (standing, seated, reclining, in profile, or face to camera). The impression created is of a studied professionalism informed by a keen aesthetic sensibility.

OPPOSITE
NO.208 Dante Gabriel Rossetti, *Mrs William Morris (The Blue Silk Dress)* 1868, oil paint on canvas, 101.5 × 90.2

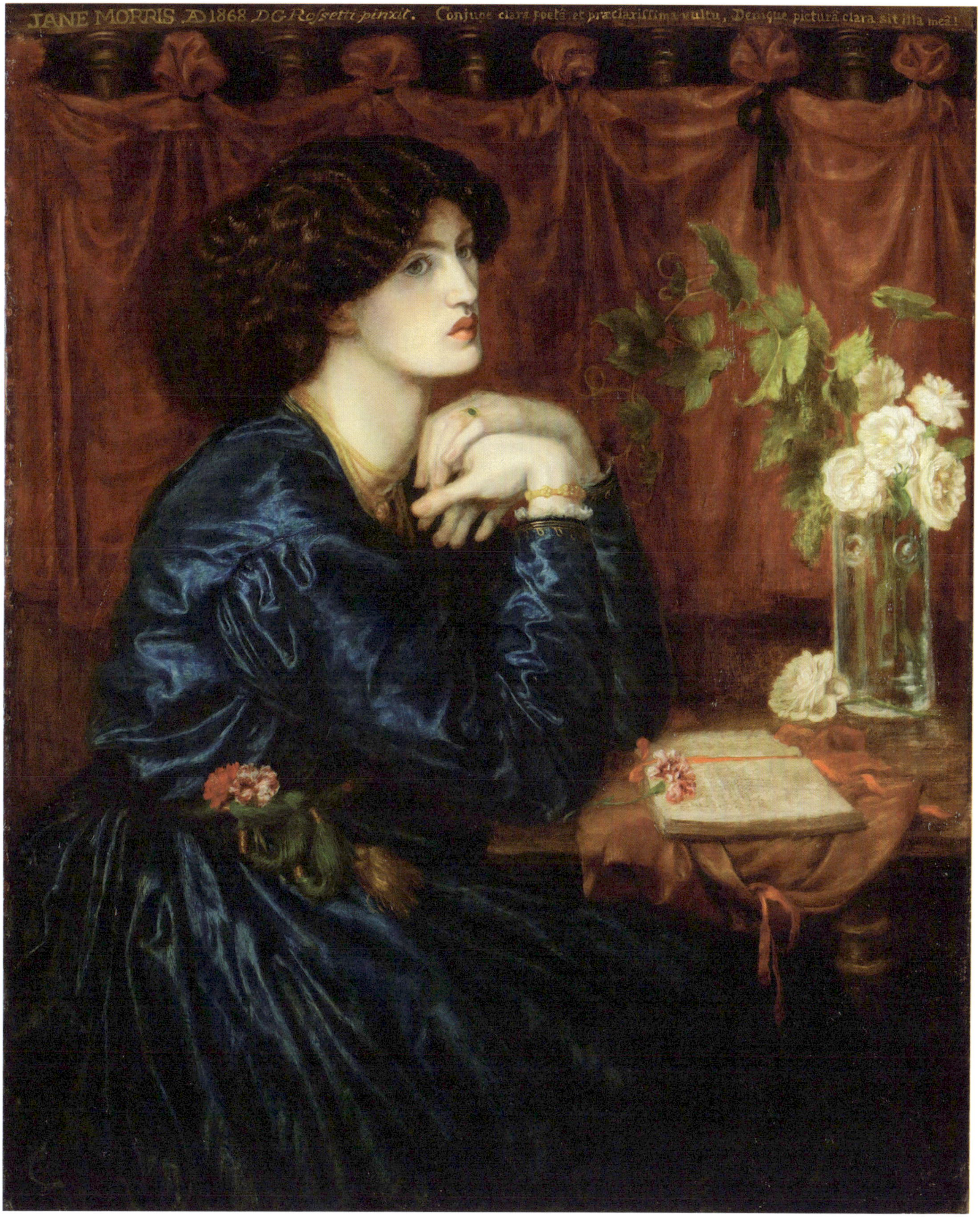
JANE MORRIS AD 1868 DG Rossetti pinxit. Conjuge clara poetâ et præclarissima vultu, Denique picturâ clara sit illa meâ!

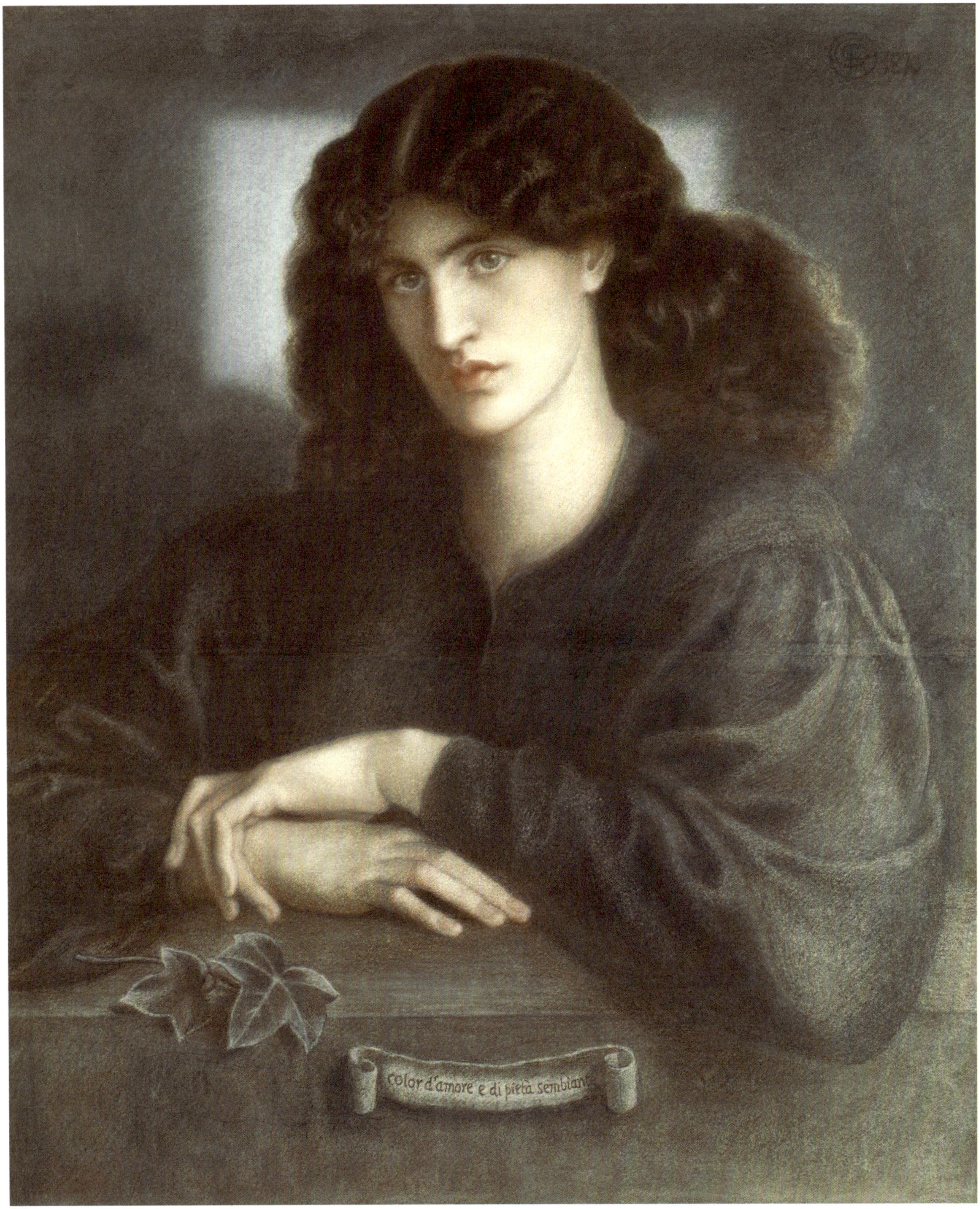
color d'amore e di pietà sembiant

'It's hard to say whether she's a grand synthesis of all the Pre-Raphaelite pictures ever made ... whether she's an original or a copy.'

Henry James

OPPOSITE
NO.209 Dante Gabriel Rossetti, *La Donna Della Finestra (The Lady of Pity)* 1870, pastel on paper, 84.8 × 72.1

Further evidence, both on canvas and in correspondence, suggests that Jane Morris was not a passive bearer of the artist's vision but actively fashioned a personal style as well as a professional role of her own. She sewed other costumes for modelling purposes, such as the pale overdress she made for Gabriel's *La Pia de' Tolomei*, painted the same year as *The Blue Silk Dress* portrait, and an 'oriental' dress, described in a letter by Gabriel as 'of crimson Chinese silk lined with yellow striped green [and] a green silk belt ornamented with gold thread'.[12] In later life, she took commissions to make dresses for models of the artist Charles Gere.[13]

As so often with the work of craftswomen, however, we are left to infer from their work itself the investment of time, skill and creativity, or the degree of satisfaction and achievement attained by the maker. Perhaps the most poignant insight into the aesthetic significance of such dressmaking for Jane Morris comes from her daughter, the designer and craftswoman May Morris, who later recalled that Gabriel's picture of the blue silk dress:

> perpetuates a delicious, simple silk gown of shot blue and brown that was a great favourite with the little girls [i.e., May and her sister Jenny]. It had some fragile ornament of gold thread at the throat and wrists, and was of a delicate, faintly-rustling texture, that we never tired of stroking.[14]

The close, tactile association between mother and daughters in this memory of childhood evokes a home where beauty and creativity were treasured, as had been the case at Red House, the first real home of William and Jane Morris after their marriage. Friends - including Gabriel and his wife Elizabeth Siddal (who died in 1862), and Edward and Georgiana Burne-Jones - worked on the decoration and furnishings of Red House, and it was there that Jane Morris first studied the traditional embroidery in which she would excel. Reflecting on the early experiments in embroidery she undertook with her husband at Red House, Jane Morris later wrote:

> There were no lessons to be had, everything had to be laboured at for a time often unsuccessfully ... but the failures were amusing too. The first stuff I got to embroider on was a piece of indigo-dyed blue serge I found by chance in a London shop... I took it home and he [William Morris] was delighted with it, and set to work at once designing flowers. These we worked in bright colour in a simple rough way - the work went quickly and when finished we covered the walls of the bedroom at Red House to our great joy.[15]

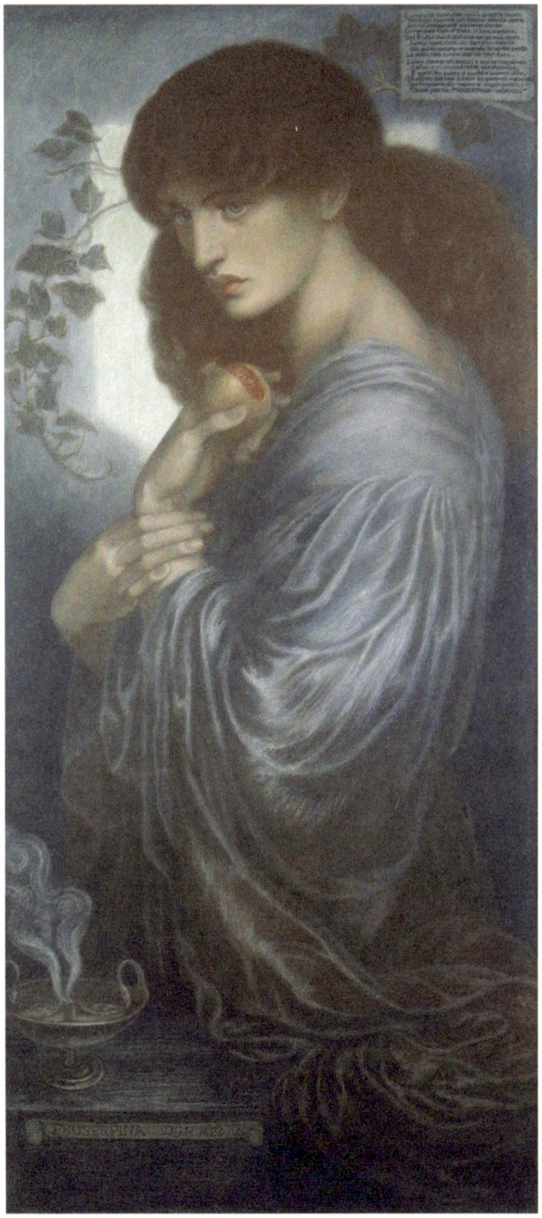

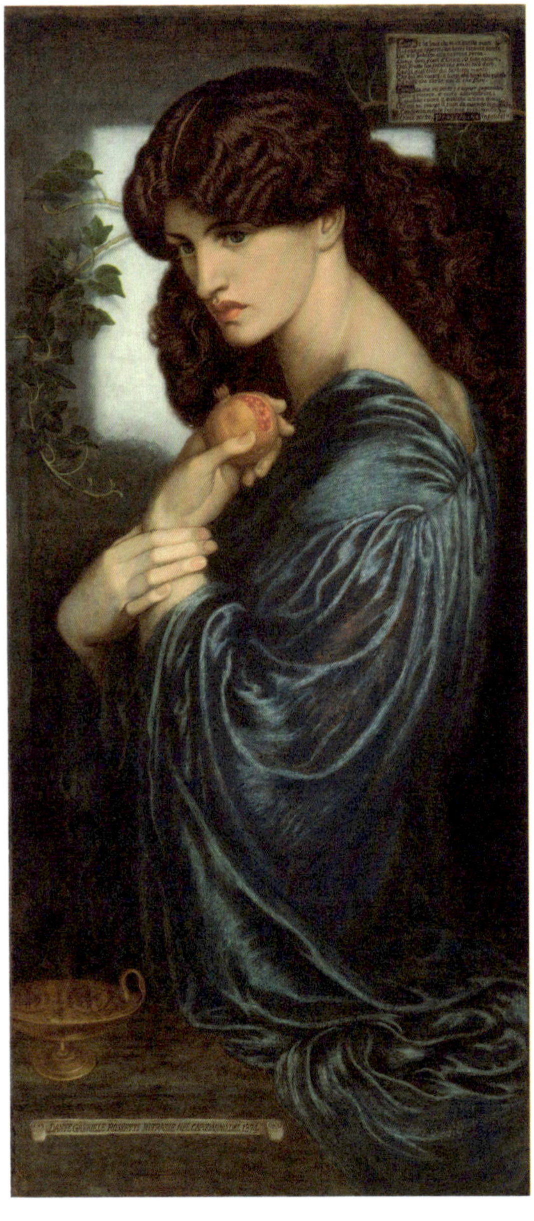

OPPOSITE LEFT
NO.210 Dante Gabriel Rossetti, *Proserpine* 1874, oil paint on canvas, 125.1 × 61

OPPOSITE RIGHT
NO.211 Dante Gabriel Rossetti, *Proserpine* 1880, coloured chalks on paper, 120 × 56

RIGHT
NO.212 Dante Gabriel Rossetti, *Proserpine* 1877, oil paint on canvas, 116.8 × 55.9

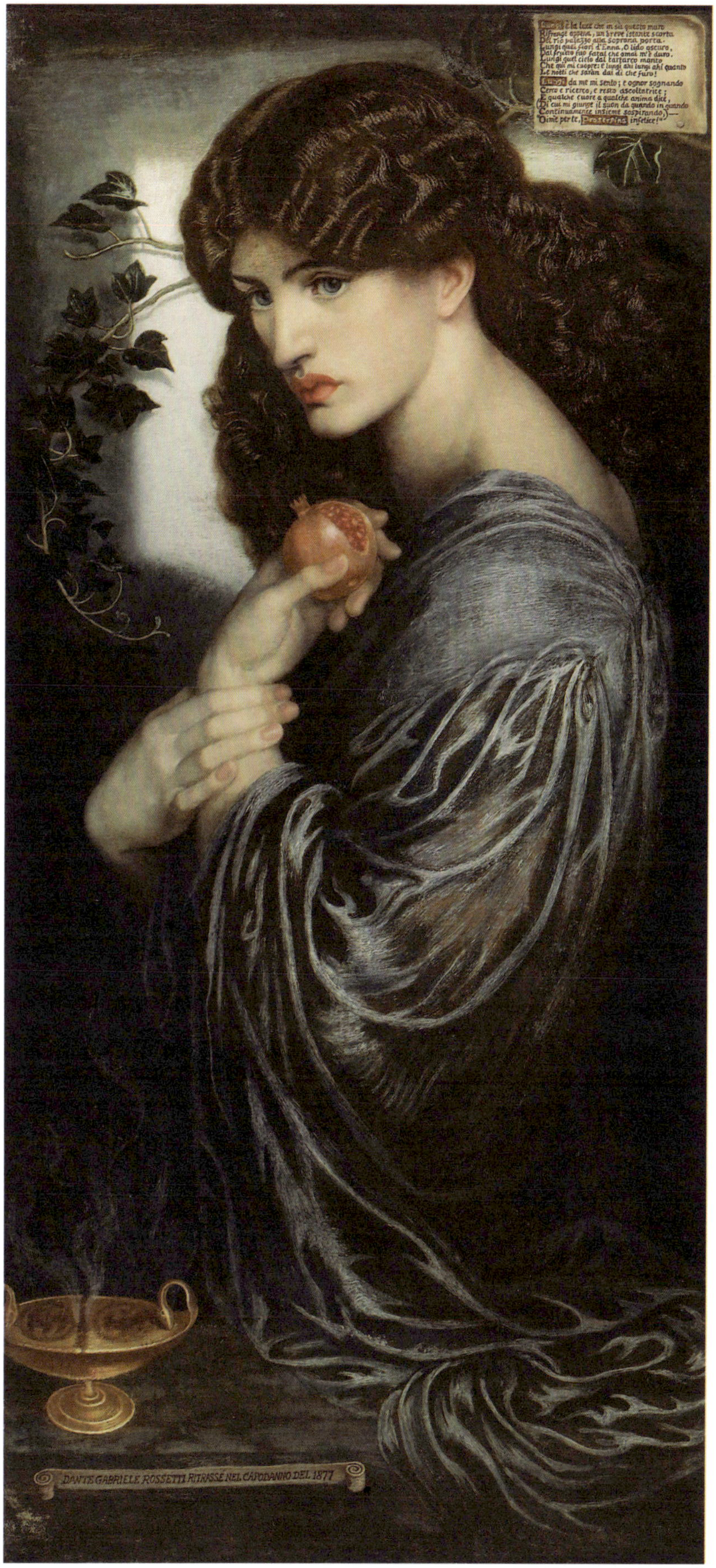

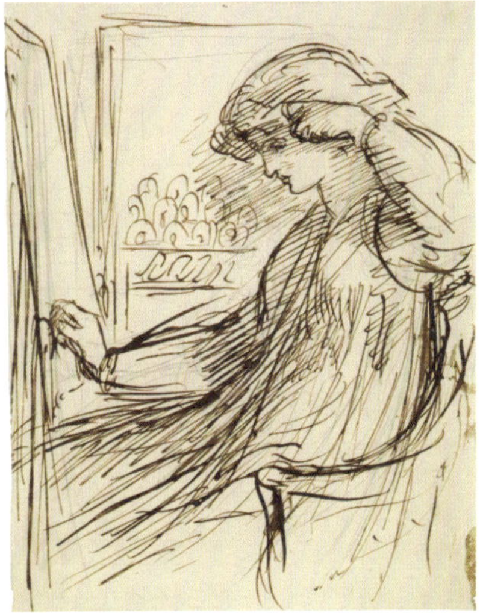

NO.213 Dante Gabriel Rossetti, *Woman seated at an embroidery frame or easel* 1870, brown ink, over graphite with faint indication of a grid, on note paper, 21.6 × 17.1

NO.214 Jane Morris, 'Honeysuckle' embroidery, designed 1876, made 1880s

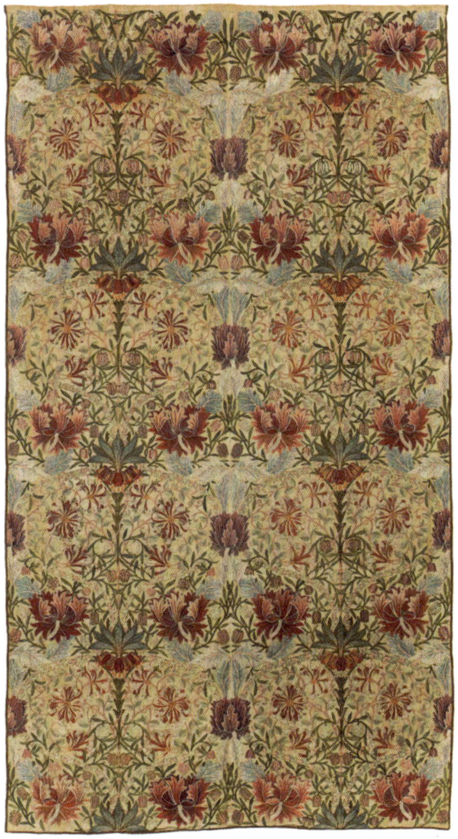

This first effort (the 'Daisy' wall hangings now displayed at Kelmscott Manor) would soon be followed by other projects, like the almost life-size series of seven women embroidered for the dining room of Red House, on which Jane Morris is believed to have worked with her sister Bessie Burden (who lived with the Morrises for a time and was herself a professional needlewoman). This theme of 'eminent women', derived from medieval sources Christine de Pizan and Geoffrey Chaucer, was a favourite of the circle, and a feature of the casket painted by Dante Gabriel Rossetti and Elizabeth Siddal and given to Jane and William Morris upon their marriage (see NOS.156, 157). Jane Morris would go on to play a leading role in the production of complex and ornate textiles and embroideries for Morris & Co., later in conjunction with her daughter May, and her embroidery was displayed in Arts and Crafts exhibitions in the 1880s and 1890s in London and Europe.

All this time – up until his death in 1882 – Jane Morris continued to be muse and model for Gabriel, even after their affair ended. From the 1870s onwards, the paintings featuring Jane Morris encompassed a range of styles, not always the monumental or mythic, and it is tempting to read them as, at least in part, reflecting the vicissitudes of Gabriel's feelings towards Morris. In the deceptively simple *Water Willow* 1871 (NO.215), Morris is posed against a background of the river landscape near Kelmscott Manor, where Gabriel spent long periods alone with Jane in William Morris's absence at the height of their affair. In *The Daydream* 1880 (NO.217), we can still see continuities with Gabriel's very first sketches of her in Oxford. The simple styling of the hair, the angle of the head and neck, the pensive expression on her distinctive facial features: all these remain, although Morris is now clad in a dark green silk dress that closely connects her with the bower-like setting of a sycamore tree. But in his final painting featuring Morris, completed at Birchington-on-Sea a few days before his death in April 1882, Gabriel reverted to depicting her as a Joan of Arc – an eminent woman drawn from the writings of Christine de Pizan, combining physicality, spirituality and femininity (NO.218). Gabriel had already painted several versions of Joan of Arc in the 1860s but at the end of his life, and in his more mannered late style, he painted the virgin soldier-saint once more, with the features of Jane Morris.

If Morris has still too often been depicted almost as a figment of Gabriel's imagination – a woman to desire and worship, elevated to mythic proportions – we need to look beyond the canvases to seek a fuller, flesh-and-blood story of this remarkable woman. Some of Gabriel's sketches showed her in more mundane settings or occupations, such as sewing or reading a newspaper. In fact, Morris was an enthusiast for books, and widely read (see NO.203). Shared literary interests are evidenced by the edition of Robert Burton's seventeenth-century *Anatomy of Melancholy* which Gabriel gave Morris for Christmas in 1873. The subject matter, and the portrait he drew in the flyleaf (NO.205), resonate with *Proserpine*, on which he was working at the time. Her book reminds us that while Jane Morris is silent in Gabriel's paintings, she was not in life, and sittings were likely informed by conversations between them, if we may judge by the lively, almost playful tone often evident in Morris's correspondence.

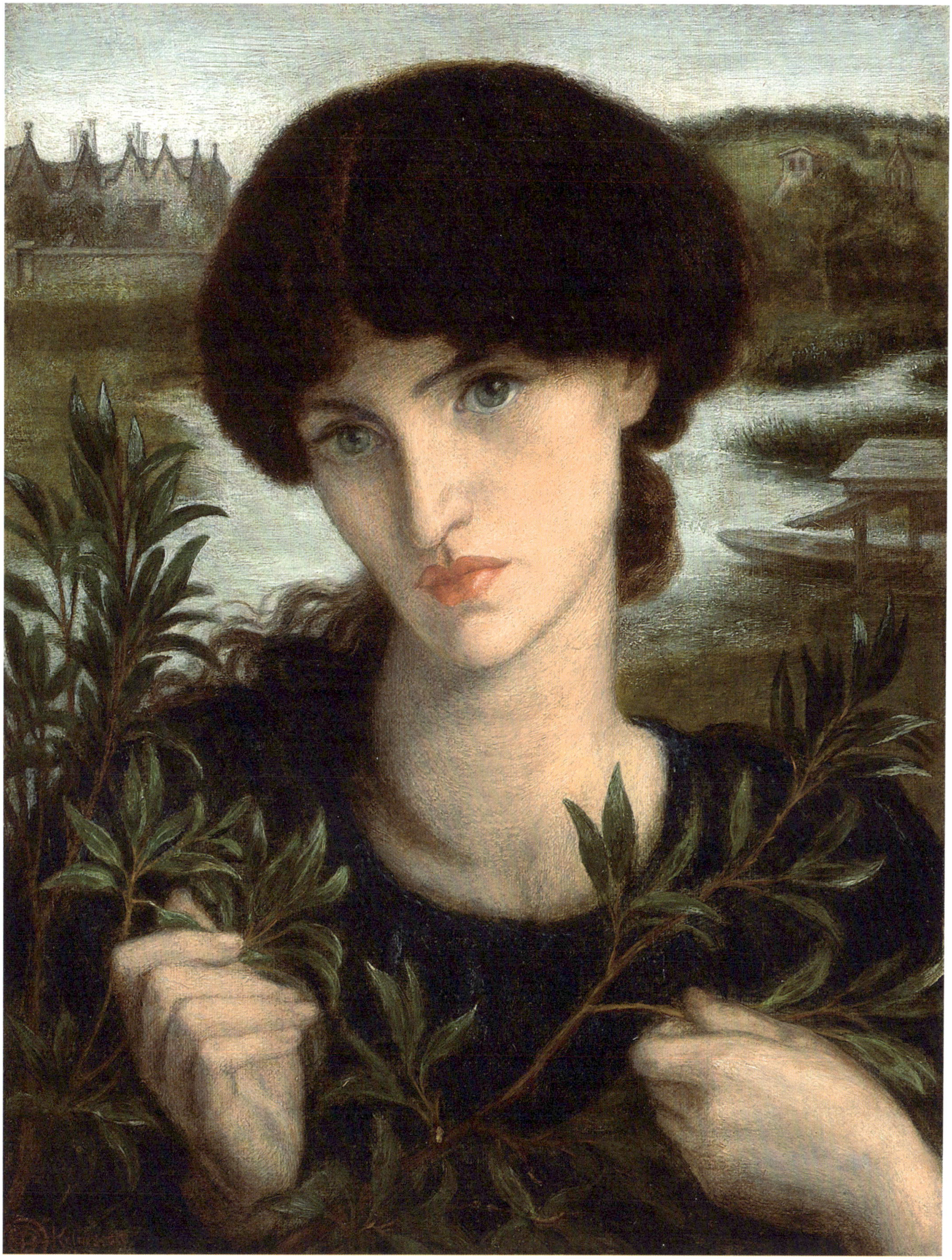

'Afar from mine own self I seem, and wing
Strange ways in thought, and listen for a sign:
And still some heart unto some soul doth pine ...'

Dante Gabriel Rossetti, 'Proserpina', 1880

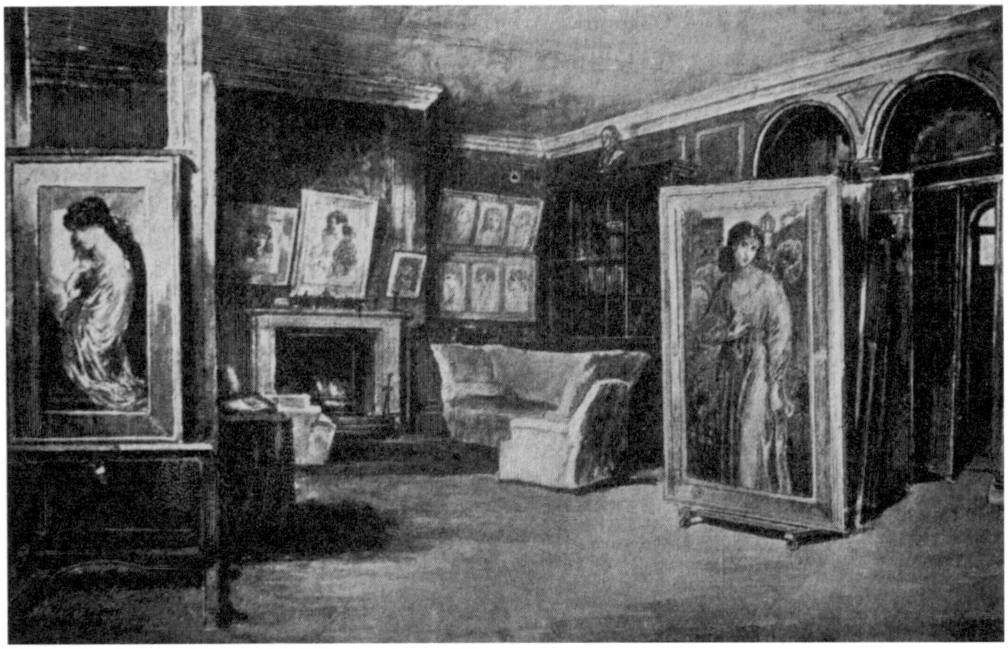

PAGE 221
NO.215 Dante Gabriel Rossetti, *Water Willow* 1871, oil paint on canvas, 33 × 26.7

LEFT
NO.216 H.C. Marillier, *Dante Gabriel Rossetti: An Illustrated Memorial of his Art and Life* 1899, book, open to reproduce painting of Rossetti's studio by Henry Treffry Dunn

OPPOSITE
NO.217 Dante Gabriel Rossetti, *The Daydream* 1880, oil paint on canvas, 195.3 × 128.8

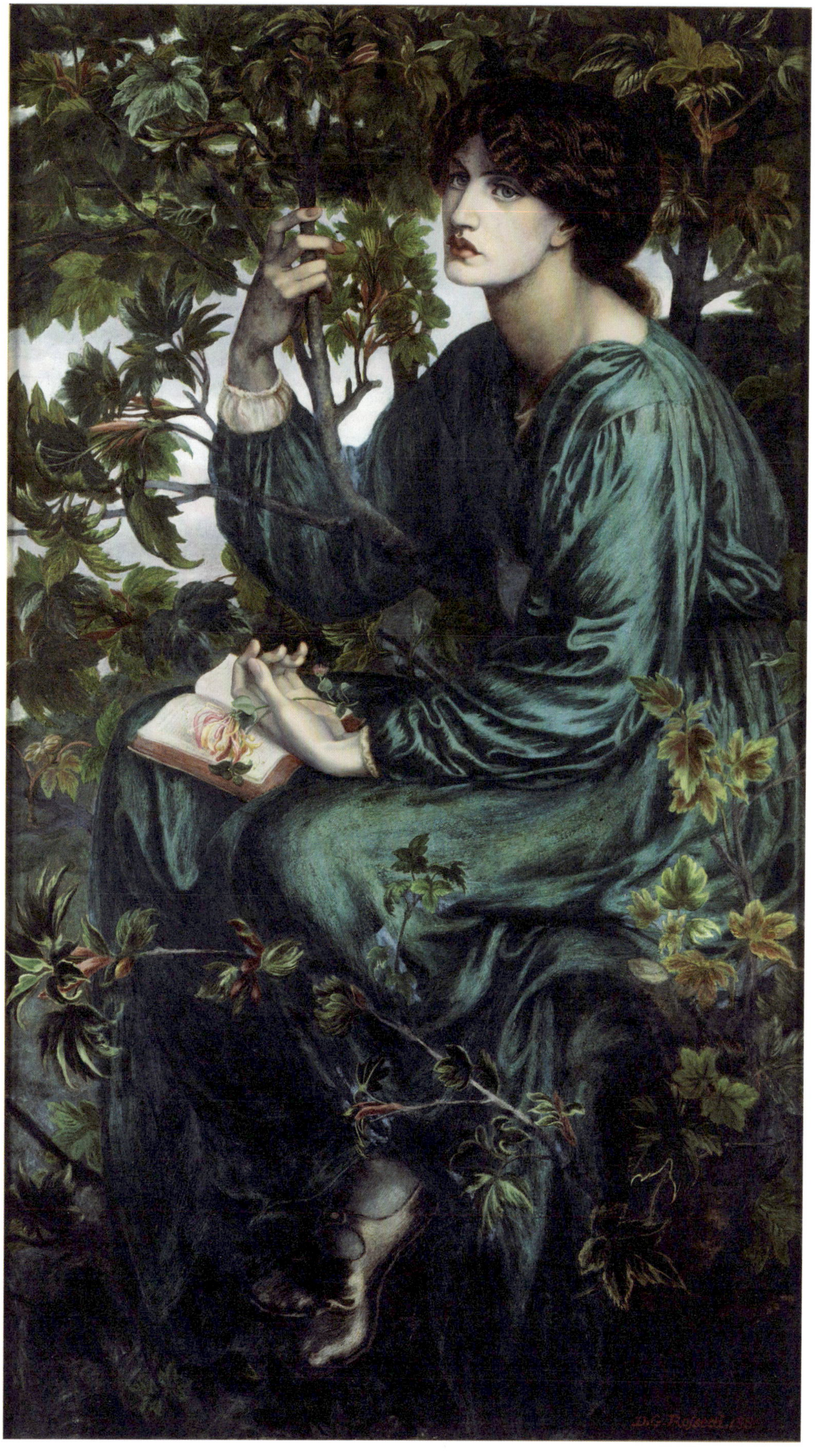

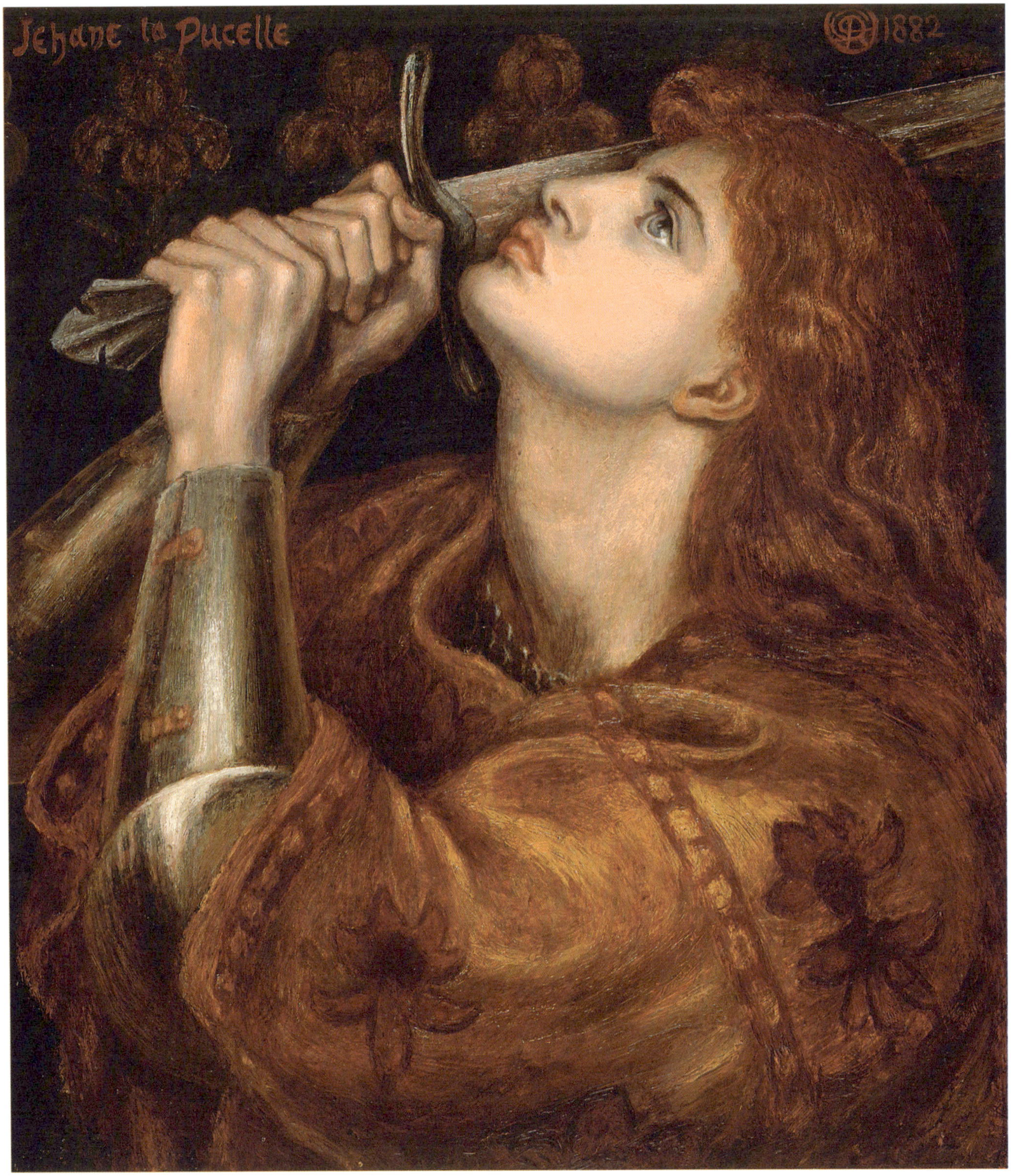

ABOVE
NO.218 Dante Gabriel Rossetti, *Joan of Arc* 1882, oil paint on panel, 52.7 × 45.7

OPPOSITE
NO.219 Frederic James Shields, *The Dead Rossetti* 1882, coloured chalks on paper, 33.7 × 28

Scholars have recently begun to piece together the evidence of Morris's daily life, work and relationships in more complex ways.[16] This research seeks to gain a better historical understanding of the agency of women who lived alongside famous men; women whose own creativity was both enabled and obscured by such relationships, and whose daily lives closely entwined the domestic with the aesthetic.

After Gabriel's death, when Jane Morris began to read some of the negative reviews that his work received, she wrote to friends to express her strong objections to such harsh assessments, taking a keen interest in the posthumous exhibition and sale of Gabriel's work. The voice that emerges from such letters is of a woman not only claiming for herself the right to adjudicate Gabriel's art but also trusting that she knew the artist as few others had done. 'I don't know why I am writing this to you,' one such letter reads, 'but I feel that I want to talk to someone about him.'[17] For Jane Morris and Dante Gabriel Rossetti, the imbrication of art and feeling, in the creative process as well as in the finished work, was a tale demanding to be told but always evading simple interpretation

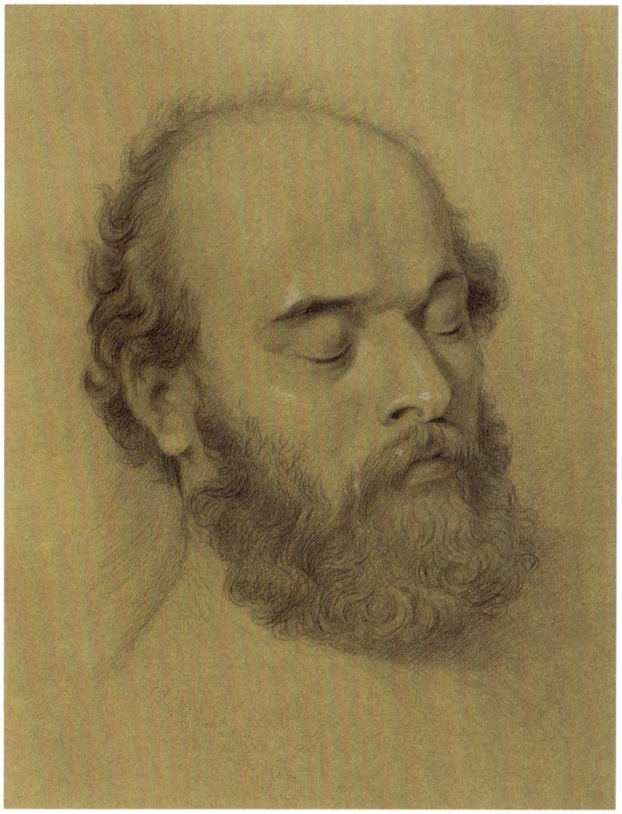

The title 'The works are there to tell their own tale' comes from William Michael Rossetti, *Dante Gabriel Rossetti: His Family-Letters with a Memoir*, 2 vols., London 1895, vol.1, p.245.

1 Ibid.

2 Ibid., p.199.

3 Percy Lubbock (ed.), *The Letters of Henry James*, New York 1920, p.17.

4 Whistler, quoted in E.R. and J. Pennell, *The Life of James McNeill Whistler*, London 1920, p.84; du Maurier, quoted in Oswald Doughty, *A Victorian Romantic: Dante Gabriel Rossetti*, London 1949, p.372.

5 William Tirebuck, *Dante Gabriel Rossetti: His Work and Influence*, London 1882, p.31.

6 John Bryson (ed.), *Dante Gabriel Rossetti and Jane Morris: Their Correspondence*, Oxford 1976, p.54. The completed watercolour was intended for sale to a private collector, Leonard Rowe Valpy.

7 For more on Dante Gabriel Rossetti's friends' views of Jane Morris during Gabriel's health crisis, see Wendy Parkins, *Jane Morris: The Burden of History*, Edinburgh 2013, pp.24–41.

8 David Hannay, 'The Paintings of Mr Rossetti', *National Review*, vol.1, no.1, March 1883, pp.133, 128.

9 Theodore Watts-Dunton, 'The Truth About Rossetti', *The Nineteenth Century*, March 1883, pp.404–23.

10 Bryson 1976, p.3.

11 Colin Ford, 'A Pre-Raphaelite Partnership: Dante Gabriel Rossetti and John Robert Parsons', *Burlington Magazine*, vol.146, no.1214, May 2004, p.311.

12 See Leonée Ormond, 'Dress in the Painting of Dante Gabriel Rossetti', *Costume*, vol.8, 1974, p.28. See also William E. Fredeman (ed.), *The Correspondence of Dante Gabriel Rossetti*, 10 vols., Cambridge, Woodbridge and Rochester, NY 2002–15, vol.6, p.419; alas, the letter records that the 'oriental' dress was lost in transit.

13 See Jane Morris's letter to Charles Gere, in *The Collected Letters of Jane Morris*, ed. Frank C. Sharp and Jan Marsh, Woodbridge 2012, p.248.

14 May Morris, 'Introduction', in *The Collected Works of William Morris*, 24 vols., London 1910–15, vol.3, p.xxxv.

15 British Library, Add. Ms. 45341.

16 See, for example: Parkins 2013; Sharp and Marsh 2012; Wendy Parkins, 'Feeling at Home: Gender and Creative Agency at Red House', *Victorian Literature and Culture*, vol.15, no.1, 2010, pp.61–81; Wendy Parkins, 'Feeling for Beauty: Tactile Aesthetics and the Childhood of May Morris', *The Senses and Society*, vol.10, no.1, 2015, pp.26–38; Suzanne Fagence Cooper, *How We Might Live: At Home with Jane and William Morris*, London 2022.

17 Jane Morris to Theodore Watts-Dunton, 1883, in Sharp and Marsh 2012, p.127.

Chronology

1783
28 February: Gabriele Pasquale Giuseppe Rossetti born in Naples.

1800
April: Frances Mary Lavinia Polidori born in London to Gaetano Polidori and Anna Maria Pierce.

1824
Gabriele, in political exile from Naples, arrives in London.

1826
10 April: Gabriele and Frances Polidori marry. The couple live at 38 Charlotte Street, Portland Place, London.

1827
17 February: Maria Francesca Rossetti born in London.

1828
12 May: Gabriel Charles Dante Rossetti born at family home. Gabriel would change his name to Dante Gabriel in 1849 following the death of his godfather, botanist Charles Lyell, for whom he was named.

1829
25 July: Elizabeth Eleanor Siddal born at family home in Holborn, London.

25 September: William Michael Rossetti born in London.

1830
5 December: Christina Georgina Rossetti born in London.

1842
27 April: Christina composes 'To My Mother on Her Birthday', her first known poem.

July: Gabriel enrols at Henry Sass's drawing academy.

1843
Maria, Christina and their mother begin attending Christ Church on Albany Street in London, which practised High Church Anglicanism. Gabriel's poem *Sir Hugh the Heron* is printed on his grandfather's press.

October: Gabriel stays with family friends the Maenzas in Boulogne while recovering from illness.

1844
February: Maria takes a post as a governess and leaves home.

1845
February: William Michael, having left school, is employed at the Excise Office as a clerk, in order to accommodate financially for their father Gabriele's increasingly poor health. Meanwhile, Christina becomes Gabriele's primary carer, the stress of which likely contributes to her breakdown in the summer.

1846
July: Gabriel is admitted to the Royal Academy Antique School.

1847
June: Christina's poetry collection *Verses* is privately printed on her grandfather's press. Gabriel is also steadily writing poetry by this period, having completed 'The Blessed Damozel', 'Jenny', 'The Portrait' and 'Retro me, Sathana'.

1848
January: Gabriel forms the Cyclographic Society, a sketching group, with Walter Deverell. William Holman Hunt and John Everett Millais are also members.

September: A meeting at the home of John Everett Millais in Gower Street, which both Gabriel and William Michael attend, leads to the formation of the 'PRB' ('Pre-Raphaelite Brotherhood'), a group founded on a commitment to painting in a naturalistic style based on that of early Renaissance artists. The group also included William Holman Hunt and Walter Deverell, among others.

By *November*: Christina, Gabriel and William Michael are all working collaboratively as part of the PRB, with Christina sitting for the Virgin Mary in Gabriel's *Girlhood of Mary Virgin* and *Ecce Ancilla Domini!*, while Gabriel and William Michael both sit for John Everett Millais.

31 December: First official meeting of the PRB.

1849
By this time, Elizabeth Siddal is working at a milliner's shop in Cranborne Alley, where she becomes familiar with the mother and sister of Walter Deverell, and his father, the principal of the London School of Design, to whom she likely showed her sketches and expressed an interest in an artistic career.

28 March: The Free Exhibition opens in Hyde Park Corner, including Gabriel's *Girlhood of Mary Virgin*. The other members send their pictures to the Royal Academy, whose exhibition opens on 7 May.

December: Elizabeth is introduced to the PRB and agrees to model for Deverell's *Twelfth Night*, which Gabriel helps to complete.

1850
January: Publication of the first volume of the PRB's magazine *The Germ*, which would have three further volumes this year. Gabriel, Christina and William Michael are all contributors. Christina's poetry is published under the pseudonym Ellen Alleyn. William Michael takes on the role of manager and editor of the publication.

February: William Michael takes the position of art reviewer at *The Critic* and at *The Spectator* in October, both of which he holds throughout this decade.

1851
13 May: In the wake of several negative reviews of the PRB, influential art critic John Ruskin writes a letter in defence of the group of artists.

1852
Elizabeth decides to stop modelling, wishing to focus on her own artistic production. She continues to sit only for Gabriel, who becomes both her instructor and romantic partner.

1853
August: Elizabeth begins work on *St Agnes' Eve*, which she intends to send to the Royal Academy.

September: Gabriel begins work on *Found*.

By *November*: The PRB has essentially dissolved. Christina commemorates it with a sonnet: 'The PRB is in its decadence.'

1854
13 April: Ruskin calls on Gabriel at his studio and promises to help his career. He is likewise impressed by Elizabeth's work.

26 April: Gabriele Rossetti dies. All four Rossetti siblings are present.

1855
12 April: Ruskin offers to buy all of Elizabeth's completed and future work for a salary of £150 per year.

23 September: Elizabeth departs for Nice. She will spend the rest of the year in the South of France and Paris.

1856
Gabriel meets Edward Burne-Jones, William Morris and Frederic Leighton, with whom he will collaborate.

1857
25 May: Semi-public exhibition of Pre-Raphaelite works at 4 Russell Place, Fitzroy Square, including seven by Gabriel and several by Elizabeth. Elizabeth's painting *Clerk Saunders* is purchased by an American collector. This month, also, the *Poems by Alfred Tennyson* is published, including illustrations by Gabriel and others.

August: Gabriel is in Oxford working on a mural for the Union Debating Hall with William Morris. There, the two meet Jane Burden. Also, this summer, Elizabeth attends the Sheffield School of Art.

1858
8 July: The Hogarth Club, a members-only exhibition space, is established at 178 Piccadilly. Gabriel exhibits his work here, the limited audience and lack of critical reviews suiting his aversion to publicly displaying his work.

1859
26 April: Jane Burden and William Morris are married in Oxford. Soon after, William Morris begins plans for the construction of Red House, which would serve both as a family home and as an outlet for his and his wife's creative pursuits.

23 July: Gabriel begins work on *Bocca Baciata*, which Fanny Cornforth sits for and which is shown at the Hogarth Club the following year.

1860
February: Maria becomes an Associate Sister of the All Saints Sisterhood, an Anglican order. She composes *Letters to my Bible Class*, which is published in 1872.

23 May: Elizabeth and Gabriel are married, and travel to Paris for their honeymoon.

1861
Gabriel co-founds Morris, Marshall, Faulkner & Co., which William Morris will develop into Morris & Co.

2 May: Elizabeth gives birth to a stillborn daughter, and afterwards suffers from postpartum depression.

December: Gabriel's volume *Early Italian Poets* is published.

1862
February: Elizabeth dies from a laudanum overdose. She is buried in the Rossetti family plot in Highgate cemetery with the manuscript of Gabriel's poems.

March: Christina's *Goblin Market and Other Poems* is published, with illustrations by Gabriel.

22 October: Gabriel moves to 16 Cheyne Walk, in Chelsea.

1864
December: Gabriel begins to attempt to contact Elizabeth Siddal by séance, and works on *Beata Beatrix*, based on her.

1865
February: William Michael publishes his translation *Comedy of Dante Alighieri: Part 1, The Hell.*

Gabriel begins work on *The Beloved.*

7 June: Gabriel poses Jane Morris in his garden for a series of photographic portraits by John Robert Parsons.

October: Gabriel first meets Frederick Leyland, a shipping magnate from Liverpool who will become a key patron and collector of his works.

1866
June: Christina's collection *The Prince's Progress* is published.

August: Gabriel begins work on *Lady Lilith*, which Frederick Leyland purchases for 450 guineas.

1868
March: Jane Morris sits for Gabriel's *La Pia de' Tolomei*. Letters indicate that a romantic relationship between the two begins this year.

1869
September: Intent on renewing his focus on poetry after persuasion by art dealer Charles Augustus Howell, Gabriel requests that his poems be exhumed from Elizabeth Siddal's grave. The exhumation is completed on 10 October.

1870
Gabriel publishes *Poems*, about which critic Robert Buchanan publishes the scathing 'Fleshly School of Poetry', criticising the indelicacy of Gabriel's work.

1871
October: Publication of Maria's *A Shadow of Dante.*

June: Gabriel and William Morris settle on a joint-tenancy of Kelmscott Manor, a house in Oxfordshire. Soon after, Morris departs for Iceland and Gabriel spends much of the summer at the house with Jane Morris. Gabriel begins work on the first version of *Proserpine.*

18 November: Christina's *Sing-Song*, a collection of nursery rhymes, is published.

1872
June: Gabriel has a nervous breakdown and attempts suicide.

1873
June: William Michael travels to Italy with artist Ford Madox Brown and his daughter Lucy, to whom William Michael proposes the following month.

September: Maria enters the All Saints Anglican Sisterhood as a novice.

1874
31 March: William Michael and Lucy Madox Brown are married.

1875
March: Edition of Christina's collected poems issued.

20 September: Olivia 'Olive' Frances Rossetti, daughter of William Michael and Lucy, is born.

October: Maria becomes full sister of the All Saints Sisterhood.

1876
24 November: Maria dies of cancer and is buried in the Order's grave at Brompton Cemetery.

1879
10 November: Helen Maria Rossetti, daughter of William Michael and Lucy, is born.

1880
Gabriel finishes *The Daydream*, one of his latest completed works.

1881
William Michael composes *Democratic Sonnets*, but, on advice from Gabriel, withholds them from publication due to their radical political content. They are eventually published in 1907.

22 April: Mary Elizabeth and Michael Ford Rossetti, twin children of William Michael and Lucy, are born.

1882
9 April: While staying with an old friend in Kent, Gabriel dies.

30 December: An exhibition of 84 of Gabriel's paintings opens at the Royal Academy.

1883
24 January: Michael Ford Rossetti dies of meningitis.

1889
William Michael publishes *Dante Gabriel Rossetti as Designer and Writer*, the first of several publications recording the works of his siblings.

1891
September: Olive, Helen and Mary Rossetti publish the anarchist journal *The Torch of Anarchy*, which would continue until 1895.

1894
12 April: Death of Lucy Madox Brown Rossetti.

29 December: Christina dies of cancer.

1895
William Michael publishes *Dante Gabriel Rossetti: His Family-Letters with a Memoir.*

1904
Publication of the *Poetical Works of Christina Georgina Rossetti*, edited by William Michael and including his memoir of her.

1906
William Michael publishes *Some Reminiscences*, his own memoir.

1919
5 February: William Michael Rossetti dies.

Compiled by Taryn Power

List of Exhibited Works

1
Christina Rossetti 1830–1894
Verses
1847
Book
17.1 × 10.8
The British Library
TATE ONLY

Dante Gabriel Rossetti 1828–1882
Christina Rossetti
1848
Chalk on paper
28.8 × 21.5
British Museum
TATE ONLY

Dante Gabriel Rossetti 1828–1882
Study for 'Ecce Ancilla Domini! (The Annunciation)'
c.1849
Graphite on paper
19.4 × 13.7
Tate. Purchased 1959

Dante Gabriel Rossetti 1828–1882
Ecce Ancilla Domini! (The Annunciation)
1849–50
Oil paint on canvas
72.4 × 41.9
Tate. Purchased 1886

2
William Blake 1757–1827
Dante Gabriel Rossetti 1828–1882
The Notebook of William Blake ('the Rossetti manuscript')
1787–1847
Graphite and ink on paper
19.7 × 15.9
The British Library
TATE ONLY

Filippo Maenza 1825–1862
Portrait of the young Dante Gabriel Rossetti, seated in an arm-chair
1843
Graphite on paper
22.2 × 19
Peter and Renate Nahum

William Michael Rossetti 1829–1919
Colnbrook Dale
c.1844
Charcoal and chalk on paper
24 × 34
Jane Cohen
TATE ONLY

William Michael Rossetti 1829–1919
On Yarmouth Beach, Norfolk
c.1844
Charcoal and chalk on paper
25.5 × 35.5
Jane Cohen
TATE ONLY

Dante Gabriel Rossetti 1828–1882
Homeward Bound
1844
Ink on paper
18.7 × 15
National Trust

Dante Gabriel Rossetti 1828–1882
Man with Woman Wearing Trousers
1844
Ink on paper
19 × 16
National Trust

Dante Gabriel Rossetti 1828–1882
The Bivouac after the Ball
1845
Ink and graphite on paper
22.5 × 18.5
National Trust

Dante Gabriel Rossetti 1828–1882
Hermia and Helena
c.1846
Ink on paper
21 × 15.5
National Trust

Dante Gabriel Rossetti 1828–1882
The Shadowless Man
c.1846
Ink on paper
17 × 12.5
National Trust

Paul Gavarni 1804–1866
Les gens de Paris: petit commerce
1846
Lithograph on paper
26.3 × 17

Dante Gabriel Rossetti 1828–1882
Faust
1846
Ink on paper
24 × 23.5
National Trust

Dante Gabriel Rossetti 1828–1882
The Raven: Angel Footfalls
1846
Ink on paper
28.5 × 22
National Trust

Dante Gabriel Rossetti 1828–1882
Lady Anne Bothwell's Lament
1846–7
Graphite, brown ink and wash on paper
29.2 × 23.2
Peter and Renate Nahum

Dante Gabriel Rossetti 1828–1882
The Sleeper
1846–7
Ink and wash on paper
26.6 × 17.4
British Museum
TATE ONLY

Dante Gabriel Rossetti 1828–1882
Paolo and Francesca da Rimini
1846–8
Ink and graphite on paper
28 × 23
National Trust

Dante Gabriel Rossetti 1828–1882
Girl Walking or Flying
1846–50
Ink on paper
22 × 16.5
National Trust

Dante Gabriel Rossetti 1828–1882
The Raven: Angel Footfalls
c.1848
Pen and brown ink on light brown paper
22.9 × 21.6
Victoria and Albert Museum, London. Given by Mrs Felix Moeller

Dante Gabriel Rossetti 1828–1882
Faust: Margaret in the Church
1848
Ink on paper
17.8 × 12.1
Tate. Presented by E. Percival Allam 1946

Dante Gabriel Rossetti 1828–1882
Retro me Sathana – Get thee behind me Satan
1848
Ink on paper
24.1 × 17.5
On loan from Bolton Library & Museum Services

Paul Jonnard 1840–1902
Dante Gabriel Rossetti
1889
Line engraving on paper
12 × 11.5
Tate. Purchased 2022
TATE ONLY

3A
William Holman Hunt 1827–1910
Rienzi Vowing to Obtain Justice for the Death of his Young Brother, Slain in a Skirmish between the Colonna and Orsini Factions
1848–9, retouched 1886
Oil paint on canvas
86.4 × 121.9
The Ramsbury Manor Foundation
TATE ONLY

Dante Gabriel Rossetti 1828–1882
The Girlhood of Mary Virgin
1848–9
Oil paint on canvas
83.2 × 65.4
Tate. Bequeathed by Lady Jekyll 1937
TATE ONLY

Dante Gabriel Rossetti 1828–1882
Portrait of Christina Rossetti
c.1848–50
Graphite on paper
14.9 × 11.4
Private Collection
TATE ONLY

Dante Gabriel Rossetti 1828–1882
Study of a Man Smoking a Long Pipe
c.1849
Ink and watercolour on paper
19 × 9.2
Tate. Bequeathed by J.R. Holliday 1927

Sir John Everett Millais, Bt. 1829–1896
Study for Christ in the House of His Parents
c.1849
Graphite on paper
19 × 33.7
Tate. Bequeathed by H.F. Stephens 1932
TATE ONLY

The Germ: Thoughts Towards Nature in Poetry, Literature and Art, vol.1
London: Aylott & Jones
1850
Periodical
21.6 × 14
Mark Samuels Lasner Collection, Special Collections, University of Delaware Library

Hand and Soul (proof sheet from The Germ, vol.1)
1850
Ink on paper
23.3. × 14
Mark Samuels Lasner Collection, Special Collections, University of Delaware Library

James Collinson 1825–1881
The Child Jesus
1850
Engraving on paper
12 × 18.5
Tate. Presented by Edmund Houghton 1898

William Holman Hunt 1827–1910
Frontispiece to The Germ
1850
Etching on paper
20.3 × 12.1
Tate. Bequeathed by H.F. Stephens 1932

Sir John Everett Millais, Bt. 1829–1896
A Baron Numbering his Vassals
1850
Graphite, ink and watercolour on paper
29.2 × 40.6
Tate. Bequeathed by J.R. Holliday 1927
TATE ONLY

Frederic George Stephens 1827–1907
The Proposal (The Marquis and Griselda)
c.1850
Oil paint on canvas
80.6 × 64.8
Tate. Bequeathed by H.F. Stephens 1932
TATE ONLY

Dante Gabriel Rossetti 1828–1882
Thomas Woolner
1852
Graphite on paper
15.5 × 14.6
Lent by the National Portrait Gallery
TATE ONLY

Dante Gabriel Rossetti 1828–1882
Self-portrait
c.1853
Ink and graphite on paper
17.7 × 10.8
Private Collection

After Dante Gabriel Rossetti 1828–1882
Elizabeth Siddal with Dante Gabriel Rossetti
c.1853
Photogravure on paper
14 × 19.5
Lent by the National Portrait Gallery
TATE ONLY

Dante Gabriel Rossetti 1828–1882
William Michael Rossetti
1853
Graphite on paper
28.2 × 21
Lent by the National Portrait Gallery
TATE ONLY

Dante Gabriel Rossetti 1828–1882
John Ruskin
c.1860
Ink on paper
11.5 × 5.7
Mark Samuels Lasner Collection, Special Collections, University of Delaware Library

The Germ (facsimile reprint)
London: Aylott & Jones
1901
Four periodicals
21.6 × 14
Stephen Calloway
TATE ONLY

3B

Dante Gabriel Rossetti 1828–1882
Taurello's First Sight of Fortune
1849
Ink on paper
27.9 × 27.9
Tate. Bequeathed by H.F. Stephens 1932

Dante Gabriel Rossetti 1828–1882
Study for 'Giotto Painting the Portrait of Dante'
1852
Ink on paper
19 × 16.8
Tate. Bequeathed by J.R. Holliday 1927

Dante Gabriel Rossetti 1828–1882
Dante Drawing an Angel on the Anniversary of Beatrice's Death
1853
Watercolour and bodycolour on paper
42 × 61
The Ashmolean Museum, University of Oxford. Bequeathed by Mrs Thomas Combe, 1893

Dante Gabriel Rossetti 1828–1882
Hesterna Rosa
1853
Ink on paper
21.9 × 26.3
Tate. Bequeathed by H.F. Stephens 1932

Dante Gabriel Rossetti 1828–1882
Elizabeth Siddal
c.1854
Graphite and watercolour on paper
18.1 × 16.2
Delaware Art Museum, F. V. du Pont Acquisition Fund, 1985

Dante Gabriel Rossetti 1828–1882
Dante's Dream at the Time of the Death of Beatrice
1856
Watercolour on paper
48.7 × 66.2
Tate. Bequeathed by Beresford Rimington Heaton 1940

Dante Gabriel Rossetti 1828–1882
St Catherine
1857
Oil paint on canvas
34.5 × 25
Tate. Bequeathed by Mrs Emily Toms in memory of her father, Joseph Kershaw 1931

Elizabeth Siddal 1829–1862
The Woeful Victory
c.1860
Ink and graphite on paper
16 × 12
Mark Samuels Lasner Collection, Special Collections, University of Delaware Library

William Michael Rossetti 1829–1919
The Comedy of Dante Alighieri, Part 1, The Hell
London: Macmillan
1865
Book
16 × 10
Stephen Calloway
TATE ONLY

Maria Francesca Rossetti 1827–1876
A Shadow of Dante
London: Rivingtons
1871
Book
20 × 13
Stephen Calloway
TATE ONLY

3C

Dante Gabriel Rossetti 1828–1882
Found
1853
Ink and wash on paper
20.5 × 18.1
British Museum. Bequeathed by Colonel William James Gillum
TATE ONLY

Dante Gabriel Rossetti 1828–1882
The Gate of Memory
1853–4
Graphite on paper
14 × 8.6
Delaware Art Museum, F. V. du Pont Acquisition Fund, 2002

Dante Gabriel Rossetti 1828–1882
Found
c.1854
Oil paint on panel
30.3 × 35.8
Tullie House Museum and Art Gallery

Dante Gabriel Rossetti 1828–1882
Found
1854–5/1859–81
Oil paint on canvas
88.9 × 76.2
Delaware Art Museum, Samuel and Mary R. Bancroft Memorial, 1935

Dante Gabriel Rossetti 1828–1882
George Price Boyce with Fanny Cornforth in Rossetti's Studio, Chatham Place
c.1858
Ink on paper
22.2 × 31.8
Tullie House Museum and Art Gallery

Dante Gabriel Rossetti 1828–1882
Mary Magdalene at the Door of Simon the Pharisee
1858
Pen and Indian ink on paper mounted on fine linen on a stretcher
50.8 × 45.7
The Syndics of the Fitzwilliam Museum, University of Cambridge
TATE ONLY

Dante Gabriel Rossetti 1828–1882
Bocca Baciata
1859
Oil paint on panel
32.1 × 27
Museum of Fine Arts, Boston. Gift of James Lawrence
TATE ONLY

Dante Gabriel Rossetti 1828–1882
A Sketch for 'Found'
c.1860
Ink on paper
18.1 × 11.1
Delaware Art Museum, Acquisition Fund, 2014

Dante Gabriel Rossetti 1828–1882
Fanny Cornforth (study for 'Fair Rosamund')
1861
Chalk on paper
32.2 × 25.9
Cecil Higgins Art Gallery, Bedford
TATE ONLY

Christina Rossetti 1830–1894
Goblin Market and Other Poems
London: Macmillan
1865
Book
22.9 × 15.2
Tate Library and Archive
TATE ONLY

Henry Treffry Dunn 1838–1899
Study for the background of 'Found' by Dante Gabriel Rossetti
c.1869
Graphite, crayon and watercolour on paper
31.8 × 58.7
Delaware Art Museum, Acquisition Fund, 2010

Henry Treffry Dunn 1838–1899 and Dante Gabriel Rossetti 1828–1882
Found
1870s
Oil paint on canvas
99.1 × 81.3
Private Collection

William Downey 1829–1915
Fanny Cornforth
1863, printed 1904–11
Gelatin silver print on paper
13.7 × 10.8
Samuel and Mary R. Bancroft Pre-Raphaelite Manuscript Collection, Helen Farr Sloan Library & Archives, Delaware Art Museum

4

Elizabeth Siddal 1829–1862
Last Farewell Before Crucifixion
1850–62
Pen, black ink and brown wash on paper
19.7 × 14
Lent by David Smith

Elizabeth Siddal 1829–1862
The Macbeths
1850–62
Ink with scratching out on paper
21.4 × 13.5
The Ashmolean Museum, University of Oxford. Presented by John Bryson, 1937

Elizabeth Siddal 1829–1862
Clerk Saunders
1851
Watercolour, bodycolour and coloured chalks on paper, laid on a stretcher
28.4 × 18.1
Syndics of the Fitzwilliam Museum, University of Cambridge
TATE ONLY

Dante Gabriel Rossetti 1828–1882
Elizabeth Siddal in a Chair
c.1853
Graphite on paper
26 × 18.4
Tate. Bequeathed by H.F. Stephens 1932

Dante Gabriel Rossetti 1828–1882
Carlisle Wall (The Lovers)
1853
Watercolour on paper
24.1 × 16.8
Tate. Bequeathed by Miss E.K. Virtue Tebbs 1949

Elizabeth Siddal 1829–1862
The Lady of Shalott
1853
Ink on paper
16.5 × 22.3
The Maas Gallery

Elizabeth Siddal 1829–1862
St Agnes' Eve
1853–60
Gouache on paper
16.5 × 12
National Trust

Elizabeth Siddal 1829–1862
The Gay Goshawk
c.1854
Graphite on paper
10 × 7.5
Private Collection
TATE ONLY

Elizabeth Siddal 1829–1862
Lady Clare
1854–7
Watercolour on paper
33.8 × 25.4
Private Collection
TATE ONLY

Dante Gabriel Rossetti 1828–1882
and Elizabeth Siddal 1829–1862
Sir Galahad and the Holy Grail
c.1855–7
Watercolour on paper
28 × 23.8
Private Collection

Dante Gabriel Rossetti 1828–1882
Paolo and Francesca da Rimini
1855
Watercolour on paper
25.4 × 44.9
Tate. Purchased with assistance
from Sir Arthur Du Cros Bt
and Sir Otto Beit KCMG through
the Art Fund 1916

Elizabeth Siddal 1829–1862
Lady Affixing Pennant to a Knight's Spear
c.1856
Watercolour on paper
13.7 × 13.7
Tate. Bequeathed by W.C. Alexander
1917

Elizabeth Siddal 1829–1862
The Haunted Wood
1856
Gouache on paper
12 × 11
National Trust

Elizabeth Siddal 1829–1862
Sir Patrick Spens
1856
Watercolour on paper
24.1 × 22.9
Tate. Purchased 1919
TATE ONLY

Dante Gabriel Rossetti 1828–1882
The Damsel of Sanct Grael
1857
Watercolour on paper
34.9 × 12.7
Tate. Purchased with assistance
from Sir Arthur Du Cros Bt
and Sir Otto Beit KCMG through
the Art Fund 1916
TATE ONLY

Dante Gabriel Rossetti 1828–1882
Mary Nazarene
1857
Watercolour on paper
34.3 × 19.7
Tate. Purchased 1911

Alfred Tennyson 1809–1892
Poems
London: E. Moxon
1857
Book
22.9 × 16.8
Tate Library and Archive
TATE ONLY

Dante Gabriel Rossetti 1828–1882
Sir Galahad, Sir Bors and Sir Percival receiving the Sanc Grael, but Sir Percival's Sister died by the Way
1857
Ink, chalk, graphite and wash on paper
25.1 × 35.2
British Museum. Bequeathed by
Colonel William James Gillum
TATE ONLY

Dante Gabriel Rossetti 1828–1882
The Tune of the Seven Towers
1857
Watercolour on paper
31.4 × 36.5
Tate. Purchased with assistance
from Sir Arthur Du Cros Bt
and Sir Otto Beit KCMG through
the Art Fund 1916

Dante Gabriel Rossetti 1828–1882
The Wedding of St George and Princess Sabra
1857
Watercolour on paper
36.5 × 36.5
Tate. Purchased with assistance
from Sir Arthur Du Cros Bt
and Sir Otto Beit KCMG through
the Art Fund 1916

Dante Gabriel Rossetti 1828–1882
Writing on the Sand
1858–9
Watercolour on paper
26.3 × 24.1
British Museum
TATE ONLY

Dante Gabriel Rossetti 1828–1882
Arthur's Tomb
1860
Watercolour on paper
23.5 × 36.8
Tate. Presented by the Art Fund 1918

Elizabeth Siddal 1829–1862
Sister Helen
1860
Ink and chalk on paper
15 × 13
National Trust

Elizabeth Siddal 1829–1862
St Cecilia
1860
Ink on paper
10 × 7.8
National Trust

Dante Gabriel Rossetti 1828–1882
How Sir Galahad, Sir Bors and Sir Percival Were Fed with the Sanct Grael; but Sir Percival's Sister Died by the Way
1864
Watercolour and gouache on paper
29.2 × 41.9
Tate. Bequeathed by Beresford
Rimington Heaton 1940

After Elizabeth Siddal 1829–1862
Studies of angels and kneeling women, with study for 'The Blessed Damozel'
c.1866
Photographic reproductions
57 × 45.5
The Ashmolean Museum,
University of Oxford. Bequeathed
by John Bryson, 1977

After Elizabeth Siddal 1829–1862
Three sketches for angels and three sketches for 'St Agnes' Eve'
c.1866
Photographic reproductions
57 × 45.5
The Ashmolean Museum, University of
Oxford. Bequeathed by John Bryson,
1977

After Elizabeth Siddal 1829–1862
Three studies for 'Sister Helen'
c.1866
Photographic reproductions
57 × 45.5
The Ashmolean Museum, University of
Oxford. Bequeathed by John Bryson,
1977

Christina Rossetti 1830–1894
The Prince's Progress and Other Poems
London: Macmillan
1866
Book
17.8 × 11.4
Stephen Calloway
TATE ONLY

Dante Gabriel Rossetti 1828–1882
St John Comforting the Virgin at the Foot of the Cross
1868
Ink and wash on paper
16.4 × 15.2
Syndics of the Fitzwilliam Museum,
University of Cambridge
TATE ONLY

Dante Gabriel Rossetti 1828–1882
Sister Helen
c.1870
Graphite and ink on paper mounted
on board
21.1 × 16.7
Delaware Art Museum, Wilmington,
DE. Gift of Mark Samuels Lasner,
2002

5
Dante Gabriel Rossetti 1828–1882
The Portrait
c.1850–70
Ink on paper
20.2 × 32.2
Mark Samuels Lasner Collection,
Special Collections, University of
Delaware Library

Elizabeth Siddal 1829–1862
Madonna and Child
1850–62
Watercolour over graphite on paper
6.5 × 5.9
Lent by David Smith

Barbara Leigh Smith Bodichon
1827–1891
Elizabeth Siddal
1854
Graphite on paper
11 × 9
Mark Samuels Lasner Collection,
Special Collections, University of
Delaware Library

Anna Mary Howitt 1824–1884
Elizabeth Siddal
1854
Graphite on paper
12.8 × 11.1
Mark Samuels Lasner Collection,
Special Collections, University of
Delaware Library

Elizabeth Siddal 1829–1862
Lovers Listening to Music
c.1854
Graphite and ink on paper
37.8 × 39.8
National Trust

Dante Gabriel Rossetti 1828–1882
Elizabeth Siddal
1855
Graphite on paper
12 × 9
Mark Samuels Lasner Collection,
Special Collections, University of
Delaware Library

Elizabeth Siddal 1829–1862
Madonna and Child with Angel
c.1856
Watercolour, gouache and metallic
paint on paper
19.7 × 15.2
Delaware Art Museum, Samuel and
Mary R. Bancroft Memorial, 1935

Dante Gabriel Rossetti 1828–1882
Portrait of Elizabeth Siddal
c.1857
Graphite on paper
18.8 × 15.3
British Museum
TATE ONLY

Dante Gabriel Rossetti 1828–1882
Portrait of Elizabeth Siddal
c.1857
Graphite on paper
18.8 × 15.3
British Museum. Bequeathed by
Colonel William James Gillum
TATE ONLY

Dante Gabriel Rossetti 1828–1882
The Blue Closet
1857
Watercolour on paper
35.4 × 26
Tate. Purchased with assistance
from Sir Arthur Du Cros Bt
and Sir Otto Beit KCMG through
the Art Fund 1916
TATE ONLY

Dante Gabriel Rossetti 1828–1882
Dantis Amor
1860
Oil paint on mahogany
74.9 × 81.3
Tate. Presented by F. Treharne James
1920

Dante Gabriel Rossetti 1828–1882
Elizabeth Siddal
1860
Graphite on paper
26 × 25.4
The Syndics of the Fitzwilliam
Museum, University of Cambridge
TATE ONLY

Dante Gabriel Rossetti 1828–1882
The Early Italian Poets from Ciullo d'Alcamo to Dante Alighieri
London: Smith, Elder, and Co.
1861
Book
18 × 12
Stephen Calloway
TATE ONLY

Dante Gabriel Rossetti 1828–1882
Elizabeth Siddal
1861
Graphite on paper
24.8 × 21
Private Collection

Ford Madox Brown 1821–1893, Edward Coley Burne-Jones 1833–1898, William Morris 1834–1896, Valentine Cameron Prinsep 1838–1904, Dante Gabriel Rossetti 1828–1882, and John Pollard Seddon 1827–1906
King René's Honeymoon Cabinet
1861
Oak, inlaid with various woods, with painted metalwork and painted panels
133.4 × 252 × 87
Victoria and Albert Museum. Purchased with the assistance of Art Fund
TATE ONLY

Dante Gabriel Rossetti 1828–1882
Design for the front and back of a watch
1862
Ink and graphite on paper
11 × 20.5
Geoffrey Munn

Dante Gabriel Rossetti 1828–1882 and Morris, Marshall, Faulkner & Co.
Sofa and cushion
c.1862
Open-back sofa of wood painted black and partially gilded, the back painted with three figures in oval medallions, upholstered with contemporary green cut velvet
82.6 × 198.1 × 66
Syndics of the Fitzwilliam Museum, University of Cambridge
TATE ONLY

Lock of Elizabeth Siddal's Hair
1862
Hair
7.4 × 7.4
Mark Samuels Lasner Collection, Special Collections, University of Delaware Library

Dante Gabriel Rossetti 1828–1882
King René's Honeymoon – Music
c.1863
Clear and coloured glass with painted and stained details
64.2 × 54.7
Victoria and Albert Museum
TATE ONLY

Dante Gabriel Rossetti 1828–1882
Roman de la Rose
1864
Watercolour on paper
34.3 × 34.3
Tate. Presented by Andrew Bain 1925
TATE ONLY

Dante Gabriel Rossetti 1828–1882
Beata Beatrix
c.1864–70
Oil paint on canvas
86.4 × 66
Tate. Presented by Georgiana, Baroness Mount Temple in memory of her husband, Francis, Baron Mount Temple 1889

After Elizabeth Siddal 1829–1862
Studies for 'The Nativity'
c.1866
Photographic reproductions
57 × 45.5
The Ashmolean Museum, University of Oxford. Bequeathed by John Bryson, 1977

Morris & Co.
'Rossetti' chair
c.1870
Ebonised beech and rush
82 × 52 × 45.5
Stephen Calloway
TATE ONLY

Dante Gabriel Rossetti 1828–1882
Poems
London: F.S. Ellis
1870
Book
19 × 12.5
Stephen Calloway
TATE ONLY

Dante Gabriel Rossetti 1828–1882
Poems
Leipzig: Bernard Tauchnitz
1873
Book
15 × 10
Tate Library and Archive
TATE ONLY

Lock of Dante Gabriel Rossetti's hair
c.1882
Hair
7.4 × 7.4
The Syndics of the Fitzwilliam Museum, University of Cambridge
TATE ONLY

6

Unknown maker
Bracelet
1850
Plaited gold and rubies
6 × 6.2 × 1.1
Victoria and Albert Museum. Bequeathed by May Morris
TATE ONLY

Dante Gabriel Rossetti 1828–1882
Head of a Young Woman [Mrs. Eaton?]
1863–5
Chalk and charcoal, with stumping
46.5 × 31.5
Iris & B. Gerald Cantor Center for Visual Arts at Stanford University

Dante Gabriel Rossetti 1828–1882
Study of a Head (probably a study of Keomi for 'The Beloved')
1865
Graphite on paper
36.8 × 33.7
Victoria and Albert Museum. Bequeathed by J.R. Holliday

Dante Gabriel Rossetti 1828–1882
Study for 'The Bride'
1865
Graphite on paper
41.9 × 30.5
Tate. Bequeathed by J.R. Holliday 1927

Unknown artist
The Beloved
1865
Carbon print on paper
26.5 × 24
Samuel and Mary R. Bancroft Pre-Raphaelite Manuscript Collection, Helen Farr Sloan Library & Archives, Delaware Art Museum

Dante Gabriel Rossetti 1828–1882
The Beloved ('The Bride')
1865–6
Oil paint on canvas
82.5 × 76.2
Tate. Purchased with assistance from Sir Arthur Du Cros Bt and Sir Otto Beit KCMG through the Art Fund 1916

7

Dante Gabriel Rossetti 1828–1882
Elizabeth Siddal Plaiting her Hair
Date not known
Graphite on paper
17.1 × 12.7
Tate. Bequeathed by H.F. Stephens 1932

Dante Gabriel Rossetti 1828–1882
Portrait of Christina Rossetti
1866
Chalk on paper
79 × 63.5
Private Collection
TATE ONLY

Dante Gabriel Rossetti 1828–1882
Lady having her hair combed out
1855
Ink and wash on paper
15.3 × 11.5
Lowell Libson & Jonny Yarker Ltd

Dante Gabriel Rossetti 1828–1882
La Belle Dame Sans Merci
1855–6
Graphite and ink on paper
33.2 × 43.2
British Museum. Bequeathed by Colonel William James Gillum
TATE ONLY

Dante Gabriel Rossetti 1828–1882
Lucrezia Borgia
1860–1
Graphite and watercolour on paper
43.8 × 25.8
Tate. Presented in memory of Henry Michael Field by Charles Ricketts through the Art Fund 1916
TATE ONLY

Dante Gabriel Rossetti 1828–1882
Cassandra
1861
Ink on paper
33.1 × 46.2
British Museum. Bequeathed by Colonel William James Gillum
TATE ONLY

Dante Gabriel Rossetti 1828–1882
Study for Delia in 'The Return of Tibullus to Delia'
1860–2
Graphite on paper, mounted on card
22.2 × 19.6
The Syndics of the Fitzwilliam Museum, University of Cambridge
TATE ONLY

Dante Gabriel Rossetti 1828–1882
Fanny Cornforth
1862
Graphite on paper
38.9 × 35.6
The Syndics of the Fitzwilliam Museum, University of Cambridge
TATE ONLY

Dante Gabriel Rossetti 1828–1882
Aurelia (Fazio's Mistress)
1863–73
Oil paint on mahogany
43.2 × 36.8
Tate. Purchased with assistance from Sir Arthur Du Cros Bt and Sir Otto Beit KCMG through the Art Fund 1916

Dante Gabriel Rossetti 1828–1882
Monna Pomona
1864
Watercolour and gum arabic on paper
47.6 × 39.3
Tate. Presented by Alfred A. de Pass 1910
TATE ONLY

Dante Gabriel Rossetti 1828–1882
Sibylla Palmifera
1865–70
Oil paint on canvas
98.4 × 85
National Museums Liverpool
TATE ONLY

Dante Gabriel Rossetti 1828–1882
Monna Vanna
1866
Oil paint on canvas
88.9 × 86.4
Tate. Purchased with assistance from Sir Arthur Du Cros Bt and Sir Otto Beit KCMG through the Art Fund 1916

Dante Gabriel Rossetti 1828–1882
Lady Lilith
1866–8, altered 1872–3
Oil paint on canvas
96.5 × 85.1
Delaware Art Museum, Samuel and Mary R. Bancroft Memorial, 1935

Percy Bysshe Shelley 1792–1822
Poetical Works
London: Ward, Lock & Co.
1867
Book
18 × 13
Tate. Purchased 2023
TATE ONLY

Dante Gabriel Rossetti 1828–1882
Head of Andromeda (Aspecta Medusa)
1868
Chalk on paper
51.3 × 54.7
Victoria and Albert Museum.
Bequeathed by Constantine Alexander Ionides
TATE ONLY

Dante Gabriel Rossetti 1828–1882
Venus Verticordia
1868
Watercolour and bodycolour on paper
67 × 59
Private Collection

Walt Whitman 1819–1892
London: John Camden Hotten
Poems
1868
Book
19 × 14
On loan from The London Library
TATE ONLY

Dante Gabriel Rossetti 1828–1882
Lady Lilith
c.1869
Ink and graphite on paper
21 × 17.5
Jane Cohen

Dante Gabriel Rossetti 1828–1882
Veronica Veronese
1872
Oil paint on canvas
109.2 × 88.9
Delaware Art Museum, Samuel and Mary R. Bancroft Memorial, 1935

Dante Gabriel Rossetti 1828–1882
La Ghirlandata
1873
Oil paint on canvas
124 × 85
Guildhall Art Gallery, City of London

Dante Gabriel Rossetti 1828–1882
Ligeia Siren
1873
Coloured chalks on paper
80 × 55
Private Collection
TATE ONLY

Christina Rossetti 1830–1894
Speaking Likeness
London: Macmillan
1874
Book
19 × 15
Tate Library and Archive
TATE ONLY

Dante Gabriel Rossetti 1828–1882
Proserpine
1874
Oil paint on canvas
125.1 × 61
Tate. Presented by W. Graham Robertson 1940

Unknown photographer
Photograph of Dante Gabriel Rossetti
c.1875
Stephen Calloway
TATE ONLY

Dante Gabriel Rossetti 1828–1882
The Blessed Damozel
1875–9
Oil paint on canvas
221.5 × 139 (frame)
National Museums Liverpool
TATE ONLY

Dante Gabriel Rossetti 1828–1882
Mnemosyne
1881
Oil paint on canvas
126.4 × 61
Delaware Art Museum, Samuel and Mary R. Bancroft Memorial, 1935

Lucy Madox Rossetti 1843–1894
Mrs Shelley
1890
Book
19 × 14
Tate. Purchased 2023
TATE ONLY

8

Robert Burton 1577–1640
The Anatomy of Melancholy
1651
Book
19 × 14
Society of Antiquaries
TATE ONLY

Dante Gabriel Rossetti 1828–1882
Jane Burden
1858
Ink, graphite and wash with white highlights on paper
48.3 × 35.3
National Gallery of Ireland
TATE ONLY

John Robert Parsons c.1826–1909
Thirteen Photographs of Jane Morris Posing in the Garden of Rossetti's House
1865
Photographs, albumen prints on paper from wet collodion glass negatives
21.8 × 15.7 (each)
Private Collection
TATE ONLY

Dante Gabriel Rossetti 1828–1882
Jane Morris
1868
Chalk on paper
89 × 70
Private Collection, The Maas Gallery

Dante Gabriel Rossetti 1828–1882
Jane Morris
1870
Graphite on paper
35 × 30
Mark Samuels Lasner Collection, Special Collections, University of Delaware Library

Dante Gabriel Rossetti 1828–1882
Jane Morris (Study for 'Dante's Dream')
1870
Chalk on paper
60 × 51.1
British Museum. Bequeathed by Cecil French
TATE ONLY

Dante Gabriel Rossetti 1828–1882
La Donna Della Finestra (The Lady of Pity)
1870
Pastel on paper
84.8 × 72.1
Bradford Museums & Galleries
TATE ONLY

Dante Gabriel Rossetti 1828–1882
Proserpine
1877
Oil paint on canvas
116.8 × 55.9
Private Collection
TATE ONLY

Dante Gabriel Rossetti 1828–1882
The Daydream
1880
Oil paint on canvas
195.3 × 128.8
Victoria and Albert Museum.
Bequeathed by Constantine Alexander Ionides
TATE ONLY

Dante Gabriel Rossetti 1828–1882
Proserpine
1880
Coloured chalks on paper
120 × 56
Private Collection
TATE ONLY

Dante Gabriel Rossetti 1828–1882
Ballads and Sonnets
London: Ellis & White
1881
Book
19 × 14
Tate. Purchased 2023
TATE ONLY

Dante Gabriel Rossetti 1828–1882
Joan of Arc
1882
Oil paint on panel
52.7 × 45.7
The Syndics of the Fitzwilliam Museum, University of Cambridge
TATE ONLY

Henry Currie Marillier 1865–1951
Dante Gabriel Rossetti: An Illustrated Memorial of his Art and Life
1899
Book
25 × 15
Tate Library and Archive
TATE ONLY

9

The Torch: A Journal of Anarchist Communism, vol.2, no.1
London: H. & O. Rossetti
1895
Periodical
26 × 19
Mark Samuels Lasner Collection, Special Collections, University of Delaware Library

Sunil Gupta b.1953
Untitled #2 from the series The New Pre-Raphaelites
2008, printed 2021
Archival inkjet print
70.9 × 106.7
Hales Gallery
TATE ONLY

Works Exhibited at Delaware Only

Elizabeth Siddal 1829–1862
Sketch for 'La Belle Dame Sans Merci'
c.1855
Graphite on paper
10.5 × 7.3
Delaware Art Museum, Acquisition Fund, 2007

Dante Gabriel Rossetti 1828–1882
Mary Magdalene leaving the house of feasting
1857
Watercolour on paper
35.6 × 20.6
Tate. Purchased 1911

Dante Gabriel Rossetti 1828–1882
The Adoration
1858–64
Watercolour on paper
40.6 × 29.2
Tate. Purchased 1924

Dante Gabriel Rossetti 1828–1882
Fanny Cornforth
1859
Graphite on paper
14.3 × 14.6
Tate. Bequeathed by J.R. Holliday 1927

Dante Gabriel Rossetti 1828–1882
Fanny Cornforth
c.1862–5
Graphite on paper
33.3 × 25.4
Delaware Art Museum, F. V. du Pont Acquisition Fund, and partial gift of Mark Samuels Lasner, 2022

Elizabeth Siddal 1829–1862
Study for 'Jephthah's Daughter'
Date not known
Graphite on paper
21.3 × 12.1
Delaware Art Museum, Acquisition Fund, 2011

Dante Gabriel Rossetti 1828–1882
Joan of Arc
1864
Watercolour on board
53.3 × 57.1
Tate. Bequeathed by Beresford Rimington Heaton 1940

Information is correct at the time of publication but is subject to change.

Selected Bibliography

Broussine, Sylvie, and Christopher Newall, *Rossetti's Portraits*, London 2021

Bryson, John (ed.), *Dante Gabriel Rossetti and Jane Morris: Their Correspondence*, Oxford 1976

Caine, T. Hall, *Recollections of Dante Gabriel Rossetti*, London 1882

Chapman, Alison, and Joanna Meacock, *A Rossetti Family Chronology*, Basingstoke and New York 2007

Clifford, David, and Laurence Roussillon (eds.), *Outsiders Looking In: The Rossettis Then and Now*, London 2004

Crump, R.W., and Betty S. Flowers (eds.), *Christina Rossetti: The Complete Poems*, London 2001

Ford, Colin, 'A Pre-Raphaelite Partnership: Dante Gabriel Rossetti and John Robert Parsons', *Burlington Magazine*, vol.146, no.1214, May 2004

Fredeman, William E. (ed.), *The Correspondence of Dante Gabriel Rossetti*, 10 vols., Cambridge, Woodbridge and Rochester, NY 2002–15

Gere, Charlotte, and Geoffrey C. Munn, *Artists' Jewellery: Pre-Raphaelite to Arts and Crafts*, Woodbridge 1989

Grieve, Alastair, *The Best Years of Rossetti's Art: 1846–1862*, Norwich 2017

Harrison, Antony H. (ed.), *The Letters of Christina Rossetti*, 4 vols., Charlottesville, VA 1997–2004

Hunt, William Holman, *Pre-Raphaelitism and the Pre-Raphaelite Brotherhood*, 2 vols., London 1905–6

Marsh, Jan, *The Legend of Elizabeth Siddal*, London 1989

Marsh, Jan, *Christina Rossetti: A Literary Biography*, London 1994

Marsh, Jan, *Dante Gabriel Rossetti: Painter and Poet*, London 1999

Marsh, Jan, *Pre-Raphaelite Sisters*, London 2019

Mason, Emma, *Christina Rossetti: Poetry, Ecology, Faith*, Oxford 2018

Parkins, Wendy, *Jane Morris: The Burden of History*, Edinburgh 2013

Parris, Leslie (ed.), *The Pre-Raphaelites*, London 1984

Peattie, Roger W. (ed.), *Selected Letters of William Michael Rossetti*, London 1990

Prettejohn, Elizabeth, *Modern Painters, Old Masters: The Art of Imitation from the Pre-Raphaelites to the First World War*, New Haven, CT and London 2017

Prettejohn, Elizabeth (ed.), *The Cambridge Companion to the Pre-Raphaelites*, Cambridge 2012

Roe, Dinah, *The Rossettis in Wonderland*, London 2011

Rossetti, Christina, 'Dante, The Poet Illustrated out of the Poem', *The Century*, Feb. 1884

Rossetti, William Michael, 'Dante Rossetti and Elizabeth Siddal', *Burlington Magazine*, vol.1, no.3, May 1903

Rossetti, William Michael, *Some Reminiscences of William Michael Rossetti*, 2 vols., London 1906

Rossetti, William Michael (ed.), *Ruskin, Rossetti, Preraphaelitism: Papers 1854 to 1862*, New York 1899

Rossetti, William Michael (ed.), *Rossetti Papers, 1862 to 1870*, London 1903

Rossetti, William Michael (ed.), *The Poetical Works of Christina Rossetti*, London 1904

Rossetti, William Michael (ed.), *The Works of Dante Gabriel Rossetti*, London 1911

Sasso, Eleonora, *The Pre-Raphaelites and Orientalism: Language and Cognition in Remediations of the East*, Edinburgh 2018

Sharp, Frank C., and Jan Marsh (eds.), *The Collected Letters of Jane Morris*, Woodbridge 2012

Siddal, Elizabeth, *My Ladys Soul: The Poetry of Elizabeth Eleanor Siddall*, ed. Serena Trowbridge, London 2018

Simons, John, *Rossetti's Wombat: Pre-Raphaelites and Australian Animals in Victorian London*, London 2008

Stephens, F.G., *Dante Gabriel Rossetti*, London 1894

Thirlwell, Angela, *William and Lucy: The Other Rossettis*, New Haven, CT and London 2003

Thomas, Frances, *Christina Rossetti: A Biography*, London 1994

Treuherz, Julian, Elizabeth Prettejohn and Edwin Becker (eds.), *Dante Gabriel Rossetti*, London 2003

Walker, Kirsty Stonell, *Stunner: The Fall and Rise of Fanny Cornforth*, London 2006

Warner, Malcolm, 'The Pre-Raphaelites and the National Gallery', *Huntington Library Quarterly*, vol.55, no.1, Winter 1992

Watts-Dunton, Theodore, 'The Truth About Rossetti', *The Nineteenth Century*, no.13, March 1883

Woolley, Anne, *The Poems of Elizabeth Siddal in Context*, Manchester 2021

Youde, Glenda, and Robert Wilkes (eds.), *Pre-Raphaelite Sisters: Art, Poetry and Female Agency in Victorian Britain*, Oxford 2022

Image Credits

© Ashmolean Museum endpapers, 77, 78, 84, 89, 92, 95, 123, 126, 128, 130, 135, 137, 162
Photo by Birmingham Museums Trust, licensed under cc0 5, 6, 59, 61, 62, 66, 67, 69, 100, 101, 104, 106, 129, 153, 168, 170, 171, 172, 174, 213
© Bolton Council. From the collection of Bolton Museum 40
© Bradford Museums & Galleries / Bridgeman Images 209
© British Library Board / Add MS 49460 38; / Ashley MS 1371 44; / C.39.e.64 (1) 49
British Library, London © British Library Board. All Rights Reserved / Bridgeman Images 156
© The Trustees of the British Museum 3, 35, 43, 102, 133, 147, 160, 161, 186, 206
Christie's, 2013 / Private collection 64
The Cleveland Museum of Art 4
Delaware Art Museum / Acquisition fund, 2010 107; /Acquisition Fund, 1014 103; / F. V. du Pont Acquisition Fund, 1985 80, 88; / F. V. du Pont Acquisition Fund, 2002 99; / Gift of Mark Samuels Lasner, 2002 131; / Samuel and Mary R. Bancroft Memorial, 1935 96, 188, 195, 198, 215, 219; /Samuel and Mary R. Bancroft Pre-Raphaelite Manuscript Collection, Helen Farr Sloan Library and Archives, Delaware Art Museum 98, 112, 178
© The Fitzwilliam Museum, Cambridge 2, 55, 91, 113, 119, 143, 152, 182, 183, 218
The Mistress and Fellows, Girton College, Cambridge 148
Front cover, 193 Guildhall Art Gallery, City of London
Harry Ransom Center, The University of Texas at Austin 50, 51, 52
Harvard Art Museums, Fogg Museum / The Picture Art Collection / Alamy Stock Photo 75
© The Higgins Art Gallery & Museum / Bridgeman Images 111
Historic England Archive 194
Hulton Archive / Stringer / GettyImages 9
© Ilyanna Kerr, Illustrator / www.ilyannakerr.com / @ily_kerr 154
Iris & B. Gerald Cantor Center for Visual Arts at Stanford University; Museum Purchase Fund, 1970.390 176
Mark Samuels Lasner Collection, University of Delaware Library, Museums and Press 93, 144, 146, 149, 167, 204
Photo by Marcus J. Leith 11, 70, 140, 166
Lowell Libson & Jonny Yarker Ltd 180
The Maas Gallery 85
© Manchester Art Gallery / Manchester Art Gallery / Bridgeman Images 83
© The Metropolitan Museum of Art, New York 202
Collection of Geoffrey Munn 155b
Photograph © 2023 Museum of Fine Arts, Boston 94
Peter and Renate Nahum 18, 39, 86
National Gallery of Canada, Ottawa Photo: NGC 7, 142
Photo © National Gallery of Ireland 200
© The National Gallery, London 58
The National Gallery, London; on loan from The Ramsbury Manor Foundation, © The Capricorn Foundation 57
Courtesy National Museums Liverpool, Lady Lever Art Gallery 179, 185, 196
© National Portrait Gallery, London 20, 56, 60
© National Trust Images 13, 21, 22, 23, 24, 28, 29, 30, 31, 32, 34, 37, 136, 141, 151, 163
Private collection 45, 97
203 Private collection / Painters / Alamy Stock Photo
Private collection / Photo © Christie's Images / Bridgeman Images 14, 15, 16, 17, 109, 138, 187, 191, 207
Private collection / Danvis Collection / Alamy Stock Photo 79
Private collection / © Mary Jacobs 47, 48
Private collection / Photo © Peter Nahum at The Leicester Galleries, London / Bridgeman Images 211
Private collection / Photography David Parmiter 41, 108, 212
Private collection / Photography by David Smith 87, 120
Private collection / Sotheby's, London 189
Private collection / © Tate, 2023 / Sam Day 19, 26
© The Society of Antiquaries of London (Kelmscott Manor) 157, 205, 208
© Tate, 2023 10, 25, 27, 54, 63, 65, 72, 73, 139, 155a, 164, 169, 184, 192; / Sonal Bakrania 1, 36, 68, 71, 74, 76, 81, 110, 117, 118, 121, 125, 127, 145, 173, 181; / Lucy Dawkins and Jai Monaghan 12, 42, 82, 199, 201; / Matt Greenwood 53, 197, 210; / Matt Greenwood and Seraphina Neville 134, 165; / Joe Humphrys and Jai Monaghan 90, 116, 124, 132; / Rod Tidnam 46, 115, 122, 216
Image © Tullie House Museum, Carlisle 8, 105, 114
© Victoria and Albert Museum, London 33, 150, 158, 159, 175, 177, 190, 217
William Morris Gallery, London Borough of Waltham Forest 214

Index

Supporting TATE

Tate relies on a large number of supporters – individuals, foundations, companies and public sector sources – to enable it to deliver its programme of activities, both on and off its gallery sites. This support is essential in order for Tate to acquire works of art for the Collection, run education, outreach and exhibition programmes, care for the Collection in storage and enable art to be displayed, both digitally and physically, inside and outside Tate. Please contact us at:

Development Office
Tate
Millbank
London SW1P 4RG
Tel: +44 (0)20 7887 4900
Fax: +44 (0)20 7887 8098

Tate Americas Foundation

520 West 27 Street Unit 404
New York, NY 10001
USA
Tel: 001 212 643 2818
Fax: 001 212 643 1001

Donations, no matter the size, are gratefully received, either to support particular areas of interest, or to contribute to general activity costs.

Legacies

A legacy to Tate may take the form of a residual share of an estate, a specific cash sum, or an item of property such as a work of art. Legacies to Tate are free of inheritance tax and help to secure a strong future for the Collection and galleries. For further information please contact the Development Office.

Offers in lieu of tax

Inheritance Tax can be satisfied by transferring to the Government a work of art of outstanding importance. In this case the amount of tax is reduced. It can be made a condition of the offer that the work of art is allocated to Tate. Please contact us for details.

Tate Members

Tate Members enjoy unlimited free admission throughout the year to all exhibitions at Tate, as well as a number of other benefits such as exclusive use of our Members' Rooms and a free annual subscription to *Tate Etc.* Whilst enjoying the exclusive privileges of membership, members also help secure Tate's position at the very heart of British and modern art. Members support actively contributes towards new purchases of important art, ensuring that Tate's collection continues to be relevant and comprehensive, as well as funding projects in London, Liverpool and St Ives that increase access and understanding for everyone.

Tate Patrons

Tate Patrons share a passion for art and are committed to supporting Tate on an annual basis. The Patrons help enable the acquisition of works across Tate's broad collecting remit and support the staging of major exhibitions in the galleries. They also give their support to vital conservation, learning and research projects. The scheme provides a forum for Patrons to share their interest in art and meet curators, artists and one another in an enjoyable environment through a regular programme of events. These events take place both at Tate and beyond and encompass curator-led exhibition tours, visits to artists' studios and private collections, art trips both in the UK and abroad, and access to art fairs. The scheme welcomes supporters from outside the UK, giving the programme a truly international scope.

Corporate Membership

Corporate Membership at Tate offers companies opportunities for corporate entertaining and the chance for a wide variety of employee benefits. These include special private views, special access to paying exhibitions, out-of-hours visits and tours, invitations to VIP events and talks at members' offices.

Corporate Investment

Tate has developed a range of imaginative partnerships with the corporate sector, ranging from international interpretation and exhibition programmes to local outreach and staff development programmes. We are particularly known for high-profile business to business marketing initiatives and employee benefit packages. Please contact the Corporate Partnerships team for further details.

Charity Details

The Tate Gallery is an exempt charity; the Museums & Galleries Act 1992 added the Tate Gallery to the list of exempt charities defined in the 1960 Charities Act. Tate Foundation is a registered charity (number 1085314).

Tate Americas Foundation

Tate Americas Foundation is an independent charity based in New York that supports the work of Tate in the United Kingdom. It receives full tax exempt status from the IRS under section 501(c)(3) allowing United States taxpayers to receive tax deductions on gifts towards annual membership programmes, exhibitions, scholarship and capital projects. For more information please contact the Tate Americas Foundation office.

This information is correct as of the beginning of December 2022

Douglas S. Cramer
Cristea Roberts Gallery
Harry and Lana David
Patricia Phelps de Cisneros
De Ying Foundation
Tiqui Atencio Demirdjian and Ago Demirdjian
Department of Digital, Culture, Media & Sport
Maryam Diener
Joe and Marie Donnelly
Peter Dubens
The Easton Foundation and Osiris
Leontine Ebers
Edward Eisler
Maryam and Edward Eisler
Endeavor
European Commission
Warren, Amanda and Jeremy Felson, and Lucy Sun
Jeanne D Fisher
Wendy Fisher
Fondation Walter & Nicole LeBlanc
Ford Foundation
Eric and Louise Franck
Helen Frankenthaler Foundation
The Estate of Lucian Freud
Frith Street Gallery
Amanda and Glenn Fuhrman
Mala Gaonkar
Garcia Family Foundation
Garfield Weston Foundation
Candida Gertler
The Golden Bottle Trust
Nicholas and Judith Goodison's Charitable Settlement
Lydia and Manfred Gorvy
The Granville-Grossman Bequest
Greater London Authority
Dr Philip Greider
Wang Guangyi
Alexandra and Guy Halamish
Paul Hamlyn Foundation
The Hartfield Foundation
The Drue Heinz Charitable Trust
Barbara Hepworth Estate
Damien Hirst
David Hockney
Michael Hoppen
Alexandra Howell
Huo Family Foundation (UK) Limited
Denise Hurst-Hastings
The IHS Markit Charitable Foundation
Lyndsey A Ingram
Egill and Evelyn Jacobsen Foundation
Catriona Jeffries and Duane Linklater
Pamela J. Joyner and Alfred J. Giuffrida
Elizabeth and William Kahane
Mari Katayama
Peter and Maria Kellner
J. Patrick Kennedy and Patricia A. Kennedy
The Elie Khouri Art Foundation
Jack Kirkland
David Knaus
Samuel H. Kress Foundation
Peter Kulloi
Lachaise Foundation
Edward Lee in memory of Agnès Lee
Miyoung Lee and Neil Simpkins
Legacy Trust UK
Kiyoko Lerner
The Leverhulme Trust
Ruben Levi
The Linbury Trust
James Lindon in honour of Khalid bin Sultan Al-Qasimi
The Deborah Loeb Brice Foundation
Lillian and Jon Lovelace
LUMA Foundation
Manet (London) Charitable Trust
Kim Manocherian
The Estate of Sir Edwin Manton
The Manton Foundation
Matt's Gallery / 303 Gallery / Galleria Franco Noero / Mike Nelson
Lord McAlpine of West Green
David McDermott and Peter McGough
Steve McQueen
Paul Mellon Centre for Studies in British Art
The Andrew W. Mellon Foundation
The Estate of Ana Mendieta
Adrian Mibus
Gregory R Miller
Ronald Moody Trust
Robert Moon, Benedick Moon and Georgina Moon
Henry Moore Foundation
Mottahedan Family
The Estate of Tish Murtha
National Heritage Memorial Fund
The National Lottery Heritage Fund
National Philanthropic Trust
New Carlsberg Foundation
Simon Nixon and Family
Michael and Sukey Novogratz
Open Hand
OUTSET Germany_Switzerland
Pace Gallery
Yukiko Pajot
Maureen Paley
Midge and Simon Palley
Irene Panagopoulos
Martin Parr
Estate of Carl-Henning Pedersen
Catherine Petitgas
Pi Artworks
The Stanley Picker Trust
The Pilgrim Trust
The Porthmeor Fund
David W. Posnett, OBE
Gilberto Pozzi
Serena Prest Fund
Joanna Rajkowska and l'étrangère
Michael Rakowitz
Alice Rawsthorn
Bob Rennie
Marsha Ribeiro
Richard Saltoun Gallery
Dianne Roberts
The Donald Rodney Estate
The Rokos Family
The gift of Peter Rose and Albert Gallichan
The Estate of Eugene and Penelope Rosenberg
Rothschild Foundation
Kristin Rey and Michael Rubel
Alin Ryan Lobo
The Michael and Nicola Sacher Charitable Trust
The Estate of Simon Sainsbury
Gillian and Simon Salama-Caro
Jean and Melanie Salata
Sammlung Hoffmann Gbr
Franca and Cosima Scheggi
Jake and Hélène Marie Shafran
Jack Shear
Syd Shelton
The Estate of Sylvia Sleigh
Matthew Slotover
Jay Smith and Laura Rapp
Emile Stipp
The Norah and Norman Stone Collection
Mercedes and Ian Stoutzker
John J. Studzinski CBE
Patrick Sun
Ministry of Culture, Taiwan
Tamares Real Estate Holdings, Inc. in collaboration with the Zabludowicz Collection
Tate 1897 Circle
Tate Africa Acquisitions Committee
Tate Americas Foundation
Tate Asia-Pacific Acquisitions Committee
Tate Central and Eastern Europe Plus Acquisitions Committee
Tate European Collection Circle
Tate International Council
Tate Latin American Acquisitions Committee
Tate Members
Tate Middle East North Africa Acquisitions Committee
Tate North American Acquisition Committee
Tate Patrons
Tate Photography Acquisitions Committee
Tate South Asia Acquisitions Committee
Tavolozza Foundation
Teiger Foundation
Terra Foundation for American Art
The Terziev Family
The Estate of Mr Nicholas Themans
Imants Tillers and Michael Nelson Jagamara
Robert and Matthew Travers
The Turner Family
Luc Tuymans
Juan Carlos Verme
Mercedes Vilardell
Marie-Louise von Motesiczky Charitable Trust
Kara Walker
Dr Anne Walmsley
The Weinstock Fund
The Michael G. and C. Jane Wilson 2007 Trust
The Lord Leonard and Lady Estelle Wolfson Foundation
Zhang Xiaogang
Qiao Zhibing, in honour of Gregor Muir
Roman Zubal
and those who wish to remain anonymous

Platinum Patrons

Eric Abraham
Walid Abu-Suud
Mr Shane Akeroyd
Celia and Edward Atkin, CBE
The Estate of Francis Bacon
Lars Bane
Alex Beard
Beecroft Charitable Trust
Francesca Bellini Joseph (Co-Chair) and Allan Hennings
Sir Nigel Boardman and Professor Lynda Gratton
Jacques Boissonnas
Natalia Bondarenko
John Booth
Rory and Elizabeth Brooks
The John Browne Charitable Trust
Mandy Cawthorn Argenio
Chargeurs Philanthropies
XiaoMeng Cheng
Victoria Chu
Lord and Lady Davies of Abersoch
Ms Miel de Botton
Pascale Decaux
Sophie Diedrichs
Valentina Drouin
Kateryna Filippi
Forster Foundation
Edwin Fox Foundation
Stephen Friedman
Alexander Green
David Herro
Kristin Hjellegjerde
Mr Yan Huo
Mr Phillip Hylander (Co-Chair) and Ms Ellie Harrison-Read
Natascha Jakobs-Linssen
Elli Jason Foster and Millie Jason Foster
Maria and Peter Kellner
Mr M J Margulies
Svetlana Marich
Scott and Suling Mead
Mary Moore
Afsaneh Moshiri
Alexandre Mouradian
Batia and Idan Ofer
Simon and Midge Palley
Mr Søren Fryland Møller and Dr Fiona Pathiraja
Jan-Christoph Peters
Alexander and Bella Petrov
Mr Gilberto and Mrs Daniela Pozzi
Frances Reynolds
Mr John Russo and Mr Jay Rutland
Jake and Hélène Marie Shafran
Andrée Shore
Maria and Malek Sukkar
Ann Tang Chiu
Pierre Tollis and Alexandra Mollof
Saffron Wace
Michael and Jane Wilson, CBE
Lady Wolfson of Marylebone
Chizuko Yashiro
Jessica Zirinis
and those who wish to remain anonymous

Gold Patrons

Karim Abdel-Motaal
Ryan Allen and Caleb Kramer
Ms Mila Askarova
Catherine Carver Dunn and David Dunn
Liza Cawthorn
Angela Choon
Beth and Michele Colocci
Harry G David
Dr Genevieve Davies
Jackie Donnelly Russell
Eykyn Maclean
Carl Faker
Hugh Gibson
Tudor Havriliuc
Mazzoleni Art
Mathew Prichard
Valerie Rademacher
Irith Rappaport
Sybil Robson Orr
Almine Ruiz-Picasso
Carol Sellars
Hahnah Seminara
Raksha Sriram
Kimberly Stallvik
Brunhild Stelter
Yuko Takano
Manuela and Iwan Wirth
and those who wish to remain anonymous

Silver Patrons

Geoffrey and Julian Agnew Charitable Trust
Jose Alcantara
Sharis Alexandrian
Marc Anani-Isaac
The Anson Charitable Trust
Toby and Kate Anstruther
Hannah Armstrong
James Arnell
Mrs Charlotte Artus
Aspect Charitable Trust
Charles Banner, QC
Peter Barham
Mrs Jane Barker
Oliver Barker
Victoria Barnsley, OBE
Jim Bartos
Ms Anne Berthoud
Madeleine Bessborough
David Blood and Beth Bisso
Harry and Fabiana Bond
Elena Bowes
Alina Boyko
Viscountess Bridgeman
Basia Briggs
Laura Brimson
Laura and William Burlington
Michael Burrell
Mrs Marlene Burston
Mrs Aisha Cahn
Timothy and Elizabeth Capon
Roger Cazalet
Lord and Lady Charles Cecil
Sandrine Chelmy
David Cheng
Dr Peter Chocian
Miss FangChing Chou
John F Clappier
Andres Clase
Frank Cohen
Mrs Jane Collins
Terrence Collis
Mr and Mrs Oliver Colman
Giles and Sonia Coode-Adams
Cathy Corbett
Cynthia Corbett
Pilar Corrias
Tommaso Corvi-Mora
Mr and Mrs Bertrand Coste
Kathleen Crook and James Penturn
Veronika Dapunt
Fiona Davies
Sir Howard Davies
Sir Roger and Lady De Haan
Giles de la Mare
Mr Damon and The Hon Mrs de Laszlo
Jean-Annet de Saint Rapt
Anne Chantal Defay Sheridan
Pier-Luigi del Renzio
Mr Robert Devereux
Maeve Doyle
Lord and Lady Egremont
Jake Elsley
Margaret Erbe
John Erle-Drax
Dr Nigel Evans
Stuart and Margaret Evans
Ernest Fasanya
Mrs Margy Fenwick
Laurie Fitch
The Sylvie Fleming Collection
Lt Commander Paul Fletcher
Mr and Mrs Laurent Ganem
Mala Gaonkar
Yasmin Gee
Ms Emily Goldner and Mr Michael Humphries
Kate Gordon
Dimitri Goulandris
Martyn Gregory
Olga Grishina
Richard and Odile Grogan
Professor John Gruzelier
Jill Hackel Zarzycki
Alex Haidas
Arthur Hanna
Mark Harris
Michael and Morven Heller
Cherine Helmy
Paul Higgins
Soo Hitchin
Muriel Hoffner
James Holland-Hibbert
Lady Hollick, OBE
Holtermann Fine Art
Jeff Horne
Tina Hughes
Josephine Jenno
Mr Haydn John
Mr Michael Johnson
Mike Jones
Jay Jopling
Mrs Brenda Josephs
Tracey Josephs
Niki Kalamida
Andrew Kalman
Ghislaine Kane
Mr David Kaskel

Dr Martin Kenig
Mr and Mrs Simon Keswick
Neha Khosla
Mrs Mae Khouri
David Killick
Mr and Mrs James Kirkman
Brian and Lesley Knox
David P Korn
Kowitz Trust
Mr and Mrs Herbert Kretzmer
Simon Lee
Tiina Lee
Leonard Lewis
Sharron Lewis
Sophia and Mark Lewisohn
Linwan Li
Yimeng Lin
Mr Gilbert Lloyd
Mrs Elizabeth Louis
Alison Loyd
Evelin Luecker
Kate MacGarry
Fiona Mactaggart
Sir John Mactaggart
Audrey Mandela
Marlborough Fine Art
Marsh Christian Trust
Daniele Mattogno
Professor Rob Melville
Shahid Miah
Victoria Miro
Mrs William Morrison
Louise Nathanson
Ms Deborah Norton
Emma O'Donoghue
Reine and Boris Okuliar
Julian Opie
Pilar Ordovás
Leslie Osterling
Desmond Page
Maureen Paley
Sir Michael Palin
Mrs Kathrine Palmer
Pierre Papet
Asta Paulauskaite
Alexander V Petalas
Frederique Pierre-Pierre
Professor Richard Portes, CBE, FBA
Graham Powell
Susan Prevezer, QC
Mr and Mrs Ryan Prince
Ivetta Rabinovich
Patricia Ranken
Carla Rapoport
Mrs Phyllis Rapp
Lady Ritblat
David Rocklin
Frankie Rossi
Mr David V Rouch
Mr Charles Roxburgh
Sir Paul and Lady Ruddock
Mr Alex Sainsbury and Ms Elinor Jansz
Mr Richard Christo Salmon
Tatiana Salomon
Cherrill and Ian Scheer
Mrs Cara Schulze
Melissa Sesana
The Hon Richard Sharp
Sadie Sherman
Neville Shulman, CBE
Oliwia Siem
Skarstedt Gallery
Grey Skipwith
Louise Spence
Mr James Swartz
Elaine Thomas
Olivia Thornton
Marita Thurnauer
Ian Tollett
Karen Townshend
Mr Philippos Tsangrides
Melissa Ulfane
Mrs Jolana Vainio and Dr Petri Vainio
Celine Valligny
Ewan Venters
Gisela von Sanden
Audrey Wallrock
Linda Waterhouse
Offer Waterman
Michael Webber
Miss Cheyenne Westphal
Professor Sarah Whatmore
Derek James Wilson
Ms Caroline Wiseman
Mr Douglas Woolf
Adam Wurr
Wen Xiao
and those who wish to remain anonymous

Young Patrons
Khaled Abu-Suud
Omar Abu-Suud
Tarek Abu-Suud
Nadine Adams
Estelle Akeroyd Hunt
HRH Princess Alia Al-Senussi
Fiona Amitai
Aishwarya Anam
Mihai Anca
Sheila Anjoree
Aurore E Ankarcrona Hennessey
Gulru Arvas (Co-Chair, Young Patrons Ambassador Group)
Nur Arvas
Miss Olivia Aubry
Colette Auyang
Katrina Beechey
Penny Johanna Beer
Eleni Beveratou
Dr Maya Beyhan
Valeria Biamonti
Dorothee Boissonnas
Jennifer Brown
Matthew Charlton
Bianca Chu (Co-Chair, Young Patrons Ambassador Group)
Charlotte Cobb
Olly Cobb
Thamara Corm
Stephanie Courmont
Huguette Craggs
Averil Curci
Helena Czernecka
Lina Daneshyar
Henry Danowski
Filipe de Almeida Assis
Countess Charlotte de la Rochefoucauld
Émilie De Pauw
Sophie Dickson
Eleanor Dilloway
Indira Dyussebayeva
Lena Economides
Alexandra Economou
Jennifer Ellis
Thomas Forwood
Jane and Richard Found
Sylvain Fresia
Brian Fu
Mr Andreas Gegner
Beth Greenacre
Richard Grindy
Ari Helgason
Patrick Hennessey
Max Edouard Friedrich Hetzler
Phoebus Istavrioglu
Eva Jurin
Miss Meruyert Kaliyeva
Mrs Vasilisa Kameneva
Melih Kaplan
Zoe Karafylakis Sperling
Miss Tamila Kerimova
Kendall Kerr Ayers
Ms Chloe Kinsman
Yoshiaki Ko
Daria Kravchenko
Natalia Kritsali
Mr Victor Kyaw Win
Nicholas M Lamotte
Megan Leckie
John Lellouche
Alexander Lewis
Ines Leynaud
Yisi Li
Hedvig Liestol
Jonathan Lim
Alexandra Lindsay
Mr J Lueddeckens
Giulia Magnani
Ms Sonia Mak
Mr Jean-David Malat
Mary McNicholas
Stefan Miesner
Amanda Millwood
Mr Fernando Moncho Lobo
Tilak Nathwani
Muchun Niu
Ikenna Obiekwe
Nnamdi Obiekwe
Hilla Olsson
Opera Gallery
Cuppy Otedola
Periklis Panagopoulos
Yioryios Papayioryiou
Divya Pathak
Alonso Peña Alfaro
Mary Pollock
Chelsea Purvis
Mitali Rakhit
Nikki Ramirez
Ariana Regalado
Dr Konrad Rotthege
Isabel Sachs
Sinclair Schäfer
Daniel Schwarz
Count Indoo Sella Di Monteluce
Wei Shi
Ms Marie-Anya Shriro
Louise Simpson
Mandeep Singh
Laura Stoloff
Jana Suhani Soin
Ilgin Surel
Molly Susman
Yaroslav Syzonov
Evangeline Tawil
Ryan Taylor
Vassan Thavaraja
Mr Leo Thetiot
Omer Tiroche
Mr Giancarlo Trinca
Ms Navann Ty
Valentina Vangelista
Zina Vieille
Marlene von Carnap
Luning Wang
Thomas Williams
Duo Zhang
Tiffany Zhang
Alexandra Zirinis
and those who wish to remain anonymous

International Council Members
Staffan Ahrenberg, Editions Cahiers d'Art
Mr Geoff Ainsworth, AM
Anne H Bass Foundation
Mrs Anita Belgiono-Nettis, AM
Nicolas Berggruen
Jo and Tom Bloxham
Pontus Bonnier
Paloma Botín O'Shea
Mr William Bowness, AO
Ivor Braka
Rory and Elizabeth Brooks
Andrew Cameron, AM
Christina Chandris
Pierre Chen, Yageo Foundation, Taiwan
Mr Euisun Chung and Mrs Geesun Chung
Mr Dimitris Daskalopoulos
Ms Miel de Botton
Suzanne Deal Booth
Tiqui Atencio Demirdjian and Ago Demirdjian
Robert and Renée Drake
Mrs Olga Dreesmann
Füsun and Faruk Eczacibasi
Désiré Feuerle and Sara Puig
HRH Princess Firyal of Jordan
Mrs Wendy Fisher
Founder of Lise Wilhelmsen Art Award
Kathrine Fredriksen
Fuhrman Family Foundation
Mrs Belma Gaudio and The Butters Foundation
Candida and Zak Gertler
Mrs Yassmin Ghandehari
Lydia and Manfred Gorvy
Bianca and Noam Gottesman
Laurence Graff, OBE
Mimi and Peter Haas Fund
Margrit and Paul Hahnloser
Mrs Susan Hayden
Marlene Hess and James D. Zirin
Ms Maja Hoffmann
Sangita Jindal
Dakis and Lietta Joannou
Ms Monica Kalpakian
Richard and Pamela Kramlich
Andreas Kurtz (Vice Chair) and Ulrike Kurtz
Ms Catherine Lagrange
Mr Pierre Lagrange
Judy and Leonard Lauder
Edward Lee
Seo Hyun Lee
Jacqueline and Marc Leland
Ms Joyce Liu
The Deborah Loeb Brice Foundation
Andrew J Love
Panos and Sandra Marinopoulos
David Meitus and Angela Westwater
Audrey and David Mirvish, Toronto
Professor Cav. Simon Mordant, AO (Vice Chair) and Catriona Mordant, AM
Mrs Yoshiko Mori
Naomi Milgrom, AC
Gael Neeson
Dr Mark Nelson
Mr and Mrs Takeo Obayashi
Mr and Mrs Eyal Ofer
Andrea and José Olympio Pereira
Hideyuki Osawa
Ms Gretel Packer, AM
Midge and Simon Palley
Irene Panagopoulos
Véronique Parke
Yana and Stephen Peel
Catherine Petitgas
Sydney Picasso
Ana Pinho
Lekha Poddar
Miss Dee Poon
Smita Prabhakar
Ms Miuccia Prada and Mr Patrizio Bertelli
Laura Rapp and Jay Smith
Maya and Ramzy Rasamny
Patrizia Sandretto Re Rebaudengo and Agostino Re Rebaudengo
Frances Reynolds
Michael Ringier
Ms Hanneli M Rupert
Ms Elcin Melisa Sabanci Tapan
Rajeeb and Nadia Samdani
Alejandro Santo Domingo
Tarana and Tarun Sawhney
Czaee Shah
Dasha Shenkman, OBE
Dr Gene Sherman, AM
Jon and Kimberly Shirley
Poonam Bhagat Shroff
Uli and Rita Sigg
John J Studzinski, CBE
Maria and Malek Sukkar
Mr Christen Sveaas
Lorraine Tarabay
Richard and Maggie Tsai
Paulo A W Vieira (Chair)
Mercedes Vilardell
Robert and Felicity Waley-Cohen
Diana Widmaier Picasso
Christen and Derek Wilson
Mrs Sylvie Winckler
The Hon Dame Janet Wolfson de Botton, DBE
Terry Wu
Yang Yang
Poju Zabludowicz and Anita Zabludowicz, OBE
and those who wish to remain anonymous

Africa Acquisitions Committee
Aki Abiola
Kathy Ackerman Robins
Kola Aina
John Basnage de Beauval
The Beachum Charitable Fund
Priti Chandaria Shah
Mrs Kavita Chellaram
Harry G David
Lana de Beer David
Mrs Wendy Fisher
Diane B. Frankel
Samallie Kiyingi
Alexander Klimt
Caro Macdonald
Dale Mathias
Wissam and Hiba Nesr Art Foundation
Charlotte L. Newman
Alain F Nkontchou
Emile Stipp
Josef Vascovitz and Lisa Goodman
Mercedes Vilardell (Chair)
Alexa Waley-Cohen
Peter Warwick
and those who wish to remain anonymous

Asia-Pacific Acquisitions Committee
Shane Akeroyd
Jim Amberson
Director of Arario Museum
Arndt Foundation, Matthias Arndt
Bonnie and R Derek Bandeen
Mrs Victoria Bruhn
Lito and Kim Camacho
Mrs Marisa Chearavanont
Adrian Cheng
XiaoMeng 'Cherry' Cheng
Jonathan Cheung
Lawrence Chu
Mrs Yassmin Ghandehari
Esther Heer-Zacek
Philippa Hornby
Shareen Khattar Harrison
Mr Jung Wan Kim
Ms Ellie Lai
Alan Lau (Co-Chair)
Woon Kyung Lee
Woong-Yeul Lee
Ms Dina Liu
Alan and Yenn Lo
Ms Kai-Yin Lo
Yoonwhe Leo Moon & Young Ran Yun
Lynn Ou
Francis and Eleanor Shen
Arif Suherman
Mr Patrick Sun
Dr Andreas Teoh
Rudy Tseng
Yang Bin
Jenny Yeh
Fernando Zobel de Ayala (Co-Chair)
and those who wish to remain anonymous

Central and Eastern Europe Plus Acquisitions Committee
Stella Beniaminova

David and Kathryn Birnbaum
Attila and Emese Brezoczki
Francise Hsin-Wen Chang
Gabriela Gantenbein
Jan Hammer
Patrick Hessel
Kasia Kulczyk
Peter Kulloi (Co-Chair)
Danica and Eduard Maták
Luba Michailova
Florin Pogonaru
The Pudil Family Foundation
Ivana & Martin Ridler
Valeria Rodnyansky
Robert Runták
Ovidiu Sandor
The Terziev Family
Attila G. Vizi
Mr Jānis Zuzāns
and those who wish to remain anonymous

European Collection Circle
Mandy Cawthorn Argenio
Lonti Ebers
The Gaudio Family Foundation
Edward Lee
The Reitan Family
Danny Rimer, OBE
Stichting Hartwig Foundation
and those who wish to remain anonymous

Latin American Acquisitions Committee
Monica and Robert Aguirre
Francesca Bellini
Celia Birbragher
Countess Nicole Brachetti Peretti
Estrellita and Daniel Brodsky
Luis Javier Castro
Simone Coscarelli Parma
HSH the Prince Pierre d'Arenberg
Tiqui Atencio Demirdjian (Co-Chair)
Marta Regina Fernandez-Holmann
Heloisa Genish
Barbara Hemmerle Gollust
José Luis Lorenzo
Sofia Mariscal and Guillermo Penso Blanco
Susan McDonald
Gabriela Mendoza
Felipe and Denise Nahas Mattar
Veronica Nutting
Victoria and Isaac Oberfeld
Silvia Paz Illobre
Catherine Petitgas
Claudio Federico Porcel
Thibault Poutrel
Frances Reynolds
Erica Roberts (Co-Chair)
Renata and Roberto Ruhman
Lilly Scarpetta
Richard Weinstein
and those who wish to remain anonymous

Middle East North Africa Acquisitions Committee
Walid Abu-Suud
Rula Alami
HRH Princess Alia Al-Senussi
Abdelmonem Bin Eisa Alserkal
Marwan T Assaf
Bishoy Azmy
Perihan Bassatne
Mrs Elisabeth Bauchet-Bouhlal
Maryam Eisler
Shirley Elghanian
Dr Farhad Farjam
Hossein and Dalia Fateh
Raghida Ghandour Al Rahim
Mareva Grabowski
Mary Habib
Yasser Hashem
Fady Jameel
Rasheed Kamel
Mr Elie Khouri
Maha Kutay
Hashem Montasser
Dina Nasser-Khadivi
Mr Moshe Peterburg
Ramzy and Maya Rasamny
Maria (Co-Chair) and Malek Sukkar
Faisal Tamer (Co-Chair)
Mr Zahid and Ms Binladin
Roxane Zand
and those who wish to remain anonymous

North American Acquisitions Committee
Abigail Baratta
Dr. Eraka Bath
Allison Berg
Lewis Cheng
Dillon Cohen
J. Patrick Collins
Michael Corman and Kevin Fink
Amy Gold
Alex Grant
Joshua Greenberg
Craig Hollingworth
Peter Kahng
Patricia Kaneb Kelly
Christian Keesee
Charles Kim
Ekaterina Klim
Leon Koffler and Rachelli Mishori
Anna Korshun
Bernard Lagrange
Margarette Lee
Miyoung Lee
Marjorie and Michael Levine
James Lindon
Kathleen Madden and Paul Frantz
Matt McClure
Gregory R Miller (Co-Chair)
Mohammad N. Miraly
Sami Mnaymneh
Shabin and Nadir Mohamed
Alexander V. Petalas
Holly Peterson
Laura Rapp and Jay Smith
Stephanie Robinson
Leo Rogath
Ralph Segreti and Richard Follows
Francis and Eleanor Shen
Kimberly and Jon Shirley
Emily and Jeremy Steckler
Graham Steele and Ulysses de Santi
Ann Tang Chiu
Teresa Tsai
Charlotte Wagner
Christen Wilson (Co-Chair) and Derek Wilson
Mary Zlot
and those who wish to remain anonymous

Photography Acquisitions Committee
Ryan Allen
Nicholas Barker
Cynthia Lewis Beck
Pierre Brahm
Alla Broeksmit
Elizabeth (Co-Chair) and Rory Brooks
Lisa and Mark Caputo
Michael A Chesser
Beth and Michele Colocci
David Fitzsimons
Lisa Garrison
Emily Goldner and Mike Humphries
Natascha Jakobs-Linssen
Elizabeth and William Kahane
Jack Kirkland (Co-Chair)
Randall Kroszner and David Nelson
Nathalie Lambert-Besseddik and Cyril Besseddik
Suling Mead
Nicholas Stanley
Maria and Malek Sukkar
Sohni and Dipak Tanna
Francois Trausch, in memory of Caroline Trausch
Juan Carlos Verme
Michael and Jane Wilson, CBE
Chizuko Yashiro
and those who wish to remain anonymous

South Asia Acquisitions Committee
Dr Arani and Mrs Shumita Bose
Carolina Brossard Salve
Krishna Choudhary
Akshay Chudasama
Jai Danani
Taimur Hassan
Dr Amin Jaffer
Neha and Sumedh Jaiswal
Arushi Kapoor
Deepanjana Klein
Simran Kotak and Vir Kotak
Ms Aarti Lohia
Mohammad N. Miraly
Hiroo and Haresh Motwani
Mr Rahul Munjal and Mrs Pooja Munjal
Moklasur Rahman Pinto
Lekha Poddar (Co-Chair)
Smita Prabhakar
Alka and Amit Ruia
Isheta Salgaocar
Nadia Samdani, MBE
Rajeeb Samdani (Co-Chair)
Mrs Tarana Sawhney
Damian Vesey
Manuela and Iwan Wirth
and those who wish to remain anonymous

The 1897 Circle
Lynn Allan
Anne Berthoud
Marilyn Bild
James Birch
David and Deborah Botten
Geoff Bradbury
Charles Brett
Eloise and Francis Charlton
Paul Cumming-Benson
Alex Davids
Jonathan Davis
Sean Dissington
Ronnie Duncan
Joan Edlis
V Fabian
Ian Fletcher
Lt Cdr Paul Fletcher
Mr. and Mrs. R.N. and M.C. Fry
Richard S. Hamilton
L.A. Hynes
John Iddon
John Janssen
Dr. Martin Kenig
Vanessa Koster-Goodliffe
Isa Levy
Theo Matoff
Jean Medlycott
Tony Miller
Sonya Newell-Smith
Miss Sue Novell and Mr. Graham Smith
Martin Owen
Ruth Rattenbury
Simon Reyonlds
Dianne Roberts
Dr. Claudia Rosanowski
Ann M Smith
Alan Sprince
Deborah Stern
Jennifer Toynbee-Holmes
Estate of Paule Vézelay
D. Von-Bethmann Hollweg
Audrey Wallrock
Rosie Watts
Professor Brian Whitton
Simon Casimir Wilson
Kay and Dyson Wilkes
Andrew Woodd
Mr. and Mrs. Zilberberg
and those who wish to remain anonymous

Tate Britain Corporate Supporters
AGC Equity Partners
Bank of America
BNP Paribas
Bloomberg LP
Chanel
Deutsche Bank UK
EY
Hyundai Motor
IHS Markit
Lockton
Oaknorth Bank
PJT Partners
Sotheby's
and those who wish to remain anonymous

Tate Britain Corporate Partners
Adobe
Aspen Insurance Group
Atomico (UK) Partners LLP
Bentley Systems Ltd
Beringea
Bjarke Ingels Group
Clifford Chance LLP
Copper Technologies
CRA International (UK) Limited
fgs Global
Foster + Partners
Freshfields Service Company
Hakluyt & Company Limited
Hayfin Capital Management LLP
Heidrick & Struggles
HKA Global Ltd
Howden M&A
Imperial College Healthcare Charity
JATO Dynamics
LinkedIn Technology UK Limited
Linklaters LLP
Matthews Daniel International London Ltd
McDermott Will & Emery UK LLP
Morgan Stanley
Oliver Wyman
Portland PR Ltd
PuRe PR
St George's Hospital
State Street Bank and Trust
T. Rowe Price
The Up Group
Xynteo Ltd
and those who wish to remain anonymous

First published 2023 by order of the Tate Trustees
by Tate Publishing, a division of Tate Enterprises Ltd,
Millbank, London SW1P 4RG
www.tate.org.uk/publishing

on the occasion of the exhibition
The Rossettis

Tate Britain, London
6 April – 24 September 2023

Delaware Art Museum
21 October 2023 – 28 January 2024

The exhibition at Tate Britain is supported by

The Rossettis Exhibition Supporters Circle:
Tavolozza Foundation

and Tate Members

The exhibition at Delaware Art Museum is made possible through support from the Nathan M. Clark Foundation, the Amy P. Goldman Foundation, and the Dr. Lee MacCormick Edwards Charitable Foundation. This organization is supported, in part, by a grant from the Delaware Division of the Arts, a state agency, in partnership with the National Endowment for the Arts.

A catalogue record for this book is available from the British Library

ISBN 978-1-84976-841-2 (hardback)
ISBN 978-1-84976-842-9 (paperback)

Distributed in the United States and Canada by
ABRAMS, New York

Library of Congress Control Number: applied for

Senior Editor: Alice Chasey
Production: Bill Jones
Picture researcher: Emma O'Neill
Designed by Lorenz Klingebiel, with Louis Hunt
Typeface: Albis by Jack Niblett
Colour reproduction by DL Imaging, London
Printed and bound in Belgium by Die Keure

Front cover: Dante Gabriel Rossetti, *La Ghirlandata* 1873 (see NO.193)
Endpapers in hardback: *Glass Plate Negative of Flying Angels* 1866
Frontispiece: Dante Gabriel Rossetti, *Paolo and Francesca da Rimini* 1855 (detail, see NO.121)

Measurements of artworks are given in centimetres,
height before width, before depth

The artists and writers featured in this book shared a surname so we have named them individually by their main forenames

FSC
www.fsc.org
MIX
Paper | Supporting responsible forestry
FSC® C009115

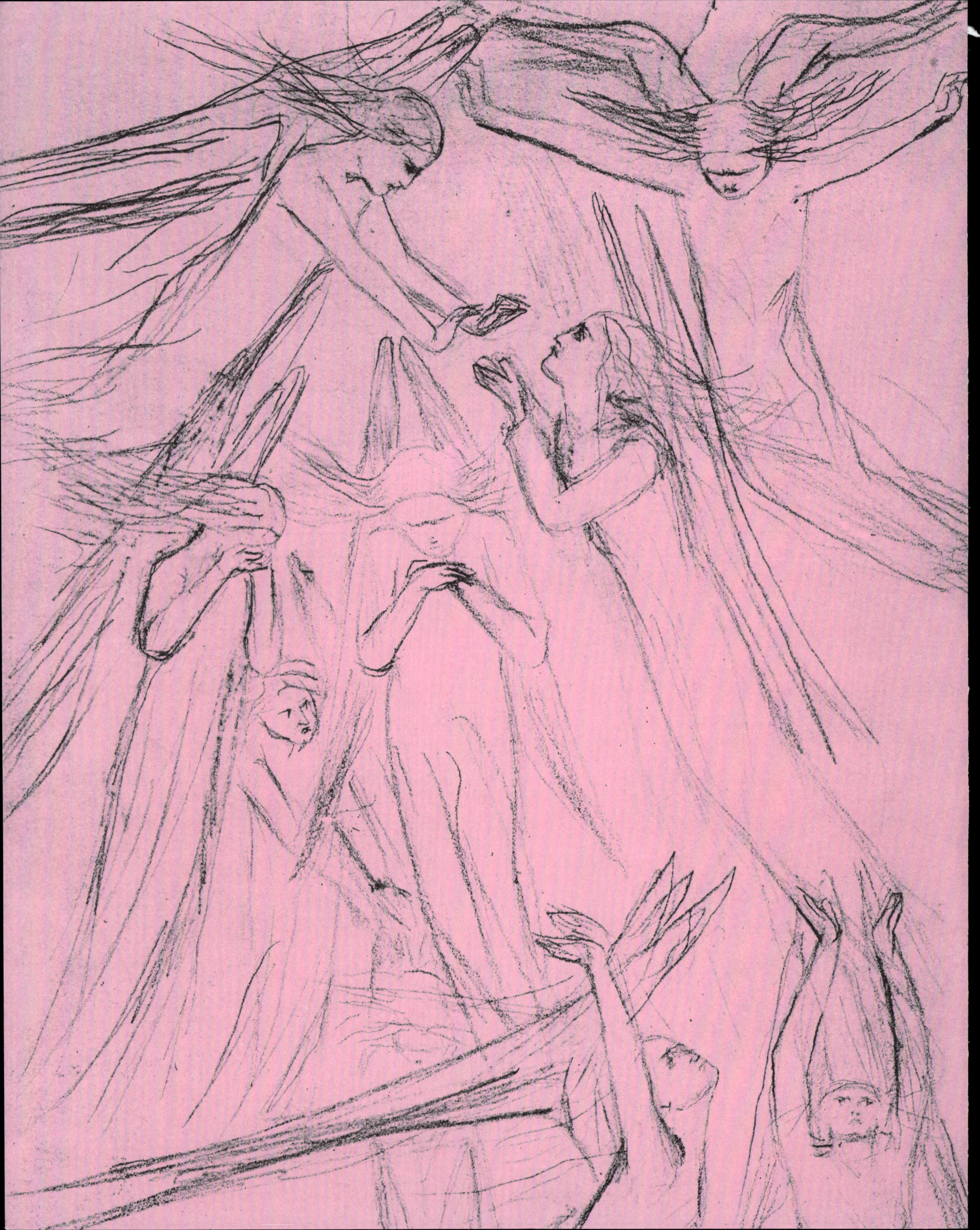